D1452445

Public Housing,
Race, and Renewal

John F. Bauman

Public Housing, Race, and Renewal

Urban Planning
in Philadelphia,
1920–1974

Temple University Press
Philadelphia

*Publication of this book was assisted by a grant
from the Samuel S. Fels Fund.*

Temple University Press, Philadelphia 19122
Copyright © 1987 by Temple University. All rights reserved
Published 1987
Printed in the United States of America

The paper used in this publication meets the minimum requirements
of American National Standard for Information Sciences—Permanence
of Paper for Printed Library Materials, ANSI Z39.48-1984

Library of Congress Cataloging-in-Publication Data

Bauman, John F.
Public housing, race, and renewal

Bibliography: p.
Includes index.
1. City planning—Pennsylvania—Philadelphia—
History—20th century. 2. Public housing—
Pennsylvania—Philadelphia—History—20th century.
3. Urban renewal—Pennsylvania—Philadelphia—20th
century. I. Title.
HT168.P43B38   1986   307.1'2'0974811   86-5907
ISBN 0-87722-444-7 (alk. paper)

For
Barbara, Cindy, and Scott

Contents

List of Maps

Preface

In 1974, the year in which President Richard M. Nixon banned further construction, there were 1.4 million units of federally built public housing in city neighborhoods. Whether high-rises or two- and three-story row houses, the graffiti-scarred buildings had the unmistakable physiognomy of public housing.

Few other features of the urban landscape have incurred greater opprobrium. One sociologist, William Moore, castigated federal housing projects as "vertical ghettoes"; another, Lee Rainwater, vilified East Saint Louis's Pruitt-Igoe towers as "federal slums"; the journalist Harrison Salisbury termed New York's public housing as "human catchpools . . . that breed social ills."[1]

Paradoxically, the idea of public housing derives from highly visionary late-nineteenth-century and early-twentieth-century designs for better housing the industrial working class and creating a village community within the modern city. In the minds of the early housing professionals, architects, and planners, public housing offered not only employment for the jobless construction worker but also the hope for a new, humane, and cooperative social order.

The key idea underlying public housing was that the construction of a better environment would improve the behavior and citizenship of the poor. The following pages attempt to illuminate the 50-year history of the public housing vision, from its early practical application during World War I to its exhaustion in the 1970s.

The book focuses on the men and women who debated, promoted, and helped shape Philadelphia's public housing and urban development policies. These people harbored the conscience of the public housing movement. Such dedicated and articulate proponents of modern housing as the author and lecturer Catherine Bauer, the Russian-born architect Oscar Stonorov, and the housing economist and executive director of the Philadelphia Housing Association (PHA), Dorothy Schoell Montgomery, championed an enlarged public housing program, pressed for racial integration, and advocated projects situated on well-planned sites located on the urban periphery.

The Great Depression produced urban housing conditions desperate enough to allow Bauer and Montgomery to entertain seriously a European-style housing revolution in America. But the early public housing projects fell short of the modern housing vision mirrored during the 1920s in such planned developments as Radburn, New Jersey, and Sunnyside, New York. Although arranged in neighborhood units replete with common walkways, community rooms, and workshops, large federal housing projects ordinarily bore a stark, cheerless appearance and accomplished more slum clearance than the deconcentration of crowded urban populations into airy, sunbathed communities.

After World War II, a changing urban economy, new racial patterns, and the ideology of urban development shattered the basic assumptions undergirding the earlier public housing policy. The disintegration of the urban-industrial economy of center-city mills and manufacturing undermined the city tax base and hastened the death of the central business district. In Philadelphia, rebuilding the city became the basis for a political coalition of businessmen, labor leaders, and ethnic groups united by a common interest in urban prosperity. Public housing became less a program to supply modern shelter to ill-housed urban dwellers and more a tool for facilitating the growth of the historic central core.

The disappointing outcome of Philadelphia's housing program can be illuminated by examining the issue of race. After World War II, Philadelphia's black population rose significantly, while the supply of low-income housing dwindled. New housing for whites mushroomed in suburban areas, but blacks crammed the aging center-city units. Public housing loomed as a critical source of shelter for the city's expanding population of under- and unemployed blacks. The city's failure to scatter public housing units in white peripheral neighborhoods disillusioned housing reformers and city officials already dismayed by public housing's failure to stabilize neighborhood redevelopment.

An ideological shift followed the demise of Philadelphia's crusade to integrate public housing. It was a loss of faith that would have tragic overtones for the future of public housing. Once portrayed as the proving ground for a new order, by the early 1960s public housing had devolved into a program for expediting the delivery of social services. A decade later, it had degenerated into a custodial operation, warehousing the poor.

Public housing was the victim of an ideological conundrum. On the one hand, planners saw the housing as the epitome of a modern community—an architect-designed neighborhood unit built to promote efficient, socially satisfying urban living. On the other hand, bu-

reaucratic-minded, politically acute housing officials trumpeted public housing's didactic function and raised expectations that it would
acculturate the poor, end crime and disease, and abolish urban slums.

In the postindustrial city, this conundrum proved devastating for
the future of public housing. The once burning faith in the power of
public housing to engineer a better city was extinguished amid boun-
tiful evidence that, more often than not, public housing projects
turned into publicly owned slums.

This study affords insight into, and some understanding of, the
policies that conceived and later ravaged public housing. Ideally, with
enlightenment may come some action to restore to existing public
housing a small trace of the vision that bathed the policy at its birth.

Acknowledgments

Like other scholars who venture into the labyrinth of American history, my quest for a deeper understanding of the social, economic, and political forces that shaped public housing policy in Philadelphia was aided by numerous people and institutions.

For their generous financial support, I wish to thank both the Samuel S. Fels Fund and the Penrose Fund (Grant 9321) of the American Philosophical Society for support of research. I am also grateful to the University of Pittsburgh's Center for Social and Urban Research, where I have been a research associate since 1982. My greatest debt is to the California University of Pennsylvania, where I have been a faculty member since 1969. Not only did the university frequently provide transportation for research trips but also through the Irene O'Brien Fund the university supported the cost of typing the original manuscript. At a critical juncture in the history of this study, the university awarded me a special yearlong sabbatical so that I could complete the book.

During the years that I was engaged in researching and writing this book I greatly benefited from an exchange of ideas with many friends and colleagues. Among those are Ronald Hoy, Sumner Ferris, Frank Edwards, Thomas H. Coode, Kenneth Jackson, Sam Bass Warner, Zane Miller, Michael Ebner, Raymond Mohl, Eugenie Birch, Theodore Hershberg, Randolph S. Klein, H. Viscount Nelson, Norman Hummon, and William Yancey.

I owe a particular debt to Mark Rose, who carefully read the final draft of the manuscript and offered valuable suggestions for improving it. I am also deeply indebted to Edward K. Muller and William F. Trimble, who read several drafts of the manuscript and spent hours sharing with me their wealth of historical insight and editorial skill.

As always, I have been graciously served by the staffs of many fine libraries, archives, historical societies, and public agencies. My special debt is to the staff of the Temple University Urban Archives, especially Fred Miller, whose knowledge of archival science is extraordinary. Allen Weinberg proved most helpful in assisting my research at the Philadelphia City Archives, and the staffs of the Historical Society of Pennsylvania and the Free Library of Philadelphia were equally generous in offering help. Shirley Parham of the Afro American Museum in Philadelphia shared many useful insights into the social structure of the black community during the 1920s and 1930s.

Considerable research for this book was done at the National Archives in Washington, D.C., where Aloah South and Jerry N. Hess were very gracious and helpful. At the local level, Robert Alotta, the chief of public relations for the Philadelphia Housing Authority in the 1970s and an historian in his own right, helped me discover housing records stored away in dark recesses of housing project basements; he also introduced me to housing project managers who could recall the early days of public housing. Also invaluable were my conversations with Dennis Clark and George Schermer.

For their work on the manuscript, I would like to thank Michael Ames, Doris Braendel, and Jennifer French at Temple University Press. For several of the map illustrations found in this book, I wish to thank the firm of Adkins and Associates, Architects, of Pittsburgh, Pennsylvania.

Over the years, I have published a number of articles that have dealt with the subjects of public housing, planning, and the black experience in Philadelphia, 1900–1970. I would like to thank the authors and editors of the following books and journals in which an earlier version of some of the facts and ideas found in this book appeared: William Cutler and Howard Gillette, eds., *The Divided Metropolis: Social and Spatial Dimensions of Philadelphia, 1800–1975* (Westport, Conn.: Greenwood Press, 1980); *Pennsylvania History; Pennsylvanian Magazine of History and Biography; Urbanism: Past and Present;* and Donald A. Krueckeberg, ed., *Introduction to Planning History in the United States* (New Brunswick, N.J.: Rutgers University Press, 1983).

I owe a very special debt to my family. Over the years, my parents, Fred and Elizabeth Bauman, both lifelong residents of Philadelphia, have shared with me their insights into the city and its history. My brother, Fred W. Bauman, Jr., a staff member of the Library of Congress, helped me enormously in providing biographical data on obscure personalities in the housing field, and in checking bibliographical references. Finally, my wife Barbara, son Scott, and daughter Cynthia Jeanne have been enormously supportive. Not only were they somewhat tolerant of rooms cluttered with books and scraps of paper, but for many years they have endured, with only moderate objection, weeks in which it appeared that I was more preoccupied with housing, race, and renewal than with them. Alas, it only seemed that way.

Part I

A Vision of
Modern Housing

1

The Roots of Public Housing

The sun shone warmly one Sunday in June 1925, and new houses sprouted like daffodils along the recently opened streets in Philadelphia's Overbrook, Northwood, Olney, and Oak Lane sections. A middle-income family, "taking a spin" in their Buick out Ridge Avenue to scout the new houses in Overbrook, found row and duplex housing situated on spacious front lawns and featuring interiors with tile bathrooms and hardwood floors. Later, perusing the Sunday newspaper, the prospective homeowners spotted an advertisement for Overbrook's "cottage type homes" that presented the dwellings as "a modern woman's home, simplifying the everyday cares with every modern convenience [and offering] the lasting sense of comfort and of friendliness . . . a real home for real folks."

Although it embodied the modernism and suburban domesticity inherent in the decade's "Own your own home" theme, the advertisement did not tell the truth about the housing boom. Beneath the veneer of real estate boosterism, and the allure of romantic bungalows gracing new city and suburban subdivisions, stood the harsh facts that most urban working-class families lacked decent housing and that, despite the housing boom, urban slums expanded in the 1920s.[1]

Two Views on Housing

Once William Penn's "greene countrie towne," Philadelphia by 1920 was an industrial city with a heavy concentration of textile and metal manufacturing. The bulk of the city's enormous stock of two- and three-story brick row housing consisted of small, unsafe tenements, lacking modern heating and plumbing, and situated amid the dark back alleys and courts of Southwark, Poplar, and the Northern Liberties areas, just north and south of the downtown. Beyond this inner ring of courts and alleys was a much larger ring of sturdy row housing, much of it built during an earlier housing boom, from 1850 to 1900 (see Map 1).

Housing reform in Philadelphia, and in other cities, began in the mid-nineteenth century when reformers saw a causal relationship be-

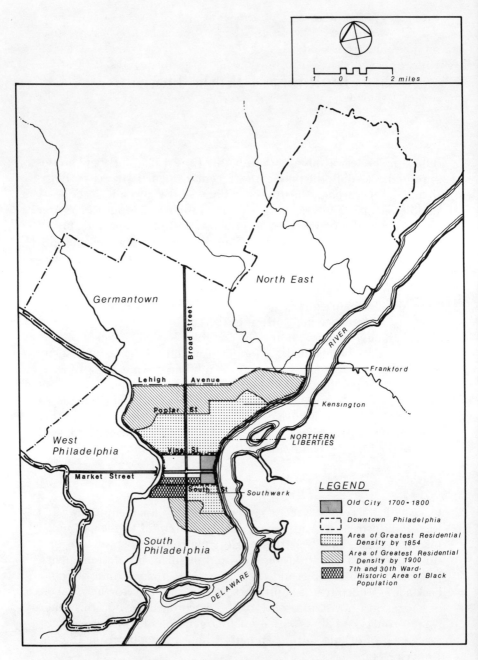

MAP 1: Philadelphia's Major Regions and Built-Up Areas, 1700–1900
Source: Adkins and Associates, Architects.

tween degrading housing environments and the incidence of crime, juvenile delinquency, prostitution, and intemperance. Progressive-minded sanitarians and housing reformers, called *professionals* in this book, attacked the housing problem by supporting the building of low-rent housing developments and by gathering reams of information on the evils of slum environments that they used to lobby for the enactment of strict tenement-house laws.[2]

A second group of urban reformers, called *communitarians* in this book, appeared in the early twentieth century. Like the professional housers, these planners, environmental philosophers, urban ecologists, and architects deplored slums, but they saw population congestion and urban chaos, rather than the tenement evil, at the root of the cancer. They traced social conflict to the dissolution of community wrought by urban industrialism, and proposed modern housing and planning as tools to restore moral order. Communitarians saw restrictive housing laws as diminishing rather than expanding the supply of good, inexpensive housing. Impressed by the European example of government-supported housing construction, and buoyed by America's World War I experience with government-built housing, they pushed for federally aided homebuilding.

The communitarians and professionals shared several tenets of the Progressive creed—a selfless concern for the commonweal, a strong belief in environmental determinism, and a commitment to use bureaucratic means to solve social and economic problems.[3] Urban Progressives believed that by bettering housing and neighborhood conditions, building parks and playgrounds, supplying clean water and public bathhouses, widening streets, and improving mass transportation, America could extend the benefits of modern science to the two-thirds of the nation's urban population occupying the aging structures that lined the narrow, treeless streets of America's cities.[4]

Professional Housing Organizations

Throughout the late nineteenth and early twentieth centuries, professional housers and philanthropic housing organizations strove to improve the housing conditions of the working class.[5] Among the more famous of their endeavors were A. T. White's Improved Dwellings Company in New York, philanthropist-realtor Jacob Schmidlapp's model tenements for blacks in Cincinnati, and the Octavia Hill Society in Philadelphia, the latter an organization for "friendly" housing management imported from England by two Quakers, Helen Parrish and Hannah Fox. In 1915 the Octavia Hill Society built model row housing in Kensington; another Philadelphia limited-dividend organization, the Whittier Center Housing Corporation, operated row housing for blacks. The philanthropic housing movement, however, provided little new, low-income housing; it also failed to convince housing speculators that slums were so wretched and slum residents so dangerous that they should risk their capital at 5 percent interest when jerry-built housing brought an easy 11 to 14 percent.[6]

In the 1890s, many settlement house people, such as Jane Addams and Florence Kelly of Hull House, Graham Taylor of Chicago Commons, and Robert Woods of Boston's South End House, undertook scientific investigations of slum housing conditions. But it was Robert Hunter, a resident of Chicago's Hull House and secretary of the City Homes Association, whose exhaustive study of housing in Chicago's inner city, *Tenement Conditions in Chicago* (1901), set the standards for future housing surveys. Following disclosures of horrible sanitation, disease, mortality, and crime, the settlement housers campaigned for legislation to help clean up the slums. They were joined by the muckraking journalist Jacob Riis and by the first professional tenement-house sleuth, Lawrence Veiller, whose exposé of New York City's tenement-house conditions produced in 1901 the first major tenement-house law.[7]

Professional housers developed a kinship with the public health movement, and the "science" of housing advanced alongside refinements in germ theory. Indeed, housers often referred to themselves as *sanitarians*. In their investigations of tenement conditions, they carefully noted the presence of overflowing privies, the hazard of fly-attracting fecal matter, and the accumulation of filth in basements and vacant lots. Like public health workers, professional housers attempted to meliorate specific housing problems one at a time, and preached that the abolition of pernicious conditions and the provision of good housing required strict enforcement of housing laws governing structural specifications, room size, electrical wiring, plumbing, and lot size.[8]

But cities would enact strict legislation only after expert investigations and public revelations about the social and economic cost of slums. By 1911 Veiller rejoiced that professionally staffed housing associations, equipped to carry out such investigations, operated in 19 American cities, including New York, Boston, Chicago, Cincinnati, Hartford, New Haven, Saint Louis, Pittsburgh, Buffalo, and Philadelphia. To provide national direction for the housing movement, Veiller and Robert de Forest founded the National Housing Association in 1909. Its board of directors represented a cross-section of the housing movement and included A. T. White, Grosvenor Atterbury of Forest Hills, New York, Helen Parrish and Hannah Fox, Jane Addams, Jacob Riis, and E. R. L. Gould. The National Housing Association endeavored to foster tenement-house legislation nationally and to provide encouragement and direction to fledgling housing associations.[9]

Philadelphia reformers officially launched a housing movement in 1909 when the Bureau of Municipal Research, Childrens Aid Society, Society for Organizing Charity, Tuberculosis Society, and Octavia Hill Society cooperated to form the Philadelphia Housing Commission (PHC). In addition to "aid[ing] the public authorities in the enforcement of existing laws affecting . . . housing conditions," the commission "pledge[d] to cooperate [with the city] in every way possible in the development of wholesome surroundings and proper home conditions throughout the city." Between 1909 and 1920 the PHC (after 1916, the Philadelphia Housing Association, or PHA) investigated and exposed the hazards of the stable fly, the insanitation of dog pure (used in the tanning industry) and manure heaps, and the health threat of 6,000 privy vaults. In 1915 the PHA helped draft the state's first housing ordinance. Like the professional housing organizations of other cities, however, the PHA clung to the belief that, if policed, private enterprise could produce decent housing for the urban working class.

In 1911 Bernard Newman became the first executive director of the PHC. Unlike many of his colleagues in the housing field, Newman never worked in a settlement house; he did, however, study at Union Theological Seminary, an experience that the historian Allen Davis found not uncommon among progressive social reformers. It was during his sojourn at Union that Newman discovered housing reform. After completing his studies for the Unitarian ministry, he continued his education at the New York School of Philanthropy and then traveled to Great Britain to study slum conditions. After landing the job with the PHC, Newman bolstered his housing credentials by taking courses in engineering and public health at Harvard and the University of Pennsylvania.

Newman trusted in private enterprise to supply inexpensive working-class housing. A housing reformer who always identified himself as a "certified sanitarian," Newman saw in Philadelphia's often maligned row housing an ideal solution to the dilemma of sheltering the low-income worker. In 1913 the PHC sponsored a competition for the best plans to build moderately priced workingmen's housing on a city lot 404 feet by 306 feet. The Octavia Hill Society built and leased 32 workingmen's houses in the city's Kensington section. Rents ranged from $8 to $10 a month.[10] For Newman, however, this was not a matter of encouraging philanthropy at 5 percent. "The value of a model block," confided Newman to a potential contestant, "would be in its being a profitable business investment."[11]

Communitarian Vision

Communitarian architects, planners, and social philosophers, whose breadth of vision transcended the more mundane interest of most professionals in platting subdivisions, designing traffic articulation patterns, and calculating the stresses of cantilevered floors, viewed planning issues as part of a broad inquiry into the evolving relationships between man, technology, and society. Such communitarians as the architects Clarence Stein and Clarence Perry, the author-philosopher Lewis Mumford, and the forester-conservationist Benton MacKaye conveyed their ideas through the Regional Planning Association of America (RPAA). Among other influences, communitarian thought reflected the organic concept of the neighborhood expressed by settlement workers Graham Taylor, Robert Woods, and Mary Simkhovitch, as well as the philosophical excursions into learning theory and postindustrial civilization undertaken by the social philosophers and economists John Dewey, Charles Horton Cooley, and Thorstein Veblen, and by the Scottish biologist and social theorist Patrick Geddes.

In the main, communitarians discovered their roots in the convergence of civic art, landscape architecture, and the anticongestion movement, the latter led by Benjamin C. Marsh, a resident of New York's Greenwich House and a former secretary of Pennsylvania's Society to Protect Children from Cruelty. At the 1907 Washington Conference on Congestion, chaired by Marsh, architects, planners, housers, and social workers explored the relationship between urban density, unplanned urban form, poverty, and the disintegration of the urban community.

During the "age of prosperity" most professional architect-planners were too preoccupied with designing middle-class housing, offices, apartment buildings, and highways to philosophize about ideal communities. In contrast, communitarians underscored the role of low-income housing in urban planning. Moreover, they saw urban housing problems in the context of a dynamic historical change. Following the seminal thought of the fathers of urban sociology—Emile Durkheim, Ferdinand Tönnies, Charles Horton Cooley, and George Simmel—communitarians believed that urban industrialism had shattered the bonds that secured the preindustrial social order and produced a morally vitiated urban society. The new industrial order upheld monetary values and scorned the affective, face-to-face relationships of the traditional neighborhood community.[12] Nevertheless, Geddes, Veblen, and Simon Patten taught that the age of brutal industrialism had ended and that an era of cooperation was dawning that would render vicious competitive practices obsolete. Technology would usher in a modern Elysium heralded by "neotechnic forces" such as electricity, the dynamo, and telegraphic communication. Communitarians saw a new, decentralized—"naturally decongested"—urban morphology, a spacious city freed from the specter of huddled masses and excrescent slums.[13]

Professionals dreamed of science and technology providing safer, more sanitary housing for working-class families; the communitarian vision ranged across entire urban regions to embrace watersheds, wilderness trails, electrical power grids, and highway networks binding urban regions into systems. Lewis Mumford and others cross-bred Geddes's biological model of social evolution with their own environmental determinism. From this philosophy, they fashioned the building blocks for their image of a "biotechnic" era, a motor age in which new communities would harness the technological power of electricity and the automobile to create a planned cooperative order.

For communitarians, technology itself became a solution to social problems. In the modern, school-centered city the sickly and uneducated child of the slums would find nourishment and knowledge; the hollow-eyed sewing-machine operator, now enslaved in a downtown sweatshop, would be transformed into a beaming mother joyously attending her child at a community playground.

Clarence Perry, Clarence Stein, and their companions in the RPAA envisioned the total restructuring of urban society around planned, school-centered communities, termed by Perry "neighborhood units." Unlike the designs for working-class housing that had so intrigued Veiller and Newman, the neighborhood unit would occupy a carefully surveyed and planned site located on the green rim of the city; the street design and housing arrangement would incorporate all the institutional, technological, and economic infrastructure of a socially and psychologically modern community.

The concept did not originate with the RPAA. In 1898 an imaginative British court stenographer, Ebenezer Howard, published a short but brilliant volume entitled *Tomorrow: The Path to Real Reform;* four years later it was republished as *Garden Cities of Tomorrow.* This utopian treatise contained Howard's plan for a new town, located outside London, girthed by a lush greensward and replete with wide boulevards, diagonal arteries, garden and industrial zones, and enclosed shopping areas. Howard's vision excited the imagination of a young British architect, Raymond Unwin; together Unwin and Howard launched the garden city movement in the industrial suburb of Letchworth in 1903 and at Welwyn Garden City shortly after World War I. Both towns reflected not only Unwin's devotion to Howard's idea of a freestanding suburban town but also Unwin's intention to provide inexpensive, low-density housing in design settings that blended the baroque and the picturesque.[14]

Between 1920 and 1930, Howard and Unwin's town planning ideas enjoyed an international appeal. They inspired the German planner-architect Ernst May, who in 1924 oversaw the development of a sprawling, modern, functionally designed workers' housing complex commissioned by the socialist city council of Frankfurt am Main, Germany. Robert D. Kohn, Frederick Ackerman, Catherine Bauer, Clarence Stein, Edith Wood, and other communitarians were enchanted by the Frankfurt model.

The most significant difference between professional and communitarian housers, therefore, was means; the two groups agreed on the ends: safe and sanitary housing for the urban working class. Professionals saw cajoling homebuilders and policing the private housing market through codes and ordinances as the means; communitarians favored positive action to increase the supply of low-cost housing and postulated the need for federal intervention to provide safe and sanitary housing for the urban working class.[15]

World War I and Housing

The importance of European housing ideas was highlighted by the severe housing shortage in America during and after World War I. Before the war, the great influx of immigrants from eastern and southern Europe and the easy access to land, capital, and cheap construction had made tenement building in the central city a profitable venture. Wartime inflation and a shortage of building supplies ended that. Between 1914 and 1917, the homebuilding industry, including tenement construction, ground nearly to a halt as military priorities drained the supply of lumber, steel, and other critical materials.

The cessation of housing construction created a desperate situation for those seeking houses. Surveys revealed that close to 300,000 workers in 76 cities searched futilely for shelter. In Philadelphia, John Ihlder, who between 1917 and 1920 managed the PHA while Newman sojourned in Washington, D.C., estimated that the war had swelled the city's population by over 200,000 people. Concurrently, new housing construction citywide plummeted from 7,762 units in 1916 to 965 in 1918.[16]

As the housing problem worsened, pressure built in the nation's capital to relieve the crisis. In 1918 Congress reluctantly approved the creation of two federal housing agencies. The Emergency Fleet Corporation (EFC) operated under the U.S. Shipping Board and included among its advisory and architectural staff such prominent architects as Robert D. Kohn, Frederick Law Olmsted, Jr., and Henry Wright. Wright helped draft the attractive baroque design for the Shipping Board's Yorkship Village project in Camden, New Jersey. Rather than actually build houses, EFC loaned its $75 million to shipbuilders, who furnished rental housing at a limited dividend of 5 percent.[17]

A second federal agency, the U.S. Housing Corporation (USHC), represented a significant and controversial departure from the American tradition of nongovernmental intervention in the realty marketplace. Convinced that efficient war production required a decently housed work force, and persuaded that the housing crisis constituted a wartime "emergency," Congress begrudgingly appropriated $100 million for the USHC to construct wartime housing. Directed by Olmstead, the USHC erected solidly built, well-designed houses.[18]

Because of Philadelphia's importance as a center for shipbuilding and military supply, the USHC and the EFC facilitated the development of several housing projects in the city. The USHC built more than 2,000 two-story, brick row houses on Oregon Avenue in South Philadelphia, arranging the dwellings tastefully in a parklike setting. Nearby, the EFC built more than 2,000 houses on Elmwood Avenue, another 634 houses on Oregon Avenue, and a hotel for single men on Hog Island. These Philadelphia projects were among 28 EFC-funded developments and 55 projects constructed nationwide by the USHC. By 1919 the USHC had housed 5,998 war-worker families and 7,181 laborers.[19]

Although professional housers such as John Ihlder and Lawrence Veiller philosophically opposed government intervention in homebuilding, they reasoned that the war projects were "being built to win the war" and applauded the high quality of the units. In fact, Veiller had drafted the *Standards for Permanent Industrial Housing Developments* used in project construction. In 1919 Veiller and Ihlder joined forces with the Women's Trade Union League, James Ford, and John Nolen to urge Washington to complete the projects. Later, Edith Wood hailed the government's World War I housing program as evidence that America, like Europe, could build well-planned, well-landscaped, and well-executed working-class housing.[20]

Despite all the kudos for Olmstead and the USHC's handiwork, Congress did not approve of the 176,000 units of wartime housing. A

1920 congressional investigation chided the USHC for exceeding its charge and building "permanent" rather than temporary structures. After the war, the EFC and USHC moved expeditiously to divest themselves of the housing. In Philadelphia the USHC sold its Oregon Avenue housing for a simple 10 percent down payment and monthly installments at 1 percent interest. By 1934 the USHC still held title to 650 of the homes; because of the Great Depression, most of the buyers were in default.[21]

Rural-Urban Migration

America's World War I housing shortage foreshadowed the deepening crisis that was to accompany postwar demobilization and economic depression. Furthermore, it fueled the discussion over how better to house low-income families. After the war, inflationary construction costs and a lack of capital for residential building discouraged new housing construction. Dwelling starts in 1919 represented only 74 percent of the prewar level, and in the following year this plunged to 58 percent. Vacancy rates in Manhattan dropped from 3 percent in 1919 to .6 percent a year later. Philadelphia's housing watchdogs portrayed an equally grim picture. In 1920 the city faced a shortage of over 20,000 houses. Although homebuilders started a record 12,000 new housing units in 1922, construction failed to match the city's estimated 30,000 annual increase in population. Moreover, to the horror of the PHA's executive secretary, Bernard Newman, between 1921 and 1923 tenement construction and conversions accounted for 20.5 percent of the new supply. Newman complained that speculators converted existing buildings into tenements faster than the city's Division of Housing and Sanitation could police the building code violations.

Housing inspectors uncovered the worst housing conditions in the city's expanding black neighborhoods. In the 24th, 35th, 36th, and 47th wards, migrants from rural North and South Carolina, Georgia, Virginia, and Florida crammed the moldering roosts that honeycombed sweltering courts and narrow alleys. Between 1910 and 1920 Philadelphia's black population grew from 84,000 to 134,000. In the 30th and 36th wards, which bordered the Schuylkill River just south of the downtown area, the black population mushroomed 55 percent and 127 percent respectively.

Numerous studies indicate that opportunity for employment attracted migrants to the city. During the war, agents from both the Pennsylvania and Erie railroads, among other businesses, lured black

workers from the South by offering good-paying jobs in Philadelphia's labor-starved industries; more than 40,000 blacks trekked
northward to the city between 1916 and 1918. From Jacksonville and
Saint Augustine alone, the railroad companies transported more than
1,100 blacks to Philadelphia and housed the new work force in tents
and boxcars. Also during the war, Midvale Steel enlisted over 4,000
unskilled black workers, Atlantic Refining recruited 1,000, and Franklin Sugar hired 700. At the height of this wartime migration, black
families camped in stables, sheds, and churches.[22]

During the 1920s few blacks retained their wartime jobs in manufacturing. By 1927 industry employed only 6.1 percent of the city's
black wage earners. Few blacks worked in Philadelphia's huge textile
industry. Instead, black males worked as low-paid laborers in the
building trades, as longshoremen, as machine operators, or as domestics. According to the 1930 census, about 20 percent of black males
worked as waiters, chauffeurs, cleaners, or porters. The same census
reported that over 52 percent of black females worked in domestic
service. Moreover, black women in Philadelphia in 1930 constituted
almost one-fifth of the low-paid machine operators in sweatshop
clothing industries, cigarmaking, and laundries.

As in Chicago and Cleveland, the large influx of rural migrants
fractured the delicate social accord that had defined the status of Philadelphia's established black families—the Bustills, Mossells, Abeles,
Wrights, and Fausets. Few of the black elite in the 1920s engaged in
business. Although R. R. Wright headed a bank, Philadelphia's black
middle class discovered opportunity mainly in the professions. John
Abele, for example, established himself as a prominent architect; the
physician Nathan Francis Bustill helped found the black Mercy-Doug-
las Hospital; Aaron Mossell was a lawyer; Arthur Huff Fauset taught
anthropology at the University of Pennsylvania. Writing in the *Annals*
in 1921, Aaron's daughter Sadie Tanner Mossell, a political scientist
and member of the city's black elite, observed that Philadelphia "had
long possessed a relatively small population of Negroes of culture,
education, and some financial means. They had always enjoyed the
same social and education facilities as the whites, and courteous treatment from them. But with the increase in population by a group generally uneducated and untrained the privileges were withdrawn."[23]

Despite the large migration to Philadelphia, Newman abjured
even flirting with the idea of government-aided housing. With a
whimsical belief that he might be even slightly interested, in 1921
Edith Wood mailed him a copy of her letter to Secretary of Commerce
Herbert Hoover, proposing a $5.5 million government housebuild-
ing–job-creating measure. To cut costs, the homebuilding agency

would fire its own bricks, mix its own concrete, and saw its own lumber. This, she told Hoover, "would cut out the legitimate profits of the entrepreneur as well as the graft and profiteering revealed by the Lockwood Committee and other investigations."[24]

As she anticipated, Newman spurned the idea as offhandedly as had Hoover: "I differ so radically from you in my belief as to the wisdom of the program you suggest that I regret being unable to do anything to further such publicity. . . . Whenever the government has attempted to do what rightly belongs to the initiative of the individual, it has run into excessive costs that become burdensome to the public. . . . [Moreover] for the government to function in this field, private initiative would lag woefully."[25]

The credit squeeze on residential housing eased in 1923, inaugurating a suburban building boom in 1924 and 1925. In Philadelphia, building and loan associations helped fuel this boom by encouraging homebuyers to take second and third mortgages. But the boom expanded the supply of middle-class housing without adding to the number of low-income dwellings. On the contrary, it tempted owners of central-city slum property to convert existing housing into tenements.

Professional housing associations protested these conversions but seemed helpless to halt the practice. Lacking the reformist zeal that had marked the Progressive era, voluntary housing organizations such as the PHA plodded bureaucratically through the decade, on the one hand as best they could helping the overworked housing inspectors to enforce the city's ordinances, and on the other trying to broaden the base of homeownership among the working class.

Few cities—in fact, only New York, Brooklyn, Cincinnati, and Philadelphia—boasted housing associations with salaried professional staffs equipped to monitor the enforcement of city housing laws. For all their efforts, professional housing organizations performed ineffectively as code-enforcement watchdogs. Social and health workers reported housing offenses to the housing association; the association's inspectors confirmed the validity of the complaints and forwarded them to the city for correction. Newman also used data gathered by social and health workers "to determine the efficiency of the municipal government in its sanitary housing work," and, in classic Progressive parlance, made "recommendations to the city" and brought "the pressure of public opinion to force them to better service."

Monitoring code enforcement pitted an understaffed housing association against the sizable host of city landlords and tenement builders. The result was a mismatch. The city's housing code was neither sufficiently comprehensive nor adequately enforced. Despite the efforts of the PHA, too few inspectors manned the city's housing service, fire marshall's office, and Bureau of Buildings. In 1926 Newman bitterly attacked the city administration's poor enforcement record. "The reason," grumbled Newman, "is probably that the workers of these bureaus, if efficient, would bring in a large number of violations against [Republican boss William S. Vare] organization supporters, owners of tenements and factories, builders, and the like who make up the rank and file of their political backers."[26]

The Better Homes Movement

Newman recognized that housing laws frequently resulted in a diminished housing supply, increased poor maintenance and overcrowding, and worsened the housing problem. To offset this, the PHA kept up-to-the-minute information on construction, promoted residential zoning, and encouraged regional planning. Newman especially touted the building of small, inexpensive houses, and he combed the pages of engineering and building trade journals to discover low-cost prefabricated materials, construction gimmicks, or clever housing designs that might solve the eternal riddle of the "small cost" house. Writing about such a house to John Dries of the Department of Commerce (which, under Hoover, encouraged close government cooperation with business), Newman suggested numerous modifications of housing plans that might price a small house at under $2,100; contractors, for example, might trim building heights by a floor, use a closed staircase, or experiment with a rubber-like roofing material.[27]

Newman's fascination with the "small cost" house attracted him to the Better Homes movement, which not only emphasized home-ownership but was concerned about home efficiency and the desirability of streamlined, "inexpensive" housing that families of modest means could live in and strive to become better citizens in. Better Homes was conceived by the Department of Labor and by Better Homes in America, Inc., a home-boosting organization founded in 1922 by Mrs. William Brown Meloney, editor of the *Delineator*, a woman's magazine. From 1922 to 1927, Herbert Hoover served as president of the Better Homes organization; Calvin Coolidge chaired its advisory council, and James Ford served as executive secretary.

The Better Homes movement functioned principally through local committees. Created to encourage "better living conditions . . . by holding up high standards in homebuilding, home furnishing, and home life," the movement urged "old fashioned" thrift for home-ownership, "the improvement of home lots, the promotions of home gardens, and the dissemination of information for home makers of

moderate means to show the best that the community can do to promote and strengthen wholesome normal home life."

Closely aligned with the home economics movement that flourished in the 1920s, the Better Homes campaign promoted housing in
which modern technology and efficient design would liberate the
modern women from the slavery of housekeeping. The movement
advocated "knowledge of the means of eliminating drudgery and
waste of effort in housekeeping . . . and . . . encourage[d] the establishment of courses in home economics in the public schools." Similarly, Better Homes in America distributed numerous books and pamphlets, including *School Cottage for Training in Home Making, Boy Built
Houses*, and *Plan of Small Houses*.[28] By 1930 Better Homes councils
existed in 7,279 small towns and cities. Through Better Homes Week,
held every spring, committees held fetes, concerts, demonstrations,
and homebuilding exhibits stressing, in Hoover's words, that the
"soundness of our social system and the stability of our country are
greatly enhanced by the development of love for a home and the creation of a home that can be loved."

The PHA closely allied itself with the Better Homes movement.
Mrs. Bernard Newman sat on Philadelphia's Better Homes committee, and the association awarded a gold medal annually to the Philadelphia builder who erected the most "practical house of the best architectural design." Newman invited builders to submit drawings for
"comfortable, artistic and sanitary" dwellings that "may be purchased
or rented at a figure within the families' means." In 1928 the committee awarded the gold medal to a Philadelphia builder whose row
housing sold for under $4,650. In 1930 the committee stipulated that
its "low-priced design" should be saleable at a cost not to exceed
$6,500, but added that "satisfactory landscaping may not be found in
connection with low-cost operations."

Although Newman harbored some doubts about the space, quality, and amenities available in Philadelphia's least expensive row housing, between 1924 and 1929 he displayed unswerving confidence that
Philadelphia builders, armed with a practical blueprint, would ultimately triumph over the slums. Between 1923 and 1929 local builders
constructed almost 70,000 new homes in the city, all but 1,211 of stone
and brick. For home seekers with incomes over $1,800 a year, builders
offered a variety of sizes and styles. By 1929 over 50 percent of Philadelphians owned or were buying their homes, up from 38.8 percent
in 1920. In 1930 a modest five-room dwelling, each of the two floors
14.8 feet by 26 feet, with hot-water heat and electric fixtures, sold for
as low as $4,000. (In 1925 only 4 percent of the new housing in Phila-
delphia sold for under $5,000, and 15 percent was purchasable at

under $6,000.)[29] To aid the homebuying bonanza, by 1930 approximately 3,500 building and loan institutions, more than in any other American city, offered second and third mortgages to low- and moderate-income families. Indeed, in 1925 the PHA founded and Newman chaired the Better Housing Building and Loan Association "to aid small home purchasers by making second mortgage loans and assisting working class families with the fees and commissions which usually make second mortgages so burdensome."[30]

Limited-Dividend Housing

Newman's faith in the Philadelphia row house deflected his attention from the large-scale garden housing ideas of the Regional Planning Association of America (RPAA) and the limited-dividend schemes of the Julius Rosenwald Fund in Chicago or the Phelps-Stokes Fund and Metropolitan Life Insurance Company in New York City. Although Newman believed limited-dividend housing had a role in providing better housing, he remained convinced that housing reform should advise, police, and encourage private-sector operations rather than spawn housebuilding subsidiaries. Not surprisingly, then, when in 1931 Roberta Williams from the Wilmington, Delaware, Traveler's Aid Society asked Newman about the wisdom of large, limited-dividend housing developments, he demurred. "You undoubtedly have in mind Radburn, New Jersey," responded Newman. "My impression of the situation in Delaware leads me to suggest that much more will be gained by way of good housing for the small wage earner through the creation of a local housing association . . . than can come through a building construction project." Months earlier, he wrote, "It is only through the education of the builder and his financial backers to the greater profits in lower sale prices that the stimulus to inventive genius is given which results in lower construction costs."[31]

Here, to restate the argument, Stein, Wright, Mumford, Wood, Bauer, and the communitarian band fundamentally disagreed with professional housers such as Bernard Newman. They regarded the Newman and Better Homes approach as a provincial response to housing problems rooted in global structural change. To give fuller expression to their broad, "neotechnical" vision of modern housing, Wright, Stein, and the editor of the *Journal of the American Institute of Architecture*, Charles Whitaker, in 1923 had formed the RPAA. During the 1920s, expanding urban populations, mass transit, the automobile, and new highways pushed the boundaries of the metropolis well beyond the built-up areas and into the countryside. Deeply concerned about the need to deliberately order regional land-use patterns, the planners of the RPAA conceived highways, parks, and electrical grids as systems for directing land use on a regionwide scale. New York undertook the massive *Regional Plan of New York and Its Environs*, while the Regional Planning Federation of the Philadelphia Tri-State District (which included Bernard Newman on its executive committee) explored the future of the Philadelphia region.[32]

But the RPAA felt that regional planning federations focused too narrowly on highway planning, bridge building, and the design of city parks, and ignored the reality of unplanned suburbanization. Unplanned metropolitan growth, argued the RPAA, left urban form at the mercy of uncontrolled market forces. Reckless subdivision on the urban periphery constituted an extravagant waste of precious environmental resources, including natural beauty. Moreover, since subdivision developers keyed their product to upper-middle-class purchasers, such private ventures ignored the housing needs of working-class families.

The RPAA rejected the slum-clearance plans and restrictive legislation of the professional housers because it contracted the supply of low-income housing, which needed to be greatly expanded. Convinced that the creation of decent working-class communities rested on curbing the exploitation of land characteristic of suburban land development, the RPAA advocated bypassing the profit system in order to achieve the efficiency necessary to house low-income families.

Therefore, in 1924 Stein and Wright joined RPAA member Alexander Bing to create the limited-dividend City Homes Corporation (CHC). Between 1924 and 1931, with the moral backing of the RPAA, they built two "model" garden communities—Radburn, New Jersey, and Sunnyside, New York. In 1931 Wright and Stein teamed with Pittsburgh's Buhl Foundation to design and build Chatham Village, the last of the three communities inspired by ideas of the RPAA. All three places embraced the communitarian ideal. CHC located Sunnyside and Radburn beyond the built-up New York City area and cordoned the towns with a fringe of undeveloped land. Wright and Stein grouped their well-designed two- and three-story attached housing units around parklike greens.

Radburn and Sunnyside were hailed as evidence that America was at last emulating the pioneering example of Europe. Throughout the 1920s these housers had heralded the progress of communitarianism in Europe, especially the modern housing principles mirrored at Unwin's Letchworth and Welwyn Gardens and Ernst May's modern state-run housing developments in Frankfurt, Germany. Government-subsidized low-income housing in Europe had deeply impressed such American visitors as Catherine Bauer, from 1934 to

1964 America's leading exponent of modern housing. During a late-1920s tour of modern housing communities, Bauer had visited Great Britain and Germany and greatly approved the bauhaus style of her mentor, Walter Gropius. Another disciple of the *Neue Sachlichkeit* was the Russian-born architect Oscar Stonorov. Only a few years after the Great Depression had shrouded Philadelphia's working-class neighborhoods in gloom, Bauer and Stonorov went there to introduce their communitarian-cooperative housing ideas to the militant jobless hosiery workers of the city's Kensington district.[33]

Foreclosures and the Challenge of the Slums

It was clear by 1930 that neither garden cities nor philanthropic housing enterprises nor even the limited-dividend enterprises of Chicago's Boulevard Gardens or New York's Knickerbocker Village had effectively penetrated the surface of low-income housing need. More than 250,000 slum dwellers still crowded the grimy tenements of New York's Lower East Side. *Fortune* magazine in 1932 charged that two-thirds of Americans earned under $2,000, yet, nationally, the average price of a house topped $4,900, with shelter in the urban built-up areas selling for more than $4,500. Moreover, by 1930 thousands of low- to moderate-income families, having secured second or third mortgages from undercapitalized building and loans, floundered in a tide of sheriff sales. Between 1926 and 1930, Philadelphia sheriffs nailed writs of foreclosure on the faded doorways of 49,062 row houses; this compared to the 39,543 writs issued in the previous 25 years. It was not only sheriff sales that added to the depression's woes. In 1931 over 5,500 Philadelphians asked the city's Legal Aid Bureau for help to fight eviction for nonpayment of rent. Even the cautious Octavia Hill Society complained in 1930 about the poor rate of rent collection in their model Kensington homes.[34]

Depression poverty and overcrowding deepened urban squalor, spurring housing professionals to entertain plans for a large-scale war on the slums. The Better Homes movement shifted its focus to clean-up campaigns and housing rehabilitation. In 1930 Newman and the PHA agitated for slum clearance and tried to raise capital for the purchase, rehabilitation, and management of 1,000 houses in the city's blighted areas.[35]

Throughout the 1920s, the building boom in middle-class housing, the failure of the housing industry to supply low-cost shelter, the ineffectiveness of housing-code enforcement, and the continued flow of black migrants into the central city engendered the growth of urban slums. In October 1928, Harold S. Buttenheim, the vigorous editor of the *American City* and member of the RPAA, initiated a national crusade to eradicate slums and provide decent housing for every American family. Few housers challenged Buttenheim's emphasis on demolishing slum areas and replacing them with small parks and playgrounds and modern houses or tenements. But one objective of Buttenheim's "away with the slums" proposal raised many eyebrows, especially since it emanated from a houser who once marched in Hoover's Better Homes army. Buttenheim's proposal empowered the government "to issue housing bonds and to loan such funds at low interest . . . to non-profit housing corporations; and to give munici-palities the right to condemn slum property or land for low cost housing."[36]

Despite the challenge of the slums, such professional housers as Newman and Veiller balked at Buttenheim's call for a national gov-ernment housing subsidy "that is common to European countries." Newman protested that "[we] have not utilized the inventive genius of America yet in solving the housing problem." Undaunted, But-tenheim pressed for large-scale, government-aided slum clearance and limited-dividend housing.

In December 1931, President Herbert Hoover convened the President's Conference on Home Building and Home Ownership. It reflected not only the concern of professional and communitarian housers for slum and substandard housing but also the belief that decent housing was tied to good citizenship. A good house assured good citizenship; slums threatened to undermine the American way of life. Therefore, the American working-class family required safe and sanitary housing, complete with controlled heating, modern plumbing, electricity, and a fully equipped kitchen.

President Hoover's theme for the conference differed from But-tenheim's or Newman's. In the face of a storm of sheriff sales and evictions, Hoover insisted that the main question facing the delegates remained "how to make a home available for installment purchase on terms that dignify the name credit." Hoover favored the Home Loan Bank idea to enlarge the loaning power of banks and building and loan companies. Nevertheless, many committee reports hinted at an undercurrent of anxiety about housing and the social volatility of the slums. As an example, the Business and Housing Committee asked that, in future research, "we . . . approach with an open mind the pro-posal that the lowest wage earning group should be provided with homes at government expense."[37]

While the conference met, Wood's book *Recent Trends in American Housing* arrived at bookstores. In it, Wood estimated that 9 million unsafe and unsanitary houses in America required demolition, and she begged Congress to shoulder the $40 billion burden of providing new working-class housing. But, as the conference demonstrated, Wood, Buttenheim, and the communitarians no longer stood alone in recommending bold government action on housing. Even the chairman of the conference, Secretary of the Interior Ray Layman Wilbur, warned that "unless business men and business groups accept the challenge of [providing good housing at modest prices] housing by public authorities is inevitable."[38]

Buoyed by the newfound support for government action, in 1931 a number of housers formed the Public Housing Conference (PHC) (later the *National* Public Housing Conference), which officially launched the drive for a federal housing program.[39] Yet, despite the PHC, public housing's constituency was relatively small and inchoate. A few months after Hoover's conference, in January 1932, Senator Robert La Follette inserted a housing construction provision in his $5.5 billion public works bill. Buttenheim and Newman shared La Follette's skepticism about the chances of passing job-creating legislation in the present session of Congress, but despite the "lack of agreement among the advocates of slum clearance and large scale housing projects as to whether any federal aid is desirable, and if so, what form such aid should take," Newman concurred with Buttenheim that some of the participants at the conference should convene to discuss "how the impetus given to housing by the Conference might . . . contribute to our whole housing movement." Newman doubted that the meeting "would result in unity of judgement as to the feasibility of a hundred million government loan to limited dividend companies for the improvement of slum areas," an obvious reference to Buttenheim's pet project. Still, in 1932 Newman, the apostle of private enterprise and foe of government intervention in housing, agreed to examine the possibility.[40]

By the fall of 1932, with building construction almost at a standstill, building tradesmen, planners, and architects faced negligible opportunity for employment and joined the throngs in job lines and at soup kitchens. The ranks of those clamoring for massive public works swelled. Public housing now seemed less an ominous forerunner of European socialism and more a chance to employ the jobless and at the same time clear the slums and rehouse the poor.

2

The New Deal Housing Projects

Franklin Delano Roosevelt took the oath of office as president of the United States on a grayish day in January 1933. In Washington and other American cities, record joblessness, grinding poverty, and abysmal housing conditions excited fears of imminent disorder. Conditions were equally bleak in Philadelphia. Between 1929 and 1933, the value of Philadelphia manufactures had plummeted 50 percent. More than 300,000 jobless heads of households shuffled from mill gate to mill gate, vainly searching for work. Sheriff's writs dispossessed more than 19,000 Philadelphia homeowners in 1933, while anxious social workers publicized such cases as a 10-member family sharing a three-room apartment with another family of 5.[1]

Meanwhile, the city's private relief structure had collapsed. Lauded by President Hoover as the epitome of voluntarism in America, Philadelphia's Committee on Unemployment Relief had exhausted its funds in June 1932 and had disbanded. A distraught professional social worker and veteran of Philadelphia's voluntary relief effort, Karl de Schweinitz, told a congressional investigating committee about hungry Philadelphia families scavenging for rotting food on the docks. Social workers feared that the effects of overcrowded housing and inadequate diets, plus the social-psychological damage of extended joblessness, would undermine family life and threaten urban civilization.[2]

From the depths of the Great Depression was to emerge the nation's first federal housing program. Although fewer than 21,000 units were built nationwide by 1936—only 2 percent of the national housing output between 1934 and 1937—the New Deal housing program achieved high architectural and planning standards.

A New Deal for Housing

In 1933 Loula Lasker, after first equating the social and physical devastation visible in American cities to the destruction caused by the Tokyo earthquake of 1923, embraced the New Deal as "a chance" for planners to "rebuild the U.S.A." Lasker, along with Robert Kohn,

Catherine Bauer, Edith Wood, and Frederick Ackerman, was part of the "Make America Over Corps" that flocked to Washington, D.C., in early 1933. During the 1920s, many of these young New Deal reformers had served apprenticeships in university settlements or in planning and architectural offices. But their ideas about massive public works, national and regional planning, and government assisted low-income housing awaited the more fertile milieu of the 1930s for fruition.

On the eve of the New Deal, the Public Housing Conference (PHC) had maneuvered to make housing and slum clearance part of Roosevelt's "bold, persistent experimentation." Yet, during his 1932 campaign, FDR kept silent on the housing issue. As president of the American Construction Council, a trade association promoting the voluntary self-regulation of the building industry, Roosevelt between 1922 and 1928 had proposed very little government intervention in housing, other than providing data on building activity. As governor of New York (1928–1932), FDR had pushed for tax relief for economically stricken upstate farmers, government development of hydroelectric power on the Saint Lawrence River, wage-and-hour legislation for child and women workers, and the construction of state hospitals and prisons. Yet he balked at matching the record of his predecessor, Al Smith, as a champion of state-aided limited-dividend housing. As governor, one of FDR's few gestures toward housing was to encourage the Amalgamated Clothing Workers' union to use Smith's 1926 law to build its 234-unit Amalgamated Houses in Manhattan. Nevertheless, as the New Deal public works program unfolded during the memorable "first hundred days," Roosevelt and his secretary of the interior, Harold Ickes, supported a program of slum clearance and self-liquidating public works geared to produce maximum employment in the shortest time. By June 1933, Title II of the National Industrial Recovery Act, the Public Works Administration (PWA), inaugurated not only slum clearance but also low-income housing. Roosevelt and Ickes envisioned government-built housing generating thousands of jobs and rescuing the "sick" building trades; for housers, the PWA housing program was to "rebuild the U.S.A."[3]

With the creation of the Housing Division of the PWA, both communitarian and professional housers heralded the dawn of a new age in urban housing, especially when Ickes appointed as housing administrator Robert D. Kohn, the chairman of the American Institute of Architects' Subcommittee on Housing and a member of the RPAA. A respected proponent of modern housing, Kohn now oversaw the disbursement of $25 million in federal funds "for the construction, alteration and repair . . . of low-cost [limited-dividend] housing and slum clearance projects." Even for the depression the sum seemed paltry, but it proved sufficient to stir imaginations.

The Great Depression had intensified interest in the limited-dividend housing idea. Under the limited-dividend scheme, companies such as City and Suburban Homes were formed with the express purpose of providing good, low-rent housing. Rents were kept low because company investors accepted a limited dividend (usually between 5 and 7 percent) on their money. New York's 1926 law chartered such companies and made them eligible to float state-backed bonds to aid their housing ventures. In 1932 President Herbert Hoover's Reconstruction Finance Corporation (RFC) allowed federal dollars to be channeled to state limited-dividend companies. Since New York was the only state with a limited-dividend law, only one project was funded—the 1,593-unit Knickerbocker Village, located on New York City's East Side.[4]

The PWA money kindled ideas of a broad limited-dividend program that would cause dozens of Knickerbocker Villages to be built in many cities. Philadelphia architects and planners worked tirelessly, drafting blueprints for limited-dividend housing. The 12 proposals submitted to Washington epitomized the latest in modern design. Most featured child-centered garden communities, attractively clustered two- or three-story apartment buildings arranged on traffic-free superblocks with curvilinear streets, secondary systems of paths and lanes, and protected play areas.[5]

The only limited-dividend project built in Philadelphia was the thoroughly modern Carl Mackley Homes, sponsored by the hosiery workers union and located in the relatively undeveloped Juniata Park section near the city's Kensington-Frankford mill district. Named for a hosiery worker killed in 1931 by a strikebreaker, the Mackley project owed its existence to the dedication of three men: John Edelman, secretary of the American Federation of Full-Fashioned Hosiery Workers; Oscar Stonorov, the young, Russian-born architect who had moved to Philadelphia in 1931; and William Jeanes, a wealthy Quaker and a disciple of functional, low-cost modern housing.

Early in the depression, Edelman became aware of the tragedy of unemployment among hosiery workers and their families who lost their homes and found their belongings dumped at the curbside. He was excited by Stonorov's idea for a workers' cooperative housing project. Stonorov helped Edelman and Jeanes construct a detailed model for such a project, based on a survey of the housing needs and desires of the hosiery workers. Despite the extensive preparation, the plan was rejected by both Philadelphia philanthropists and the RFC; but in

1933 it received financial backing from Kohn and the Housing Division as the Juniata Park Housing Corporation.[6]

The 184-unit Mackley project encompassed four International Style buildings situated on 4.5 acres overlooking Juniata Park. Mackley Homes emphasized group life. Described as "long and lean," the four *Zeilenbau* were heliocentrically ordered; "every building obtained sunlight either in the morning or in the afternoon." A community swimming pool graced a setting of tidy flower gardens and sloping lawns. A wading pool and a nursery school benefited both children and working mothers; and all tenants enjoyed the auditorium, recreation rooms, hobby workshops, cooperative gas station, parking garage, and grocery store. The buildings provided additional social space on the roofs, where "people [were] able to mingle freely for discussion and reading"; indeed, proclaimed a Mackley Homes promotional brochure, "the roof is expected to be second only to the auditorium and swimming pool in popularity."[7]

The Mackley project stirred considerable attention worldwide. More than 60,000 visitors came to Philadelphia to view the housing during its early years. The outpouring of enthusiasm and excitement encouraged Stonorov to recruit a fellow student of the Frankfurt *Zeilenbau*, Catherine Bauer. In her book *Modern Housing*, published in 1934, Bauer argued that the European experience had demonstrated that, to be successful, a housing movement must spring from the anger, militancy, and organized determination of the working class. With Edelman, Bauer formed the Labor Housing Conference (LHC) and began to rally blue-collar support for low-cost public housing. She hoped to transform the Mackley initiative into a groundswell for modern housing, and she soon established local labor housing committees in New Jersey, New York, and North Carolina. Bauer and the LHC printed countless statements and flyers and hosted numerous mass meetings and conferences to advance the cause of modern housing.[8]

According to Bauer and the Philadelphia LHC, "Good housing in the right place for everyone must be the major objective of all resource planning. . . . Only large-scale methods," pleaded Bauer, "planning for use and not for quick profits, the construction of complete community developments designed to fit the needs of real groups of people, will prevent the erection of slums."

The need for good modern dwellings attracted Bauer and her LHC compatriots much more than the problem of the slum. According to the LHC, "the housing problem in Philadelphia can never be completely solved as long as the program is limited to central slum clearance." High-priced inner-city land could never accommodate good, low-cost housing.

Interestingly, the historian Bonnie Fox Schwartz found a similar ideological gulf separating professional social workers' solutions to mass joblessness from those of civil engineers in the 1930s. Schwartz found engineers, influenced by the technocratic ideas of Thorstein Veblen and Morris L. Cooke, pressing New Deal social planners to inaugurate massive public works projects, based on sound engineering principles that would provide bona fide jobs. Social case workers, however, lobbied the New Deal for a program that would require the jobless to pass a "means test" before employment.

In Philadelphia, professionals and communitarians alike applauded Mackley and the Housing Division's limited-dividend housing program. Nevertheless, Ickes spurned the bulk of limited-dividend designs submitted to the Housing Division as too costly for low-income housing. Furthermore, sponsors of limited-dividend housing proved incapable of providing the 15 percent equity required to make the projects self-liquidating. After three months of screening and reviewing blueprints, the Housing Division approved only 17 projects, including Mackley.[9]

Slum Clearance

Newman shared Bauer's disappointment when Ickes terminated the much publicized limited-dividend program in 1934 and placed greater emphasis on slum clearance. In Philadelphia the LHC joined with the Housing Study Guild— a rump session of the defunct RPAA that included Wright, Mumford, and Carol Arnovici—to accuse Ickes of paying lip service to the cause of housing and yielding to the "pressures of organized real estate and financial interests." Bauer and her colleagues charged that the Housing Division had allowed the obstruction of its original goal of building "thousands of modern, low-rental dwellings in planned communities" and spurned "the cooperation or participation of workers and consumers."[10]

For Newman, the Housing Division's adverse limited-dividend decision compounded his disdain for the agency. He was particularly embittered at Kohn for surrounding himself with a staff of lawyers and architects rather than experts like himself. Newman traveled to Washington on June 26, 1934, to inspect personally the New Deal housing operation. On his return he typed out a stinging rebuke of the Housing Division entitled "How to Stall." His fusillade appeared just as Ickes was replacing Kohn with a new division head, Horatio Hackett, a military man and an authority on skyscrapers, but not housing, and the type of bureaucrat Newman disdained as a "library specialist."

Newman bitterly accused Ickes and the Housing Division of capitulating to greedy realtors and jerry-builders. His vilification extended to the division's recently unveiled slum-clearance plans, which he branded as too costly and as rescuing the slumlord while ignoring the objectives of sparking employment in the building trades and housing the ill housed. But, in Newman's eyes, the division's main shortcoming was its failure to formulate a comprehensive housing program. "As important as slum clearance work is," he wrote to Ickes in 1935, "it should not be allowed to be the sole contribution to better housing."[11]

Ickes's Housing Division previewed its new colors when it released $144 million in June 1934, slated primarily for slum clearance and secondarily for the construction of housing projects. The abandonment of the limited-dividend program and the apparent lack of ardor for any large-scale housing program instigated the creation in 1934 of the National Association of Housing Officials (NAHO). Seeking an "organizing venture" and urged by Bauer to learn from Europe's experience with government-aided housing, NAHO staged an American tour for several prominent European housing experts; it also hoped to generate a national movement to replace the temporary Housing Division with a permanent federal housing agency and spearhead the drive for a real housing program.

Accompanied by Henry Wright and Ernest Bohn, the European housers—Sir Raymond Unwin of Britain's garden city movement, Ernst May, and Alice Samuels, manager of a housing estate in Great Britain—toured 14 cities. In Philadelphia, Newman entertained the foreign housing delegation, hosting numerous meetings and conferences, and climaxing the visit by escorting the dignitaries through Philadelphia's infamous courts and back alleys.[12]

Interest in modern housing mounted during the Unwin tour, then peaked in late October at the NAHO–Housing Division co-sponsored Baltimore Housing Conference. It was the single most important assemblage of housers in American history, organized to pressure Washington into creating a permanent, large-scale housing program modeled on the European experience. Delegates from the Baltimore conference traveled to Washington to buttonhole congressmen and PWA chief Ickes.

The conference proved a landmark in housing history. Together, American housers and planners, aided by their European colleagues, sculptured a set of recommendations that pleased communitarians and professionals alike. The final report stated that "public housing

. . . should be large-scale in which every effort . . . was made to reduce the cost of dwelling construction through care in design and purchase of materials." But, affirmed the conferees, new housing must be closely related to slum clearance, and only heavy government subsidies could recoup the great expense of demolishing acres of tottering slum housing. Finally, the conference called for the creation of a permanent governmental housing agency that would function mainly to coordinate and assist activities in local communities where federal aid or credit is given. "The responsibility for securing adequate housing accommodations," concluded the report, "and for focusing to this end the various efforts to supply new low-cost dwellings, to maintain sanitary conditions in existing dwellings, and to clear slums and abate overcrowding, must rest on the local governments administering each area."[13]

In the glow of the Unwin trip and the Baltimore Housing Conference, housers had a vision of resettling the American worker and his family in modern housing. Even Bernard Newman was enthralled by the spirit of the Baltimore meeting. Years later, Dorothy Montgomery remembered him bursting into the PHA office to announce, "Well," I took a big step; I decided to be in favor of public housing."[14]

Coincidentally, Newman now had a vehicle to articulate his newfound interest in public housing and influence the direction of government-sponsored slum clearance in Philadelphia. As part of the Housing Division's $144 million slum-clearance and housing demonstration program, in June 1934 Ickes created citizen advisory committees in all cities lacking existing local housing authorities. According to Ickes, the committees should be composed of "leaders of public opinion in the community who can advise us regarding what kind of a start should be made and where, in slum clearance." The 12-member Philadelphia Advisory Committee on Housing (PACH) included housing experts as well as representatives from business, labor, education, and philanthropy. Newman, whom Ickes initially had rejected as "having a definite opinion on the subject," was recruited as secretary.[15]

At its first meeting in October 1934, in the PHA offices, PACH identified slum clearance as its foremost mission and designated several sites for renewal, among them the region of ancient tenements and warehouses around the historic Gloria Dei [Old Swedes'] Church in the city's Southwark area. The committee earmarked $4.5 million for a project to bulldoze the site and build 700 units of demonstration housing for white residents. At later meetings, convened to honor Ickes's requirement that blacks share equally with whites in any government housing program, PACH haggled endlessly over the location of a project for the city's miserably housed black residents.[16]

As the city's black population increased, housing became a more critical problem for Philadelphia blacks. From 1920 to 1930, the city's white population rose 2.4 percent; the city's black population increased 63.5 percent, from 134,229 to 269,559. Despite modest economic gains made by blacks in the 1920s, the 1930 census indicated that over 27 percent of the gainfully employed blacks toiled as laborers; 14 percent worked as chauffeurs, longshoremen, or railroad helpers; over 13 percent served as domestics or personal service workers. The Great Depression pummeled the black work force. In 1929, unemployment idled 15.9 percent of employable blacks. Three years later, 56 percent of the black work force in Philadelphia looked for work, compared to a jobless rate of 39.7 percent among whites. In 1936, blacks constituted 39 percent of the city's relief families.[17]

By 1937, PACH had made little headway supplying either black or white housing; politics and racial factors explain the sluggish pace. To begin, in order to make public housing more politically popular PACH had pinpointed the slum for its target, not the rehousing of the poor. The depression, in fact, had etched slum statistics on the public consciousness. During 1934 and 1935, the Civil Works Administration (CWA), aided by the PHA, conducted a *Real Property Inventory* in Philadelphia and other cities and made available volumes of data on slum densities, housing that lacked basic sanitary facilities, and housing unsafe for habitation. Civic leaders viewed these data as evidence that slums exacted a horrendous tribute from the city in health, crime, and welfare costs. Slum clearance acquired a growing constituency.[18]

Politics and Public Housing

Between 1932 and 1935, Philadelphia's mayor, J. Hampton Moore, championed the political opposition to public housing. Moore, who stood for economy and retrenchment, attributed the city's financial chaos to its reckless spending in the 1920s. Philadelphia was broke, argued Moore; PWA projects would only entice the city into borrowing beyond its means. In 1933 Moore vetoed an ordinance passed by the City Council vacating several streets for the Carl Mackley Homes. Moore contended that the project not only saddled Philadelphia with high taxes but conflicted with the city's image: "Philadelphia is a City of Homes," expounded Moore. "A thousand cities and industries are appealing to the Federal Government for relief. Philadelphia is not among them." Two years later, he told the American Legion that the city "was too proud to have slums. . . . There may be some dilapidated houses . . . that does not constitute slums. People are merely living within their means."[19]

Moore's thoughts mirrored those of many small builders, local bankers, and real estate people, as well as the powerful National Association of Real Estate Boards (NAREB). In their view, the city had thousands of reparable units that, if refurbished, would more than meet the city's demand for low-cost housing. These rental houses were now being jeopardized by Ickes's plan to flood the market with housing projects.

Moore's adamant opposition to government housing notwithstanding, evidence mounted that a growing segment of Philadelphia's civic and political leadership questioned the wisdom of turning down federal money. Brandishing data on Philadelphia's collapsing infrastructure, the opposition countered Moore's intransigence. Republican Councilman Clarence Crossan, for example, scored Moore's reluctance to use CWA funds for flood-control projects and to extend the subway northward. Real estate magnate Albert M. Greenfield challenged Moore's claim that shunning federal funds lightened the city's tax burden; a Greenfield report showed that blighted areas in the central city and South Philadelphia actually drained tax revenues. Slum clearance was not a welfare matter, declared Greenfield, but merely a tactic to increase tax revenue. Finally, in 1935 the Philadelphia Chamber of Commerce, which had been urging the city to use CWA aid to repair the city's archaic sewage and water systems, informed Washington that it was "not hostile to the use of Federal monies . . . for slum clearance . . . in South East Philadelphia."[20]

The revival of Philadelphia's moribund Democratic party in the early 1930s furnished the necessary political base for slum clearance and low-income housing. Between 1890 and 1932, Philadelphia's Democratic party had survived as a Republican appendage. After 1924, a lieutenant of boss William S. Vare, John O'Donnell, chaired the sham party. Although O'Donnell supported Franklin D. Roosevelt in 1932, young New Deal zealots in Philadelphia attacked O'Donnell's Vare-tainted leadership of the party. The editor J. David Stern and the builder John B. ("Jack") Kelly (father of the late Princess Grace of Monaco) unveiled a new Democratic party, built largely on the strength of New Deal relief. In November 1933 the new party teamed with the independent Town Meeting party to elect S. Davis Wilson controller and WillB (that is the correct spelling) Hadley treasurer. The Wilson-Hadley victory announced the advent of a new Democratic party, and Jack Kelly assumed the party chairmanship.

Both Jack and his brother, Patrick H. Kelly, were builders whose ardor for the New Deal was no doubt intensified by the Roosevelt administration's commitment to crush the depression under a mountain of public works. Not coincidentally, in one of his first acts as Democratic party chairman, Kelly traveled to Washington, D.C., and convinced the administration to have a new federal post office constructed in Philadelphia. Simultaneously, Kelly seized hold of Philadelphia's explosive property-tax issue and emblazoned the symbol of homeownership as brilliantly on the Democratic escutcheon as Moore had etched it on the Republican.[21]

The young Democratic politicians in Philadelphia pressed for slum clearance, not housing. For example, in January 1935 the PWA allocated over $206 million to Philadelphia and ordered the city to submit a list of urgent projects. Both Moore's and Kelly's Non-Partisan Planning Committees submitted lists calling for the completion of the Broad Street subway and the widening of such key arteries as Vine Street. Neither list mentioned public housing, although Kelly's agenda included a $52 million slum-clearance project to level the South Philadelphia slums between Pine and Bainbridge streets and the Delaware and Schuylkill rivers.

Nevertheless, even slum clearance could be politically volatile. Such slum wards as the 2nd, 3rd, and 5th, with their large clusters of black, Italian, Jewish, and Polish voters, constituted the historic bastion of Republican strength. Campaigning for George Earle in the 1934 gubernatorial race, Kelly stopped at a roominghouse in one of the city's slum wards. On inquiry he discovered that 28 Republican voters were registered in the house; preposterously, the list of names included George Earle and Joseph Guffey, the Democratic state boss.[22]

Kelly's next political foray into the slums occurred the following year during an unsuccessful bid for the mayoralty. Campaigning against S. Davis Wilson, Kelly struck just a single blow with the slum issue. In an effort to translate Moore's statement about Philadelphia being "too proud to have slums" into Democratic votes, Kelly accepted a PHA invitation to tour the slums around Fourth and Bainbridge streets. There he tilted at Moore's conservatism by questioning how children raised without sunlight, running water, or toilet facilities could remain patriotic citizens. Kelly forthwith pledged to "wipe out all [the] City slums."[23]

The Democrat's loss in November 1935 hardly dampened the city's interest in the New Deal, for Mayor Wilson regularly commuted to Washington, D.C., seeking both Works Progress Administration (WPA) and PWA projects for the city. These included the building of the city's airport, originally named for the mayor, S. Davis Wilson, and the scrubbing of City Hall in preparation for the 1936 Democratic convention, which Wilson helped bring to Philadelphia. While Wilson appeared sympathetic to both slum clearance and housing, however, housing progress in the city languished. On the one hand, slum clearance and housing loomed as a political-economic issue pitting advocates of fiscal belt tightening against labor leaders and others championing public works; on the other hand, housing and slums could be viewed sociopolitically as a matter of black slums and black housing, issues that challenged the city to confront the mounting problems of racial segregation and black poverty.[24]

Housing the City's Blacks

Regardless of where they lived in Philadelphia in the 1930s, blacks occupied the oldest, least desirable dwellings, structures relinquished by the upwardly mobile German, Irish, and Russian Americans who discovered more suitable housing in the city's Logan, Olney, Oak Lane, and Lawndale sections, or in the expanding Montgomery and Delaware County suburbs.

The meanest black housing conditions prevailed in Philadelphia's center-city slums where, in 1936, over 32,000 of the 93,000 inhabitants were black. Black families crammed the tenements. Even less fortunate families inhabited miserable shacks nestled among decrepit houses honeycombed with one-room apartments. Sixty-six percent of the tenement structures were nearly a century old. Many residents still bucketed their water from yard hydrants, still poked about in murky rooms lit by flickering kerosene lamps and warmed unevenly by dangerous wood stoves. Over a quarter of the houses depended solely on outdoor water closets, sanitary artifacts frequently shared by three or four families. Close to 2,000 of the slum structures lacked electricity. Many of the houses were similar to a three-story row dwelling on Lombard Street that had been divided into 23 apartments; in them, 18 families shared 12 sinks, and 20 families used 7 water closets.[25]

Despite the miserable conditions, most black families endured in silence. Occasionally, groups of tenants took to the streets to shake their fists at a landlord, and the black press periodically denounced unsafe tenements. True outrage, however, required a consensus on race, a consensus that did not exist. As the tide of black migration rose in the mid 1920s, more and more of the black elite—physicians, merchants, teachers, social workers—withdrew from the old center-city neighborhoods to West Philadelphia. These black elites had difficulty identifying with the black migrants, who they blamed for the moral and physical degradation of black life.

Nevertheless, the depression struck not only the penniless migrant but also threatened to impoverish the entire black community. H. Viscount Nelson, a student of Philadelphia black society, noted that while the recognition of a common plight forced outcroppings here and there of race consciousness, one belief bound all segments of the black community: a hatred of discrimination.[26]

Philadelphia's Armstrong Association (the Urban League) and the city's National Association for the Advancement of Colored People (NAACP) best articulated the woes of the black community. Both organizations vigorously opposed discrimination; yet both bodies verbally flayed the slothfulness of the black migrants and urged them to seek job training and moral rearmament. These two organizations also promised to supply the leverage necessary to lift the black lower classes into a condition of respectability. Understandably, then, what interest there was in housing appeared principally among the ranks of these middle-class organizations. Like middle-class whites, bourgeois blacks subscribed to a housing rhetoric that identified disease, crime, delinquency, and other social problems with crowded, substandard housing.

Accordingly, the PWA's first housing program granting federal loans for limited-dividend projects had hardly been announced in November 1933 when Cheney State College President Leslie Pinckney Hill, Wayne Hopkins of the Armstrong Association, and Robert G. Taylor, the white Quaker president of the Whittier Center Housing Corporation, marched into Secretary of Commerce Dan Roper's office and extracted Roper's promise that the PWA not only would ignore racial lines in granting housing loans but also would "not support local efforts to segregate Negroes or any foreign group." Shortly thereafter, PWA officials commissioned Taylor to establish a Committee on DeSlumming, which in one official's words, "would meet the needs of all Philadelphia."[27]

Taylor's Committee on DeSlumming produced a spate of limited-dividend proposals, a number of them sponsored by black leaders and aimed at arresting incipient blight in West Philadelphia. One of the most celebrated plans was for the Park Court Apartments, a 14-unit complex to be built in West Philadelphia. But, like the plans for Jefferson Terrace, and the plans of the Blakiston Housing Corporation and Whittier Center (all for black housing in West Philadelphia), the Park Court plans were scrapped when the PWA phased out its limited-dividend program and turned to slum clearance and a demonstration housing program.[28]

Excluded from membership on PACH, and therefore without an official voice in the PWA housing and slum-clearance operations, in March 1935 the city's black leaders launched a campaign to publicize the black housing crisis. Both black newspapers, the Philadelphia *Tribune* and the *Independent,* ran a series of exposés of black housing conditions. Pictures of dilapidated tenements, of children playing in debris-strewn courtyards, and of ceilings threatening to collapse dramatized abominations that, according to the *Tribune,* both the federal government and the city heartlessly tolerated.[29]

Vocal Philadelphia blacks who demanded "really significant neighborhood developments" generally had in mind "fashionable housing" modeled after Harlem's Paul Lawrence Dunbar Apartments or the other attractive, limited-dividend developments constructed for New York City blacks in the 1920s by the Metropolitan Life Insurance Company. Apparently, some black slum dwellers fully comprehended the nuances of black housing rhetoric. A group of black women employed on a WPA sewing project insisted that while they could see the advantages of such a "high-classed colored neighborhood as the Dunbar project," they staunchly opposed segregation, "like they have in Baltimore." Nevertheless, asserted the women, "Negroes in Philadelphia still need better houses made available." Whatever the motive, and however stated, this simple agreement on the need for improved housing triggered the first housing campaign in 1935.[30]

Catherine Bauer's Labor Housing Conference, the PHA, and Philadelphia settlement workers joined the Armstrong Association and the black press to lead the campaign for action on housing. The Southwest Belmont YMCA, located in the heart of the city's worst black neighborhood, hosted several groups who met to protest firetrap houses. Prodded by activist settlement workers, a number of slum residents, black and white, bombarded PWA administrator Ickes and President Roosevelt with letters and telegrams deploring ramshackle housing and beseeching federal aid. One black woman pleaded that conditions in her neighborhood were so bad "we would be very glad if there would be iny [*sic*] way for better houses for ous [*sic*] to live in we has damp wall and water in the cellar the toilet on the outside."[31]

Within the black community, the housing campaign was mainly rooted in black professional, fraternal, and social welfare organizations, not the masses. Such individuals as the architect Homer Jefferson and the accountant Cornelius Garlick worked closely with the site-selection committee of the Philadelphia Advisory Committee on Housing. Black clergymen and other professionals concerned with housing fought the black housing battle as the Committee of One Hundred, while the NAACP's Slum Clearance Committee consisted of doctors, lawyers, clergymen, teachers, contractors, and other professionals. In addition, the National Negro Congress (NNC) established a housing committee.

The letter-writing campaigns kept interest alive in housing into 1936. In March of that year the Association of Philadelphia Settlements assembled 500 tenants to petition Washington for a government slum-clearance project. In October members of the Philadelphia chapter of the NNC visited Washington to demand action on housing; but the pleas of the delegation fell on the deaf ears of a New Deal harried by a budget-wary Congress. Ickes protested that there was no money; if Congress would extend the Housing Division appropriations, black housing in Philadelphia would be improved. But, for now, the administration could offer nothing.[32]

No matter how narrow its base nor how weak Washington's reaction, the black housing campaign registered an impact. Ickes had been alerted to black Philadelphia's enormous stake in the housing movement. And local and national Democratic leaders could no longer ignore the boost that former Republican black voters had given to Democratic candidates in Pennsylvania's 1934 gubernatorial election. In fact, the housing issue offered the Democratic New Deal coalition of organized labor, ethnic groups, and social welfare workers an ideal opportunity to respond to its newest constituency.

Evidence of the Roosevelt administration's new sensitivity emerged following the resignation in January 1935 of J. David Stern from his post on the Philadelphia Advisory Committee on Housing. In March—about the time of the letter-writing campaign—Washington began insisting that Stern's place be filled by a black representative.[33] Bernard Newman was scarcely evasive about the absence of a black on the committee. He confessed that "since a black project had not been considered, the committee had not seen a need for a black member." Newman's candor notwithstanding, Washington was goaded to act promptly. A PWA official in Philadelphia, Hyman Cunin, hurriedly instructed PACH concerning its "entirely new enlarged function." The official apologized that "the thought had not originally been given to a Negro project when the committee was selected." However, he continued, now that a black project was being considered, "a site selection for such a project will probably be most difficult." And this difficulty, Cunin concluded, "warrants the inclusion of at least two Negroes among the advisory committee membership."[34]

Ickes assigned his adviser on Negro affairs, the young black housing economist Robert C. Weaver, to find a replacement for Stern.

Weaver compiled a list of Philadelphia blacks suitable for the post, and on April 22, 1935, the advisory committee selected Crystal Bird Fauset, field secretary of the YWCA and the wife of Arthur Huff Fauset, a prominent black sociologist and chairman of the Philadelphia NNC. A month later, at Newman's behest, the committee chose a second black member, Major R. R. Wright, past president of the Georgia State Agricultural and Industrial Association and a former special agent in the Department of the Interior. At the time of his appointment, Wright was president of the Citizen's and Southern Bank and Trust Company. Although Wright's name had been absent from Weaver's list, Newman pressed for its inclusion, believing that the 80-year-old Wright would appease what Newman described as the older Booker T. Washington faction, which he saw as opposed to the younger W. E. B. Du Bois element of the black community.[35]

In truth, some concerned white Philadelphians counseled public housing for blacks as a more effective device than restrictive covenants or improvement associations for containing the expansion of the black community. In 1935 Walter Thomas of the City Planning Commission briefed regional Housing Division head A. R. Clas on the possibility of low-cost housing for blacks on slum-cleared land. According to Thomas, the area east of Broad Street around Girard Avenue was "heavily Negro and should remain so." He recommended "the development of a negro area having a physical outlet into Fairmount Avenue, and Girard Avenue, and Broad Street and Girard Avenue Business Area. Such a defined negro area would contribute to the stabilization of the area, . . . [and] will have a wholesome effect on the values of Girard Avenue west of Broad Street."[36]

The point was made even clearer in a letter to Bernard Newman from a Philadelphia attorney. The writer was "delighted" to read that PACH was "contemplating the establishment of a Harlem section for Philadelphia. . . . I have lived in this city my entire life-time, and I have been shocked to observe . . . great belts of what used to be fine residential sections, now densely populated by colored people. This is a serious situation, and . . . ought to be corrected, as it is resulting in large depreciation in the value of real estate in those sections."[37]

Newman, too, was blunt. When asked in 1935 about the city's plans for housing racial and ethnic minorities, the executive secretary of PACH argued that "we are ignoring racial matters entirely in our slum clearance program, except, or course, we are seeking to promote a separate slum clearance in a negro district, the new housing in which will be for negroes." A few months earlier, Newman complained that "opposition of certain negroes toward special negro housing projects . . . founded on antipathy toward anything which appears segregated, is unfortunate."[38]

Despite PACH's housing and slum-clearance mission, by late 1936 the committee had failed both to destroy the slums and to rehouse the city's blacks. Between 1935 and 1937, proposed sites for a black project were dismissed as either too costly or too racially sensitive. Land values proved exorbitant at one likely site, the grounds of the historic Pennsylvania Hospital in West Philadelphia. Another site, the vacant field adjoining Shibe Park (later Connie Mack Stadium), the city's professional baseball field located on Lehigh Avenue in North Philadelphia, alarmed the white neighborhood bordering the stadium. Whites hurriedly appropriated the site for recreational purposes.[39]

While racial and land-cost considerations militated against the discovery of a nonslum black housing site, an important court decision, the 1935 *United States v. Certain Lands in Louisville, Kentucky*, barred the Housing Division from building on more obvious slum sites. The case not only frustrated Ickes' sincere attempt to promote integration in public housing but forced the decentralization or localization of public housing decision making.

To make matters worse, federal money for PWA housing projects was always hard to come by. In December 1934, $110 million of the $150 million allotted for PWA housing was diverted to relief, and when $390 million was restored in June 1935, Roosevelt promptly slashed the amount by over $250 million and ordered the division to restrict its operations to swiftly executed projects on readily acquirable land. As a result, such decaying slum sites as the Old Swedes' Church area, which required costly and time-consuming land acquisition, had to be ignored.[40]

Clearly, obstacles had limited and confounded the goals of the Housing Division. During the three and a half years of its existence, the Housing Division built only 49 projects in 36 cities, most of them in New York, Ohio, and Illinois. Seventeen of the projects housed white tenants; 17 had mixed white and black occupancy; and 15, including the Alta Vista Homes in Virginia, the Techwood Homes in Atlanta, and the Trumbull Park and Jane Addams Homes in Chicago, housed black families. Only one housing project marked the PWA's efforts in Philadelphia. In fact, the city fathers gasped in January 1936 when the federal government broke ground for Philadelphia's lone demonstration project in Northeast Philadelphia—far from black or white slums. The Hill Creek project, which opened for occupancy in 1937, represented neither slum clearance nor true low-cost housing.[41]

After touring the Chicago PWA housing projects in June 1936,

Ickes dejectedly confessed in his diary that "from what I saw and heard I was very much disappointed with the progress that has been made. There isn't any doubt that something is wrong with the Housing Division, in fact it has been wrong for a long time. We are not getting results."[42]

Ickes's remorse aside, architecturally and socially the PWA Housing Division built good communitarian housing. A federal program in which 30 percent of the cost of labor and materials came as an outright government grant allowed ample latitude for the free exercise of architectural imagination. More often than not, the resulting housing satisfied communitarian expectations. Housing Division regulations straightforwardly defined low-rent housing as "the most economical type of dwelling that will assure the safety, health, and reasonable comfort of the inhabitants." Standards were promulgated "in terms of the minimum decent requirements of American family life." The division issued a variety of plans that accommodated local housing preferences and reflected the regional availability of materials.[43]

Philadelphia's tastefully designed Hill Creek Homes mirrored the range of opportunities that the Housing Division afforded local architects. Situated on a verdant site overlooking Tacony Creek Park, Hill Creek was located on the fringe of the city's Northeast, not far from the Carl Mackley Homes. Its communitarian features included cul-de-sac parking, curvilinear streets, integral shopping facilities, landscaping, and a two-story, two-room-deep design that satisfied the communitarian prescription for light and air. Nevertheless, Hill Creek's affinity for communitarian appurtenances mired the project in the same dilemma that had confronted such limited-dividend ventures as Mackley, Radburn, and Sunnyside. The high cost per room made it impossible to achieve truly low-cost housing. Therefore, most of Hill Creek's first tenants were white middle-class teachers, lower-echelon management personnel, and skilled and semiskilled workers.[44]

The dilemma of Hill Creek and Mackley cut even more deeply. Reconciling the architect-planner's penchant for modern housing with the amorphous requirements of minimal housing needs enmeshed the New Deal in an ideological quagmire. On the one hand, New Deal housers of the communitarian school insisted that within the PWA's land and building-cost limitations, the demonstration projects afford "the fundamentals of good clean living . . . without extravagance." Accordingly, Housing Division guidelines prescribed skillfully grouped, functionally designed, neighborhood units. On the other hand, this predilection for communitarianism among the division's corps of architects and planners contrasted with the division's vendetta against the slums. The vendetta of course reflected the traditional concerns of the division's professional housers and public health staffers, as well as the division's political sensitivity to the growing fear among central-city leaders about the rampant spread of slums. The outcome of this ideological jousting between communitarians and professionals bequeathed to the future of public housing a weak social underpinning. Public housing had to be justified as contributing to slum clearance; at the same time, it compelled housing spokesmen to justify superblock or neighborhood unit architecture for fiscal rather than social reasons. For example, Arthur DuBois, the Philadelphia district manager of the Housing Division, argued forcefully that massive, well-designed projects "created a nucleus in the slum and blighted district . . . [that served] as a spreading point for the regeneration of valuable and intensely developed districts in the heart of our cities."[45]

DuBois's words spotlighted the Housing Division's valiant effort to fuse the modern principles of the communitarians with the slum-clearance gospel of Newman and the professionals. The effort forced the division to explain every housing venture in the idiom of slum clearance. Unlike the visionary, if not utopian, excursions of Perry and Bauer, which beheld modern housing and community making as part of a social reconstruction, Housing Division literature bristled with burglars and murderers whose twisted psyches "were to a large degree formed in childhoods spent in slums." Not only would slum clearance check incipient crime, to use the division's logic, but it would also inoculate the city against tuberculosis, influenza, and other slum predators. This philosophical schizophrenia would indefinitely plague public housing policy.[46]

3

Bauhauses for the Worthy Poor

An electrifying incident was to jar the Philadelphia conscience and rally the city behind housing reform. Just before midnight on December 19, 1936, Alberta Richardson, a 28-year-old black housewife, felt her tenement building trembling. Then, with a crackling sound, huge chunks of plaster fell from the ceiling and crashed to the floor. Next came a dreadful rumble, followed by a deafening roar as the walls of the ancient structure teetered and the flooring collapsed. Seconds later, the Richardson dwelling and the adjoining tenement were a smoking rubble.[1] The disaster transformed the issue of bad housing from a local problem to a social and political cause.

In fact, it was in 1936 that urban housing came of age. Since 1933, Catherine Bauer had been lecturing friends in the housing and labor movements on the urgent need to convert their vision of modern housing into a crusade. Although the Mackley project and the 1934 Baltimore Housing Conference had engendered considerable excitement among communitarians and professionals, by late 1935 the prospects for a "real housing movement" seemed remote.

The situation changed quickly in 1937 when America joined such nations as Great Britain, Sweden, and the Soviet Union in establishing a permanent federal housing agency and developing a national program of low-income, publicly built housing. The housing built under America's 1937 law was professionally designed, solidly constructed, and, although frequently spartan in appearance, mirrored an ongoing adherence to communitarian principles.

Yet the federal government's rigid funding formula for public housing construction, as well as its strict guidelines for tenant selection and tenant retention, begged the question of public housing's mission. Was public housing to provide good housing for the working class, or was the program to build modern asylums where the poor could learn habits of thrift and cleanliness?

Tenant Protests

For two weeks following the tenement disaster of December 19, Philadelphia's slum dwellers seethed with anger. Polemical thunderings against slums and slumlords monopolized politics and the press. Heartened by the widespread public outrage, the Philadelphia *Tribune* pleaded that "indignation over the tragedy" not be allowed to die, and the paper summoned Philadelphians to "rid the city of this menace to health, life, and property."[2]

The city's mayor, S. Davis Wilson, hardly needed prodding. Recognizing a politically charged issue, Wilson lashed out at the tenement evil and promised to wreak vengeance on the slumlords. Overnight, he created the Mayor's Housing Committee, which included the respected black physician Harry W. Barnes, who had managed Wilson's mayoralty campaign among black Philadelphians. The mayor also announced an assault on unfit housing, demanding the immediate demolition of 5,000 slum houses. To dramatize his determination, he appeared, crowbar in hand, to help demolish the first house.[3]

Wilson hardly stood alone. Politicians and civic leaders, black and white, swarmed over the scene of the tenement disaster. Democratic chairman Jack Kelly blamed the tragedy on "political skullduggery" and backed up his demand for slum clearance by going to Washington for aid. Meanwhile, the city press published more scandal about Philadelphia's housing situation. One story reported that the landlord of the collapsed house had leased the tenement from a trust managed by the reputable Fidelity Philadelphia Trust Company. Moreover, as lessee and not owner, the slum profiteer had never licensed the building as a tenement. Bernard Newman, speaking for the PHA, cited statistics from the 1934 Philadelphia *Real Property Inventory* showing that the collapsed tenement was one of 14,000 unfit structures in the city.[4]

Unlike "proper" Philadelphians, the city's tenement inhabitants were too infuriated to be assuaged by Wilson's crowbar or Newman's statistics. A few days after the tragedy, a passionate National Negro Congress (NNC) summoned hundreds of mourners to the Wesley AME church to honor the disaster victims and plot war against the slums. In the wake of that gathering a group of slum dwellers who lived near the site of the collapse formed a Tenants' League; days later, the league held its first of many protest meetings at the Southwest Belmont YWCA. Present were representatives of the NNC, the Workers Alliance (an activist organization of the unemployed), and the communist-backed International Labor Defense. The protestors demanded that slum housing be razed and that displaced families be adequately housed at no added expense. The group quickly spurned Wilson's offer to shelter the homeless victims of slum demolition in the city's National Guard armories. Concerned Philadelphians deluged Wilson with letters and petitions demanding low-cost housing, as well as a list of housing vacancies for slum families frightened from their creaking homes or evicted by the mayor's crowbar.[5]

Tenant strikes, housing meetings, and protests dominated activities in 1937. The Tenants' League emerged in the vanguard of neighborhood organizations actively battling for better housing conditions in Philadelphia. Unlike other housing groups, the league boasted a grass-roots membership. Militantly and frequently, it picketed for "decent homes at low rent," while it stridently opposed both Jim Crow practices in housing and the blacklisting of relief tenants. Street demonstrations, flyers, and protest meetings were the usual weapons that the league wielded against belligerent landlords and city officials in behalf of better inner-city housing.[6]

The Tenants' League was not alone in its housing campaign. On the first anniversary of the tenement collapse, a council of housing groups hosted a citywide conference at which speaker after speaker, including Catherine Bauer and Langdon Post—the latter head of the New York Housing Authority—attacked slum housing. Yet, in commenting on the meeting, the *Tribune* contended that despite all the demonstrations, talk, and petitions, the same housing menace prevailed a year after the collapse: The city's black neighborhoods still averaged 121 persons per acre of crumbling rookeries.[7]

A City Housing Authority

By politicizing the housing issue, the tenement tragedy forced city politicians to prescribe a definite course of action on housing. That action became clearer after the state legislature passed the Housing Authorities Act of 1937, which empowered municipalities to create local housing authorities armed with the power of eminent domain and therefore legally equipped to undertake massive slum clearance and rehousing. Furthermore, local authorities were empowered to receive and spend public dollars and to acquire bonded debt.

Both Mayor Wilson and Jack Kelly had advocated the formation of a city housing authority, and toward that end had appointed separate housing committees that met together on New Year's Day in 1937 to hear testimony on Philadelphia's housing situation. Most of the witnesses favored a housing authority. Only the city's real estate industry opposed public housing; they argued that it would compete unfairly with existing property and impose an indirect tax on real estate owners, who bore over 90 percent of the city's tax burden. Despite their opposition, slum clearance and public housing enjoyed unprecedented momentum. Pennsylvania's "Little New Deal" governor, George Earle, gave top priority to slum clearance and, backed by a Democratic state legislature, successfully reversed a 1936 state supreme court decision killing the state's Housing Authority Act. On August 26, 1937, Philadelphia's City Council approved a resolution establishing a city housing authority.[8]

Nationally, the movement for public housing gained comparable strength. Mainly as a result of Bauer's energetic campaigning to form a European-style labor housing movement in the United States, by April 1936 labor housing councils existed in 75 cities, including Philadelphia. The April 1936 hearings before the Senate Committee on Education and Labor on the Wagner Housing Bill affirmed the growing consensus among housers that the hour for a large-scale public housing program had arrived. In a 1936 speech delivered at the opening of the PWA's Williamsburg Homes project in New York City, President Franklin Roosevelt, in the midst of his campaign for a second term, added his full endorsement to the Wagner housing legislation. But while unanimity appeared at one level, an ideological cleavage was to erupt. Congressional testimony on the Wagner bill by communitarians such as Wood, Bauer, and Woodbury continually emphasized good, well-designed housing and the need for children to grow up in safe and sanitary homes; in contrast, Ernest Bohn, testifying in behalf of the professionally oriented NAHO, stressed the economic and social cost of slums and denied that public housing necessarily competed with private-sector housing.[9]

The Wagner-Steagall Act, signed into law September 9, 1937, created the U.S. Housing Administration (USHA). Congress empowered the new agency to make loans to local authorities for up to 90 percent of the cost of minimal slum-clearance and housing projects. Although the act resembled the "national housing program" framed by the Baltimore conferees, and although communitarian housers praised the bill, it represented a compromise—a fusion of communitarian vision, professional empiricism, and political reality. The legislation clearly satisfied the housers' demand for a permanent housing agency, but couched the housing mission in the depression-era vocabulary of national emergency and job-creation.[10]

Moreover, to achieve a permanent housing agency and a national housing program, the communitarians surrendered much of their vision of modern housing. The Wagner Act made slum clearance a "moral obligation," in Charles Abrams's words. It tied public housing to the "demolition of an equivalent number of slum units" and confined the program to poor families "who cannot afford to pay enough to induce private enterprise to build safe and sanitary housing for their use." Therefore, contrary to the wishes of the communitarians, the act did not assert that Americans have a right to decent housing but only that society must provide minimum shelter to low-income families who find the private market beyond their reach.[11]

Furthermore, in deference to the American desire for local control over decisions involving taste, custom, or tradition, the Wagner-Steagall Act decentralized the administration of public housing. Federal regulations established guidelines for site selection, building material standards, and per unit cost. Government manuals also specified minimal health, safety, and other environmental standards. Beyond that, Washington carefully honored local traditions in architecture, as well as local patterns of racial segregation and local customs for determining which applicants for admission were socially and economically "worthy" or "unworthy" to live in public housing.

Significantly, this decentralization of public housing gave free rein to politics of another sort including the intrusion of extralocal pressure from Harrisburg into local affairs. A clash between Governor Earle and Mayor Wilson over the selection of Philadelphia's five Housing Authority members illustrated the conjunction of localism, public housing, and state politics. At first the state legislature, which created the Philadelphia Housing Authority, allowed only the governor the right to appoint members. Wilson furiously charged Earle, Jack Kelly, and Joe Guffey with "gang rule" and tyranny by remote control. The battle over "state dictatorship" versus "home rule" raged until Harrisburg conceded Wilson two appointments to the authority.

Earle's and Wilson's records of appointments reflected not only the authority's conservative slum-clearance orientation but also the political sensitivity of the public housing issue in Philadelphia. The first five authority members were James McDevitt, Roland Randall, Frank Smith, Harry Barnes, and Joseph Greenberg. (Barnes and Greenberg were Wilson's choices.) None of those selected won the unqualified endorsement of Philadelphia housing reformers. Although McDevitt represented labor and Barnes the black community, it was Roland Randall, a past president of the Philadelphia Real Estate Board, who typically reflected the sympathies and outlook of the authority.[12]

The unpaid, five-member board met twice monthly. Board meetings usually dealt with tenant selection, site decisions, staff hiring, awarding of contracts, and such city–authority issues as zoning variances, street vacatings, and the size of the annual payment to the school board in lieu of the property taxes the federally funded authority was constitutionally forbidden from paying. In time, the authority oversaw a bureaucratic empire, including a large downtown headquarters that housed the offices of the executive director and the directors of finance, development, management, community affairs, and personnel. Finally, each housing project evolved its own bureaucracy of managers, aides, maintenance staff, and project police.[13]

Public Housing Sites

Between 1937 and World War II, most urban housing authorities seized the opportunity to use available federal dollars to combat urban blight and erect low-cost housing. Thanks to the political acumen and personal ambition of a young Texas congressman, Lyndon Baines Johnson, the first USHA project, the Santa Rita Homes, arose in the Mexican American section of Austin, Texas. Cincinnati's housing authority located its first housing on slum-cleared land in the city's "black basin" area. Chicago's first prewar USHA project demolished 47 acres of ramshackle Southside slums and replaced the aging clapboard tenements with the 1,662-unit Ida Wells Barnett Homes, a two- and three-story brick row and apartment housing complex for black residents.[14]

Catherine Bauer relentlessly opposed this propensity of city housing authorities for siting low-income housing projects in slum areas. Convinced that technology made urban decentralization inevitable, as a USHA consultant Bauer urged the federal government to force cities to locate housing projects on vacant sites. The NAHO also promulgated public housing site standards that prescribed ample open space, proximity to schools, and freedom from noise and industrial pollution. Writing for the NAHO, the architect-planner Henry S. Churchill asked that housing projects "be conceived as an integral part of the city or metropolitan district . . . [and] be based upon knowledge of general community development, . . . and utilize comprehensive city and regional planning." Unfortunately, all too frequently Bauer's and Churchill's pleas went unheeded.[15]

Although not a member of the Philadelphia Housing Authority, Bernard Newman chaired the authority's subcommittee on sites and, as a professional crusader against the slums, campaigned to have projects located on clearance sites rather than in vacant areas. To Newman's chagrin, Washington steadfastly discouraged building on slum sites, especially those costing over $1.50 per square foot. Federal strictures forced Philadelphia to erect two of its first three projects, the James Weldon Johnson and the Tasker Homes, on vacant land; only the city's third site, Richard Allen, required extensive slum clearance.

Yet, all three projects were located in or near the center of the city, and all served the authority's policy of social and sanitary control. In addition, all three satisfied the authority's mandate that projects have a "positive impact" on the surrounding neighborhood, for each was over 15 acres and protected on at least one side by a natural boundary: railroad tracks, a wide street, a park.[16]

Newman had hoped that the Housing Authority's first white housing project would clear the tenement-infested neighborhood around the historic Old Swedes' Church, but he soon discovered that decades of protest against such putative slum evils as delinquency, high tuberculosis rates, and stunted physiques paled before the politics of neighborhood opposition. The Octavia Hill Society had joined area settlement houses and John Roak, the church rector, in a campaign to demolish 668 "decadent" buildings and erect 950 two- and three-story low-income units on a 26.3-acre site at Front Street and Washington Avenue. The project boosters, however, overlooked the social dynamics of an area whose Italian population had remained fairly stable. Many (38 percent in 1930) owned modest but well-kept homes valued at between $2,000 and $7,000. Although these homes frequently lacked modern sanitary facilities and needed repairs, 48 percent were mortgage free in 1934. The Italian homeowners made up much of the opposition to the project. When its proponents declared that a "whites only" project would guarantee neighborhood stability, Italian homeowners pleaded for their homes, pointing to their vineyards and vegetable gardens nestled in the rear. Supplications aimed at such symbols of homeownership carried political weight in Philadelphia, and another site was chosen.[17]

The city's white Tasker project would sit atop 44 acres of graded trash in the industrial "neck" area of South Philadelphia. The filled land presented an engineering nightmare for large-scale construction, and securing a foundation for the project required the builder to drive more than 1,000 pilings, some of them as much as 58 feet deep. For years, telltale remnants of the refuse heap insulted the eyes and noses of the tenants. Furthermore, and contrary to another NAHO standard, the project abutted the giant Atlantic and Gulf oil refineries, whose sulfurous emissions regularly inflamed the sinuses.[18]

Designed by an architectural group headed by Walter T. Karcher and Carl Zeigler, Tasker's 1,077-dwelling units were arranged in a peculiarly baroque fashion. Rather than order the 131 buildings about a system of curvilinear pedestrian walks, the planners created three huge quadrangular superblocks, each inclined along one of three diagonal axes. Within each superblock, the two- and three-story brick flats and row houses were aligned perpendicular to a central court or play area. A junior high school and Lanier Park anchored two corners of the triangular site, while a small grocery and drugstore shared the interior of the site with the project management offices and community building. Secluded streets, drives, and cul-de-sac parking gave the site a taste of communitarian ambience.[19]

However, building the white Tasker project ranked second to the authority's primary mission; for in Philadelphia, as in Chicago, a black housing project headed the agenda. Both Philadelphia black Housing Authority member Harry Barnes and Harold Ickes's racial watchdog, Robert Weaver, considered the new public housing program the high point of the New Deal. Standing before a meeting of the National Negro Congress (NNC) in 1938, Weaver praised the USHA for inaugurating a new era in black housing. Black Americans, said Weaver, were the real beneficiaries of the program. Yet this enthusiasm for public housing ignored the prospect that black projects might simply become black housing.[20]

Philadelphia's James Weldon Johnson Homes illustrated how easily public housing evolved into black housing. Great pomp and circumstance attended the May 1939 groundbreaking for a housing project named in honor of the famed playwright and author. The white police and fireman's band, USHA head Nathan Straus, and a scattering of white officials scarcely detracted from the distinct blackness of the affair. Surrounded by a crowd of black parents and schoolchildren especially released from class to be present, Harry Barnes and Charles Lewis, president of the National Negro Congress, helped Straus turn the first spadeful of earth. When the $3 million housing complex opened on October 1, 1940, 1,800 people—well over 95 percent of them black—were housed in the 535 units.[21]

For three years, Philadelphia's Advisory Committee on Housing (PACH) had combed North and West Philadelphia unsuccessfully for a "Negro project" site. In 1938 the Philadelphia Housing Authority followed Ickes's uncomplicated formula for determining whether a project would be white or black: The racial composition of a project should conform to the "prevailing racial composition of the surrounding neighborhood."

The task of finding a black project site had baffled PACH, which had considered the Glenwood Cemetery site in 1935 and then pigeonholed it as "too near a white district." A huge Odd Fellows cemetery situated in North Philadelphia, the Glenwood site was skirted on one side by railroad tracks and bordered on the remaining two sides by black neighborhoods. Nevertheless, some Philadelphians protested that the site "would be a great blow to West Philadelphia and jeopardize adjacent institutions like the University of Pennsylvania and Convention Hall." Despite these objections, in 1936 PACH chose the 22-acre site, but its decision arrived too late; federal housing was stalled.

Glenwood was resurrected again in 1938. The new Housing Authority had planned to locate its first black project on a slum site, but Washington's cost restrictions forced the Philadelphia authority to dust off the Glenwood proposal.[22]

Work had no sooner begun at Glenwood when plans were readied for a second black project, to be called the Richard Allen Homes. The Allen site meant clearing 27 acres of ramshackle slums from around Fairmount Avenue and Poplar Street—a heavily populated black neighborhood just below Temple University. In 1940, black families constituted 51.5 percent of the West Poplar neighborhood; other inhabitants were foreign-born Jews, Lithuanians, and Germans, who preserved the vestige of an ethnic past in an area notorious for its alley dwellings and ancient courts. The Richard Allen Homes replaced eight blocks of the neighborhood's most scabrous hovels and aging tenements. Of the structures cleared from the site, 68 percent lacked indoor toilets and almost half were without central heat. Of the 868 families displaced from the site, 88 percent were black and wretchedly poor.[23]

Low-Cost Public Housing

Freeing the slum dwellers from the bondage of unsafe and unsanitary tenements constituted only part of the challenge. The principal task remained rehousing the displaced in low-cost, modern housing. In the past, well-meaning, often visionary limited-dividend housing ventures had produced housing too expensive for the low-paid wage earner. Now, government had entered the lists as a supplier of mass housing. In setting design standards for low-income housing, the USHA adhered to the advice of Churchill, the NAHO, and the American Public Health Association (APHA). To avoid strait-jacketing architect-planners with federal regulations, NAHO recommended that public housing cover only 20–35 percent of the site, and, following Ernst May's advice, that planners arrange the housing "to obtain the maximum of wanted sunlight." Elements of the Perry, Wright, and Stein "neighborhood unit" concept also appeared in the NAHO standards: Discourage through-traffic patterns, provide pedestrian overpasses, and incorporate protected play areas, clubrooms, workshops, and assembly rooms.[24]

Increasingly, in the late 1930s, such housers as James Ford and Elizabeth Wood (who until 1954 headed the Chicago Housing Authority) envisioned the neighborhood unit, or superblock, as the critical design model for public housing. A modern urban community form first propounded by the French architect Le Corbusier and incorporated into the Bauhaus community designs of Walter Gropius and Ernst May, these bold, large-scale, comprehensively planned, freestanding superblock communities, the communitarians claimed, would exert a salutary impact on the residents of the project and the surrounding region.

Unfortunately, the social-cost justification for the superblock comported too easily with the conservative inclinations of local housing authorities. Dorothy Montgomery recalled that as an impressionable young woman, she had been captivated by the early promise of public housing. "Some of us who supported public housing [in 1937 and 1938] really had a notion that we were going to improve the quality of urban design. We were quickly disabused of that. [Much of the] reform purpose of public housing was defeated in the first couple of years. . . . When the PHA was formed," recalled Montgomery, "one of the first acts these five new board members did was to travel to North Philadelphia to see the PWA project called Hill Creek. When they came back after the meeting, and sat around the table, to a man they said, 'Well, we'll never do another like that: it's too good.' "[25]

Although, as Gwendolyn Wright has observed, much of the early public housing reflected "innovation as well as economy" (Wright singled out as an example architect William Wurster's Valencia Gardens project in California, with its continuous balconies overlooking an interior court), nevertheless, more often than not, the economy, especially the closed book on "frills," branded the buildings as poorhouses rather than pioneer community developments.[26]

With the exception of the New York City authority, during the pre–World War II years local housing authorities abjured high-rise public housing architecture and built two-, three-, and four-story row and apartment housing. In all three prewar Philadelphia housing projects, the architects arranged the low-rise buildings in communitarian fashion—facing a grassy court or "commons" area where they hoped neighbors would gather.

Because of the novelty and risk of large-scale public housing undertakings, as well as the compensation formula employed by USHA, in Chicago, Philadelphia, and other large cities architectural consortia designed the early housing projects. W. Pope Barney, the prominent architect involved with Stonorov in the communitarian inspired Carl Mackley project, headed the design group that produced the drawings for the 589-unit Johnson Homes. At Johnson, Barney arranged 58 two- and three-story red brick buildings around pleasant courts and tree-lined, grass-planted walkways. Amortized over 60 years—this was true of all prewar USHA projects—Johnson embodied sturdy construction, utilizing such durable materials as flagstone sills, concrete floors, steel double-hung windows, and structural steel frames and studding. Sturdiness aside, Barney's modest architectural flourishes—gabled roofs, white canopies over the doorways, landscaped walks—endowed Johnson with a communitarian heritage. Thus, while the Johnson buildings turned their backs on the neighborhood, Johnson's amenities earned the project an enduring reputation for distinctiveness and helped instill in the project an aura of neighborhood pride and acceptability only briefly enjoyed at Richard Allen, the city's second black project.[27]

In fact, Allen never achieved the degree of liveability attained at Johnson. More than Tasker, Allen epitomized the no-frills functionalism that project architects borrowed from the Bauhaus. It also reflected one of the tenets of modern housing in the 1920s and 1930s: Efficient or functional environments have positive behavioral consequences. The more streamlined the kitchen, the more carefree, happy, and productive the housewife. Architects viewed floor moldings and ceiling cornices and other architectural appendages as "dust catchers." Modern housing was to liberate the family from the cluttered, overstuffed, emotionally stifling Victorian residential environment; it was to provide housing for the "machine age."[28]

While few of Richard Allen's future residents would own automobiles, euphemistically "machines," nevertheless, they would live in streamlined housing. Allen's 53 three- and four-story red and yellow brick buildings were arranged in eight quadrangles. Each quadrangle *zeilenbau* encompassed a city block in which abandoned streets and alleys became pedestrian walks and driveways, achieving the communitarian goals of self-containment and traffic-free play areas. However, defying the caveat that housing authorities should never increase building densities to absorb the higher cost of slum clearance, Richard Allen—where land acquisition costs averaged $1,300 per unit—housed 42 families per acre, in contrast to the 26 per acre at Johnson. The sturdy Bauhaus structures ringed the entire perimeter of the Allen superblocks, leaving barely sufficient interior space for the parallel alignment of two additional buildings. Rather than the usable, carefully designed spaces that seemed to invite social intercourse at Radburn, Mackley, Hill Creek, or the Johnson Homes, Allen's open space paled in the shadows of the project's three- and four-story building heights, which seemed to suffocate the little patches of green tucked away in the interior courts.

Neither Allen nor Tasker achieved the warmth of design visible at Johnson. Although Tasker's walkways seemed friendlier than Allen's, and the arrangement of Tasker's buildings encouraged greater tenant interaction, nevertheless, as at Allen, the massiveness of the project, the unadorned and repetitive Bauhaus architecture, and the undifferentiated community and private space placed tremendous social and psychological burdens on the low-income tenants. At both Allen and Tasker, superimposing a social and moral order on the physical space proved exceedingly difficult.[29]

Notwithstanding the economy-induced lapses, Philadelphia's prewar housing projects mirrored a basic loyalty to the neighborhood concept. The Housing Authority equipped all three projects with central heating, a cost-saving technology praised by Frankfurt's Ernst May and utilized at Carl Mackley. Each project enjoyed its own spacious community building, which enclosed not only management offices but also handicraft workshops, classrooms, a nursery, an auditorium, and, in Allen's case, a branch of the Free Library. Moreover, mindful of Perry's, Wright's, and the settlement house movement's stress on the public school as the vital center of community life, Philadelphia's three projects were built with school location as a strategic consideration.

Despite this package of social appurtenances, the Housing Authority's unrelenting adherence to a strict code of austerity branded the large superblock complexes as islands of poverty. The standard of "sturdy . . . no frills" structures enormously influenced project interior and exterior design. In prescribing the acceptable appearance for low-income housing, Newman, for one, shunned even a hint of luxury. Writing in 1937 on "Factors in the Housing Problem," the PHA's solemn executive director deprecated the "extras" that raised the selling price of working-class houses. He deplored the "garish ornaments, colored bath tiles, stall showers, parquetry floors, and inlaid linoleum. These are luxuries," insisted Newman, "not necessities for safe hygienic occupancy."[30]

Therefore, what survived the authority's scalpel were the stark Bauhaus structures that furnished the basic human needs of clean air and light, while too often economizing on the psychological needs for living space and amenities. Shaved footage left small living rooms and cramped bedrooms; alcoves became dining rooms, and curtains substituted for closet doors. The Housing Authority also discouraged the use of ceramic tile, and only an eleventh-hour plea by Raymond Rosen, a Philadelphia appliance dealer and authority member, convinced the board to install small refrigerators in the projects rather than the iceboxes specified in the original proposals. Moreover, the authority designed durability and low maintenance into the project, including walls washable with soap and water, steel doors, and casement windows.

The spartan code infused project life. Units were laid out so that each family could learn responsibility and self-reliance by maintaining an assigned area. Workshops encouraged residents to practice frugality by decorating their units with salvaged furniture. Project community centers taught civic spirit, and tenant organizations promoted citizenship. Any unseemly behavior, such as gambling on the premises, even for pennies, was strictly forbidden.[31]

"Worthy" Tenants

The Housing Authority's assumptions about slum clearance and housing were expressed not only in its policies regarding site selection and project design but also in its standards for tenant selection. Since the authority intended to rehabilitate the city socially and economically, selecting "worthy" tenants for the new housing was crucial. Although the USHA earmarked public units for the low-income earner, this did not prevent an intricate scoring system from selecting tenants with ample redeeming qualities. The scoring system, developed to test "housing need" objectively, in effect favored an upwardly mobile member of the lower class, a "working adult known to have regularly lived as an inherent part of a family group whose earnings are an integral part of the family income."[32]

Washington required prospective tenants to have lived at least a year in substandard housing, and from this tenant pool preference was awarded to families dispossessed by slum clearance, occupying the worst housing, having the lowest income, and rearing children under the age of 18. Furthermore, to placate the real estate industry, federal law set maximum income levels for eligibility 10 percent below the plateau necessary to rent the least expensive private housing. Beyond that, Washington permitted local authorities considerable latitude. The authorities developed their own set of moral standards for tenant acceptability and determined as well the distinctive racial configurations of project populations.

Clearly, both Washington and the local authorities intended public housing to be a temporary refuge, a way station or foothold for the working class on its way to homeownership and middle-class respectability. Ironically, then, the authority's goal was not to build stable communities but to facilitate movement out of the projects and into the housing mainstream. Typically, tenants who entered public housing during the brief period (1938–1941) between the opening of the first

USHA projects and World War II represented a cross-section of the white and black working class, not an underclass. The first Allenites, for example, regarded themselves as fortunate, and whether their income was derived from earnings or assistance, they assumed the primary obligation imposed by the project management: to pay their rent on time. About a fourth of the employed heads of households living at Allen in 1941 worked as domestics, porters, cleaners, bellmen, or chauffeurs. About 40 percent were engaged as helpers or common laborers; a smaller group, 15 percent, worked in manufacturing, mainly in the city's reviving shipbuilding and munitions industries.[33]

Only a fortunate minority of the city's ill-housed working class gained residence in Philadelphia's small stock of prewar public housing, and this was particularly true for blacks. In 1939 Philadelphia blacks constituted 60 percent of those eligible for public assistance or work relief. A WPA *Real Property Inventory* that year, sponsored by the PHA and the Housing Authority, revealed that 89 percent of black households rented their homes, compared to 54 percent of whites. But while 51 percent of the black rental units were substandard (and 6 percent both substandard and overcrowded), only 14 percent of the housing rented to whites was unfit. Urging a larger participation for blacks in the public housing program, Harry Barnes pointed to grim statistics showing a juvenile delinquency rate four times higher for blacks than for whites. Tragically, blacks occupied the bottom rung of the city's rickety economic structure. "It is doubtful whether private enterprise will ever build for the marginal ethnic groups," bemoaned a pessimistic Barnes in 1939. "As for the sub-marginal, one is perhaps safe in saying private enterprise will never build."[34]

Again, the paradox of public housing loomed. Both communitarians and professionals resisted defining public housing as a welfare program—that is, a program aimed at alleviating the desperate housing needs of the urban poor. Edith Elmer Wood announced in 1939 "in no uncertain terms" that public housing should not foster "colonies of dependents." Nor did many middle-class blacks in 1939 view public housing as a poorhouse; instead, they perceived it as good housing, as a means of strengthening and enforcing traditional values.[35]

Opposition to Public Housing

By 1940 the public housing issue, in Philadelphia and elsewhere, had lost the urgency that made it politically palatable in 1937. Conservatives who had reluctantly supported public housing as a works program lost interest as war mobilization revived the city's lethargic economy. The Philadelphia Real Estate Board, which in 1937 had at least grudgingly tolerated the prospect of low-income housing for the poor, undertook a campaign in 1938 spotlighting the work of member Arthur Binns, who had renovated 20 old dwellings in North Philadelphia and called them the Linmore Project. The National Association of Real Estate Boards dispatched him on a national tour, and Washington summoned him to testify at the Temporary National Economic Committee hearings. Binns was a prophet without honor in the city slums, however. Bernard Childs of the Tenants' League scored Linmore as "jerry-built hovels"; Binns's tenants vilified the units as damp, rat infested, and dilapidated. What is more, Binns's so-called low rents—between $27 and $75 per month—were out of the reach of most of the city's ill housed.

Still, the Tenants' League saved some of its sharpest barbs for the city officials whom it accused of criminally disregarding the city's housing and sanitation needs, and of complicity in the eviction and blacklisting of tenants who complained about housing conditions. Although Childs sat on a Housing Authority subcommittee, he bitterly criticized the authority for overemphasizing slum clearance in a city where a housing shortage existed. The league demanded housing at rents the poor could afford.[36]

In truth, the City Council never willingly acquiesced in the public housing program. Required by law to pass ordinances vacating streets and providing city services to public housing projects in return for an annual payment by the authority in lieu of taxes, the council at every opportunity delayed passing the enabling legislation. Any possible incentive for council cooperation with the housing program fizzled when S. Davis Wilson died unexpectedly in 1938. At the same time, the Democratic party, whose star seemed on the ascendancy in 1936, splintered into rival factions that upbraided each other for using the WPA and PWA for political ends. Anti–New Dealer Robert Lamberton's victory in the 1939 mayoralty merely sealed the doom of public housing.[37]

Therefore, regardless of the authority's effort to arouse interest in public housing through education sessions and such films as *Housing in Our Time,* the housing effort floundered on the eve of World War II. The authority had fixed the city's need for low-cost housing at 50,000 units; the city's Tasker, Allen, and Johnson projects provided 3,000. Politically, these few projects had stretched the city's symbolic tolerances. Mayor Lamberton reflected this when in April 1940 he directed a statement to the council lambasting public housing as "highly experimental" and urging the council to reject proposed projects. References to Philadelphia's symbolic heritage laced Lamberton's communiqué: "Slum areas exist because some people are so utterly shiftless, that any place they live becomes a slum. . . . But [in Southwark and Germantown] many own their own homes. . . . Their owners take the same pride in their homes that I do in mine. In the Project all will be renters, no one can own his own home. The home owner is the backbone of our people."[38]

Philadelphia remained faithful to tradition, rejected federal aid, and preserved homeownership on a pedestal. On June 11, 1940, while jeering building trades workers demonstrated outside City Hall, the City Council voted 12–10 against further cooperation with the Housing Authority.[39]

As World War II approached, the glow of communitarian vision seemed to be fading. Mumford, Bauer, Stein, and Wright had prophesied a new civilization where the worker, liberated from a stultifying environment of filth and slums, would participate in a purposeful group life. Roosevelt's New Deal had aroused hope among professionals and communitarians that slum clearance and public housing might rid America of the tenement evil and rehouse the working class. But the hoped-for beneficiary of public housing was scarcely the oppressed victim of the slum, but, in the authority's language, "a fellow citizen on a socially desirable level," a person, that is, deemed capable of "regeneration."[40]

Moreover, after the first burst of enthusiasm for public housing in 1937, wrangling over sites and land costs replaced glib talk about modern housing, and the flush of excitement waned. Once war in Europe churned the American economy in 1939 and 1940, and new housing developments began dotting the suburban landscape, talk of slums seemed passé. Yet the war boom ultimately resurrected the housing crisis, and by 1943 the issue of government housing would again occupy the limelight.

4

Housing America's Homelines

World War II transformed such cities as San Diego and Seattle into hubs of war production and rejuvenated the aging industrial economy of Philadelphia. Just as important, the war redefined the federal-city relationship that had emerged during the 1930s.[1] War-spawned conservatism led housing planners to abandon their hopes for a centralized federal housing administration or the early development of a national (or regional) housing policy. It also weakened the New Deal's tenuous attachment to the communitarian rationale for public housing.

In the face of a conservative tide, federal and local housing planners made highly functional, minimal housing an acceptable standard for wartime houses. Moreover, wartime housing was generally racially segregated and helped imprint the invidious pattern of postwar ghettoization. This wartime reign of minimalism aside, however, many government wartime housing projects displayed good design and, given the wartime prosperity, public housing communities often assumed a sprightly appearance.[2]

On the Brink of a Crisis

Notwithstanding Mayor Robert Lamberton's canard that Philadelphia has no slums and that people are just living within their means, the city in 1940 teetered on the brink of a monumental housing crisis. Amid a large-scale industrial retooling requiring a sizable expansion of the city's work force, nearly 7,000 families shared living space with another family; 62 percent of those "doubled-up" occupied dilapidated housing. Most appalling, in South Philadelphia, the site of the city's military complex (including the Navy Yard and the Quartermaster's Depot), the 1939 Works Progress Administration (WPA) *Real Property Inventory* branded 35 percent of the residential structures as "substandard" and indicted the city for forcing thousands of families to live in buildings "unfit for human habitation."[3]

The first portent of the seriousness of Philadelphia's housing crisis appeared June 13, 1940, just seven days before the City Council repudiated the $19 million in federal housing money. The commandant of the Philadelphia Navy Yard, Rear Admiral A. E. Watson, petitioned the Housing Authority to quarter navy families in the soon-to-be-completed Tasker project. Watson complained that many enlisted naval personnel, who earned under $1,400 a year, had been forced to occupy crowded South Philadelphia tenements.[4] The problem rapidly worsened after Germany's invasion of France. Congress coupled approval of the first peacetime draft with a billion-dollar appropriation for fighter planes, guns, and other war materiel. On September 19, 1940, Coordinator of Defense Purchases Donald Nelson announced that military contracts totaling over $6 billion would be distributed among cities, including Philadelphia, that had experienced the highest rates of Great Depression unemployment.

Nelson's multibillion-dollar contracts breathed new life into Philadelphia's moribund textile and garment industries and revitalized the city's heavy manufacturing sector. In 1940–1941, contracts for city-milled mosquito netting, service coats, flannel shirting, flying vests, and serge and khaki coats topped $22 million. Philadelphia's Frankford Arsenal commenced doubling its work force, and the Navy Yard disclosed that it would add at least 7,000 more workers to its payroll. Indeed, war plants such as Cramp Shipbuilding, Midvale Steel, the Budd truck body and railcar works, Philco, Westinghouse Electric, and Kellett Aircraft received war-related orders totaling almost $43 million. From October 1940 to October 1941, the government poured nearly $131 million into Philadelphia plant expansion, enabling city defense plants to enlarge their work forces by 27,000 workers.[5]

Budd, the Frankford Arsenal, and the Bromley textile mills, among others, tapped the pool of skilled labor present in the city. After all, over 100,000 jobless remained on the local State Employment Service Registry in 1940. Philadelphia's sizable jobless pool explains why, during the first year of defense mobilization, only 10,400 families, less than 1 percent of the 1940 population, migrated to Philadelphia. By April 1942, in-migrants still constituted only slightly more than 1 percent of the city's population.[6]

Philadelphia's existing labor supply falsely implied a weak demand for additional housing. In truth, demand was high. During the 1930s, the city's housing industry built very few units of inexpensive housing for either renters or owners. Steady income caused families previously doubled-up to seek separate housing; moreover, in-migrant labor, no matter how small the flow, added to the pressure on

Philadelphia's inadequate stock of vacant units. In the face of this rising demand for shelter, Philadelphia's housing vacancy rate plummeted from 25,000 units in April 1939 to under 15,000 units in April 1940. Low-cost, low-rent housing hardly existed.[7]

In November 1940 a concerned Philadelphia Housing Association (PHA) mailed a letter to city industrialists warning about the shortage of decent housing. Explained the PHA, it was not to suggest that Bendix Aviation, for one, "confronted a problem housing its workers . . . but because we believe that you share our concern that the facts of the housing situation should be known." Bendix drew its labor supply from Brewerytown, Strawberry Mansion, and the North Central neighborhoods where in 1939 there were 3,557 housing vacancies, of which 36 percent were in substandard dwellings.[8]

Black families occupied the bulk of substandard housing near the Bendix works. Philadelphia's black population had increased 14 percent during the 1930s, from 220,000 to 251,000. Between 1934 and 1941, approximately 364 new black families crowded into the Poplar, Hawthorne, and Southwest Central areas, and more than 1,200 black families moved into West Philadelphia. In 1940 blacks represented 12.5 percent of the city's population. But the prospect of good wages lured many more black families into the city. Philadelphia became especially desirable for black migrants after a threatened march on Washington by A. Phillip Randolph of the black Sleeping Car Porters' union persuaded Franklin Roosevelt to enact Executive Order 8802 forbidding employment discrimination in all industries holding defense contracts. While the order was never fully enforced, Philadelphia's Navy Yard, Quartermaster's Depot, and large private suppliers of steel, aviation, and shipbuilding material made an effort to comply. As a result, by 1943 the black Southwest Belmont YWCA reported difficulty staffing its programs "because jobs [in the city] were plentiful, and higher wages were easily available."[9]

Philadelphia's expanding black population pressed against the boundaries of the city's racially circumscribed neighborhoods. From 1940 to 1943, the black work force grew from 74,000 to 130,000; yet private builders supplied only 74 houses to the black housing market. Such a dearth of new housing for blacks exacerbated the predicament of black families segregated in unfit housing. In 1939 Works Progress Administration (WPA) investigators classified 47 percent of black housing as substandard; over a third of black-occupied structures lacked private bathing facilities. As defense and war mobilization doubled the volume of black migration into Philadelphia, the black city increasingly became coterminous with the black slum, a fact that inevitably carved deep fissures in the rocky terrain of a broadening housing crisis.[10]

Housing and the War Effort

As early as Christmas 1940, housers and planners implored the federal government to coordinate a worker housing program with the war mobilization. In an effort to alert local and federal officials to the impending housing crisis, the PHA, the Housing Guild, the Tenants' League, the American Institute of Architects, and the Building and Construction Trades Union convened a citywide meeting on housing and defense. Among other things, the meeting aimed to expose the facts of the housing shortage and determine which defense workers most desperately needed housing. Housing and labor union people urged the immediate development of well-planned, privately and publicly financed workers' housing communities, and voiced overwhelming support for S. 591, the Lanham defense housing legislation then in the House Rules Committee.[11]

Notwithstanding the concern for carefully planned defense housing expressed by the architect Louis Kahn and others attending the meeting, very little of the vibrant communitarian spirit of the 1930s infused the debate over wartime housing. On the contrary, housers in Philadelphia and throughout the nation approached the subject of defense housing dispassionately. They still cared about planning but were more intent on the logistics of housing and plant location, on mass building technology, and on the migration patterns of war workers than on the social-psychological elements of housing. Whereas some housers nurtured a vision of good housing and social betterment, for most it was a vision set in the future, and increasingly skewed to the postwar redevelopment of the blighted urban core.

As the war commenced in Europe, American housers embarked on a gradual retreat from their collectivist designs for rehousing urban America. Although 1940–1945 witnessed extensive federal involvement in war plant production, monitoring population movements, and the construction of housing, the history of World War II defense and war housing reveals a steady shift of initiative from the public to the private sector.

The shift occurred on several fronts. America's decision to allow drift rather than mastery to govern postwar suburbanization, as well as its refusal to either guide the rehousing of millions of veterans or disrupt the pattern of black ghettoization, dated from 1941. As Chapter 5 explains, the war years witnessed the birth of urban renewal, which yoked government and private enterprise in behalf of urban modernization. Housers, planners, and business leaders joined civic leaders and agency heads to forge the basis for a postwar alliance wherein housing would emerge as a tool for urban redevelopment.

By 1941 the cooperation and compromise that had produced the 1937 Wagner-Steagall housing legislation and molded Philadelphia's public housing program overshadowed the ideological differences that earlier distinguished professional from communitarian housers. Some of the housers who had enlivened the depression-era debate were no longer living; others had left Philadelphia. Catherine Bauer took a teaching post at the University of California at Berkeley. Bernard Newman died in October 1941.

A commitment to planning still remained, and the defense housing crisis hardened the planners' resolve. Significantly, Edmund Bacon, who replaced Newman as executive director of the PHA, had served brief apprenticeships under both Oscar Stonorov and Pope Barney, the architects of the Carl Mackley Homes. Until he accepted a commission in the U.S. Navy in 1942, Bacon campaigned hard to alert Philadelphia officials to the critical link between housing and defense production.[12]

In correspondence and in articles published in social work, planning, and architectural journals, housers nationwide joined Bacon in emphasizing the role of good housing and good planning in the defense effort. Writing in *Survey* magazine, John Gavit heralded the home as "the seedbed and abiding place of the nation's spirit," making it "a legitimate military objective." Housers and planners such as Albert Mayer advertised "building our home-lines" as a chance to revive the city by fostering a spirit of cooperative planning, a chance to replan "our urban life to the human scale."[13]

From her oceanside home in Cape May, New Jersey, Edith Elmer Wood lent her plea for Washington to address the housing crisis forthrightly and creatively. Wood never doubted the need for federal defense housing, nor that the most "ordinary common sense required that [defense housing] should fit into the city plan, meet a continuing local need, and be a permanent asset to the community."[14]

To give fuller expression to such ideas and to planning in general, in 1941 Harold Buttenheim, Coleman Woodbury, Charles Abrams, Bauer, and Wood banded together with other concerned housers to form the National Committee on the Housing Emergency (NCHE, later the National Committee on Housing Inc.). In the main, the committee publicized the vital role of housing in the defense effort and campaigned for federal coordination of the housing effort in each community. The committee struck a chord heard frequently during the war years, and one that reflected not only the housers' wartime sensitivity to privatism but also their allegiance to a lingering goal of *communitas*. "New housing," stated the recommendations of the NCHE, "need not be a blight on the community creating ghost towns after the war. . . . There is now an opportunity to build much of the war housing so that it will be useful after the war." While admitting the need for temporary ("demountable") housing, dormitories, and even trailers, NCHE stressed that good, permanent housing "in well-planned communities of sufficient size to constitute neighborhood units" should be built "where there is reasonable expectation that the need will last beyond the war."[15]

Despite the planner-housers' overtures to the private sector, Philadelphia's conservative real estate establishment, which savored a bullish market for new housing, reviled the "viciousness of the socialistic attempt to have erected thousands of tax exempt properties." In a five-part series on "Defense Housing Problems in Philadelphia" that appeared in the *Evening Ledger* during the fall of 1940, an industry spokesperson attacked the $100,000 recreation rooms, auditoriums, razor blade strops, and other "frills" bedecking Philadelphia's three prewar public housing projects. In his parting broadside the *Ledger*'s Maxey Morrison excoriated the Housing Authority for having on its advisory board "known communists" such as Bernard Childs of the Tenant's League and Emil Rieve of the American Federation of Full-Fashioned Hosiery Workers.[16]

Antagonists of public housers protested that a plentiful supply of housing existed, that large homes could be subdivided, and above all, that in Philadelphia, "private capital and private enterprise were willing and able to provide the great body of defense housing . . . more rapidly than any other body."[17] In addition, private housers counted the loss of city property-tax revenue against public housing and asserted that even the threat of new public housing deterred the private sector from producing new housing. Unfortunately, such vitriol carried great weight with the public.

Sensitive to the conservative mood of the nation, Congress and the president steered federal housing policy rightward. Roosevelt responded cautiously to the plea of the president of the Industrial Union of Marine and Shipbuilding Workers, John Green, for "speedy" government action to assure production of defense housing. FDR "worried about" a "speedy" shipyard housing program, especially the creation of a housing division within the Navy Department, and the navy's "absurdly excessive" plan to build housing for Philadelphia and Norfolk Navy workers costing $3,500 per unit. In FDR's eyes, the cost should be closer to $2,000. Instead, in August 1940 the president ordered $10 million pumped into the Reconstruction Finance Corporation (RFC) to provide equity capital for private homebuilding. "It is believed," read an August 1940 press release, "that a large proportion of defense housing can be produced by private enterprise, functioning within each community and using local capital, labor and contractors."[18]

Both Congress and the president showed little sympathy for USHA head Nathan Straus's design to meet the need of Philadelphia and of the nation for defense housing by accelerating public housing construction. In September 1940 southern Democrats, with Republican support, blocked the $5 million annual subsidy for the USHA. Next, as Straus and other housing watchdogs groaned in despair, congressional opponents of public housing emasculated the USHA's role in defense housing. In October 1940 Congress drafted and passed the Lanham Act, which assigned to the Federal Works Agency (FWA)—not the USHA—full discretion in spending the $150 million defense housing appropriation.[19]

The assault on Straus and the USHA had started months earlier. In July 1940, after conferring with his National Advisory Commission on National Defense, Roosevelt established the Division of Defense Housing Coordinator within the Office of Emergency Management. Bowing to private enterprise, FDR appointed as defense housing coordinator Charles F. Palmer, head of the Atlanta, Georgia, Housing Authority. Palmer accurately mirrored the anti–New Deal mood of the nation. Four months after taking office, he announced to the National Association of Real Estate Boards (NAREB) that private enterprise must build defense housing. Consistently, he minimized the task of the USHA and focused on stimulating the private sector through the FHA, HOLC, and RFC. He never doubted that private builders, encouraged by FHA generosity, could supply all the housing needs of a heated wartime economy. Palmer conceded only that Washington should provide temporary shelter to isolated rural industrial locations—such as Willow Run, Michigan—where sudden defense mobilization drew massive numbers of low-paid unskilled and semiskilled workers.[20]

Palmer's biases notwithstanding, from September 1940 to early 1942 a conspicuous absence of coordination marked the federal defense housing effort. Palmer not only lacked real power but also oversaw a bewildering array of interlocking housing activities involving nearly a dozen agencies—including the RFC, Home Owners Loan Corporation (HOLC), Federal Housing Administration (FHA), Farm Security Administration, Federal Home Loan Bank Board, Defense Housing Corporation, USHA, FWA, and the Navy and War departments. Instead of easing the defense housing bottleneck, Palmer epitomized it.[21]

Nor were local housing authorities prepared to fill the breach. Certainly in Philadelphia the Housing Authority disappointed those awaiting a heroic wartime performance. At least one authority board member, the electrical appliance tycoon Raymond Rosen, publicly announced that private enterprise—not the public authority—should build defense housing. The Housing Authority pursued a "wait and see" attitude, and by May 1941 had accomplished nothing more than to agree to act as a construction agent for the Lanham Act housing approved for Navy Yard workers. Authority members mechanically executed Washington's directives, even relinquishing to the navy 60 of its recently opened low-rent units in the Tasker project. Unquestionably, in 1941 the Philadelphia authority welcomed the opportunity to surrender its imperium over public housing to a quasi-public body created by Acting Regional Defense Housing Coordinator B. Frank Bennett.[22]

Bennett was a former Baltimore building contractor with a notorious antipathy for public housing. Shortly after his appointment in April 1941, he traveled to Philadelphia, and after consulting with the Philadelphia Real Estate Board, he formed the Philadelphia Defense Housing Committee (the Bennett Committee), which unabashedly catered to private real estate interests.

The FHA regional director, Leo Kirk, chaired the Bennett Committee, which included Phillip Knisker of the Real Estate Board, several representatives of the Philadelphia Chamber of Commerce, an executive of the Philadelphia Electric Company, and two labor representatives. At a committee meeting unattended by the two labor members—Carl Bersing of the Congress of Industrial Organizations (CIO) and James McDevitt of the American Federation of Labor (AFL)—the Bennett Committee banned government defense housing construction "except as a last resort." Kirk affirmed that the committee "would look to private enterprise throughout new construction and through rehabilitation of substandard housing and conversion of single dwellings into apartments to meet most if not all the needs of incoming defense workers and their families. . . . [If we] 'MUST' have government help, we are going to ask that it be housing of a temporary nature preferably demountable."[23]

After Kirk's renunciation of public housing, Bersing and McDevitt resigned, denouncing the committee for exploiting them as "window dressing" for a "fifth column activity . . . [aimed] at hinder[ing] the entire defense program of the city." Bersing protested that the committee actions echoed the sentiments of real estate moguls and speculators "whose interests as merchants and businessmen should not be used to sabotage the program of much needed housing for the workers who will carry on a successful defense program for our country." McDevitt assailed the committee's bias in favor of demountable housing. "Labor," charged McDevitt, "is unalterably opposed to any temporary shelter. We don't want any cardboard homes here. . . . If defense workers are to be housed, they should be housed decently."[24]

Philadelphia's Council of Social Agencies, the PHA, and the liberal press joined labor in deprecating the Bennett Committee and its affinity for temporary construction. Enough outrage erupted in the wake of the McDevitt-Bersing affair that only 15 days after its creation, Jacob Crane, the assistant defense housing coordinator, dissolved the Bennett Committee and formed a committee chaired by Housing Authority member Raymond Rosen. The new committee drew as much fire as the old one had, especially from the PHA. The Rosen Committee included housing, social work, and labor representatives; but it was the homebuilding, real estate, and business interests that clearly dominated. Washington and the city Housing Authority were sacrificing the goals of good housing and defense to the particular interests of the homebuilding and real estate industries.[25]

The Philadelphia Plan

In areas where real estate people and private builders felt secure, Philadelphia's defense housing program scored some modest successes. In August 1941 the city established a Fair Rent Committee to combat the "unpatriotic" practice whereby speculators acquired substandard houses and profiteered by doubling the rents. Following tenants' complaints, the committee was empowered to subpoena rent-gouging landlords and force them to justify their actions.[26]

But the new housing committee spurned government-built housing. Instead, in June 1941, amid much ballyhoo, it announced the Philadelphia Plan, and touted it as the city's newest example of "self-reliance and civic enterprise." The Philadelphia Plan envisioned fully utilizing all available existing housing before succumbing to federal construction. At its first meeting, the committee created the Philadelphia Homes Registry Office (PHRO), which technically operated under the aegis of the Coordinator of Defense Housing but in reality was funded by private donations. William Mudge, an executive of the United Gas Improvement Company, directed the PHRO. Amid a barrage of radio and newspaper publicity, Mudge launched a citywide vacant-housing survey, which aimed to list every unused room in the city, and convert third-floor attics into apartment units. Mudge's house-to-house canvas and his inquiries among defense contractors convinced him that the city needed 20,000 houses and 5,000 rooms to meet the housing demand.[27]

The PHRO's so-called Shelter Wrap-Up lasted through August and culminated in a September 15 luncheon meeting held at the city's Bellevue Stratford Hotel. There, to the cheers of an admiring throng, Mudge issued his findings, later published as a pamphlet entitled *There's Always Room for One More.* Five months earlier, the PHA had circulated a report warning that the city desperately needed at least 10,000 Lanham Act units. Mudge publicly repudiated the PHA findings by proclaiming that actually a housing surplus existed in Philadelphia.[28]

The PHA challenged Mudge's roseate findings as palpably "fallacious." According to the association, the PHRO had based its housing need estimates on the city alone, and had ignored the housing demand generated by the many defense establishments outside the city limits. Moreover, at the very moment Defense Housing Coordinator Palmer chose to praise PHRO, he was receiving a memorandum from his regional agent, Henry Solotow, detailing the flaws in Mudge's report. First, the report encompassed fewer than 146,000 of the more than 831,000 workers employed in Philadelphia on January 1, 1941. Second, Solotow challenged Mudge's assumption that only 60,000 new workers would enter the city's labor force during 1941 and directed Palmer's attention to an FHA study showing that an expected 145,000 laborers (190,000 if the Philadelphia market area was included) would enter the city's work force. In fact, asserted Solotow, "it should be emphasized that insofar as the PHRO study limits its analysis to Philadelphia county alone, it assumes a highly unrealistic view of the Philadelphia labor market." While Mudge calculated a demand for only 14,000 family units from October 1, 1941 to June 30, 1942, Solotow fixed the demand at 65,000 in the Philadelphia region and 50,000 for the city alone. Commenting on Mudge's faith in the conversion of three-story dwellings into apartments, Solotow said that "the use of all vacant dwellings as a substitute for new construction would cause overcrowding and confusion."[29]

In-Migration, Blacks, and Wartime Housing

The truth of Solotow's assessment became clear in early 1942. America's entry into the war forced Philadelphia and the nation to examine every economic activity—especially housing construction—against the overriding goal of full production. Total war unleashed a frenzy of industrial activity in Philadelphia. The War Production Board ordered $52 million in plant expansion for the city's Baldwin Loco-motive Works, Budd Manufacturing, Cramp Shipyard, Philco Electronics, Bendix Aviation, and the Frankford Arsenal.

Expanding war production swelled the stream of in-migrant labor and magnified the city's housing problem. Washington added to the tide of itinerant labor by moving the offices of several nondefense agencies out of the District of Columbia and into Pittsburgh, Chicago, New York, and Philadelphia. Since Philadelphia was the nearest city with available office space, the federal government transferred to Philadelphia the offices of the Bureau of Immigration, the Department of Justice, and the Securities and Exchange Commission. Therefore, in addition to welders and sheetmetal workers, in 1942 more than 4,100 government office workers scrambled for lodging in the city's YMCAs, small hotels, and roominghouses. Transient industrial workers poured into centers of war production throughout the country. Federal Manpower Commissioner Paul McNutt estimated in 1942 that, nationally, the war had triggered a migration in which 1.6 million workers—many accompanied by families—traveled toward war-industry centers.[30]

Total war forced Washington to concede the extent of the nation's housing need. In late May 1942 Roosevelt told Congress that "victory" in "total war" required government housing. While "private enterprise is being relied upon to serve a large proportion of the need . . . there remains the irreducible requirement for . . . new public construction . . . , largely temporary in nature and designed to serve the low-income bracket of war workers." FDR charged Congress to increase Lanham Act funding by $600 million.[31]

The war also eliminated much of the verbiage that had clouded the earlier defense housing debate. It obliterated the distinction between war workers and nonwar workers. Such devout houser-planners as Edmund Bacon fully acknowledged that in wartime plane and tank production surpassed housing in importance; he strongly recommended billeting war workers in commandeered boarding schools and college dormitories. Nevertheless, Bacon just as patriotically espoused the urgent need for government-built war housing. His reasons had a familiar ring; as during World War I, the new war intensified the Progressives' concern for bureaucratization and scientific efficiency. Bacon linked decent housing to both efficiency and internal security. Substandard housing posed the threat of impaired efficiency in output, and, much worse, it threatened "a massive breakdown in morale." According to Henry Propper, "There is more danger of this country being defeated by a breakdown of the home structure and the internal morale than there is a physical defeat in battle by the Nazis and Japanese."[32]

Philadelphia's faith in the superiority of the private marketplace thwarted substantial war housing activity. Policy discussion at the DHC remained divided, albeit still in favor of the Mudge-Rosen free enterprise alternative. Then, too, as long as the Roosevelt administration linked national unity and defense mobilization with business leadership, no federal agency or local authority forcefully defended the need for well-planned, publicly built defense housing. At the war's outbreak in December 1941, Philadelphia had a paltry six projects either open or under construction: the 1,000-unit Passyunk Homes in South Philadelphia for Navy Yard workers, Bartram Village in West Philadelphia (a 500-unit development for white defense workers), Pennypack Woods and the 200-unit Oxford Village in Northeast Philadelphia, the 700-unit Abbottsford Homes located on the old Altemus Estate in the Nicetown area, and 1,000 units of Navy Yard housing.[33]

In January 1942 Philadelphia faced an expected in-migration of more than 100,000 war workers; and the war's alarums portended an even greater influx of transient labor. Yet citizen protest, City Council obstructionism, and political sabotage delayed government housing at every turn. By fomenting demonstrations against a proposed defense housing project in the Mayfair section of the city, a solitary councilman blocked its construction. Only the stalwart support of the city's AFL and CIO leadership, backed by social workers and the PHA, salvaged the Altemus Estate site located in the shadow of the critical defense complex encompassing Midvale Steel, the Budd and Bendix works, and the Signal Corps Depot.[34] The opponents of the Abbottsford project protested that the Altemus Estate was a city landmark—especially its popular gardens decorated with wooden Indians.

Delays such as the government faced at Abbottsford plagued the city's public housing efforts. Leaders of the Amalgamated Clothing Workers, who spoke for the thousands of men and women making uniforms, parachute cloth, and other textile military supplies, complained that more than 20,000 members paid exorbitant rents to live in substandard housing. In-migrant workers crowded hotel rooms and tourist houses. Shabby, frequently unhealthful trailer camps sprang up throughout the city. Fifty percent of trailer residents had skilled jobs at either the Navy Yard or the Frankford Arsenal, and most explained that they could not find other housing. Finally, in February 1942, with rents skyrocketing, Mudge grudgingly admitted that the city faced a critical housing shortage of about 2,800 units. Two days later, he suddenly fixed the shortage at 3,950 units, described it as "tremendous," and joined the Housing Authority in begging Washington to build 18,000 additional Lanham Act housing units.[35]

Stunned and embarrassed by the dimension of the housing short-age, Philadelphia's housing officials maneuvered to impress the newly opened Richard Allen Homes for use as a white defense housing pro-ject. The insensitive action shocked the black community. By 1941, more than 4,300 black families had applied for units in the Allen pro-ject, and more than 1,000 of the applicants had been residents of the former slum site. Many were elderly and infirm, and were occupying dingy rooms in the area's courts and alleys. Therefore, the news that USHA administrator and key New Deal economist Leon Keyserling planned to impound the Allen Homes for use by white defense work-ers both astounded and embittered the city blacks.[36]

As early as October 1941 Mudge had privately suggested con-verting Allen into defense housing. The Housing Authority had re-fused Mudge's request then, as they did a second request at the end of December. With available housing in Philadelphia practically nonexis-tent in January 1942, authority members Rosen and Randall traveled to Washington, D.C., and dangled the Allen deal before Palmer and Keyserling. Despite Palmer's previous support for Mudge's claim that Philadelphia had a surplus of vacant housing, he now joined Rosen and Mudge in persuading Keyserling that Philadelphia desperately needed the Allen project for war housing.

Crassly denying the new housing to low-income black slum resi-dents reeked of injustice and distressed conservatives and liberals alike. Long-standing critics of the city's housing program assailed the Allen deal as "incontrovertible proof that Philadelphia's war housing needs [had] been unmet." In an editorial entitled "Paying for Defense the Hard Way," the ordinarily stiff-collared Philadelphia *Inquirer* said of the Allen deal that it was "a crying shame [to] make poor families suffer in order to adequately house defense workers." Washington Rhodes, editor of the Philadelphia *Tribune,* blamed the usurpation on "some wise fellows who decided it would be an excellent thing to rob the underprivileged people of decent housing in the name of de-fense." Blacks, he reminded the city, were denied admittance to the segregated Passyunk Homes for Navy Yard workers. Arthur Huff Fauset, the prominent black anthropologist, scolded city blacks for their temerity. After condemning all the city defense contractors who barred blacks from employment, Fauset denounced the ignominy of shutting blacks out of the only decent housing available. Blacks were being forced to make more than their share of the sacrifice, charged Fauset.[37]

Nevertheless, unlike in Detroit, where the struggle to preserve the Sojourner Truth housing project for blacks ended in a bloody riot, Philadelphia resolved the issue peacefully. Backed by the city press, the PHA, and the Armstrong Association, the Committee to Preserve the Richard Allen Homes launched a crusade to keep the project for low-income families. By mid-January a chastened Palmer asked Keyserling and the USHA to reconsider the Allen decision. Several weeks later, Defense Housing Coordinator Rosen offered a compromise whereby not more than 200 defense workers, all black, would be housed in the Allen project. Significantly, Rosen coupled the offer with a public confession that the city faced a major housing shortage and that private builders had so far failed to fill the defense housing need.

Much of the support for low-income black housing evidenced by the Richard Allen affair can be interpreted racially. If, as Richard Dalfiume observed, 1942–1945 represented the "Forgotten Years of the Black Revolution," these were also the formative years of the modern urban ghetto. The two phenomena were not unrelated. As a slum clearance project, Allen had been designed to rehouse blacks in the heart of North Philadelphia's growing black neighborhood. The homes were located many long blocks from the bulk of good wartime jobs in the Navy Yard, Cramp Ship, Budd, or Midvale Steel. Therefore, changing the project to houses for white war workers not only constituted an affront to blacks but also disregarded the historic housing and jobs nexus of the white working class. It suggested that Philadelphia's sudden solicitude for black welfare represented less a mollification of city race relations than a desire to preserve the existing boundaries of the emerging black ghetto.[38]

The National Housing Agency (NHA)

The Allen incident illuminated the blundering of an overly cautious federal housing bureaucracy whose obsession with privatism had indirectly precipitated the fiasco. Observers of the Allen incident suspected bureaucratic inefficiency as the culprit. In an effort to eliminate the disorganization that he believed responsible for widespread blundering on the home front, FDR in 1942 commissioned his good friend Samuel I. Rosenman to unsnarl the housing mess. Over Nathan Straus's strenuous objection that defense housing must be planned as part of the USHA's long-range slum clearance program, Rosenman abolished the Federal Loan Agency, converted the USHA into the Federal Public Housing Agency, and centralized control over all 16 federal offices concerned with housing into one superagency, the National Housing Agency (NHA). To head the new body Roosevelt selected the housing expert John B. Blandford, an efficiency-minded federal bureaucrat credited with putting the Tennessee Valley Authority on a "business basis."[39]

Social worker Mary Simkhovitch and houser Coleman Woodbury greeted the birth of the NHA as a "notable date in history." Initially, at least, Blandford's actions vindicated their support. He banned almost all nondefense housing, placed a ceiling of $6,000 on private-home construction in nondefense areas, and tightened the coordination of the national defense effort by allocating federal housing projects to cities on the basis of data specifying the volume of in-migrant single men, single women, and numbers of two-person families.[40]

Blandford centered his campaign for efficiency on restricting the movement of in-migrant labor, thus minimizing the need to construct new war housing and lessening the demand for materials. Instead of new housing, the NHA administrator favored house conversion, billeting, and campaigns to register every vacant housing unit. In fact, Blandford charged the Federal Public Housing Administration (FPHA) "to use the conversion [of large hotels, commercial buildings, and warehouses into residential units] as a means of supplying units programmed by the Administrator's office wherever possible."[41]

Despite the ban on nonresidential construction, which forced many private builders out of work, Philadelphia home builders and realtors backed the NHA programs. However, the early flush of enthusiasm for Blandford among union people, social workers, and housers faded. Blandford, like Palmer, geared his program to the private sector. Congress even aided Blandford's cause by boosting funding for the FHA Title VI program, which furnished $500,000 in mortgages for privately built war housing.

Blandford measured war housing progress by calculating the level of private involvement; he gloated that the NHA supplied barely 20 percent of the accommodations for war workers while "consistently maintain[ing] standards under which private enterprise could build." Not surprisingly, in the fall of 1942 Blandford announced that private builders would furnish 15,000 of the 23,700 new units programmed for Philadelphia; to placate realtors, who dreaded a post-war glut of half-empty project housing, he pledged that the bulk of government-supplied war housing would be demountable.[42]

The realtors sighed in relief, but labor and housing liberals were aghast. R. J. Thomas, chairman of the United Auto Workers Housing Committee, denounced the NHA for relying more on private construction under Title VI than on high-speed operations by the government: "Title VI of the FHA is in the opinion of the UAW-CIO nothing more than an attempt by Real Estate and building people to *make business better than usual during the war crisis* [italics added]." Despite the ouster of Palmer, Thomas complained that the "NHA is continuing the fatal policy of helping private enterprise produce war housing despite the obvious fact that private enterprise is not able to do so in time, or at the right place, or at rents and costs which war workers can afford."[43]

Other labor leaders and housers denounced the NHA for coddling private builders. William Green, head of the AFL, charged that Blandford's deference to big real estate resulted in a dearth of low-cost war housing that impaired war production by causing high labor turnover and abnormal absenteeism. Green also assailed Blandford for denying labor and the public at large any meaningful role in determining war housing policy. Unruffled by the charges, Blandford defended NHA's policy of assigning private builders the pivotal role in war housing. According to Blandford, the NHA was successfully "channeling private war housing at a cost . . . [affordable] for the majority of war workers, [and] greatly increasing the production of rental housing, and . . . making a start in private financing of housing for Negroes."[44]

Blandford's words assuaged few of his critics. One of the heaviest brickbats aimed at the housing czar came from Helen Fuller, a nationally known houser. Like her labor colleagues, she rebuked Blandford for being a "stooge of the real estate interests" and for overlooking labor support for a massive public war housing program. Among other opponents, Philadelphia's Edmund Bacon reproached NHA's "milk and water policy," based on voluntary compliance and obeisance to privatism. Bacon pleaded with the NHA to impose compulsory measures; certify all vacant dwellings; commandeer country clubs, hotels, and warehouses; and register all renter-occupants. Bacon also assailed Blandford's policy of temporary construction. Was it possible, he asked rhetorically, to secure adequate standards of site selection and construction for temporary developments, or would the war bequeath to American cities acres of slums that would not be torn down?[45]

Bacon's wartime solicitude for housing standards and planning priorities masked a subtle but distinguishable ideological shift. Despite their carping at the NHA for its failure to supply decent housing, between 1941 and 1945 housers and planners lobbied less on behalf of ill-housed human beings than for the functional or economic utility of good housing. With victory as the nation's singular cause, housers adapted their environmentalist arguments about the social utility of housing to the new war-worker clientele. Housers now contended that rather than breed crime and disease, dilapidated housing, located far from defense plants, imperiled job performance. Thomas stated the position exquisitely: "Labor's interest in housing does not derive from peacetime sentiments of moral reformation or social uplift. We are interested in housing as a war tool."[46]

Temporary Versus Permanent Housing

Whether built as "permanent" additions to the city's housing stock or slapped together in the fashion of the temporary Shipyard Homes, Philadelphia's "homelines" left their imprint on the city. First, the racial configuration inscribed by war housing presaged the segregated postwar ghetto-neighborhood/urban-suburban residential pattern. Then, too, such war-worker communities as the Tacony, Passyunk, and Shipyard introduced young rural in-migrants to a new lifestyle; these projects became laboratories for an emergent urban-suburban lifestyle, nourishing all the aspirations for a more affluent postwar society.

By war's end, the federal government had built in Philadelphia 4,630 units of defense and war housing, accommodating more than 17,630 people. Other thousands of war workers lived in projects dotting the city's periphery in Hatboro, Johnsville, and Camden.

The houser-planner Albert Mayer at first envisaged war housing as a chance to order attractively the American urban landscape. Yet, as early as February 1942, Mayer registered deep misgivings about the drabness of many of the newly built defense housing projects. He feared that in the rush to build war housing conveniently located near plants and offices, the government was ignoring housing's role in making "our human power as efficient as our splendid physical production plant by creating broad-gauged living conditions."[47]

Philadelphia's war housing experience demonstrated that Mayer's fears were well founded. Of the five large, permanent housing projects built by the government in Philadelphia, only the 700-unit Abbottsford Homes featured distinctive architecture and a carefully landscaped setting. Passyunk Homes in South Philadelphia, the 500-unit Bartram Village in West Philadelphia, and the 200-unit Oxford Village in the city's Northeast were at best unimaginative. Bartram Village, for example, consisted of 43 "durable" three-story red brick buildings arranged on either side of a long, curving street. Although the project featured interior walkways, a community building, a commons, and proximity to Bartram Gardens, the oldest botanical gardens in America, the uniform height and sameness of the buildings gave the village a dreary, regimented appearance. Pennypack Woods, the fifth project, followed the so-called Camden Plan by which residents cooperatively owned and maintained their units. Although of clapboard construction, Pennypack was attractively landscaped and possessed distinctive architectural integrity.

From 1943 to the end of the war, the FPHA built only 350 permanent housing units in the city; meanwhile, to the consternation of housers and planners, it slapped together more than 2,600 temporary dwellings. These "demountable" units exhibited little concern for the provision of vital services and even less for planning. Urgency supplied a weak framework for housing blueprints. Less than six months after Blandford awarded the city $9 million to build 750 units of permanent war housing, he reversed his stand and started temporary construction at Oxford Village II, Tacony, Juniata, and Shipyard.[48]

Families of war workers and military personnel fortunate enough to be housed in either the city's five permanent war housing projects or the prewar Allen, Johnson, or Tasker complexes discovered services, even a few amenities (e.g., hardwood floors at Passyunk), together with bustling activity and brimming communal solidarity. True, the government permitted war workers only at Abbottsford, Pennypack Village, Oxford Village I, Passyunk, and Bartram Gardens, and adjusted rents there to conform to wartime wages, but the Housing Authority that managed the projects displayed sensitivity to tenants' postwar aspirations. More particularly, it advertised and deliberately cultivated a "suburban atmosphere." The 197-unit Pennypack Woods complex, designed by Oscar Stonorov and Louis Kahn, embodied, according to the literature, "a suburban atmosphere within the city."[49]

The Pennypack wartime milieu stemmed as much from the modern architecture, the tasteful WPA landscaping, and the gleaming newness of the interiors as it did from sharing a demographic youthfulness and a common involvement in the war effort. Most residents were under age 35, were raising families, and were earning wages sufficient to afford both the $25–$35 monthly rents and the initial $700 outlay that local department stores advertised would "comfortably" furnish a Pennypack unit. On weekdays in 1943, knots of working wives escorted their small children to the project's day-care center. On the way, we can hypothesize, they gossiped about their jobs, about their neighbors, or about their occasional anxiety over prospects for employment after the war.

Such war-born anxieties, however, were tempered by a whirl of activity. Scout troops, hobby clubs, meetings in community rooms, and community newspapers quickened the pace of life for families at Abbottsford, Oxford Village, Bartram Gardens, and Richard Allen.

73

In addition, Tasker residents engaged in victory gardening, dramatics programs, dancing and cooking classes, home management courses, bowling, softball, and the Tasker Tiger football team.[50]

While the few permanent war housing projects afforded decent housing and a suitable arena for socialization, the many acres of temporary units in the city underscored the worst fears of housing critics. Announcing the opening of the temporary Oxford Village II, Tacony, and Shipyard Homes, Roland Randall confessed that the authority designed the housing to be "purely functional, to preserve the health, efficiency and morale of those who will produce munitions for our armed forces to crush the enemy." Most temporary war housing struck observers as jerry-built and stultifying. In such places as Oxford II and Shipyard or the massive 1,500-unit Lacey Park Gardens, located outside Philadelphia in Warminster, Bucks County, FPHA contractors built unit after unit of barrack-like structures with flat roofs or low-angle gabled roofs. Regulations from the Supplies and Allocation Board dictated the use of sparse and flimsy materials. Few units had separate dining areas, and most utilized oil-fired space heaters or primitive wood stoves for warmth. Built to house the overflow of Navy Yard workers, the 1,000-unit Shipyard Homes epitomized the tawdriness of demountable war housing. All Shipyard housing consisted of single-story, two- or three-room structures built out of comp-board (a compressed paper product) and seated on a concrete slab atop an abandoned city dump. Blacks at the Shipyard Homes were segregated in flat-roofed buildings while whites lived in hardly superior gable-roofed units. The flat-roofed units leaked badly, and compounding the misery of the cold and dampness, rats and other vermin infested the entire project. Moreover, the houses were situated in the "neck" of South Philadelphia at an inconvenient distance from the Broad Street–Snyder Avenue commercial axis. Few stores served the area, and for entertainment residents enjoyed only an unpartitioned comp-board recreation hall and two neighborhood theaters (which refused admittance to blacks).[51]

More than the inheritance of acres of flimsy, often unsightly war housing, by the end of the war NHA's policy of localism and privatism had bequeathed to the city a more segregated pattern of black housing. Many white war workers had avoided the government-built temporary war housing, while Philadelphia blacks protested their exclusion from the half-empty "white" projects. The NHA's unwillingness to move black families into this vacant housing mirrored the reluctance of wartime housing policymakers to pursue social objectives at the expense of private interests; in the end, the policy contributed toward firming the boundaries of the black ghetto.[52]

During the war, the Philadelphia branch of the National Association for the Advancement of Colored People (NAACP) berated the Housing Authority for "refusing to provide housing facilities for Negro Workers." The executive secretary of the local NAACP, Carolyn Davenport, argued in 1942 that the exclusion of blacks from the Abbottsford Homes made it "fairly clear that the Housing Authority does not have the interests of Negro defense workers at heart." Yet the authority merely reflected the mood of the city—and the nation. The year 1943 witnessed not only riots in Detroit—in part the result of the Detroit Housing Authority's efforts to move white defense workers into the Sojourner Truth housing project—but also a major transportation strike in Philadelphia caused by the city's effort to hire black streetcar conductors. Racial tensions in Philadelphia heightened in August 1943 when the city established an interracial commission in an attempt to defuse the conflict. Still, in October 1943, talk that black families might be admitted to the Tacony Homes sent the neighborhood's Polish community to a protest meeting at Kaczynski Hall. Thus, while war housing projects on the urban fringe, such as Oxford, Tacony, and Pennypack Woods, introduced working-class whites to suburban living, by excluding blacks they helped congeal the racial pattern of postwar urbanization.[53]

World War II bequeathed to Philadelphia and other American cities a strengthened pattern of racial segregation as well as an enlarged stock of government housing. Few houser-planners perceived the invidiousness of those trends. Instead, fully expecting a postwar housing shortage, they looked to the future with hope. Just as the "homes-front" experience of World War I had inspired Louis Mumford, Clarence Stein, and Henry Wright to fashion a glorious vision of regional planning and "machine age" garden cities, so World War II kindled among planners and housers the vision of a revitalized, redeveloped, and rehoused postwar urban America.

Part II

Public Housing and Urban Renewal

5

Race, Redevelopment, and Rehousing

John B. Blandford's National Housing Agency (NHA) bequeathed to postwar urban America an unimpressive record of defense and wartime housing production. Philadelphia, like other major American cities, celebrated final victory over the Axis burdened with an enormous housing shortage. In addition, the war had diverted attention from the basic maintenance of city property. Blight and decay engulfed an ever-widening region of the central city.

Nevertheless, the war had greatly enlarged Washington's urban role. Moreover, it had kindled a vision of federally aided urban redevelopment that quickly dominated the postwar urban agenda.

Although the end of the war saw urban America in a housing crisis, cities dreaded more the host of related problems—blight, suburbanization, a severely eroded tax base, and the specter of an expanding black ghetto. With urban manufacturing firms migrating to the suburbs, or to sunbelt sites in the South and West, downtown bankers, lawyers, business executives, and others—people whom Harvey Molotch and William Domhoff identified as the backbone of the postwar "growth machine"—explored ways to shore up sagging downtown land values and restore the historically pivotal role of the central business district.[1]

After World War II, the economic concerns of downtown businessmen dovetailed with the reform agenda of housers, planners, and organized labor. In Philadelphia, all these groups favored federal involvement in urban redevelopment; moreover, all believed that the city's ancient Republican machine prevented the social, economic, and physical revitalization of the city. The political scientist John Mollenkopf saw this postwar marriage of civic leaders and Democratic reformers forging a "progrowth coalition."[2] Like the earlier communitarians, progrowth evangelicals confronted the reality of a mushrooming black ghetto. Increasingly after 1946, the urban ill housed were not the Polish, Italian, Jewish, or Irish American tenement dwellers, but black renters who occupied the oldest, most substandard housing, which was situated in or near the downtown area. Therefore, as the historian Arnold Hirsch made clear in his study of the making of Chicago's "second ghetto," the fate of the black community rested with those who mapped the growth plans for the postindustrial city.[3]

Planners and redevelopers in Philadelphia seemed deeply sensitive to the sociological ramifications of urban development, especially the need to rehouse displaced black families in unsegregated housing. Philadelphia anchored its postwar housing and redevelopment dreams to a solid foundation of political and social reform. Indeed, the city's redevelopment program, which unfolded in the early 1950s, was nationally celebrated for its outstanding design and for being "shelter oriented." The area development plans of Philadelphia's nationally recognized planner-architects—Edmund Bacon, Louis I. Kahn, and Oscar Stonorov—featured public housing as an integral part of the renewed neighborhood fabric, and reflected a consensus among postwar planners that public housing must occupy a critical position in any overall urban redevelopment strategy.[4]

Urban Blight

The gritty, forlorn landscape of America's manufacturing cities scarcely hinted at an urban renaissance. Wartime Pittsburgh, for example, still groaned from the St. Patrick's Day flood of 1936, which swirled the waters of the Allegheny and Monongahela rivers across the length and breadth of the city's smoggy downtown. In Boston, downtown bankers and merchants, faced with high taxes, reduced services, and fewer customers, prepared to abandon the city. Philadelphia businessmen were dismayed not only by the grime, the unrepaired street lamps, and the high taxes but also by the barely potable city water. Philadelphia, Cleveland, Boston, and St. Louis had all experienced slight population declines during the 1930s, which fed the recurring nightmare that untrammeled slum growth might obliterate the urban tax base. And in 1946–1947, Doomsday seemed at hand. The Philadelphia Housing Association (PHA) counted 80,000 of the city's 550,000 occupied structures as "substandard." Property values had plummeted in the 1930s, depressing Philadelphia real estate assessments from 35 to 40 percent in most center-city neighborhoods. Forebodings of the coming "necropolis" haunted businessmen and civic officials.[5]

Yet, notwithstanding the bleak city streets, urban planning had flourished during World War II. Charles S. Ascher, a consultant to the National Resources Planning Board, wrote in 1942 that the "war has given a new intensity to thinking about the future of cities." He noted that "in Great Britain the impetus seems to be the destruction wrought by enemy bombers. . . . Though the United States hopes to be spared the rain of death from the sky, there is the same ferment at work here: the determination that the communities of the future must be nobler embodiments of the democratic respect for the worth of the individual, if our war effort is to be justified."[6]

Interestingly, the "new intensity" that enthralled Ascher catalyzed a vigorous wartime dialogue about housing and urban redevelopment and recast the role and meaning of public housing in America. Involving housers, federal economists, and members of the real estate industry, the wartime debate spawned visions of the future modern city. The National Association of Real Estate Boards (NAREB), through its think tank, the Urban Land Institute (ULI), in February 1942 published a brochure entitled *A Proposal for Rebuilding Blighted City Areas*. The ULI planners proposed to establish a federal urban land commission empowered to make 99-year loans at 1.75 percent interest to local land commissions chartered to rebuild blighted central-city areas and "restore livability to wasted urban neighborhoods." Critics of the ULI plan charged that while seemingly broad in scope, the program focused exclusively on the blighted urban core and assured developers enormous publicly underwritten profits.[7]

The NAREB took its "Urban Land Triple A" proposal to the Federal Housing Administration (FHA), whose formula for the creation of city realty companies sharply resembled the ULI's land commission plan. The FHA directed NAREB to the National Resources Planning Board (NRPB) where Charles Merrian, excited about realtors' interest in postwar planning, created an Urban Section to act as an incubator for all postwar planning ideas. Headed by Robert Mitchell, who later directed the Philadelphia Planning Commission, and staffed by houser-economists Charles Ascher, Guy Greer, and Alvin Hansen, the Urban Section, in addition to undertaking neighborhood rehabilitation demonstration projects in cities such as Baltimore, Tacoma, and Salt Lake City, assembled a digest of postwar planning. Ascher summarized these plans in a pamphlet entitled *Better Cities*, which entertained a broad view of the modern city and stressed the primacy of the neighborhood unit. According to Ascher, urban rebuilding must be on a large scale, not merely the replacement of a few decaying structures.

The NRPB viewed the government's rehousing task just as broadly, and called for reshaping the federal housing program to achieve the desired community pattern. Ascher wrote that public housing must be freed from its present income limitations in order to "provide homes on a self sustaining basis for a great number of badly housed Americans above the minimum income level."[8]

Following conservative charges of socialism and accusations that the NRPB was usurping Congress's responsibility for planning, FDR shut down the agency in 1943, the same year that the NHA created the Division of Urban Studies (DUS). Described by its administrator, Jacob Crane, as a "rather obscure name for a staff unit which functions to develop methods and advises the administration on all matters relating to urban development and city building," the DUS staff included such distinguished consultants as Ernest Bohn, Frederick Law Olmstead, Jr., and Lewis Mumford. But the DUS never became a central clearinghouse for postwar urban planning. Instead, after the dissolution of the NRPB, Washington lodged comprehensive postwar planning within the NHA, which, under Blandford, saw the postwar housing task "as predominantly a job for private enterprise and a local responsibility."[9]

Neither ULI's free-enterprising cure for urban blight nor Ascher's grand view of the future satisfied Catherine Bauer, the wartime president of the National Public Housing Conference. Dorothy Rosenman, president in 1943 of the National Committee on the Housing Emergency, and R. J. Thomas, president of the United Auto Workers and chairman of the UAW-CIO Post-War Planning Committee, were equally unimpressed. Bauer, Rosenman, and Thomas rallied support for stricter government control over metropolitan land use and housing production. Automobility, the wartime suburbanization of industry, and postwar defense needs dictated, in Bauer's words, "planned urban decentralization." Bauer labeled all the talk about a postwar rebuilding of blighted downtown areas as "unrealistic." "I say this with regretful realism," explained Bauer, "because I like cities and hate suburbs." Together Rosenman, Bauer, and Thomas pressed for a massive postwar housing program, including public housing built in planned neighborhood developments within and outside the central city. In their view, mass homebuilding and rigorous code enforcement in slum areas had to precede urban redevelopment in order to stop the large speculator profits identified with slum ownership and facilitate a truly comprehensive urban rebuilding.

Clearly, the war years had produced among housers, planners, and housing industrialists some common ground and some basic differences of opinion. All viewed the city as disease ridden and traced the cancer to the neglect of city planning and unchecked decentralization. Moreover, all the participants in wartime housing reform recommended federal aid. But while the Bauer-Rosenman-Thomas cure hinged on mass rehousing and embodied elements of broad, federal ownership and control over city and suburban land reminiscent of the British Uthwatt Report for rebuilding England's wartorn cities, the

ULI prescriptions focused on blight and private initiative, and a federal role limited to underwriting and insuring risk taking by private central-city land developers.

Between 1941 and 1945, the key ingredients of this planning appeared in several pieces of state and federal legislation. In 1941, New York passed urban redevelopment legislation containing eminent-domain provisions enticing enough to lure the Metropolitan Life Insurance Company into clearing 61 acres of Lower East Side Manhattan slums and building the massive Stuyvesant Town project. Other states passed similar laws. But all these redevelopment ordinances lacked the land-cost write-down clause that planners and developers considered vital for large-scale urban renewal. Both the pigeonholed Federal Urban Redevelopment Act of 1943, introduced by Senator Elbert Thomas (D.-Utah), and the 1945 Wagner-Ellender-Taft legislation, which languished in Congress until 1949, called for federal aid for urban land acquisition.[10]

Planners at ULI, however, conceded the inevitability of postwar suburbanization. Modern suburbs had appeared as early as the 1920s. While suburban growth slowed in the 1930s, it quickened to minor boom proportions on the eve of World War II. The automobile, the FHA's preference for unattached suburban houses and residential homogeneity, the favorable tax environment of early suburbia, and the popular equation of suburbs with homeownership all foretold an explosion of postwar homebuilding on the "cool, green rim" of American cities. All the wartime planners dreaded that a postwar suburban boom would siphon off urban middle-class families. In their scary scenario, commerce would trail its select customers to Greenbelt Knoll or Cherry Hill, depriving the city of the last remnants of its tax base.[11]

An eroding tax base and a suburban tide mirrored only half the crisis facing urban America in the postwar years. Mollenkopf and Jackson described the forces of postindustrialism transforming the postwar social, economic, and political landscape of such old commercial cities as Philadelphia. During and after the war, much of the city's surviving pharmaceutical, metal manufacturing, food processing, and electronics industries moved outside the city. White engineers, technicians, managers, data analysts, and other members of the new middle class, together with white working-class beneficiaries of New Deal labor legislation, joined the hegira of commerce and industry to Cherry Hill, King of Prussia, Plymouth Meeting, and Fairless Hills.[12]

Meanwhile, a rising population of black migrants crammed into central-city courts and alleys and into the North and West Philadelphia row housing left behind by fleeing whites. As Hirsch emphasized in Chicago, the spirit of downtown renaissance stemmed in part from the fears of city leaders concerning the encroachment of the black population into the central city.[13]

Blacks and Urban Renewal

As the black population in America's cities grew, interest in urban renewal and public housing rose accordingly. Chicago's black population increased 80 percent between 1940 and 1950. In the same decade, Detroit's minority population rose 101 percent; Los Angeles added over 150,000 blacks to its population. And 126,000 new black residents moved into Philadelphia, making the black population in 1950 almost 380,000 and giving the city the third-largest black population in America (see Map 2). By 1960, Philadelphia's black population exceeded 500,000, and it rose above 650,000 by 1970.[14]

Many thousands of the black in-migrants from South Carolina, North Carolina, Virginia, and Georgia moved to South and West Philadelphia; but a significant proportion located in North Philadelphia. In 1940 this area held a mixture of first- and second-generation German, Irish, Russian-Jewish, Polish, and Ukranian Americans, in addition to a 39 percent black population. Beween 1945 and 1970, the old North Philadelphia area, bounded by Spring Garden Street on the south, Ninth Street on the east, Lehigh Avenue on the north, and the Schuylkill River on the west, emerged as the city's principal black ghetto; by 1970, 93.3 percent of the residents were black.[15]

Poverty severely limited the ability of blacks to find decent housing in postwar Philadelphia. Although many had traveled to the city searching for work, Philadelphia's meager postwar opportunities thwarted the ambitions of migrant and native blacks alike. After the war, the large firms that had hired blacks, such as Budd and Cramp Ship, either left the city for suburban locations or closed. Increasingly between 1945 and 1970, the large pool of unskilled black labor competed for a dwindling supply of good jobs. Throughout the period, unemployment gnawed at the fabric of the North Philadelphia black community. A 1956 "environmental survey" of city blocks along the largely black Girard and Poplar streets discovered 37 percent jobless and 42 percent working irregularly as domestics, service employees, and common laborers.[16]

As late as 1960, low-wage manufacturing jobs supplied work for 45.6 percent of the employed laborers in the North Philadelphia ghetto. But between 1940 and 1970, service and domestic employment escalated in importance, especially for black women. Until the mid 1950s, black women principally toiled in laundries and in the kitchens of Philadelphia's major hotels and restaurants. Combined,

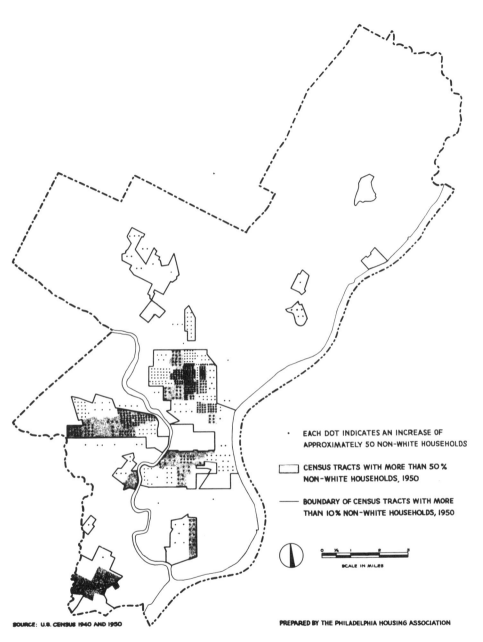

EACH DOT INDICATES AN INCREASE OF
APPROXIMATELY 50 NON-WHITE HOUSEHOLDS

CENSUS TRACTS WITH MORE THAN 50%
NON-WHITE HOUSEHOLDS, 1950

BOUNDARY OF CENSUS TRACTS WITH MORE
THAN 10% NON-WHITE HOUSEHOLDS, 1950

SCALE IN MILES

MAP 2: Increase in Nonwhite Households in Philadelphia, 1940–1950

Source: Housing Association of Delaware Valley, Urban Archives Center, Temple
University Libraries.

the percentage of the North Philadelphia work force employed in service and household work grew from 21.6 in 1940 to 46.7 in 1970; less than 15 percent of employed blacks worked in white-collar occupations in 1960, although the percentage increased to 22.5 in 1970.[17]

Whatever their jobs, most blacks subsisted near the bottom of the economic ladder. True, they retained some of the income gains from the city's wartime economy; but in 1950, 32 percent of the North Philadelphia area households earned less than $1,000 a year. A decade later, the percentage had improved only slightly, to 20 percent. Citywide in 1960, 43 percent of black families, and 32 percent of whites, lived on incomes under $2,000. And 78 percent of Philadelphia black families earned less than the $4,000 deemed necessary to purchase an inexpensive house.[18]

Notwithstanding the heavy wartime migration of blacks to Philadelphia, by 1950 the city still did not have the black concentrations that characterized the ghettos of New York, Chicago, Cleveland, and other cities. Many black Philadelphians lived on all-black streets, but these streets lay not more than a block or two away from white neighbors. Consequently, a study done at that time found black residents in all but a third of Philadelphia's 404 census tracts. After 1950, however, the tide of the postwar migration began to carve a new and odious residential configuration in Philadelphia—one that was unmistakenly segregated.[19]

Studies of postwar suburbanization and segregation have shown that the massive growth of the black population in northern cities paralleled a concomitant white population boom in the sprawling suburbs. As white families occupied the new, low-density tracts of single-family dwellings in the suburbs, blacks jammed the high-density row housing in and at the edges of existing black settlements. Wartime pressures on the bulging frontiers of Philadelphia's three principal areas of black concentration had forced some expansion. After the war, in North Philadelphia low-income black renters poured into the aging row housing between Girard and Columbia avenues and Tenth and Eleventh streets. Blacks with stable, albeit modest, incomes bought or rented the better housing in Nicetown and Strawberry Mansion, actually stabilizing and even increasing housing values in neighborhoods threatened by the rapid exodus of German and Irish American families.[20]

It was clear by 1953 that the wartime and postwar growth of the city's black population had produced a different urban form—what Robert Weaver called in 1947 "the Negro ghetto." A Philadelphia study completed two years later observed: "While many white families live in inadequate housing, the white slum as a mass-phenomenon has disappeared, and substandard housing occupied by whites is scattered rather than concentrated. . . . The concentrated slums today are largely Negro areas."[21]

Urban blacks in America had historically occupied overcrowded slum housing. Descriptions of black slums in nineteenth-century cities emphasized the often fetid alley dwellings occupied by blacks in Chicago, Washington, D.C., Detroit, and Philadelphia. World War II exacerbated already horrendous housing conditions. Although the black population's share of wartime housing improved from 1.4 percent of the 331,567 units built by the end of 1941 to 8.6 percent of the 1,336,140 units by the end of 1944, less than 4 percent of those dwellings were private. In Philadelphia, whites opposed housing projects for black war workers; private developers built only 74 houses for blacks. With the exception of those blacks fortunate enough to find shelter in Philadelphia's two black housing projects, most of the city's black war workers shared the old housing in the city's central city.[22]

As segregation patterns hardened, crowding, dilapidation, and general housing quality worsened. Maps prepared in 1953 by the PHA, based on the 1950 census, illustrated the gross nature of black housing conditions in the city (see Maps 3 and 4). Substandard housing prevailed in every area with a high concentration of blacks. Compounding the dilapidation, lack of sanitary facilities, and crowding, black enclaves witnessed wretched neighborhood conditions—intensive land use, sparse play space, narrow streets, proximity to noisy and dangerous industrial plants and railroad yards. The PHA found the data on overcrowding and dilapidation most shocking. Crowding (more than one person occupying a single room) occurred three times more frequently among blacks than among whites. Many of the overcrowded black households doubled-up or shared already inadequate dwelling space with relatives or friends. Often, the congested space consisted of little more than two back rooms on the third floor of a North Philadelphia row house. Very frequently, black dwellings lacked such basic sanitary facilities as running water or a private bath.[23]

Clearly, in Philadelphia and other cities, a new migration of blacks and whites compounded the seriousness of the housing crisis. Shortly after the war, veterans scoured American cities for available housing, living in automobiles, converted trolley cars, and large boxes. To solve the crisis, President Truman in 1946 appointed a former mayor of Louisville, Wilson Wyatt, to the post of housing expediter. Wyatt created the Veterans Emergency Housing Program, which trumpeted private enterprise and the housing miracles to be achieved by prefabrication. But fanfare and wild ideas for mass-produced igloos failed

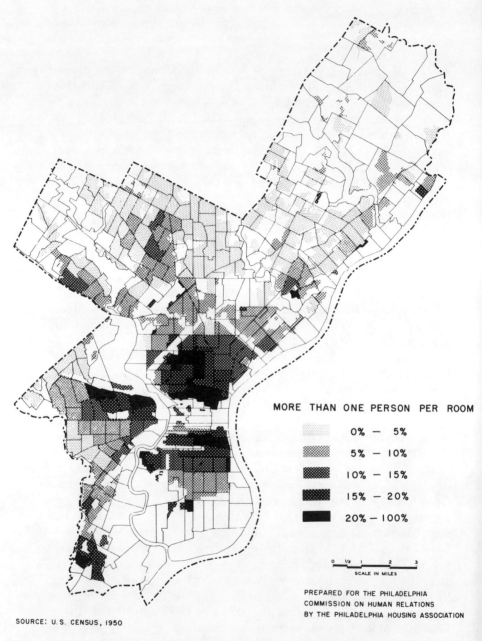

MORE THAN ONE PERSON PER ROOM

0% — 5%

5% — 10%

10% — 15%

15% — 20%

20% — 100%

SCALE IN MILES

PREPARED FOR THE PHILADELPHIA
COMMISSION ON HUMAN RELATIONS
BY THE PHILADELPHIA HOUSING ASSOCIATION

SOURCE: U.S. CENSUS, 1950

MAP 3: Crowding in Residential Areas of Philadelphia, 1950

Source: Housing Association of Delaware Valley, Urban Archives Center, Temple
University Libraries

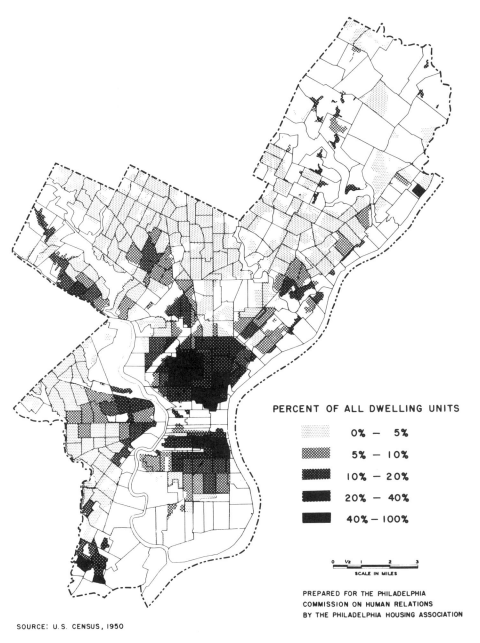

PERCENT OF ALL DWELLING UNITS

0% — 5%

5% — 10%

10% — 20%

20% — 40%

40% — 100%

0   ½   1   2   3
SCALE IN MILES

PREPARED FOR THE PHILADELPHIA
COMMISSION ON HUMAN RELATIONS
BY THE PHILADELPHIA HOUSING ASSOCIATION

SOURCE: U.S. CENSUS, 1950

MAP 4: Dilapidated Dwelling Units in Philadelphia, 1950

Source: Housing Association of Delaware Valley, Urban Archives Center, Temple
University Libraries

to shelter the nation's homeless veterans. In 1945, under pressure from veterans' organizations, Congress appropriated $191 million for the Temporary Emergency Housing Program. Operating through the Federal Public Housing Administration, federal officials contracted with city mayors and local housing authorities to make military barracks, trailers, Quonset huts, and other forms of "demountable" housing available to veterans and their families. Philadelphia received 1,781 demountable units from Camp Reynolds, a military encampment located outside Pittsburgh. Quickly erected on wooden piers, these structures became the 1,405-unit Northeast Village and the smaller Belmont, Lehigh, Pulaski, and Luzerne Homes.[24]

The Philadelphia Housing Authority managed only the city's veterans' housing program. Between 1945 and 1960, low-income veterans received first preference in all public housing, and to expand its stock of low-income housing, the authority literally wrested from Washington the 4,549 units of defense and wartime housing that, to "promote homeownership," the federal government proposed to sell to young veteran families. By 1947, despite the sprouting of temporary barracks and trailer communities for veterans, and despite the infusion of VA and FHA mortgage stimulants, Philadelphia's postwar housing malaise lingered.[25]

Professional Urban Planning

By 1948, the consensus sharpened on the need not only to rehouse low-income families but also to rebuild urban America. Although sympathetic to progrowth rhetoric about the importance of urban prosperity and the goal of a blight-free city, housers and labor leaders viewed this rebuilding task more in human than in economic terms. To them, blight meant wretched housing, not the collapse of central-city property values. Although planners in many cities enjoyed a kinship with urban developers and bankers, in Philadelphia the historic role of the PHA in planning and housing would keep planners philosophically attuned to the houser ideology.[26]

In 1948, most planners were professional designers, landscape architects, and civil engineers. During the Great Depression, planners necessarily made their opportunity base the public sector. They labored on the payrolls of the Public Works Administration, the Resettlement Administration, the Tennessee Valley Authority, the National Resources Planning Board, and local housing authorities, agencies that afforded them the opportunity to design and create free of the whims and biases of patrons and guided only by housing standards and department budgets.

World War II elevated the status of the career planner. Cities enhanced the power of their planning commissions, and universities established departments of planning and urban studies. Out of this milieu emerged the master planner, a public servant eager to express, architectonically and spatially, the optimal urban landscape.[27]

This outcome was hardly peculiar to urban planning. Between 1935 and 1960, the authority of the so-called expert burgeoned and infused a larger and larger sphere of American life. David Reisman detected the glorification of expertise among the "lonely crowd," as did fellow sociologists John R. Seely, F. W. Loosey, and Alexander Sim in their study of a Toronto, Canada, suburb. Universities credentialed expertise, and professional organizations—the American Society of Planning Officials, for example—certified the planner's claims and lobbied to preserve the standards of the profession.[28]

Housers occupied a less certain niche, one that rendered their status as professionals murky at best. Nevertheless, as members of respected housing associations and as champions of garden cities, housing codes, zoning ordinances, parks, playgrounds, and other reputable forms of community development, housers had enjoyed a long history of urban involvement, and in the immediate postwar era they basked in the publicity showered on the housing crisis. Nevertheless, denied the coveted mantle of the "expert," one group of housers, led by Catherine Bauer, found legitimacy by aligning itself with familiar colleagues in public health and new associates in the social and behavioral sciences, people such as Robert K. Merton, Robert McKenzie, and Kurt Lewin.[29] Other housers—Ernest Bohn, John Ihlder, and Elizabeth Wood, among them—found sanctuary in the growing housing bureaucracy now represented by the National Association of Housing Officials. California planner-historian Mel Scott observed that by 1948 NAHO had linked itself closely with the ideas and goals of urban planning and redevelopment.

The academic housers and the planning and redevelopment group mingled as members of citizen advisory boards, housing commissions, and ad hoc housing groups; but clearly the specialist/practitioners and housing scholars carved separate spheres. Bauer's name was missing from the list of prominent housing officials attending the 1948 Chicago conference on "Obstacles to Urban Redevelopment." Bauer and her housing gadfly friends, such as Dorothy Montgomery, observed the postwar housing and redevelopment spectacular from the near sidelines, shouting advice, criticizing here and there, prodding, and occasionally goading.[30] In an outpouring of articles and reports, Bauer exhorted redevelopment officials to apply the findings of social and psychological research to community planning. She referred planners to new sociometric studies, especially the investigation by the Massachusetts Institute of Technology Research Center for Group Dynamics of "Group Formation in a Housing Community" (a study of 270 veteran-student families residing in a temporary housing project) and Robert Merton's Lavenburg-Columbia research on human relationships in a married students' housing complex. To Bauer, both projects demonstrated the significance of face-to-face interaction and yielded convincing evidence that community design could facilitate neighborhood formation in public housing. Bauer constantly appealed to planners and redevelopers to cross-fertilize their design ideas with the theoretical insights of social science.[31]

What the academic houser-planners shared with urban leaders was despair over the inexorable spread of central-city blight. Ordinarily, planners following the progrowth economic logic diagnosed the urban malady in strictly physical terms. For example, planner-redevelopers attending a 1948 Chicago conference described the blighted core as victimized by structural deterioration, obsolescent land use, and population loss. Significantly, only the Philadelphians in attendance urged the broadening of the definition of blight to embrace "social deterioration."

Most planners and redevelopers fit low-income housing into their model of the remade city. Clearing away and replanning the city, argued the 1948 conferences, "could never become a reality in most localities without a continuous public housing program on a major scale." Aware of the importance of public housing for the uprooted victims of massive slum clearance, redevelopment officials depicted public housing as short-term, low-income shelter, ideally located on vacant or clear land in or near the redevelopment site, and "close to . . . friends, institutions and places of employment." Many displaced families "would return to the old area after redevelopment," predicted the officials, "providing, of course, re-use were for housing that they could afford."[32]

While redevelopers and planners regarded public housing as only an appendage of the redevelopment process, Bauer and Montgomery hailed it as vital to urban rebuilding. Bauer in 1949 advocated redesigning the social fabric of the entire city-region to achieve a new spaciousness. Using social and behavioral research, housers and planners hoped to design a cooperative, efficient, and productive society free of crime, delinquency, and the human alienation spawned in the dense, anomic, unplanned cities of the industrial age.

In these early postwar years, Bauer and her friends remained wedded to the idea of the neighborhood unit. Bauer disagreed with

Reginald Isaacs and Svend Reimer that the neighborhood concept was outmoded and encouraged social and racial exclusiveness. According to Bauer, the whole emphasis of social science pointed to the significance of face-to-face groups. Bauer stressed the importance of designing heterogeneous communities featuring varied housing types, including public housing, which would be located on vacant land as part of a "sensitive community development."

Despite ideological differences, however, Bauer, Montgomery, and the housing academy could close ranks behind their associates in the world of planning and redevelopment. Both parties agreed that the central city was blighted and urgently needed redevelopment, that urban revitalization hinged on a large-scale public housing program, and that only federal intervention could muster the power and resources required for the rebuilding task.[33]

The Housing Act of 1949

Between 1947 and 1949, every group anxious about the future of cities and the progress of housing and redevelopment made a pilgrimage to Washington to voice support or disapproval of the pending Wagner-Ellender-Taft bill. Finally passed in 1949, the legislation not only revivified a dormant public housing program and created a federal-urban partnership in city rebuilding but also exposed ghettoization and racial integration in public housing as key issues.

The Wagner-Ellender-Taft legislation had endured a long trial in Congress. As part of his Fair Deal, Truman had assigned a high priority to shepherding the legislation safely through a hostile Congress. The legislation was basically the bill drafted in 1943 by Greer and Hansen, providing federal grants to local redevelopment authorities to purchase and clear urban slum areas; but respecting the severe postwar housing shortage and the intensity of the prohousing lobby, the 1948 bill mandated that redevelopment activity be for "primary residential" purposes, and it incorporated a large public housing program.

Only a diffuse opposition surfaced to the redevelopment provisions of the Wagner-Ellender-Taft legislation. But the NAREB, the National Association of Home Builders, and the American Savings and Loan League assailed the public housing provisions as "communistic." Senators Jesse Wolcott and Joseph McCarthy, among others, vilified public housing as "a key to opening the door to Socialism in America," and they masterminded the antihousing strategy in Congress.[34]

From 1945 to 1948, the NAREB's withering anti–public housing barrage plagued the bill. In 1948, Wolcott's machinations on the Rules Committee again shattered Truman's hope for comprehensive housing and urban redevelopment legislation. This time, the sharptongued Missourian shot back, castigating Congress for its slothfulness and parading its "do-nothing" record on housing as a front-line issue in his successful bid for reelection.

Scenting imminent victory for housing legislation in 1949, the prohousing forces mobilized to seal the bill's passage. As in past campaigns, the National Public Housing Conference (NPHC), headed by Lee Johnson, led the housing forces into battle. Johnson provided daily news reports that kept local housing groups apprised of the legislation's progress. On one critical vote, in response to a Johnson plea, Montgomery shifted her Philadelphia letter-writing machinery into high gear, flooding the city's fence-riding congressmen with mail. At long last, in July 1949, the Wagner-Ellender-Taft bill was enacted, and Truman signed it into law.[35]

The Housing Act of 1949 for the first time established a national goal of "a decent home in a decent environment for every American." Title I of the law authorized a first-year appropriation of $1 billion in federal loans to local redevelopment authorities for the purchase of slum land. The law allowed $500 million to local authorities for grants (not to exceed two-thirds of the loss on a redevelopment project) to assist cities to write-down the cost of purchasing, clearing, and preparing land for private redevelopment. Opponents complained that the write-down clause rewarded slumlords. But William Slayton, commissioner of urban redevelopment, called the controversial provision the "cost of achieving a public purpose—the elimination of slums." Significantly, the law required cities to rehouse all families displaced by redevelopment activities in decent, safe, and sanitary dwellings. To this end, Title II of the Housing Act resuscitated the public housing program by scheduling the construction of 810,000 units of new public housing, 135,000 yearly for six years.[36]

While the Housing Act of 1949 called for well-planned, well-integrated residential communities, it failed to enact strong land-use provisions over suburban development, which had been sought by both planners and housers. Charles Abrams also noted that the new law surpassed the 1937 law's emphasis on local initiatives and the role of private enterprise in the redevelopment process.[37]

William Domhoff viewed the 1949 law as a triumph for the urban growth machine. The law awarded lump sums to local communities, in effect precluding a close federal monitoring. And, against the wishes of many planners and labor leaders, the law allowed redeveloped land to be sold as well as leased to private developers, giving speculators potential windfall profits from rising land values.[38]

Despite these concessions to corporate developers, Title I, insisted Senator Robert Taft, remained primarily a housing bill. Both titles of the law underscored the main intention of the bill's authors and supporters to rebuild urban America not only by destroying slums but by housing the ill housed. As a locally based program that demanded that city officials back their requests for federal funds with "workable plans" and evidence of "citizen participation," the final mix of public housing and redevelopment mirrored the social and political environment of a particular city.[39]

Multiracial Housing?

For the NAACP and the Urban League, which lobbied hard for its passage, the Housing Act of 1949 promised not only a significant increase in the supply of desperately needed housing but also the possibility of multiracial housing. The legislation heightened the belief of housers and civil rights reformers that the federal government could create an interracial society. Housers and intergroup activists preached that federal action offered the best hope for bettering the living conditions of black urban America. Both Robert Weaver and Charles Abrams believed that public housing would blaze the trail for a racially integrated America.

Yet, from the outlook of 1950, it took tremendous optimism to imagine the federal government as a champion of black housing interests. Indeed, Kenneth Jackson, among recent historians, has shown that after its creation in 1934, the Federal Housing Administration (FHA) worked assiduously to promote segregated and not integrated patterns of urban residence.[40] Not only did the FHA draft blatantly discriminatory racial guidelines for property appraisal (preferring to insure housing in racially homogeneous neighborhoods as opposed to areas of mixed occupancy), but between 1937 and 1939 the FHA, along with its sister agency, the Home Owners Loan Corporation (HOLC), took steps to foreclose investment in all central-city neighborhoods where blacks lived.

Although leery of the FHA, housing reformers placed considerable trust in the Federal Public Housing Administration (FPHA); yet, before 1950, the effect of the public housing agency's decentralized policymaking apparatus rendered it only slightly less racially discriminatory than the FHA or HOLC. Even under the original liberal and racially sympathetic administration of Nathan Straus, the U.S. Housing Agency (USHA) proved more sensitive to local prejudice than to black needs. Straus did inaugurate a Racial Division, headed by the black poet and teacher Frank S. Horne. When USHA became part of the National Housing Agency (NHA) during World War II, however, Horne's job became so narrowly circumscribed as to be ineffective.[41]

After World War II, the FPHA clung to its decentralized system of site selection, in effect preserving Ickes's old "neighborhood composition" racial formula. In 1946, FPHA Commissioner Herbert Emmerich undertook to diminish the already limited influence of Horne and the Race Relations Division. Notwithstanding the rancor of black leaders such as Robert Weaver, the division was eliminated. Horne's job was redefined as adviser to the commissioner. Bitterly, Horne wrote to Emmerich that "apparently there has never been any particular enthusiasm from the operating branches concerned with the solution [to the race problem]."[42]

Before 1950, public policy at the local level regarding race and housing seemed equally unenlightened and unpromising. Only a massive publicity campaign prevented the NHA from commandeering the newly completed Richard Allen Homes for use by white war workers instead of the intended black families. By 1944 Philadelphia's local housing administration supplied only 2,300 of the city's 11,862 wartime housing units to the families of ill-housed black war workers, and true to the sentiment expressed by a South Philadelphia realtor, that "it is more fitting that persons of various classes of people be kept segregated so that we can enjoy the freedom afforded by our glorious constitution and country," the 2,300 units were segregated. As early as 1946, the Philadelphia Housing Authority recognized that because of the shortage of black housing, poor black families made homeless by urban redevelopment confronted a serious "racial problem" that threatened the sanctity of the "neighborhood pattern." "Any project which the authority was likely to build," stated the authority, "would face the same racial problem." Yet the authority remained oblivious to black housing needs. When the Reverend W. L. Johnson, chairman of the local NAACP, visited the offices of the authority in 1946 inquiring about their policy for racial occupancy, Executive Director James Kelly confessed that "neighborhood patterns are observed and this pattern is one of segregation"; however, he could "do nothing about this."

Philadelphia was hardly unique. Ninety miles north, in New York City, the Metropolitan Life Insurance Company with state redevelopment assistance built the 18-square-block Stuyvesant Town apartments, which excluded blacks "as a matter of business and economics."[43]

The shameful truth of restrictive covenants, FHA redlining, and the existence of neighborhood formulas tempered expectations about a new mood in race relations. But in 1948 an event occurred that convinced blacks and housing reformers that America took seriously the goal of decent housing for all. The U.S. Supreme Court, in *Shelly v. Kraemer et al.*, agreed to review two lower-court decisions that had upheld the enforcement of racially restrictive covenants. The Court ruled that while such racial covenants were not unlawful between private parties, they were unenforceable in the nation's courts. *Shelly v. Kraemer* forced the FHA to amend its rules. A new 1949 FHA directive to its appraisers and banking affiliates stated that "a mortgage must establish that no restriction upon the sale or occupancy of the mortgaged property, on the grounds of race, color, or creed, has been filed on record at any time subsequent to 1949." Yet, despite the triumph for open housing represented by *Shelly v. Kraemer* the FHA persistently insured properties subject to racial covenants.[44]

Black leaders considered the Housing Act of 1949 to be a second breakthrough. It promised not only a significant increase in the supply of black housing but also the possibility of interracial housing. Black hopes for improved housing soared.[45]

Pennsylvania's Redevelopment Laws

A progrowth coalition had emerged in Philadelphia in the late 1930s. Called the Young Turks, the band of galahads included Walter Phillips, a liberal patrician and recent graduate of Princeton University; such vibrant houser-planners as Dorothy Schoell Montgomery and Henry Beeritz; G. Holmes Perkins, a professor of fine arts at the University of Pennsylvania; Edmund Bacon; Oscar Stonorov; and several crusading lawyers, including Abraham Freedman, Joseph Clark, and Richard Dilworth. Phillips promoted physical planning as a nonpolitical, noncontroversial way to stir the city from its lethargy and accomplish reform. Phillips, Montgomery, Stonorov, Freedman, and Bacon were all associated with the PHA. Accordingly, with considerable help from PHA fellow members, in 1939 Phillips transformed the Young Turks into the City Policy Committee, which met biweekly. Bacon performed much of the staff work, and when Bernard Newman died in 1941 it was Phillips who maneuvered Bacon into the executive directorship of the PHA.[46]

In 1941 the City Policy Committee, the Junior Board of Commerce, and the Lawyers' Council on Civic Affairs formed the Joint Committee on City Planning, which vowed to overhaul Philadelphia's existing 15-member planning commission. Using Bacon's technical expertise, the committee drafted a comprehensive city plan and submitted it to Mayor Robert Lamberton. Lamberton authorized the group to undertake the reorganization of the city's moribund planning commission, but his sudden death delayed action on the formation of a new commission. Finally, on December 2, 1942, the City Council approved legislation establishing a new planning commission, and auspiciously, the new mayor, Bernard Samuels, endowed the body with a substantial budget. To head the reborn commission Samuels appointed the distinguished patrician Edward Hopkinson, great-grandson of a signer of the Declaration of Independence. For its executive director Phillips recruited Robert Mitchell, a professional planner who had recently headed the Urban Section of the National Resources Planning Board. Its primary task completed, the policy committee reconstituted itself into the Citizens' Council on City Planning (CCCP), which retained a close relationship with the PHA, even sharing adjoining offices at the housing group's Sansom Street headquarters.[47]

In contrast to Domhoff's findings about the differences between housers and planners, from the outset Philadelphia illustrated the cross-fertilization of housing, planning, and redevelopment ideas. Philadelphians drafted Pennsylvania's 1945 Redevelopment law, whose authors included Abraham Freedman, a member of the PHA's board of directors, Hans Blumenthal, research director of the new planning commission, G. Holmes Perkins, and Dorothy Schoell (who in 1949 married the architect-planner Newcomb Montgomery). In 1943 John A. MacCallum, president of the PHA, appointed Schoell executive director of the housing organization to replace Bacon, who had accepted a commission in the navy. Educated at the University of Pennsylvania and the London School of Economics, Schoell had worked at the PHA and as a field representative of the FHA. In 1942 she was head of planning and review for the NHA's Home Use Service.[48]

In 1946, a year after passage of Pennsylvania's Redevelopment Act, Philadelphia established a Redevelopment Authority (RA). A taxpayer's challenge to the constitutionality of redevelopment in the state (*Belovsky* v. *Redevelopment Authority of the City of Philadelphia*) delayed the commencement of authority activity until July 1946. Significantly, *Belovsky* highlighted not only the breadth of support for the postwar crusade against blight but also the city's emerging concept of redevelopment. A host of Philadelphia civic and business organizations appeared as *amici curiae* of the Philadelphia Redevelopment Authority. In his brief before the state supreme court, counsel for the RA, Abraham Freedman, argued that slums produce a profound social and economic injury not only to those who dwell in the areas but to the entire city. He observed that the flight from slum-ridden cities endangered the enormous investment in municipal facilities. Freedman pronounced the goal of redevelopment to be restored urban livability and the creation of a modern, attractive community that would entice people to remain in cities.[49]

Freedman's argument, which linked slums, suburbanization, and the erosion of the municipal tax base, appealed to the five men Mayor Samuels had appointed in 1946 to the new authority. With the exception of Irwin Underhill, a distinguished black missionary and theologian who managed the Richard Allen project, all the other members—John P. Crisconi, Kevy Kaiserman, Joseph McDonough, and Earl Barber—were realtors. Dorothy Schoell Montgomery deplored the real estate bias of Samuels's "political choices," but hoped that under the tutelage of the planning commission's director, Robert Mitchell, the board would operate effectively.

Pennsylvania's redevelopment law required the City Planning Commission to certify neighborhoods for redevelopment. To the delight of Montgomery and the PHA, the RA and the planning commission collaborated from the outset on an area survey using the Public Health Association's Neighborhood Environmental Standards.[50] Nevertheless, Montgomery seemed perplexed in October 1947 when she wrote Catherine Bauer Wurster (Bauer had married the architect-planner William Wurster); her letter indicated that, despite outward harmony, Philadelphia housers harbored serious ideological differences with their progrowth planner colleagues. The team "may have come up with some good recommendations from the APHA survey," Montgomery informed Wurster. But "they may only be interested in central city commercial areas with high potential tax yield. We [the PHA] will be pleasantly surprised if we do not have to disagree with the recommendations, which will be out pretty soon." Indeed, Montgomery was "pleasantly surprised." The RA's first program involved neighborhood-level code enforcement and the type of housing rehabilitation program historically identified with the PHA.[51]

The CCCP served as a watchdog agency overlooking the activities of the reconstituted planning commission. The CCCP founder, Walter Phillips, wrote that the purpose of the organization was "to criticize or praise from the citizen's standpoint, proposals of the City Planning Commission." In reality, through its neighborhood forums, high school and college seminars, newsletters, and radio broadcasts, the CCCP became both a sounding board and an advertising agent for the planners' vision of the postwar city.

Delegates from more than 100 community organizations formed the membership base of the CCCP. Its broad representation made it an ideal vehicle for creating the illusion of citizen participation in the planning process and imparting legitimacy to the city's housing and redevelopment plans. Listed among CCCP members were not only the Philadelphia chapter of the American Institute of Architects, the Philadelphia Building and Construction Trades Council, and the chamber of commerce but the Germantown Settlement, the NAACP, the League of Women Voters, and such grass-roots organizations as the Kensington Community Council and the Greater Olney Civic Association.

The CCCP called its primary goal to restore Philadelphia to a "bright, clean city," and it prescribed planning as the means. By 1950 the council voiced the aspirations of the city's leaders for comprehensive physical renewal involving the revitalization of the downtown and the building of a modern highway system.[52]

In 1947 the CCCP helped with a spectacular Philadelphia planning event that overshadowed everything else on the civic affairs calendar. The CCCP and the planning commission had hunted for a means to stir the public's imagination about the city's future and underscore the importance of city planning. The two organizations decided on a Better Philadelphia Exhibit, and entrusted its design to two architects, Louis Kahn and Oscar Stonorov. Philadelphia-based corporations raised over $400,000 for the exhibit. Gimbels Department Store graciously provided exhibit space. The show, which ran for two months, proved to be extraordinarily successful. More than 400,000 people paid a $1 fee to gaze at Philadelphia's grim past and behold its planned and magnificent future. Stonorov's model of Philadelphia revealed glimpses of the changes planned for the city, including an Independence Mall and a tree-lined riverside promenade. Elsewhere at the exhibit, with the help of the PHA the planning commission erected a full-size, rehabilitated Philadelphia row house.

The Better Philadelphia Exhibit accomplished its purpose. Years later, in 1960, Bacon traced the city's renaissance to the vision of a planned city shown at the exhibit. Montgomery praised the "super-duper planning exhibit," yet she registered some slight apprehension. "I could make some carping comments as to the very small amount of housing that got into the show," but, by and large, she added, "it was a remarkable promotion."[53]

In many respects, Montgomery's estimation of the Better Philadelphia Exhibit served to encapsulate Philadelphia's first housing and redevelopment program, 1945–1952. During these years, solving the housing problem remained a city priority; and while little actual public housing construction or urban redevelopment occurred, planning proceeded.

As early as May 1945, the Philadelphia Housing Authority sought to fashion a postwar housing program by convening several public meetings at the Bellevue Stratford Hotel. At these meetings, representatives of business, labor, the real estate industry, and the PHA advanced proposals to allay the housing crisis. The PHA forecast a five-year need for 50,000 new houses, and saw a need for 19,500 immediately. Nevertheless, most conferences envisioned a limited role for public housing. Evoking the faith in the power of free enterprise that infused postwar America, Montgomery assured the audience that "private enterprise can and should build the overwhelming majority of these dwellings." Montgomery relegated public housing to the poor and extolled the program mainly as a boon to full employment and a means for abolishing city slums.[54]

Ignoring the demand for an immediate program of 19,500 units, as well as labor's plea for a yearly target of 4,000 publicly built houses, the Housing Authority scheduled 19,500 units over six years, and trusted the specious "filter system" to "trickle down" additional housing to low-income families. According to the authority, the mythical "filter" would relieve the acute shortage, since presumably the private housing "industry will engage in one of the largest private construction programs . . . resulting in the considerable exodus of citizens in surrounding neighborhoods."[55]

The Philadelphia Housing Authority predicated its postwar housing program on the expected passage of the Wagner-Ellender-Taft legislation. With hopes for that legislative relief dashed from 1945 to 1948, the authority limped along, attempting to soften the housing crisis through such Band-aid measures as purchasing the four permanent wartime housing projects and managing 2,000 units of temporary veterans' housing.

Funding difficulties aside, between 1945 and 1950, the Philadelphia Housing Authority displayed none of the efficiency and professionalism evident in the city planning department. In fact, the demoralized and graft-ridden Republican administration, which controlled Philadelphia's City Hall between 1945 and 1952, treated the housing authority as just another political satrapy.[56] From 1945 through 1949, critics of the authority protested its use of political patronage to fill many of the 450 jobs, often with "unqualified" personnel. Opponents also inveighed against the authority's "closed meetings" and denounced its failure to spend the $71,119 earmarked for preliminary site studies in anticipation of the eventual passage of federal housing legislation.[57]

Political Reform in the City

In January 1949 Philadelphia's progressive business community, the city's social notables (among them Quaker and Catholic leaders concerned about human relations), and PHA and CCCP "do-gooders" mobilized for another assault on the Republican machine. Slum blight and the departure of middle-class taxpayers had deepened the social and economic malaise overwhelming the city. Despite the Better Philadelphia Exhibit, the city's "filtered filth" water, unrepaired street lamps, unsolved murders, and outrageous political scandals kept urban morale at a low ebb. Therefore, when in 1948 the perennial fiscal crisis forced Mayor Samuels to beg the City Council for additional operating funds, the council exacted a promise to impanel a blue ribbon Committee of Fifteen to investigate corruption in city affairs. The committee's findings of gross governmental mismanagement and criminal conduct among officials mortified the usually unflappable Philadelphians; more important, the findings provoked the drafting of a new city charter.[58]

Indignation over the political corruption seethed, and in 1948 the whole city talked of reform. Concerned about inefficiency in city government and impressed by Pittsburgh's business-oriented Allegheny Conference on Community Development's success in overcoming civic lethargy, Philadelphia's locally based corporate leadership formed the Greater Philadelphia Movement (GPM).

The GPM prided itself on having a small staff and operating principally through its large, "working" board of directors. Leaders of the GPM realized that the city's future growth hinged not only on the prospect of federal redevelopment aid but also on the cooperation of city government with enlightened business and civic leadership. The GPM's board of directors mirrored the organization's downtown orientation. In the 1950s and early 1960s it included C. Jared Ingersoll, president of the Kansas, Oklahoma and Gulf Railroad; Edward Budd of the Budd Company; William F. Kurtz, chairman of the Pennsylvania Company; Nicholas Roosevelt, who chaired the prominent architectural firm of Day and Zimmerman; Stuart Rauch of the Pennsylvania Savings Fund Society; Gaylord Harnwell, president of the University of Pennsylvania; and the chief executives of Atlantic Refining Company, Jefferson Medical College, John Wanamaker Department Stores, and major life insurance companies, building trades unions, and downtown law firms.

Dedicated to bettering urban living conditions and fostering the growth of business and industry throughout the Philadelphia metropolitan region, the GPM, like the CCCP, focused on revitalizing the central city. Although it supported planning and redevelopment through educational programs and publicity extravaganzas, the GPM concentrated on mobilizing the city's social and financial resources in behalf of urban growth.

Both the GPM and the CCCP espoused efficient government and pressed for highway development and slum removal. The GPM campaigned especially for the eradication of such social and physical eyesores as skid row, graffiti-scarred tenements, and juvenile delinquency, which it considered blotches on the city's image and impediments to economic progress. Therefore, the GPM supported public housing as a useful tool, on a par with highway building and new office construction. Not surprisingly, over time, GPM board member William Kurtz chaired the city's Redevelopment Authority, while board member P. Blair Lee of the Western Savings Fund Society chaired the Philadelphia Housing Authority.[59]

Two years after Richardson Dilworth failed to unseat Mayor Samuels, the GPM spearheaded a second drive to oust the city's Republican machine. Allied with the PHA and the CCCP, the GPM mobilized an army of social and political reformers to elect Joseph Clark as city controller and Richardson Dilworth as city treasurer.[60]

City reformers in 1949 pounded the housing issue, especially the inaction of the Housing Authority. William Jeanes, president of the PHA, complained that the housing authorities of other cities had already "swung into action," expanding their staffs and hiring architects, while Philadelphia's housing staff seemed barely able to manage existing projects. Since as city controller he would be authorized to appoint two members to the authority, Clark campaigned on the promise that, if elected, he would immediately appoint the "white knight" of Philadelphia reform, Walter Phillips.

With the passage of the Housing Act in July 1949 and the prospect of from $1 million to $2 million available for a housing program in Philadelphia, the exuberant GPM-PHA-CCCP coalition launched a crusade to overhaul and streamline the Housing Authority. The coalition forced the authority's realtor head, William Reinhardt, to resign.

Political chicanery at the authority matched the reform juggernaut of Clark and Phillips against a tired remnant of aging machine politicos left barricaded behind the walls of the Philadelphia Housing Authority. The machine at last surrendered, and by 1952 Clark and his reform were in control. As promised, Clark appointed Phillips to the authority board, and shortly afterward Phillips installed in the authority a merit hiring system.[61]

The Triangle Plan

Philadelphia's renaissance began discreetly. Encouraged by the Real Estate Board and by downtown bankers and business groups, the RA first targeted for revitalization the "Triangle area," a parcel of urban land adjoining the city's early-twentieth-century beaux arts masterpiece, the Benjamin Franklin Parkway. Architects Kahn and Stonorov authored the Triangle Plan, whose text contained allusions to the earlier City Beautiful Movement and the more scientific postulations common to growth rhetoric. The plan involved clearing approximately 50 acres of old warehouses, sheds, and tenement housing, and undertaking "the biggest single promotion job for the Better Philadelphia of today which begins today." Decrying the "indiscriminate use of land" in the Triangle as "inefficient and uneconomical," the architects assured the city that once redeveloped, annual tax levies in the area would increase from the $956,000 raised in 1947 to over $4 million. The area was already the site of such major institutions as the Art Museum and Franklin Institute; the architects promised to add a civic center and attract private capital to adorn the planned Pennsylvania Boulevard with tall hotels and office towers.[62]

Urban gateways, embellished with City Beautiful monumental architecture, impressed the city's business and civic elites. At the same time, the heady prospect of private investment and fresh tax dollars awakened the promise of a revived downtown economy and a refurbished city pride. And no individual's imagination soared higher than Edmund Bacon's.

Bacon and his colleagues at the planning commission shunned Robert Moses's preference for magisterial central-city development.[63] Between 1947 and 1952, both housing and redevelopment authorities were immobilized by politics, the dearth of federal funds, and the big developers' scorn for the residential land-use constraints built into the Housing Act of 1949. Consequently, first under Hopkinson and then Bacon, the planning commission pioneered an innovative approach to city development that emphasized low-income housing. David Walker, executive director of the RA, informed the city's architectural community in 1950 that "Philadelphia's redevelopment stresses housing." Agreeing that the Triangle project offered "dramatic possibilities equal to those anywhere," he stated, "the Redevelopment Authority must take first things first, must meet the most urgent needs—those pertaining to housing." An alternative hardly existed. Although it would not be fully completed until 1951, Philadelphia's APHA *Housing Quality Survey* disclosed central-city housing conditions that were "predominantly substandard; and to a serious degree." Therefore, with housing as much as slum clearance in mind, between 1948 and February 1952 the planning commission certified 16 areas for redevelopment. Both Eastwick, a swampy, relatively undeveloped section of Southwest Philadelphia, and Aramingo, a region of mixed industrial and residential land use located in the Kensington-Richmond section of North Philadelphia, lay on the periphery of the central city. The other areas—Temple, Poplar, Mill Creek, Powelton, Southwest Central, Passyunk, Old City, Triangle, North Central, Fairmount, Lombard, and Lehigh—with few exceptions embraced aging, largely black wards that originally had been developed in the nineteenth century as the city's industrialized streetcar suburbs (see Map 5). Excluding the Triangle area, planning in all these areas accentuated housing.[64]

Faced with homeless veterans, spreading black slums, and an impotent public housing authority, Bacon, Stonorov, and Kahn helped devise a nationally recognized approach to urban redevelopment that focused on code enforcement, housing rehabilitation, and neighborhood conservation. In addition, the city's program reflected the design preoccupation of Philadelphia planners and their ingrained beliefs about urban form and the etiology of urban blight.

Charged with "projectitis" in the 1960s, and accused later of ignoring the "social concerns" of planning, between 1947 and 1953 Edmund Bacon and the Philadelphia Planning Commission masterminded a unique, "shelter oriented" redevelopment program. Bacon, a graduate of the Cornell University School of Architecture, had apprenticed as a designer in Shanghai before returning in 1935 to Philadelphia, where he joined the architectural firm of Pope Barney. He worked only briefly for Barney, leaving in a year to accept a fellowship to study city planning at Elliel Saarinen's Cranbrook Academy in suburban Detroit. After leaving Cranbrook, Bacon worked three years as a city planner and housing expert in Flint, Michigan, then returned to Philadelphia, first to practice as an architect under Oscar Stonorov and then to manage the PHA.[65]

Saarinen's ideas stirred the young Bacon. In addition to espousing functionalism and the International Style in architecture, Saarinen preached a gospel of urban form and planning that followed closely Patrick Geddes's concept of "organic decentralization." Modern technology, argued Saarinen, had exploded the compact city and challenged modern architects to plan for the orderly dissolution of old, densely settled cities and the genesis of new, functionally arranged communities. Since the virus of blight flowed from one organ of the urban anatomy to another, urban design must be continuous. It must also be flexible and afford protection. As such, planning should

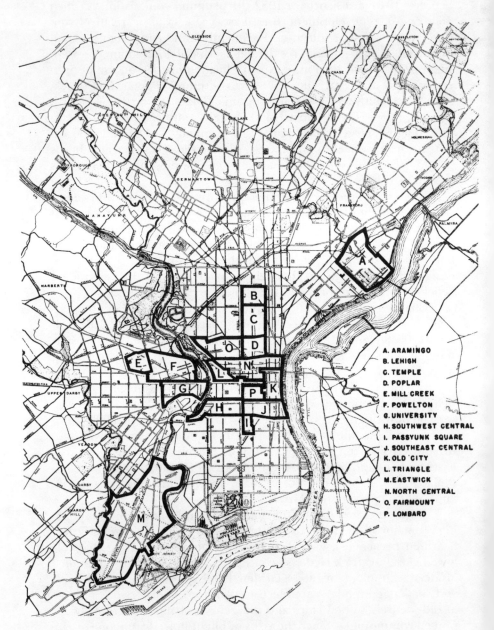

A. ARAMINGO
B. LEHIGH
C. TEMPLE
D. POPLAR
E. MILL CREEK
F. POWELTON
G. UNIVERSITY
H. SOUTHWEST CENTRAL
I. PASSYUNK SQUARE
J. SOUTHEAST CENTRAL
K. OLD CITY
L. TRIANGLE
M. EASTWICK
N. NORTH CENTRAL
O. FAIRMOUNT
P. LOMBARD

MAP 5: Philadelphia Redevelopment Areas, 1952

Source: Philadelphia City Planning Commission; in possession of the author.

establish "no-man's-lands (or buffers) between areas of different function and spirit." Finally, organic planning involved what Saarinen
termed "revaluation," a recognition that the transition from a compact to a decentralized city compelled planners to "revaluate" old
ideas and "replan" for a new set of social, cultural, educational, and
artistic problems.[66]

"Human-Scale" Projects

Philadelphia's early housing-oriented program, like Baltimore's, attacked blight "with penicillin, not surgery." Under Bacon, Kahn,
Hopkinson, and David Wallace (who was replaced by Francis Lammer
in 1951 when Wallace moved to Baltimore), and aided by the CCCP
and the GPM, Philadelphia's redevelopment planners shunned mon-
ster projects in favor of smaller, "human scale" ones. They believed
that the "penicillin" approach would produce "spores" of renewal that
would grow and multiply, ultimately regenerating the entire blighted
area.

Bacon vigorously denied that his distinctive area designs resulted
in disharmony, muddle, or "projectitis." By engaging prominent architects skilled in the art of design rather than practitioners of "spot"
architecture, Bacon's planning interwove separate projects into an
organically conceived urban tapestry, making whole areas, in the director's words, "harmonious."

In the spring of 1948, shortly after the planning commission announced locations for its first nine redevelopment areas, the RA
launched a neighborhood redevelopment program modeled closely
on Baltimore's prewar Waverly project. Accordingly, instead of slum
clearance and rebuilding, the Philadelphia program emphasized vigorous code enforcement, housing rehabilitation, and citizen involvement.[67]

The Mayor's Committee on Neighborhood Improvement, which
worked closely with the city's Department of Housing and Sanitation
(the enforcer of city housing codes), selected for rehabilitation a two-
block slum in the East Poplar redevelopment area. A year later, the
committee's strenuous efforts to take action against the 430 housing
code violators in the area failed. Curiously, an article in *McCalls* magazine about "Yardville," the magazine-sponsored experiment to rehabilitate backyards in a North Philadelphia neighborhood, triggered
the second phase of the plan. Using "Yardville" as a rallying cry, the
mayor's committee, armed with RA technical advisers and modest
contributions from neighbors, landlords, and tenants, transformed
the trash-cluttered backyards of the two-block area into a parklike

commons.[68] Believing that the Yardville idea might be contagious and that such self-help endeavors could eliminate large areas of urban blight, the mayor's committee announced Operation Fix-Up, a plan with a citywide goal of rehabilitating 50 neighborhoods in 1950. Unfortunately, Operation Fix-Up hinged on landlord cooperation and an outburst of self-help fervor within the community. It did not happen. By the end of 1951, only 8 neighborhoods had organized backyard projects, and only 1 backyard area had been rehabilitated.[69]

Operation Fix-Up represented the low-budget, fanciful stage in the saga of Philadelphia redevelopment. The next stage marshaled the city's planning and redevelopment energies as much against blight as for improved housing. While Operation Fix-Up had targeted an entire blighted region, the RA now singled out one severely blighted 50-block region in East Poplar, a section bounded on the south by Spring Garden Street, on the north by Girard Avenue, on the east by Fifth Street, and on the West by Ninth Street.

The idea of East Poplar originated during World War II, not in the city planning office, but in the halls of the Friends Neighborhood Guild, a 75-year-old settlement house situated at the corner of Eighth Street and Fairmount Avenue. Once a fashionable nineteenth-century residential neighborhood, by 1943, the year Francis Bosworth arrived as director of the settlement, East Poplar's four-story brick townhouses had been partitioned into overcrowded tenements. A tangle of icehouses, coal yards, and warehouses snarled the area, and the din of horse-drawn wagons on the cobblestone streets, plus the factories, railroads, and trolley lines, expunged all but the barest trace of the area's dignified past.[70]

Emboldened by the success of Penn Craft, a Quaker-sponsored community project undertaken during the 1930s in strike-torn southwestern Pennsylvania, Bosworth determined to employ the self-help philosophy to transform four blocks of East Poplar's most decayed townhouses into a mutually owned and collectively rehabilitated interracial housing development. In addition to preserving the grandeur of the 93 three- and four-story dwellings, Bosworth aimed to achieve low rents and retain the area's indigenous leadership.

Bosworth's self-help proposal was the centerpiece in the planning commission and RA Poplar scheme (see Map 6). However, action on the East Poplar plans had to wait for the federal largesse bestowed in 1949. Using the write-down provision of Title I, the RA acquired the four-block slum site for $257,552 and forthwith resold it to the nonprofit Mutual Housing Corporation for $78,400. Later, in 1952, the Housing and Home Finance Agency approved the Quaker corporation as the first recipient of funds under the rehabilitation provisions

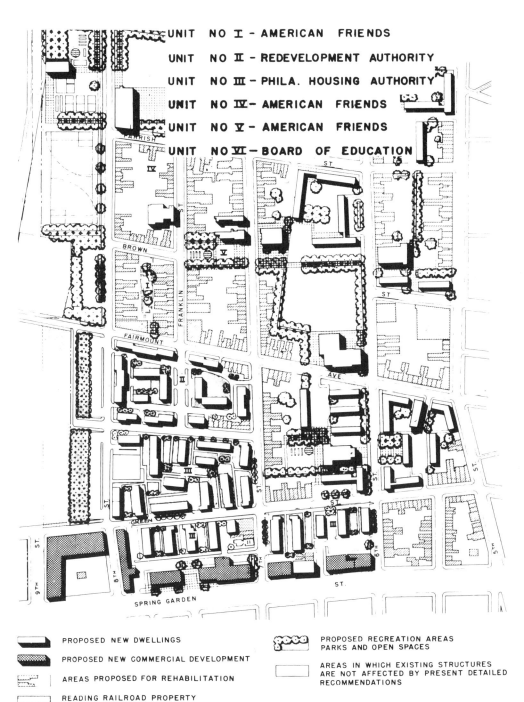

UNIT NO I - AMERICAN FRIENDS
UNIT NO II - REDEVELOPMENT AUTHORITY
UNIT NO III - PHILA. HOUSING AUTHORITY
UNIT NO IV - AMERICAN FRIENDS
UNIT NO V - AMERICAN FRIENDS
UNIT NO VI - BOARD OF EDUCATION

PROPOSED NEW DWELLINGS

PROPOSED NEW COMMERCIAL DEVELOPMENT

AREAS PROPOSED FOR REHABILITATION

READING RAILROAD PROPERTY

PROPOSED RECREATION AREAS
PARKS AND OPEN SPACES

AREAS IN WHICH EXISTING STRUCTURES
ARE NOT AFFECTED BY PRESENT DETAILED
RECOMMENDATIONS

Map 6: East Poplar Redevelopment Area Plan, 1953

Source: Philadelphia Housing Authority Records; in possession of the author.

of the Housing Act of 1950. Still, Bosworth dreaded that the malignant East Poplar slums would inevitably engulf his small pocket of restored housing. Accordingly, aided by state and federal dollars, the RA complemented Bosworth's mutual housing project by building the very attractive 173-unit Penn Towne Apartments, a privately managed, garden housing complex for middle-income families. Completing the residential fabric of East Poplar, the RA conveyed redeveloped land to private developers for sales housing, and to the Housing Authority for construction of Spring Garden Homes, a 203-unit, low-rise public housing project.

The design of East Poplar, included many open spaces, as well as the provision of grassy buffer zones and the preservation of historic and socially significant buildings, such as the Edgar Allen Poe House, the Labor Lyceum, the St. Nicholas Russian Orthodox Church, and the Wister and Kearny schools. Moreover, unlike the "Yardville" scheme, the Bacon and Stonorov design for East Poplar sought to reshape the whole texture of the area to, as Saarinen had taught, create harmonious order out of the unplanned chaos of the urban past.[71]

East Poplar's respect for history, its human-scale architecture visible in the two- and three-story Penn Towne and Spring Garden Homes, and its Quaker sensitivity to social, economic, and racial diversity earned the project the praise of contemporary urban planners and housing reformers. Unfortunately, the ideal of East Poplar as a pioneer urban community never fully materialized. Although visitors traveled from Europe and Japan (including Japan's Prince Akihito) to study Philadelphia's "penicillin" approach to housing and neighborhood design, East Poplar fell short of supplying Philadelphia's need for sufficient low-cost housing. Even with an annual $10,000 grant from the American Friends Service Committee to nourish the "self-help [sweat] equity" that enabled low-income cooperators to exchange their labor for a "stake" in the corporation, few neighborhood people moved into the Friends housing. The average cost of $9,300 per unit for the rehabilitation of the 93 houses drove the rent far beyond the reach of most Poplar residents. One black family with nine children, three of whom had college educations, moved into the Friends Cooperative when it opened in 1953. More typically, the new tenants were adventuresome and liberal-minded people, such as the young engineer with Leeds and Northrup and the owner of the Harley-Davidson motorcycle franchise. Conversely, state-aided Penn Towne suffered from a dearth of middle-income tenants. Consistent with postwar trends, more affluent families preferred buying or renting the new row or single housing springing up in Olney or in the

New Northeast or in the suburbs. East Poplar developers scrounged to retain neighborhood leaders and attract middle-income families. Meanwhile, low-income families jammed the waiting list for such public housing projects as Spring Garden and Richard Allen or crowded into the surrounding neighborhoods. Indeed, the poor collected on the outer edges of the East Poplar area. In one instance, a group of slum occupants displaced from East Poplar packed up and moved to an old slum building that their former landlord had purchased to house them.[72]

Although East Poplar's low-rise architecture and mix of public, private, and rehabilitated housing affirmed certain beliefs and ideals about postwar urban developments, the concept failed to ease the city's crisis in low-income housing. From a national perspective, however, the integration of public housing into the East Poplar plan was exceptional. And, indeed, between 1949 and 1952, public housing dominated area planning in Philadelphia.

Anxious in 1950 to get redevelopment underway, the CCCP viewed housing as "the city's number-one headache" and saw public housing as the solution. The CCCP urged the housing authority to "be prepared to build on open or vacant sites as a general policy or at the very least to make possible the rehousing of families for redevelopment and other planning purposes."[73] In fact, the Housing Authority programmed its first three projects—the 77-unit Arch Homes, the 1,122-unit Raymond Rosen Homes, and the 742-unit Wilson Park Homes—on occupied land. And the 714-unit Schuylkill Falls project and 412-unit Liddonfield Homes, which opened the same year (1955) commanded open sites (see Map 7).

Regardless of project location, Philadelphia prided itself on its public housing architecture. In August 1949 the Philadelphia Housing Authority appointed George Lowatt, then vice-president of the Philadelphia chapter of the American Institute of Architects, consulting architect. Moreover, for its first 10 postwar projects, the authority commissioned prominent architectural firms and "encouraged them to do their best individual design." W. David Morgan designed Arch Homes; Wigham and Tilden, the architects of Northeast Village, produced the Raymond Rosen Homes blueprints; and Oscar Stonorov created Schuylkill Falls. W. Pope Barney and Roy W. Banwell, who landed the commission for Wilson Park, had not only worked as architects on buildings for Haverford and Swarthmore colleges but had been the architects for both James Weldon Johnson and the Abbottsford Homes.[74]

The Housing Authority also strove to build low-rise housing in its early projects. While site problems and even the federal land cost-unit

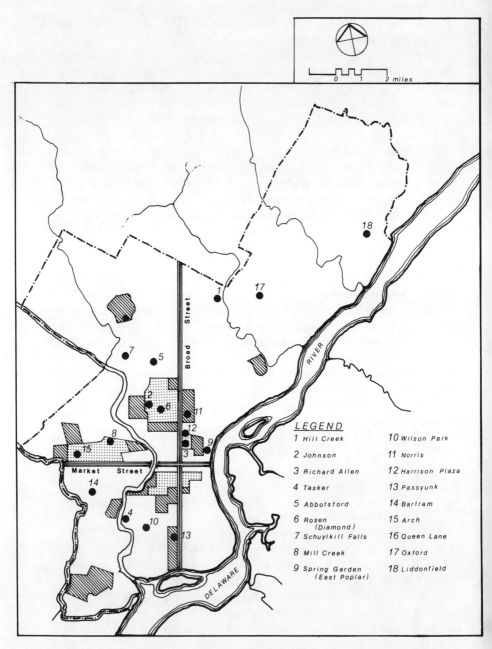

MAP 7: Pre-1956 Housing Authority Projects and Racial Change, 1940–1950
Source: Adkins and Associates, Architects

equation militated against the use of row housing, on the whole Philadelphia's housing projects reflected a greater sensitivity to low-rise design than was evident in cities of comparable size. Both David Wallace
and Catherine Bauer Wurster commended the Philadelphia Housing
Authority for its sincere effort to mute the scale of its housing projects. Of the 10 projects designed and built between 1949 and 1955,
only the 120-unit Queen Lane in Germantown loomed as a solitary,
16-story elevator building, uncomplemented by adjoining row
houses. Three projects, including Spring Garden Homes, featured
row housing exclusively. In the remaining projects, Philadelphia architects endeavored to preserve "human scale and a sense of neighborhood" through a judicious mixture of row housing and elevator
structures.[75]

Such projects as Wilson Park exhibited not only Philadelphia's
concern for low densities and row housing but also the persistent appeal of the neighborhood principle. Located in the Point Breeze
neighborhood of South Philadelphia, in the shadow of several Philadelphia oil refineries, Wilson Park featured four eight-story International Style elevator buildings surrounded by two-story flat-roofed
and three-story hip-roofed, low-rise units. Typically, the buildings
were arranged heliocentrically to assure maximum sunlight. Housing
literature emphasized the "openness," "orderly feeling," and
"livability" of the design, which "should be a positive asset to the appearance and values of the surrounding community." Reminiscent of
Wright and Stein's Radburn, interior driveways were arranged to discourage through traffic. Typical of the neighborhood-unit concept, a
community building, with space for a child-care center, well-baby
clinic, and recreation, served both tenants and nearby residents. The
playgrounds, tot lots, and community facilities served "as meeting
places to foster harmonious relations between the new families and
the older residents."[76]

Wilson's "ultramodern" design paled beside the "experimental"
composition of color, mass, and texture in Stonorov's award-winning
Schuylkill Falls project. Called on the eve of its opening in late 1954
"the unique housing project in the nation," the 714-unit complex occupied a magnificent 26-acre site in Germantown, overlooking the
Schuylkill River. In neighborhood-unit style, and with a nod toward
Wright and Stein, Stonorov grouped two 15-story towers together
with several clusters of 2- and 3-story red and white brick row houses
around an elementary school, a community building, and a playing
field. Harmonizing the design, a serpentine drive wound past the pic-
ture-windowed row housing units and attempted to integrate the low-
rise buildings with the high-rise structures towering above.[77]

113

While such Philadelphia architects and planners as Henry S. Churchill, Wallace, and Bacon applauded Stonorov's use of "imagination and courage" at Schuylkill Falls, they spoke little about Wigham and Tilden's 1,122-unit Rosen project. A true urban island, the project erupted like some craggy mountaintop from the sea of North Philadelphia blight. Eight 13-story cruciform-shaped elevator buildings and 308 gable-roofed, 2-story row housing units loomed above the 27-acre site at Twenty-second and Diamond Streets. Wigham and Tilden stationed the eight towers symmetrically along an east-west axis formed by grassy sitting areas interspersed with asphalt play spaces. The row housing occupied an independent triangular site and was arranged around a large court. Despite the tot lots, generous play areas, community building, trees, and exterior parking, Rosen's giant scale exuded an air of regimentation, evoking the worst of the Bauhaus.[78]

Kahn's Mill Creek in West Philadelphia stood in sharp contrast to the Raymond Rosen Homes. Kahn was deeply committed to achieving quality design in public housing. At Mill Creek, he attempted to incorporate public housing into the social and physical fabric of the existing neighborhood. Therefore, in his composition the housing project became an integral part of the Mill Creek area plan in which streets were abandoned and transformed into tree-lined promenades; plazas, shopping areas, and greenways completed the orchestration of a holistic design. The Mill Creek I housing project consisted of three 17-story, modern-style buildings staggered around a large open square. Reflecting his strong belief in the continuity of space, Kahn designed Mill Creek without boundaries, making it, ideally, part of the whole tissue of Mill Creek life.[79]

Kahn's philosophy appeared just as vividly in the design for the Temple area, where he showed his flair for widened streets, greenways and promenades, and cul-de-sac parking. Unquestionably, the streets, low-rise housing, and greenery imbued the area with light and openness; but it also created an incongruously nonurban environment in the heart of the city.[80]

Two large public housing projects impressed Kahn's Temple design, but, unlike Kahn's Mill Creek, neither Northwest Temple's Norris Homes I nor Southwest Temple's Harrison Plaza warranted special architectural distinction. Both projects, built on costly slum land acquired by the Redevelopment Authority, featured a mixture of low- and high-rise buildings. For Norris I, at Tenth and Norris streets, architects Atrim and Etter conventionally positioned an 11-story apartment building and 68 2- and 3-story row units on a two-block site. The flat-roofed, low-rise housing grimly fronted the street. The chain-link-fenced recreation area seemed the lone concession to the "neighborhood unit" concept in this spartan design.

Unfortunately, the 300-unit Harrison Plaza that opened in 1956 lacked even Norris's unity of design. Instead, Harrison's 15-story tower and the 188 row house "flats" sprawled over parts of four city blocks; and its tot lots and sitting areas fronted a broad but forbidding concrete plaza. A few blocks away, in the North Allen redevelopment area, the twin 18-story Corbusian towers of Cambridge Plaza bore project stigmata identical to Harrison: untapered, unfluted concrete columns; slab canopies over doorways; the ubiquitous chain-link fencing; and the scattered little plots of famished grass and shrubbery gasping for life in a concrete sea.[81]

The Social Benefits of Public Housing

It would be misleading to interpret the vapidity of the Norris, Cambridge, and Harrison Plaza designs as evidence that Philadelphia had disavowed its faith in public housing. On the contrary, between 1949 and 1954 housing and redevelopment planners in Philadelphia harbored a deep faith in public housing. When, on occasion, some Philadelphians complained of trash and litter around such prewar projects as Richard Allen, city officials and housers rushed to the project's defense. Dorothy Montgomery toured Allen in 1949 and marveled at its cleanliness. Evidence of poverty abounded, but she thrilled at the "signs" of middle-class respectability, "especially the effort [of the tenants] to adorn the walls with pictures."[82]

Montgomery and others doggedly clung to the belief that the cost of slums could be measured in human pathology, especially in the rates of crime and delinquency. Throughout the 1940s, 1950s, and 1960s, the Philadelphia Housing Authority gathered crime and delinquency data from the local police districts to affirm the social and economic benefits of public housing. Certainly the social-benefit arguments resounded at the numerous public hearings held in Philadelphia in 1951–1952, on the redevelopment program. At one hearing, Blair Lee, chairman of the Housing Authority, explained that the Norris project would "give families [in the area] the advantage of healthful surroundings to raise children." He also proclaimed the Housing Authority "a vital factor in Philadelphia [for it] has added much to the lives of those who otherwise would be forced to live in dwellings that blight not only the city's appearance, but the minds of those who have to inhabit them." At another hearing, David Walker, having noted the dismal citizen turnout and having praised the "real demonstration of cooperation between the Housing Authority, Redevelopment Authority and the Planning Commission," spoke about the significance of Philadelphia's war on blight. "Here for the first time," rejoiced Walker, "will be the joining together of facilities and abilities to bring normalcy into areas [such as Norris] which today do not have normalcy."[83]

The call for "normalcy" echoed in authority rhetoric. Drayton Bryant, the Housing Authority's director of public relations, insisted in 1952 that public housing aimed to develop "as near to normal communities as possible within a range of different incomes and occupations, rather than creating a sort of transient poorhouse." Bryant was not repudiating public housing's historic way-station mission. Housing management in 1952, as in 1939, hoped for a resident turnover as upwardly mobile families left the projects and were replaced by others. Public housing projects such as Schuylkill Falls were described as "Dream Home[s] for famil[ies]." For a Philadelphia cab driver and his family, the Schuylkill Falls project meant less rent, a modern kitchen for his wife, and a safe play area for his children. As in 1937 this tenant, Mr. Hart the cab driver, a World War II veteran who earned just $50 per week and had several commendations from the Yellow Cab company for heroism, was the hero of public housing.[84]

Nevertheless, despite the housers' faith that public housing would save families from the tragedy of slum living, invidious social and economic forces operated in America's large cities. Racial segregation and discrimination played a crucial role, as Hirsch points out in his study of Chicago; but so did America's deeply embedded abhorrence of poverty, which produced a set of attitudes highly detrimental to the success of public housing. Among the most important of these was the belief that minimalism sufficed in the provision of low-income shelter; there was also the conviction, discussed by Constance Perrin, that when "everything is in its place," the poor would be isolated from the not-so-poor, preferably in the central city.[85]

These beliefs strengthened the planners' determination to wed public housing to area planning, even in the face of Wurster's exhortation that the marriage would inevitably prejudice public housing. Despite assistance in assembling land for public housing, tight building regulations and the high cost of central-city sites created unreasonable population densities and quality compromises. Housing and rehabilitation architects and planners constantly dickered over cost, shaving footage here and adding and subtracting a floor there. In order to enhance the Harrison design, explained Lancelot Sims, a Housing Authority engineer, it "may be necessary to increase the elevator buildings to 15 stories and squeeze in a few additional row houses." It is interesting that Montgomery, who was present when Sims made the suggestion, offered no objection.[86]

Removing a closet from the living room, eliminating wall enclosures from the heater, and excluding splashboards in the kitchen seemed understandable when the priority was cost rather than quality. Housing Authority official George Dunn stated the rationale when discussing the wisdom of using "glass walls" in the Harrison row housing. "Such a departure from normal construction may be highly desirable where the occupants have the financial ability to provide the extras to take advantage of this type of design," explained Dunn, "but where income is low and furnishings and space limited, I doubt its advantage." Needless to say, glass walls were not used.

Nor was the project landscape spared poorhouse planning. The landscape architect for the Spring Garden Homes in East Poplar had urged the Housing Authority to plant hedges. The authority refused, arguing that no shrubbery "will survive in this location. . . . No part of the ground of our projects . . . are [sic] inviolate from the traffic of children and adults. . . . If grass or sod will not stay, the area should be covered with granite block, black top or concrete."[87]

Although in 1952 none of Philadelphia's 10 postwar housing projects had yet opened for occupancy, Philadelphia housers and planners still nurtured the belief that public housing had a vital role to play in shaping the new city. That view was soon to change.

6

The "Sunlit Years"

Joseph S. Clark's election as mayor inaugurated what sentimental Philadelphians have called the Golden Age of city reform. Clark's 1951 victory was a high point in the city's halting crusade for sound government. Over the years, urban progressivism had scored isolated victories along Philadelphia's social and political reform fronts, but it was not until after World War II that a flagging urban economy and a fear of suburbanization forced city leaders to modernize the creaking political machinery and restore vitality to the central district.[1]

Philadelphia's reform movement exuded a strong social conscience and a deep concern over racial discrimination. Indeed, because of discrimination and the absence of sufficient housing for minorities, blacks in 1952 constituted over 75 percent of the low-income families eligible for public housing. The reformers emphatically subscribed to the idea that interracial contact promoted brotherhood. Moreover, they preached that integrated public housing could stabilize declining neighborhoods, serve as the nucleus for modern urban development, and help accomplish the social and physical revitalization of the city.[2]

While housing reformers attempted to use public housing to engineer a more just and brotherly Philadelphia, progressive housing theory strained under a mounting burden of data discounting the positive effects of good housing. Other challenges also undermined the housers' faith. For one, postwar prosperity and a return to individualism eclipsed the heady social experimentalism of the 1930s that had inaugurated public housing as a tool for building a modern community. Assailed by its enemies as socialism and by its friends as oppression, by 1956 public housing had devolved into the unloved stepchild of urban renewal.

The New Regime

In 1949 the state legislature authorized Philadelphia to draft a new city charter. Promoted by the City Charter Commission, the Greater Philadelphia Movement (GPM), and the Citizens' Council on City

Planning (CCCP), and approved by city voters on April 1, 1951, the new charter stripped away the City Council's sovereignty and vested power in a strong mayor-and-council form of government. Consistent with postwar urban reformers' fascination with efficiency, the charter lodged four powerful administrative posts in the mayor's office: a managing director, a director of finance, a city solicitor, and a director of commerce. It also created a "cabinet status" Commission on Human Relations (CHR). The charter preserved the City Planning Commission as an independent board but more carefully defined the commission's duties to include the production of an annually updated six-year comprehensive plan, the preparation of a detailed zoning ordinance, and the development of an annual capital program and budget.[3] Only months after Philadelphians voted to approve the new charter, they elected Clark as mayor and chose as district attorney Richardson Dilworth. Philadelphia's "sunlit hour" had dawned.[4]

Clark's support was broad, including downtown businessmen; organizations such as the GPM, CCCP, and PHA; and university, hospital, and other institutional administrators convinced that Philadelphia's survival hinged on expertly managed government and a rebuilding of the city's decaying core. Clark's political reach extended further to embrace the traditional New Deal Democratic constituency: organized labor, racial and ethnic minorities, and groups such as the Fellowship Commission, dedicated to improved race relations. Liberal middle- and upper-middle-class households living in fashionable Mount Airy and Chestnut Hill also flocked to Clark's colors.[5]

Philadelphia's indefatigable band of housers and planners exulted at the mayor's election. Dorothy Montgomery hailed Philadelphia's rebirth and begged her friend, the prominent houser, Bryn Hovde to join in the crusade by filling the newly vacant position of executive director of the CCCP. Hovde answered: "After all those years wandering in wilderness, so to speak, you see the promised land. Now, clearly, you are set up to really get things done." But Hovde did not wish to leave his present position, and Aaron Levine took the CCCP job.[6]

In the estimation of Dennis Clark, a human relations specialist with the Housing Authority, Joe Clark "lacked a political bone in his body." Fortunately, James Finnegan, the powerful Democratic party chairman, reinforced Mayor Clark's political flanks and helped navigate Clark's social programs through the treacherous waters of City Hall.

In the fashion of his political idol, Franklin Roosevelt, Clark's liberalism had aristocratic underpinnings. Educated at Harvard College and the University of Pennsylvania Law School, Clark belonged to an old Philadelphia family of investment bankers. Throughout his life, Clark clung to an unshakable faith in class, authority, and tradition; but he also trusted that republicanism and gentility alike survived at the sufferance of common man. Therefore, good government operated to serve human needs, which, according to Clark's interpretation of American history, had too often been recklessly ignored by selfish and imprudent oligarchs. Generations of corrupt politicians, piratical landlords, and scheming utility magnates had fashioned a vicious urban form that thwarted opportunity and segregated racial and ethnic minorities in wretched slum housing.[7]

Clark assigned to government the task of creating a more socially inclusive as well as a more spatially and structurally efficient urban system, which would foster the individual's quest for dignity and wealth.[8] Clark shared with his colleagues in the National Conference of Mayors the conviction that urban renaissance began by transforming aging downtowns into modern centers of commerce and finance. Clark envisioned a center city of multistory steel and glass towers rendered accessible by interconnecting beltways, expressways, cloverleafs, and ramps.[9]

Despite his devotion to free enterprise, Clark rejected the idea that the nation's business leaders possessed the wisdom, determination, and social conscience to solve the urban crisis. He suspected capitalists of being incapable of mediating and harmonizing the multitude of conflicting social interests that made up the modern city. Notwithstanding the vehement protestations of innocence from the National Association of Real Estate Boards (NAREB), Clark accused private bankers and homebuilders of habitually ignoring the squalid housing conditions of over 70,000 Philadelphians.[10]

Clark not only insisted that the fouled wellsprings of urban opportunity be unclogged but that the plumbers be "the best men"—professionals, planners, and university-trained administrators. He filled key city posts, especially those dealing with housing and city planning, with people who had demonstrated competence and had a record of professionalism. Abraham Freedman, counsel for the Philadelphia Housing Authority, accepted Clark's appointment as city solicitor. Next Clark strengthened the Redevelopment Authority (RA) by tapping former U.S. Senator Francis J. Meyers to chair it and naming as new members Dorothy Montgomery and William F. Kurtz. On Freedman's advice, Clark established within the mayor's office a new post of housing coordinator, and selected for housing czar his young executive secretary, William Rafsky.[11]

Urban reform movements thrive on drama and visibility. Clark rallied the city around the alluring image of a "better Philadelphia," the same phrase used by Bacon and Stonorov in the 1947 exhibit. Clark expedited such symbolically potent and already planned undertakings as sandblasting the grimy exterior of City Hall, demolishing the forbidding Chinese Wall, and building fire stations and sewage treatment plants. At the same time he enthusiastically promoted Edmund Bacon's plans for the Triangle area and the redevelopment of "Old Philadelphia."[12]

Clearly, the problem of black housing ranked high on the reform agenda of the new administration. Several years earlier, as city controller Joseph Clark and his liberal friends had lobbied the City Council and the Housing Authority to abandon the notorious "neighborhood formula" for housing project racial composition and inaugurate a nondiscriminatory policy in public housing. The so-called Cooperative Agreement resulted from the 1949 Wagner-Ellender-Taft legislation that had allocated 10,000 units of low-income housing to Philadelphia conditional on a signed statement assuring the city's "cooperation" with the Housing Authority in vacating intruding city streets and delivering water, sewerage, school, and other vital services to otherwise tax-exempt project neighborhoods.

The Philadelphia Council of Churches, the Race Relations Committee of the Society of Friends, and the Committee on Democracy in Housing (CDH), among other liberal groups dedicated to improving race relations, saw the federally mandated Cooperative Agreement as a perfect opportunity to achieve integrated public housing. The newly formed CDH pleaded that "the living relationships [in public housing] are as important to the people who live there as the roof over their heads." Sidney Schulman, counsel for the CDH, referred to the privately built Marshall Field interracial housing project in Chicago as evidence that "non-segregated housing develops understanding between groups, while segregated housing continues traditional prejudices. You can only know your neighbors by really being a neighbor and working together."[13] Although city politicians whose neighborhoods were potential targets for public housing fought the interracial impact of the Cooperative Agreement by attempting to give the City Council a veto over public housing site selection, Controller Clark worked successfully to block the veto provision.[14]

In its final form the agreement required the Philadelphia Housing Authority to rent the 10,000 housing units "on a non-discrimination and non-segregated basis, without regard to race, religion and national origin," language similarly found in Pennsylvania's Urban Redevelopment Law. When the Housing Authority formally adopted nondiscrimination and nonsegregation as a policy, Mayor Clark issued a press statement that "the City of Brotherly Love has now become a City of Brotherly Living."[15]

Clark's rhetoric notwithstanding, the agreement highlighted merely the first round of Philadelphia's crusade for improved race relations. Fearing the growth of the black ghetto and shocked by almost daily reports of racial incidents, most of them triggered by the movement of blacks into formerly all-white working-class neighborhoods, Clark led a campaign for integrated housing and interracial harmony.[16] To Clark, the racial ghetto not only suffocated life within it but threatened to crush the city's postwar renaissance. In a 1955 speech on "The Future of Urban Shelter," he condemned the private homebuilding, banking, and real estate establishments for imprisoning Philadelphia's 400,000 blacks in the city's three large ghettos. "Unless we can break through some of these barriers at a much more rapid rate than heretofore," warned Clark, "the unsolved minority shelter problem will remain an ominous cloud over the whole urban renewal concept."[17]

Clark showed the full weight of his concern when in 1952 he selected George Schermer to be the first permanent director of the CHR, the city's new human relations commission. Schermer began his career with the Chicago Housing Authority where he gained a reputation for expertise in dealing with racial issues. During World War II he was summoned to the racially torn motor city to head the Mayor's Interracial Committee. His effectiveness there in "tension control" earned him a national reputation. Although Schermer and the CHR dealt with a variety of incidents stemming from racial, religious and ethnic tensions, housing constituted a major concern of the new city agency.[18]

In addition, to Clark, Schermer, and the CHR, numerous organizations played critical roles in the crusade to promote a large-scale, interracial housing program in Philadelphia. World War II racial tensions in Philadelphia, particularly the 1943 transit strike, had induced such organizations as the Federation of Churches and the NAACP to create an emergency City-Wide Interracial Committee, which had an active Subcommittee on Housing.[19] Moved by the example of the wartime interracial committee, and desiring a permanent agency to coordinate the city's antidiscrimination campaign, in 1946 several organizations dedicated to racial and religious harmony formed the Philadelphia Fellowship Commission (FC). Among the constituent members were the Citizens Council on Democratic Rights, the National Conference of Christians and Jews, the Philadelphia Council of Churches, the Catholic Interracial Council, the Jewish Community

Relations Council, and the Society of Friends. A Quaker activist in the social welfare movement, Clarence Pickett, first presided over the FC, while the dynamic Maurice Fagan occupied the post of executive director. By 1949, with the Reverend George Trombridge as president, the FC spearheaded the drive to secure a city human relations commission and outlaw discrimination in urban housing.[20]

Philadelphia's Quaker Yearly Meeting, like the Council of Churches and the Catholic Interracial Council, coordinated its housing integration activities through the FC; the Friends interracial housing endeavors, however, reached far beyond the realm of the commission. Philadelphia Quakers exerted their greatest moral force for interracial housing through funding individual projects such as the Friends Neighborhood Guild and the interracial cooperative housing in East Poplar.[21]

Restrictive Covenants

Philadelphia's organized movement for interracial housing, and its Cooperative Agreement, seemingly exuded a mood of tolerance abroad in the nation in the early 1950s and a positive social climate for public housing integration. Such Supreme Court cases as *Shelly v. Kraemer, Brown v. Topeka, Kansas, Board of Education,* and a flurry of local court cases hinted that urban America might relax its opposition to racial integration in housing as well as education. A closer examination of the nation's housing situation produced a less optimistic assessment. Abrams in 1958 charged that, notwithstanding the FHA's recantation, the agency had bequeathed an enduring lifestyle of restricted homogeneous living in suburbia. Generations of Americans had entered positions in government and real estate psychologically prepared to enforce racial segregation and to view black occupancy as a threat to property values. Moreover, much of America's urban housing stock remained subject to restrictive covenants. Indeed, in 1952 Republican vice-presidential candidate Richard M. Nixon and his wife coexecuted an agreement that the house they purchased would never be sold or rented to a black, Jewish, Armenian, Persian, or Syrian family.

Within the Housing and Home Finance Administration (HHFA), only the anemic Racial Relations Office monitored the civil rights record of the housing agency.[22] Despite its precarious status in the early 1950s, under Joseph Ray the office analyzed black demographic patterns, black employment opportunities, black homeownership trends, and other data relevant to black access to housing. President Eisenhower's Advisory Committee on Housing Policies and Programs expressed "deep concern" that the "opportunities of minority group families to obtain adequate housing are extremely limited or non-existent." A month later, HHFA Administrator Albert Cole confessed that regardless of what measures were developed to clear slums and meet low-income housing needs, "the critical factor . . . which must be met is the factor of racial exclusion from the greater part of our housing supply." In a similar vein, Foley exhorted, "We are simply not living up to the standards of a free economy and a democratic society. . . . The real problem lies with the citizen, the businessmen, the builders, the lender, the realtor."[23]

In 1954 Cole himself indicated that neither the FHA nor the Public Housing Authority was assuming its proper responsibility for aiding black housing. Whereas, noted Cole, "statistics [revealed] an increasingly free mobility of nonwhite families . . . where Federal aids are the exception," the FHA continued to guarantee mortgages in racially restrictive markets. Significantly, in the face of evidence that blacks depended heavily on public housing for decent shelter, the Race Relations Office reported that "except where state statutes or local ordinances prohibit discrimination or segregation by race . . . racial exclusion and segregation predominate in local [public housing] programs." Moreover, while black demand increased for public housing, a free market enterprise-oriented Congress in 1954 cut appropriations for the housing program.[24]

For whatever reason, throughout urban America, as the black demand for public housing rose, public housing became increasingly segregated and less politically acceptable. Several studies, one by Alene Simkins, supervisor of tenant selection in the Newark Housing Authority, ascribed racial segregation in public housing to the attitude of public housing officials who had internalized deep-seated racist beliefs about the negative effect of black occupancy on urban property values.[25] Nevertheless, during an August 1954 field trip to inspect Philadelphia's proposed interracial Eastwick Redevelopment Area, HHFA race relations officer George Nesbitt heaped praise on Philadelphia. Nesbitt marveled that "Philadelphia happens to be a city with a distinctively favorable level of readiness for racially unrestricted housing development." After reviewing demographic data indicating that 25 percent of Philadelphia's white households already lived in mixed blocks, Nesbitt concluded that whereas interracial housing requires "leadership resources [that] are informed and well positioned . . . it seems evident that [in Philadelphia] . . . an excellent framework of such leadership exists."[26]

The progress in interracial housing reported by Nesbitt failed to increase the supply of housing for low-income blacks; nor did it solve the dilemma that enmeshed redevelopment and public housing in the invidious process of ghetto building. In fact, public housing fit comfortably into this redevelopment-ghettoization equation because, after 1954, it served the unenviable function of sheltering the poor, usually black, victims of inner-city slum clearance.

Reevaluating Public Housing Policy

Several years before the Housing Act of 1954 helped make urban redevelopment more attractive to private land developers, houser-planners, with the aid of contemporary sociological theory, had begun stripping away the lingering traces of communitarian idealism that once undergirded the vision of public housing. In truth, Joseph Clark's election in 1951 coincided with a thoroughgoing reassessment of the nation's public housing policy. While Harry Truman had salvaged from Congress the basic social welfare edifice of the New Deal, including the Tennessee Valley Authority, most of the trappings of the collectivist stage of New Deal "experimental democracy" had succumbed during the war years.

Postwar America exalted the heroic individual, the "other-directed" self who pursued socially defined goals in a world that David Reisman described as the "lonely crowd." Reisman, like William H. Whyte and Morris Janowitz, supplanted Robert Park's and Ernest Burgess's organic view of the city with a mechanistic one in which the individual negotiated the urban wilderness guided by little more than the media and a few cultural symbols. Reisman's individualism proved lethal to the environmental determinism that underlay the concept of the neighborhood unit. Indeed, Janowitz in 1952 described the city not as a community but as a congeries of perpetually shifting and overlapping localities; none of these unstable little worlds had any autonomy, explained Janowitz, but embodied "communities of limited liability." Individuals in these worlds not only freely chose which neighborhoods to live in, but, acting simultaneously in many roles—for example, as student, employee, union member, church parishioner, and taxpayer—also belonged to numerous communities. Furthermore, argued Whyte, since individuals voluntarily selected their neighborhoods, their preferences for homogeneous communities deserved the same degree of respect as the desire of others for racially diverse localities.[27]

While Janowitz and Whyte were redefining the urban neighborhood, other scholars were demolishing the logic connecting housing with social and psychological well-being. In 1951 prominent homebuilders, architects, and planners gathered in Lansing, Michigan, to talk about housing, living environments, and people. After several days of discussion, they concluded that families routinely interacted with their housing environment, that modern housing environments were deficient, and that architects must design shelter that provided families with a functional and emotionally satisfying mode for family living. Significantly, the Michigan conference focused on individual needs and totally ignored the housing community. Summarizing the conference findings, Frederick Gutheim amplified the delegates' singular concern for the "individuality" of families. "Some families," he mused, "have natural homemaking abilities, others don't. Some are teachable, others are marooned in bad living habits and routines. Individuality is an important factor in relating particular families to a particular type of house." Having masterfully deflected attention from the environment to the individual, Gutheim subtly obliterated the principal sociological argument once undergirding the housing movement. Instead of "good housing making good people," Gutheim proposed that the opposite might be true. Possibly, hypothesized Gutheim, housing administrators could "best help families to improve their way of living by helping [them] to make changes in living habits that would allow [them] to make the most of a new type of house."[28]

Neither Edmund Bacon nor John Dean agreed with such apostasy from the canons of public housing doctrine. Yet, even their once evangelical fervor had mellowed. Dean's 1949 article on the "Myths of Housing Reform" affirmed that public housing "had provided rehoused families with structures more comfortable and decent . . . to live in," but he glumly confessed that the expected "improvements in social welfare . . . have failed to materialize." He blamed the defeat on "laissez faire individualism" and current real estate practices; but he mainly criticized those housing reformers who had succumbed to the myth that clearing slums and rehousing slum dwellers in gigantic public housing projects would eradicate social ills. Declaring better housing alone insufficient, Dean, like Gutheim, recommended greater emphasis on social programs and community organizing.[29]

Catherine Bauer Wurster admired Dean, especially his analytical approach to housing. But Wurster's vision of public housing still glowed in 1950, while Dean's merely flickered. In her address before the American Institute of Planners Conference, Wurster rejoiced that the 1949 Housing Act had freed planners from their ancient bondage to land-cost formulas and bestowed on them the weighty responsibility to make serious decisions about housing and urban form. Yet, her image of public housing in 1950, while burnished, lacked its earlier ecstatic quality. It was clearly more reasoned, more pragmatic. Title I, she exhorted her planner friends, had unfettered the public housing market and afforded cities the opportunity to build attractive low-rise complexes both within the central city and on the urban periphery. Wurster urged that creative planners overcome vicious patterns of social and economic segregation by interspersing new low-income housing with middle-income housing. "It is possible," explained Wurster, to tear down slums and erect one-story bungalows. "Any decision to stick [in] a tall elevator apartment is a real choice to be justified on social and civic grounds, not mere cost accounting." Planners must collaborate with such social scientists as Robert K. Merton, must grapple with the sociologically desirable ends of planning.[30]

Three related issues graphically illustrated the precarious balance between the ends and means of Philadelphia's housing policy. The first issue concerned integrated public housing; the second involved public housing design, particularly the wisdom of building high-rise structures; the third dealt with housing so-called problem families. All three issues were related to a process that began when Philadelphia secured its Title I funding and moved aggressively to carry out its East Poplar, Mill Creek, and Southwest Temple redevelopment projects.

By 1953, the RA had mailed eviction notices or orders to vacate to 342 families and 138 single persons living in the East Poplar area; 117 families in Mill Creek received orders to vacate beginning in November 1952. Altogether, between 1950 and 1957, 1,074 families were displaced by slum-clearance action in the southwest Temple area.[31] The RA had opened a Rehousing Bureau in 1950 to help relocate families uprooted by the Friend's Mutual Housing Corporation project in East Poplar; similar rehousing bureaus aided victims of Mill Creek and Temple redevelopment.

The Rehousing Bureau diligently verified that most displaced families previously occupied "dark, dingy, vermin infested, overcrowded, health destroying, and vice-breeding tenements." Data substantiated that blacks constituted 90 percent of the families displaced from East Poplar. All of the Mill Creek uprooted families were black, and of those, 56 percent earned less than $399 a month. To lessen the trauma of displacement the Philadelphia Housing Authority awarded first preference "to families . . . displaced by any low-rent project or by any public slum clearance or redevelopment project initiated after January 1, 1947."[32]

Significantly, Philadelphia's new charter had ordered the Housing Authority to develop a policy of integration in rehousing uprooted families. After two years of prodding from the FC and the PHA, in early 1952 the authority officially installed integration as part of its housing policy. According to the text of Resolution 3630, the authority would henceforth rent all housing units "on the basis of need within preferences declared by law . . . to all applicant families alike without regard to race, color, creed, religion or national origin."[33]

The Housing Authority's program involved work on 11 projects encompassing almost 4,600 units. The 77-unit Arch Homes in 1952 awaited its first occupants; Raymond Rosen, Norris, and Schuylkill Falls were under way; and at East Poplar, Mill Creek, North Allen, Harrison, Liddonfield, Queen Lane, and Wilson Park, only the absence of an official signature on a federal loan contract delayed the start of construction. Rosen, Norris, East Poplar, and Harrison made up the housing phase of Philadelphia's urban redevelopment program, which involved the extensive clearance of black slums and the rehousing of many displaced families (see Map 7).[34]

Two of the 11 projects—Arch Homes and Wilson Park—were slated for integration, and as the deadline for signing the funding contract with the federal government approached, the authority's interracial planners met their first test, one that compelled them to enunciate more clearly their integration plans. Final approval of a $9 million federal loan for Wilson Park required the City Council to rezone the South Philadelphia site from industrial to residential use. Located at Twenty-sixth Street and Snyder Avenue, the mere designation of the 24-acre site for interracial public housing incurred the wrath of the area's Italian and Irish American homeowners, who argued that the 742-unit project threatened the value of their property. Local priests and powerful South Philadelphia politicians led the crusade to block the building of the project, but on March 4, 1952, undaunted by the shouts and curses of over 300 protesters, who packed the City Hall gallery, the City Council approved the site for residential use. Although an important victory for public housing integration, the contest over Wilson Park boded ill for the future of the city's integration program.[35]

As its first action toward the implementation of its Resolution 3630, the Housing Authority created a Neighborhood Relations Committee composed of, among others, representatives of the CHR, the Catholic Interracial Council, the FC, and the American Friends Service Committee. Following recommendations made by the Tenant Selection Committee, particularly the prominent black attorney Sadie T. M. Alexander, the Housing Authority conducted staff orientations and initiated education sessions. Further, to aid in laying the delicate groundwork for integration and to assist in staff training, the authority hired as a consultant Edward Rutledge of the National Committee against Discrimination in Housing. On June 4, 1952, the authority publicly announced its adoption of an integration policy and consummated its declaration by hiring several blacks for positions in the central office.[36]

In July 1952 the Housing Authority opened the 77-unit Arch Homes in West Philadelphia. On "move-in" day, 40 "stable" black families joined 30 white families as the first residents. A number of the white tenants were families of veterans attending the University of Pennsylvania. At the same time, the Housing Authority moved several black families into the previously all-white Hill Creek Homes.[37]

Perhaps the authority believed it could as easily integrate the lily-white Abbottsford Homes located in a working-class section of East Falls, only a few blocks from Midvale Steel and the Budd works. More likely, as Anna McGarry hinted, Housing Authority executive director Allesandroni had tired of her and Maury Fagan's badgering and finally had said, "The hell with it; we'll give them what they want, and let them worry about how it works!" Nevertheless, integration day at Abbottsford occurred August 1, 1952. On that sweltering evening a black tenant family consisting of a Mr. Bernadino, his wife, and their two children arrived at the Abbottsford Homes. Sticking to the Tenant Selection Committee's recommendations, the authority had carefully selected an "attractive" black family; Mr. Bernadino was a veteran and a student at Temple University. Unfortunately, the Bernadinos did not slip into Abbottsford unnoticed. Their arrival at Abbottsford ignited a disturbance that was quelled only after city police "swarmed" over the project and a providential rainstorm cooled neighborhood tempers.[38]

A later survey of the Abbottsford incident disclosed white attitudes similar to those Arnold Hirsch discovered in his study of housing tensions in postwar Chicago. The white tenants at the Abbottsford project felt that the Housing Authority had surrendered to NAACP pressures, that the Bernadinos were "paid block busters," and that the white public housing tenants were victims of a "test case." Tenants worried about black and white intimacy at the project's youth dances, about blacks and whites attending the same schools, and about the negative effect of integration on property values of nearby white homeowners.[39]

Philadelphia's integration program culminated with the entry of black families into Abbottsford, Arch, and Bartram Village Homes. While the Housing Authority continued to place black families in selected projects, the progress of public housing integration was agonizingly slow. The authority combed tenant rolls searching for black families whose middle-class profile qualified them as likely candidates for integration. By 1954, despite the ballyhoo surrounding Resolution

TABLE 1: Percentage of Black Occupancy in Philadelphia Housing Projects, 1950–1954

Project	Year of Occupancy	Percentage Black				
		1950	*1951*	*1952*	*1953*	*1954*
Hill Creek	1938	0	0	0.7	2.3	2.3
Johnson Homes	1940	97	97.0	98.8	98.8	99.0
Richard Allen	1942	99	99.7	99.9	99.9	100.0
Tasker	1942	10	10.0	9.0	11.9	17.6
Abbottsford	1942	0	0	0.4	2.3	3.3
Bartram	1942	0	0	0.8	2.8	4.4
Oxford	1942	0	0	0	0.4	0.6
Passyunk	1942	0	0	0	2.4	4.1
Arch	1952	—	—	51.9	50.7	53.0
Wilson Park	1954	—	—	—	—	10.0
Norris	1954	—	—	—	—	99.0
Raymond Rosen	1954	—	—	—	—	89.6

Source: Federal Public Housing Administration, Statistical Branch, *Reports on Occupancy*.

3630 and "the City of Brotherly Living," the Housing Authority's integration record proved unexceptional (see Table 1).[40]

The High-Rise Issue

Another thorny issue confronting public housing policymakers in the early 1950s concerned the use of high-rise architecture. The high-rise housing issue had first been broached in the spring of 1951 when the Housing Authority prepared to build postwar housing projects. Rebuffed in its early efforts to locate vacant peripheral sites for public housing projects, constrained by high center-city land costs, and deluged by low-income applicants, the authority announced its intention to employ high-rise architecture.

Word of the Housing Authority's high-rise decision rumbled through the headquarters of the PHA and the CCCP, causing groans and cries of outrage from Montgomery and Freedman and the CCCP executive director, Aaron Levine. Even in the thick of battle against the ignominious slum, housers in the 1920s could at least salute Philadelphia as "the City of Homes"—and affordable row homes at that. Suddenly, Philadelphia, historically wedded to low-rise housing design, had capitulated to the New York City solution of building elevator apartments. Montgomery complained to Wurster that the authority's 1951 blueprint proposed furnishing 65 percent of its federally allocated 20,000 units in 11- to 13-story buildings. In chorus with Wurster, Montgomery implored the authority to abandon its madness and make greater use of Title I funds to preserve the city's "human-scale" tradition.[41] Convinced that public housing bureaucrats in Washington had instigated the elevator-building craze, Wurster and Montgomery helped arrange the fall meeting of the American Institute of Architects (AIA) in Philadelphia, where Wurster blasted "those God Damned Skyscrapers!" But the meeting "did little more," grumbled Montgomery. She grimly admitted to Wurster that "while we [in Philadelphia] have not given up, we are fighting a losing battle."[42]

Philadelphians overwhelmingly sided with Montgomery. Undoubtedly, city policymakers entered the skyscraper age grudgingly. In fact, half the members of the Housing Authority opposed high-rise construction. Prodded by Montgomery, the authority commissioned a "scientific" study to investigate the "implications of multi-story, low-rent, public housing projects for such social matters as family life, child development and race relations." Rather than rehash old arguments on the evils of slums and the safety and health benefits of improved housing, the authority sought an impartial but rigorous analysis of the "livability" of elevator apartments for low-income families. To conduct the study, it hired Anthony F. C. Wallace, a young anthropologist from the University of Pennsylvania.[43] Wallace brought to the study of housing unique research skills and unquestionable impartiality. His specialty in 1952 was the study of the North American Indian, particularly the culture of the Eastern Woodlands nations, whose characteristic shelter had been the long house. Therefore, he approached the public housing community as an exotic culture, "merely shifting . . . [his] angle of vision," he later quipped, "from long houses to tall houses." Using field investigation techniques, Wallace compared the cultural attributes he discovered at the 1,077-unit, low-rise Tasker housing project in South Philadelphia with the social patterns found among families living in New York City's 19-tower, 1,768-unit Jacob Riis Homes.[44]

To the dismay of both the Philadelphia Housing Authority and Wurster, Wallace's study, *Housing and Social Structure*, "seemed to imply," wrote Wurster, "pretty basic and objective failure on the part of public housing in general."[45] Wallace's report acknowledged the superiority of public housing over slum housing, but while clearly favoring the low-rise world of Tasker over New York's aerielike Riis, the study discovered severe deficiencies in both projects. At Tasker, Wallace uncovered evidence of oppressive management, on the one hand, and weakening family authority, on the other. Here was a "landlord-ridden place," he wrote, with "asphalt streets and lots crowded with unsupervised children." Signs abounded of tenant apathy and low morale, of vanishing pride and the absence of community social norms concerning the care and use of open space. He decried the ponderous management rules that stripped fathers of their freedom to garden and their dominion over the maintenance of their homes. The low-income residents he interviewed at Tasker regarded the project "as simply a port in an economic storm, and they are embarrassed to even admit they live there."[46]

Albeit poorly kept and filled with sullen people, Tasker at least displayed traces of human activity. Tenants gossiped on doorsteps, and congregations of children rough-housed on the half-planted grass plots. Wallace observed none of this amid the towering high-rise buildings of Riis Homes. On the contrary, Riis impressed Wallace as an inhumane, hostile world characterized by fear, "fear of children falling out of windows," "fear of death in crossing a super-highway to get to a playground." He portrayed Riis Homes as crisis ridden and attributed this mood of despair to the high-density buildings and the limited contact between mothers and children—all stress-producing phenomena inherent in what Wallace called the "overextended urbanism" of high-rise public housing environments.[47]

Rather than offer specific recommendations, Wallace postulated a number of hypotheses. For one, he hypothesized that public housing densities above 12 to 20 units per acre forced tenants to make difficult social and physical adjustments. Furthermore, speculated Wallace, dwelling units without privately controlled yard space inhibited family unity by constricting the father's role as "star boarder." Finally, "the more homogeneous the population, the more difficult an organized community structure." His study begged the Housing Authority to reassess its aims.[48]

Joined by Montgomery and Wurster, Wallace urged the authority to reexamine its standards and define precisely the goal of a "decent home and a decent environment for every American." In 1952, housers no longer exuded the same cocksureness about the goals of public housing. Clearly, Wurster, like Wallace, abominated "super-tenements," high-density elevator buildings that, in her eyes, not only defied the trend toward decentralization but were inexpedient in a nuclear age and rudely ignored humankind's "overwhelming preference for ground-level living." Multiple-family structures, she charged, required a commitment to cooperative living that was lacking among today's American families. Her youthful faith in Carl Mackley and the cooperative spirit of the American working class had disappeared.

Cloistering low-income families together in elevator towers, she wrote in 1952, will not "suddenly transform [project buildings] . . . into models of Dutch neatness, German discipline, Scandinavian co-operative genius, and Latin urbanity. Twenty years ago," she confessed, "this was much less clear. At that time there was a widespread feeling among progressive housers and planners that social, economic, and technological forces would push us inevitably in a single direction: toward a more collective mode of life."[49]

Echoing the prevailing *weltgeist* of individualism, Wurster evoked the image of contemporary urban-suburban society where the "child psychologist (while still respecting the nursery school) puts primary emphasis on the emotional ties between the child and his immediate family. Mothers are no longer supposed to abdicate in favor of supervised playgrounds, and fathers are summoned home early to play with these offspring. It is now believed the personal security which makes society possible—particularly democratic society—is a home developed quality at base." Therefore, instead of large-scale project communities arranged in neighborhood units—Mackley, Richard Allen, and Tasker, for example—Wurster encouraged "much smaller, more varied public housing developments with a bona fide domestic character." Finally, she concluded her pummeling of "supertenements" by applauding Philadelphia for planning some well "balanced [project] neighborhoods," which by mixing low- and high-rise housing escaped the look of standardized barracks.[50]

"Problem Families"

Both Wallace's brief for "father-maintained" backyards and Wurster's invective on "supertenements" touched on another issue troubling housers in the early 1950s: the "normalness," or what many housers saw as the "normlessness," of public housing. Faint-hearted housers wondered whether "normalness" was an attribute incompatible with public housing. Could public housing provide safe and sanitary dwellings, promote social and psychological well-being, and simultaneously afford way stations for economically disadvantaged families?

This conundrum of the normative poorhouse arose in its most enervating form with the discovery that more and more public housing tenants fit the prevailing sociological model of "problem," or "special," families rather than the stereotype of the hardworking, upwardly mobile families promised in the public housing literature of the 1930s. By 1952 the Housing Authority had already defined problem families as those having too many children, or as those "who make a great deal of noise, quarrel among themselves, indulge in hostilities with neighbors . . . are chronic alcoholics, narcotics addicts, active T.B. cases, lack control over children, tear up the physical structure [or] engage in prostitution, or random relationships which resemble it."[51]

There is another side to the study of these families. Carol Stack, Joyce Ladner, and others have emphasized the adaptive strengths of black public housing families. This malleability has enabled such families to employ kinship networks and family employment strategies to cope on a day-to-day basis with the ordeal of low income. Currently, I am at work on a longitudinal study of the life experiences of more than 1,000 black families who lived in Philadelphia's Richard Allen Homes between 1941 and 1965. Tentatively, the data vindicate the findings of malleable black families, but the data also underline the enormity of the economic and social burdens borne by black families living in public housing during the postwar era. Housers responded to the evidence of social and economic distress among black tenant families and ignored the signs of family durability.[52]

The "problem" family issue was first seriously broached at a fall 1952 meeting of the Housing Authority's Advisory Committee on Tenant Selection and Occupancy, called to discuss the 342 families to be relocated from the East Poplar site. Although the law gave priority in public housing to all families dislocated because of RA action, the question arose whether those families should pass the authority's "social criteria" test. For example, should those families present a valid marriage certificate? According to the advisory committee minutes, "it was the general feeling that the problem was not a piece of paper [the marriage certificate], but the definition of reasonably stable family groups with some strengths which appeared capable of progress as distinguished from those families with deep, long term problems which would cause continuous disturbance in a low-rent housing community."

If the overarching responsibility of public housing was to provide a decent environment in addition to safe and sanitary shelter, and to afford "improved opportunity for family living," then, asked the committee, to what degree should public housing be forced to accept "problem" families? To what degree should public housing supply skilled case work? "It should be realized that many of these problem families are not afflicted with temporary neuroses, but have continuing and deep problems upon which little progress may ever be made." In other words, pleaded the advisory committee, treating problem families may not only exceed but actually destroy the way-station mission of public housing. "A chronic alcoholic," observed the committee, a "wife-beater, or a woman with several children and generally unacceptable behavior will create such tensions among many surrounding families that the objective of housing will be defeated in many ways."[53]

Apparently neither side claimed victory in the problem family debate. Philadelphia housing policy listed and defined the characteristics of "undesirable" tenants and actively discouraged the admission of families with these traits; despite the proscription, often displaced or otherwise needy problem families were steered into such slum-bound projects as the Richard Allen Homes.[54]

By 1953 a worried director of public relations, Drayton Bryant, forwarded a memo to Walter Allesandroni that debunked another belief about public housing: that housing projects existed as "islands of good amidst a sea of bad." "Our experience has shown," wrote Bryant, "that neighborhoods have a strong effect upon public housing developments." Richard Allen by 1953 had become a place littered with trash, graffiti-scrawled, noisy, and vandalized. Bryant ascribed the devolution to "a changed type of applicant." Taking an increased proportion of families out of clearance areas or other slum sites had "changed the pattern of behavior to one of less control of children, less family stability and less sense of civic responsibility." Bryant deplored the frustration, rejection, hostility, and violence he found at Richard Allen, and attributed this behavior to the concentration of people of low income, low education, lack of opportunity, racial segregation, and "enforced pattern of behavior over many generations." In effect Bryant conceived a "culture of poverty" theory a decade before it became academically fashionable.[55]

Clearly, uncertainty or skepticism confounded the notion that good housing could transform human behavior; nor did housers any longer assume uncritically that housing projects could make a garden spot out of a slum. Yet, despite these gnawing doubts, a consensus still prevailed among city housers, planners, and business and civic leaders that public housing was urgently needed to replace slums. Furthermore, the consensus dictated that low-rise public housing was sociologically superior to project towers and that concentrations of the poor in large-scale central-city housing projects of any type invited the signs of disintegration visible in Tasker and Richard Allen. More ominously, the problem-family issue raised suspicions about the very nature of public housing.[56]

Shifting Ideologies

Between 1949 and 1954, shifting currents in local housing and urban renewal policy debuted in the national political arena. Maturing ideas about the role of the atomized individual, racial change, and the central city produced significant revisions in housing and urban redevelopment policies. Philadelphia's experience, like that of other cities, illustrated that during the Truman years, federal urban policy excited a bevy of area plans and project blueprints, but few tangible results. Even when cities had active redevelopment authorities, inexperience and awkwardness in coordinating public- and private-sector planning, the confusion of relocating thousands of displaced families, and the novelty of assembling and financially packaging large redevelopment parcels hobbled renaissance efforts. Some redevelopment authorities, commanded by czars such as New York's Robert Moses or possessed of powerful institutional or political support, shepherded projects into operation. Yet, by 1953 there were fewer than 52 cities with redevelopment projects either under contract or in the building stage.[57]

Nevertheless, nurtured by progrowth coalitions, urban redevelopment enjoyed relative popularity in the early 1950s; not so public housing. Even in the "cooperative" social environment of the 1930s, Americans had responded phlegmatically at best to public housing. During the individualistic postwar years, opposition to public housing stiffened. Seemingly, the fortunes of public housing fluctuated inversely with the index of economic indicators, which climbed steadily in the early 1950s.[58]

Following passage of the 1949 Housing Act, the National Association of Real Estate Boards (NAREB) moved its crusade against public housing from Congress into city halls, corporate boardrooms, and local neighborhoods. There, at the grass roots, the real estate industry erected its redoubts against creeping socialism. Pamphlets for distribution to working-class homeowners posed the simple question, "Can you afford to pay someone else's rent?"[59]

Yet, as the historian Richard O. Davies has noted, it was principally the outbreak of the Korean war and not the NAREB's campaign that undermined Truman's public housing program and slowed funding for urban redevelopment. On July 18, 1950, in order to conserve building supplies, Truman directed the HHFA to curtail all FHA credit and reduce public housing allocations from the 135,000 units authorized in the 1949 Housing Act to a mere 30,000 units. In 1951 Truman relented somewhat and urged Congress to increase the low-income housing quota to 75,000 units; but a deadly wedge had been inserted. The conservative Republican congressman Everett Dirksen goaded the House to dispatch the wounded public housing program by reducing the 1951 program to a token 5,000 units. In Philadelphia, infuriated labor unions, housers, and prohousing politicians charged that by dooming public housing, congressional opponents were preventing Philadelphia from becoming a better city. Congress ultimately relented, but trimmed Truman's 75,000-unit request to 50,000 units.[60]

The war against "socialistic" public housing enervated the program in other ways. Calling public housing the "road to serfdom," such congressional enemies as Ralph Gwinn in 1952 accused the program of harboring and coddling communists. The resultant Gwinn Amendment provided that no public housing apartment should be occupied by a person belonging to any organization identified as "subversive" by the U.S. Attorney General. From 1952 to 1954, all public housing residents were compelled to swear their innocence of radical taint, upon which the project manager filed their signed and notarized statement in their tenant folder.[61]

But the red-baiting hardly stopped there. The Los Angeles Housing Authority discharged its assistant executive director, Frank Wilkinson, for refusing to name all the organizations to which he had belonged from 1932 to 1936. In 1952 the Philadelphia authority fired Henry Marter, a Korean war conscientious objector, "because too many veterans lived in public housing." That same year, an article appeared in the Philadelphia *Daily News* alleging that Drayton Bryant once taught at a University of Southern California based "People's University" and that his affiliation with Philadelphia's Pennypack Woods Mutual Home Ownership Association indicated an affinity for "socialistic" cooperative ventures. Bryant confessed that he had lectured on "Important Neighborhood Factors in Home Ownership" at the USC People's Education Center, but he vigorously denied that "he was a member of the Communist Party or that he had ever engaged in illegal, disloyal or subversive activities." Bryant kept his job but he was forced to sever his ties with the Pennypack Woods association.[62]

Whittled down to a fraction of its intended size and caught in the crossfire of the McCarthy witch hunts, public housing limped from the Truman years into the Eisenhower era. All the signs were inauspicious. Eisenhower had been swept into the White House in 1952 on a rising conservative tide. Although he had personally disavowed McCarthyism, it had tapped a deep vein of anticommunism in America. Cold-war politics and atomic diplomacy aside, the early fifties were prosperous years of new General Electric appliances, sleek Chevrolets, and Levitt-built suburbs. By 1952 America reveled in suburbanization; indeed, almost half of the 1,396,000 new homes built in America in 1950, as well as the 2,218,300 erected in 1951 and 1952, were in the suburbs. The suburban lifestyle fostered an intensive family lifestyle and social conservatism.[63]

While Eisenhower's "dynamic conservatism" branded public

housing, together with New Deal farm and welfare programs, as socialistic, Eisenhower sanctioned government assistance to help the urban poor escape the un-American environment of the slum. Rejecting public housing, Eisenhower favored tax- and interest-rate incentives to encourage more private-sector participation in the city-rebuilding process.[64] In 1953 the outline of his new "dynamically conservative" housing and redevelopment program appeared. The principal architect of the new strategy was the urban scholar Miles Colean. Dissatisfied with the sluggish pace of the 1949 housing and redevelopment plans, Colean presented an alternative approach in his book *Renewing Our Cities* (1953). He rebuked urban planners for their "narrow intermittent surgery" tactics and proposed instead to attack the causes of blight and decay through a coordinated program of conservation, code enforcement, and rehabilitation.[65]

Colean's program struck a familiar chord in Philadelphia, where code enforcement and housing rehabilitation had historically ranked high on the housers' agenda. Philadelphia's new city charter had reorganized the city's code-enforcement machinery, and in 1953 the PHA presented to the City Council the first considerable revision of the housing code since the association had drafted the ordinance in 1915. And Operation Fix-Up and the strong rehabilitation component of the acclaimed East Poplar plan situated Edmund Bacon, David Wallace, and Robert Mitchell among the vanguard of planners preaching conservation and housing rehabilitation.[66]

By executive order, in 1953 Eisenhower established the Advisory Commission on Government Housing Policies and Programs, chaired by Baltimore developer James Rouse. In addition to a distinguished representation of banking, construction industry, and real estate people, including Rouse, John J. Scully, and Norman Mason, the commission counted among its members Cincinnati's prominent director of city planning, Ernest Bohn, and the influential author of *Renewing Our Cities,* Miles Colean. A probusiness, progrowth point of view emerged from the deliberations of the commission, which advocated, among other things, the conservation and renewal of aging neighborhoods, government-backed home repair and modernization loans to preserve existing housing, and only lastly the provision of new and rehabilitated public housing for low-income families.

The commission seemingly ignored the ominous implications of the growing black ghetto and focused instead on rehabilitating urban America. Without success, HHFA's Frank Horne and Clarence Mitchell of the NAACP begged the advisory commission to include black housing needs within the framework of comprehensive urban renewal. Mitchell reminded the commission that the great bulk of

FHA- and VA-assisted housing excluded black families and that to date "no city . . . had developed a comprehensive housing program which coordinated slum clearance, rehabilitation, and code enforcement with public housing. No city had developed a really fair and consistent program for dealing with the housing and rehousing problems of non-white families."[67]

Later, Horne lamented that the Eisenhower committee's final report expressed deep concern for the housing problems of minorities, while leaving their solutions to "changes in the attitudes of private investors." The committee failed, said Horne, "to face up to the fact that the only real solution is the removal of restrictions which prevent [black] families from bargaining in the open market for their shelter." Furthermore, argued Horne, large-scale slum-clearance and conservation and rehabilitation activity, emphasized in the committee's recommendations, "will displace even larger numbers of minority families requiring even larger quantities of new and sound existing housing. . . . Failure to meet these needs adequately will not only result in a further decrease of living space and debilitation of housing now available to minorities, but also hamper and distort the entire urban renewal program."[68]

As Horne and Mitchell predicted, the 1954 Housing Act gave black America neither its rightful place in urban comprehensive planning nor a reasonable consolation prize for enduring discrimination. Clearly, from the vantage point of HHFA, those racial considerations were waning in importance and, in 1955, HHFA emasculated the Race Division by dismissing Horne.

New FHA mortgage and loan assistance programs assigned private enterprise the primary responsibility for assisting low- and moderate-income families to either rent or purchase all the good housing Washington imagined would flourish in urban America's "renewed" gray areas. To enforce comprehensiveness in renewal planning and discourage the "intermittent surgery" approach, the 1954 law created the Urban Renewal Administration (URA), which required all communities seeking federal renewal funds to submit a detailed "workable plan."[69]

Therefore, in the Housing Act of 1954 Congress did not abolish redevelopment; rather, it chose to marry the city rebuilding idea more solidly to the comprehensive plan for economic revitalization. In fact, the 1954 legislation represented a triumph for the progrowth agenda. For developers and investment bankers, the act transformed redevelopment into an engine for profit. Whereas the 1949 law had ordered redevelopment authorities to undertake "primarily residential" projects, under the new law 10 percent of redeveloped land could be used for nondiscretionary-nonresidential purposes, including schools, recreational facilities such as stadiums, and office towers. (Five years later, the 1959 Housing Act raised the nondiscretionary allotment to 20 percent.) Moreover, for urban areas to be certified as "blighted," and therefore eligible for redevelopment, cities had only to declare 20 percent of the area buildings "substandard."[70]

Although it mandated planning and bureaucratic efficiency and promoted business participation, the 1954 Housing Act proved disastrous to the public housing program. No longer the bride, public housing after 1954 devolved into the handmaiden of urban renewal, and with the expected invidious consequences for black and other ill-housed urbanites. A conservative Congress pared the output of public housing to 35,000 units and channeled that meager supply to meet the desperate housing needs of families displaced by the acceleration of government-aided slum clearance.

Philadelphians reacted ambivalently to the 1954 law. On the one hand, city housers and planners gloated that Congress had actually enacted the "Philadelphia approach"; on the other hand, they deplored the demotion of public housing to a stepchild of urban renewal. A distraught Mayor Clark brushed aside Republican Congressman Hugh Scott's remark that the 1954 act really opened more private housing to the poor. In Clark's opinion, and that of others, the 1954 legislation emasculated public housing at a time when Philadelphia, like other cities, had an urgent need for more low-income housing. William Wheaton, head of the urban studies department at the University of Pennsylvania, calculated that America actually needed 400,000 low-income units annually—a figure promptly incorporated into National Housing Conference literature. Likewise, the Philadelphia *Daily News* observed that the city's present 10-project program only "scratched the surface" and warned that with 7,000 poor families cramming the Housing Authority's waiting lists, "Philadelphia's public housing program seemed headed for a quick death."[71]

That fear proved baseless. Washington kept the anemic public housing program—if only barely.

A Statement on Housing

Actually, Philadelphia's housers and planners did not require Eisenhower's advisory commission to pinpoint the chinks and blemishes in the city's housing and redevelopment program. As soon as Mayor Clark's three appointees to the RA—Montgomery, GPM member William Kurtz, and Francis J. Meyers—were seated in 1952, the new board created a Development Committee, whose members included Aaron Levine of the CCCP, University of Pennsylvania political scientist Martin Meyerson, University of Pennsylvania Dean of Fine Arts G. Holmes Perkins, Robert Mitchell, and Montgomery herself.[72] During the course of their discussions, the Development Committee produced a new, more inclusive definition of redevelopment, which Meyerson detailed in a May 1955 "Memorandum to the Development Committee." Meyerson recommended that the RA bypass the worst slums and concentrate on renewing areas threatened with blight. Slum clearance should be delayed until the supply of housing for minority groups could be substantially increased. Meanwhile, he entreated the authority to expand its geographical range of operations and replace its scorned project approach with a comprehensive, 15-year blight-removal program embracing code enforcement, housing rehabilitation, spot clearance, government aid in relocating slum families, and the construction of low-income public housing on vacant land.[73]

The Development Committee also urged Mayor Clark to create an Office of Housing. In January 1954 Clark announced the creation within his office of a new position of housing coordinator and named William Rafsky to the post. Rafsky exercised enormous influence in shaping Philadelphia's renewal program. Endowed with superhuman energy and an insatiable appetite for precision and control, Rafsky dashed from planning committee meetings here to RA sessions there, only to consume late evenings wrangling with the Housing Authority.

Washington had mandated "citizen participation" in renewal planning as part of the 1954 law. But, much earlier, Rafsky and the city's Housing Authority initiated a "democratic exchange" on housing and planning through the city's citizen organizations, among them the PHA, the GPM, and the CCCP. Aided by their respective housing and redevelopment committees, these agencies functioned well in the "citizen participation" capacity. Nevertheless, while the GPM in 1955 considered "housing the biggest problem facing American cities," it termed the problems of public housing site selection "beyond belief" and confined its advisory role to redevelopment.

In late March 1955 the PHA and CCCP forwarded to the Housing Authority "A Recommendation for Policy on Site Selection for Public Housing." Noting that since "low-rent public housing is now part of urban renewal . . . [the Housing Authority program] should be regarded as a means of providing much needed additional housing accommodations," Montgomery and Levine pressed their demand for small, low-rise housing projects built on undeveloped land on the periphery of the city, or on cleared sites "reduced in cost through the redevelopment process." Small projects, observed Montgomery and

Levine, "prevent economic ghettos," assist in the acceptance of sites, "and assist in racial integration."[74]

Finally, in the fall of 1955, a PHA-sponsored committee made up of 11 of the city's most prominent housing and planning experts framed "A Statement on Housing and Urban Renewal Policy for Philadelphia." The presence on the committee of city planner David A. Wallace, as well as Meyerson and Montgomery, underlined the fraternity and consensus that oversaw the birth of urban renewal in Philadelphia. Among others, the architect Henry S. Churchill, the law school dean Jefferson Fordham, Howard Hallam, William Ludlow, Dean Holmes Perkins, and William Wheaton helped author the 1955 Statement.

The document repeated many of the points about comprehensive planning, code enforcement, and public housing scale and location spelled out in earlier CCCP-PHA memoranda. But a tone of foreboding had been injected into the text. Describing the city as "threatened" and "losing the battle with blight," the housers and planners accused Philadelphia of neglecting code enforcement and starving its housing program. Unless Philadelphia provided decent low-rent housing for relocating slum dwellers, read the Statement, "urban renewal [would] fail." Anxious about the high densities and the racial segregation that prevailed in the existing centrally located projects ("which will almost certainly be regarded as substandard twenty years hence"), the authors of the Statement advanced the bold idea that the Housing Authority acquire "good, older private dwellings" for public housing. Moreover, they speculated that existing public housing might be sold to private owners, especially if "by doing so high income groups can be introduced into the neighborhoods where low income families predominate."

The Statement's authors attached an astounding $230 million price tag to their 10-point renewal program, adding that without such a sizable outlay, the irreversible "decline in the city's tax base will make it increasingly impossible to finance the city's essential services and the city will not be a place where people will live."[75]

When Jefferson Fordham smuggled an early draft of the Statement to Clark in August 1955, the mayor displayed understandable pique. He resented his housing and planning friends chiding him and his progressive administration for lax code enforcement and for not having a housing policy. Clark, however, was to run for Congress in November. It was his long-time friend Richardson Dilworth who would inherit the mayor's office.

Immediately after Dilworth's election, G. Holmes Perkins and Montgomery arranged a meeting with the new mayor to discuss his

1956 funding priorities for low-income housing and code enforcement. The meeting apparently satisfied everyone. Dilworth staunchly supported "housing for human needs." An obviously elated Montgomery wrote Dilworth in early January 1956 that although "the size and scope of Philadelphia's big city urban renewal problems are almost beyond comprehension . . . they will surely be licked if you stick to your determination to do so." In replying to her note, Dilworth thanked Montgomery for her "very kind letter regarding . . . [my] position on public housing. This is one thing," he affirmed, "on which I do not think we can compromise."[76]

Montgomery's enthusiasm for Dilworth's views on housing signaled the changes that had occurred in public housing during the first four years of Philadelphia's urban renaissance. Economic prosperity and a resurgence of individualism had shorn the public housing ideal of its last vestiges of communitarian innocence. Harsh economic and political realities had forced housing authorities to squeeze massive elevator towers on costly slum land, producing at best the blending of high-rise buildings and row housing visible at Schuylkill Falls and Mill Creek. Scorned by even its friends for inflexibility, unimaginative management, and sterile architecture, and reviled by its conservative enemies as "socialistic," public housing found a useful niche in the heady world of city rebuilding.

7

Public Housing and Roundhouse Renewal

In the mid-1950s the din of wrecking balls and the roar of bulldozers reverberated through the streets and alleys of Central, North, and West Philadelphia. The city's leaders had a bold blueprint to rebuild the central city. The Central Urban Renewal Area (CURA) plan involved an extensive program of public housing.

Central Urban Renewal Areas

Unveiled in 1956, the CURA plan linked the city's goal of saving the downtown with its mission of salvaging the outer ring of neighborhoods in West and North Philadelphia.[1] Yet the plan suffered from conceptual flaws. First, it operated on a dangerous premise that certain neighborhoods should be bypassed as unsalvageable. Second, it presumed, somewhat naively, that city bankers would invest in marginal neighborhoods merely on the planners' assurance that they were "conservable." Third, it trusted that public housing not only would house families displaced by renewal activities but also would disperse the inner-city black population.

The faith of Philadelphia planners in the ghetto-obliterating potential of public housing was not unique. Arnold Hirsch had discovered the same determination to engineer improved race relations among the "liberal environmentalists" staffing the Chicago Housing Authority in the 1950s. Because of Philadelphia's Quaker tradition and the strength of its housing reform, planning, and fellowship organizations, however, the city's commitment to desegregation and racial harmony seemed appropriate.[2]

In early 1956, nine days after Richardson Dilworth's inauguration as mayor, William Rafsky exchanged his housing coordinator's hat for wider brimmed headgear as urban development coordinator. Rafsky's dominion now extended far beyond housing, encompassing not only slum clearance but also the reinvigoration of the city's shrinking economy and the development of a modern central business district.[3] Unquestionably, Rafsky proudly announced in February 1956, the CURA plan represented a path-breaking "shift in policy from redeveloping to renewing the city." Like Philadelphia's previous urban redevelopment strategy, CURA operated mainly in the blighted central city; but, consistent with the goals of Philadelphia's Workable Program, the Redevelopment Authority (RA) considered CURA as merely one segment of a future comprehensive plan for the entire city.

Following the city Planning Commission's earlier land-use analysis, CURA assigned an *A, B,* or *C* classification to every residential section of the central city (see Map 8). Then, using a method of evaluation strikingly akin to the Ernest Burgess/Chicago School "concentric ring theory" of urban form, the plan branded most of the inner-city neighborhoods as *A* (most blighted) or *B* (moderately blighted). Fringe neighborhoods warranted a *C* (conservable) code. These "conservable" sections, north of Lehigh, west of Forty-fourth Street, and south of Tasker, had recently been entered by blacks, and to CURA analysts, the bumper crop of *For Sale* signs signaled white flight, high vacancy rates, imminent apartment conversions, and incipient blight.[4]

Earlier redevelopment efforts had channeled city resources into *A* and *B* sections; CURA reversed that strategy and "concentrated a substantial portion" of available renewal funding into those "conservable" areas that promised the greatest chance of success. CURA brandished a $15.2 million bag of tools for redevelopment in these *C* areas. Slum clearance (using Title I) would excise the one or two bad spots, while housing-code enforcement would stem further deterioration. Ideally, displaced families would find refuge in public housing built in small, neatly scattered clusters of units wherever it fit in with the neighborhood plan. Anchored to stable neighborhoods, and uncontaminated by surrounding substandard housing, conservable areas afforded redevelopment the protection from adverse conditions missing from the Richard Allen, Raymond Rosen, and East Poplar projects.[5]

Philadelphia planners, bankers, and developers therefore, unabashedly retreated from the decrepit and primarily black *A* and *B* zones. Earlier housing surveys had identified over 51,000 dwellings in these "gray" areas as substandard, indicating that effective redevelopment would necessitate massive block-clearance operations, demolishing between 40 and 100 percent of the standing structures. Therefore, Edmund Bacon and David Wallace recommended completing only existing area *A* projects such as East Poplar, Southwest Temple, and the large Eastwick development that had been undertaken as a public-private housing site for mixed black-white residency. Other-

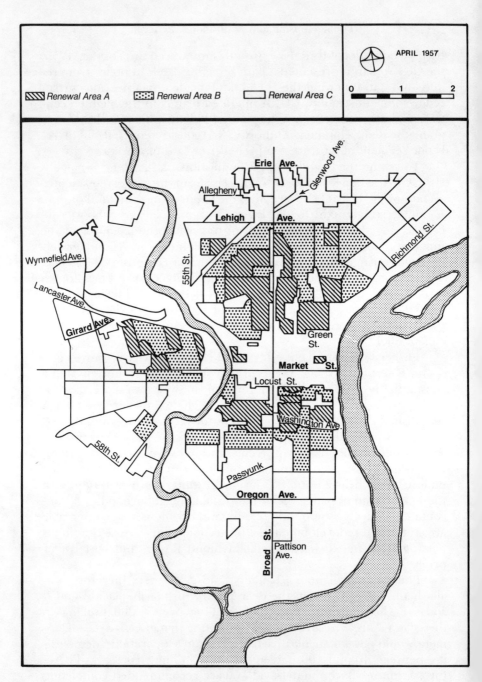

Map by Heidi Perry.

MAP 8: Renewal Areas, 1957

APRIL 1957

Renewal Area A   Renewal Area B   Renewal Area C

0   1   2

Erie Ave.

Glenwood Ave.

Allegheny

Lehigh   Ave.

Richmond St.

55th St.

Wynnefield Ave.

Lancaster Ave.

Girard Ave.

Green St.

Market   St.

Locust St.

Washington Ave.

58th St.

Passyunk

Oregon Ave.

Broad St.

Pattison Ave.

wise, suggested activity in *A* and *B* areas amounted to a strategy of formalized public disinvestment. Bacon labeled it an "open spaces program." Critics of CURA, such as Dennis Clark, decried it as "urban triage" or "roundhouse renewal."

The CURA plan had ominous implications for the city's black community. In fact, the plan involved nothing less than surrounding "graying" or "blighted" central-city neighborhoods with buffer zones of urban renewal. Dennis Clark protested to Rafsky that CURA "deliberately bypassed the most notorious slum conditions," thus preserving "these sore spots as symbols of Negro deprivation. The aggravating effect that this would have upon Negro Leadership," explained Clark, "should not be lightly discounted. [Moreover], the postponement of activity in the worst areas in all probability will lead to the 'intensification of misery' . . . and an increase in the already spectacular rate of crime, family disorganization, and social disabilities concentrated in these slum locales."[6]

Clark's apprehensions were well founded. The plan intended little more for the *A* areas than seizing and demolishing tax-delinquent property and utilizing the cleared land for parking, playgrounds, and tot lots. This "limited action" was intended to spread the relocation burden over a longer period, and to reduce the eventual cost of property acquisition.

While Rafsky ballyhooed the city's shift from spatterdash redevelopment to neighborhood conservation, he likewise encouraged continuing the city's large-scale undertakings in cooperation with Drexel, Temple, and the University of Pennsylvania. At Dilworth's urging, the RA also mobilized resources to protect the city's investment in the Triangle area, namely Bacon's and Kahn's grandiose plans for Penn Center. Penn Center not only begged for protection, it became the centerpiece for CURA. Wallace and Bacon underscored the importance of the "downtown" in renewal and contended that revival must radiate from the central core outward, as well as from the fringe inward. Theoretically, with a renewed, economically prosperous, and architecturally dazzling downtown as the keystone, and with the fringe neighborhoods conserved, the unlovely "gray" areas would afford a potentially lucrative opportunity for capital investment.[7]

A strong progrowth consensus fortified CURA, but from the beginning a nagging disagreement over tactics harried the program. Rafsky, Dilworth, and the liberal phalanx, including the PHA, backed the comprehensive neighborhood conservation approach. Proceeding with the CURA plan, in early 1957 Rafsky selected five neighborhood conservation areas: Morton in Germantown, Nicetown on the North

Philadelphia border, Mill Creek and Haddington in West Philadelphia, and Hawthorne in the Frankford section. Each community had participated in the RA's Leadership Area Program to strengthen its social infrastructure and enhance the opportunity for successful revitalization. For example, as part of the Hawthorne Leadership Area Program, between 1953 and 1956 the United Neighbors Association, a settlement organization, undertook an intensive housing-code-enforcement campaign. In Germantown the Morton Neighbors sponsored both code enforcement and housing rehabilitation.[8]

Yet, while Rafsky pressed his intensive neighborhood strategy, throughout 1956 Wallace and Bacon determinedly lobbied for a "scattered," as opposed to a concentrated, approach to renewal. Persuaded that any renewal operation in the fringe areas represented little more than a "holding action," they advocated surgically removing the worst spots of decay in those areas to check further deterioration and perhaps stimulate private rehabilitation. In the meantime, Bacon and Wallace exhorted the city to "scatter" redevelopment projects among one or two favored sectors, such as the university area of West Philadelphia or the downtown.[9]

Both Temple University and the University of Pennsylvania viewed urban redevelopment as vital to their continued existence in the city. Each institution had high-ranking representatives on the boards of the GPM and the CCCP. With no less ardor, city businessmen dreaded the blighting effect of a black invasion, and following the lead of the FHA, they steered mortgage and home improvement dollars away from neighborhoods occupied or being "invaded" by black home seekers.

Not surprisingly, during 1956 most of the businessmen and financiers consulted by Rafsky about the CURA strategy supported the scattered-site approach. Real estate spokesmen, bankers, and others candidly informed Rafsky of their reluctance to invest in black areas. Realtor Roland Randall for one warned Rafsky that, despite federal loan guarantees, few financiers would put up venture capital for rehabilitation in such black areas as Hawthorne.[10] Randall's remark touched the core of the urban dilemma. Only a massive infusion of local, state, and federal money into housing and blight removal could make city neighborhoods ripe again for private investment; but private investors (in concert with the FHA) shunned those areas as untouchable. Henry Beeritz, the new president of the PHA, in October 1956 reminded Dilworth that the 1955 Statement had called for sinking tremendous money and human resources into neighborhood conservation, and that without such a commitment, blight would continue.[11]

Clearly, neither Dilworth nor Rafsky possessed the determination or political strength to divert a staggering amount of public and private investment from downtown renewal projects and new white developments on the edge of the city into the eroding black central city. Later, in 1961, Wallace noted that Rafsky had championed neighborhood conservation in vain. Indeed, Rafsky once dreamed of annually multiplying the number of conservable areas; by 1960, however, money for conservation and code enforcement had dwindled to a token sum. Just one CURA plan "rang the bell"; it was the downtown.[12]

CURA floundered because the progrowth consensus that guided renewal regarded the downtown as the critical, if not the only, element of the comprehensive plan. Also, Philadelphia, like other cities, failed to resolve the dilemma of rehousing the thousands of poor blacks uprooted by redevelopment activities.

Rehousing the Displaced

Planners and politicians saw displacement as the regrettable human cost of any large-scale urban renewal. Not only downtown projects, but also increased code-enforcement activities and "spot" slum clearance in the conservable areas displaced families. Between May 1955 and April 1957, the enforcement of the housing code, the Temple and North Allen redevelopment projects, and slum clearance for the Fitzwater project forced the relocation of families from more than 2,000 dwellings. Of the families known by the city's Relocation Bureau to have been displaced by this renewal activity, 25 percent lived as single persons; the remaining families contained two or more persons. The Relocation Bureau reported that 21 percent of the displaced families found "satisfactory" housing; thus, 26.2 percent were relocated in "unsatisfactory" housing, that is, in buildings in violation of the city's housing code. An astounding 52.8 percent of the uprooted families either refused to cooperate with the bureau or "disappeared."[13]

As black leaders angrily charged, urban renewal amounted to black removal. In Philadelphia, as elsewhere in urban America, the royal highway of urban renewal invariably ran through the black ghetto. In 1956 George Nesbitt of the HHFA Race Relations Office confronted his boss, James W. Follin, with data portraying the effect of urban renewal on 39,729 families living in 54 project areas in 31 American cities. According to Nesbitt's information, black families constituted more than two-thirds of the total population living in the affected zones; and in some places, such as Chicago's huge Lake Meadows renewal area, blacks represented 100 percent of the displaced population. In 1956 half of the families living in Philadelphia's 17 areas certified for redevelopment were black, and within the city's 5 key areas—Temple, Poplar, Mill Creek, Powelton, and Southwest Central—black families made up between 59 percent and 84 percent of the population.[14]

Unquestionably, federal and city officials foresaw the disastrous social consequences of undertaking urban redevelopment without first solving the dilemma of rehousing displaced families. Indeed, the housing and redevelopment legislation of 1949 commanded local housing authorities to submit relocation plans to Washington before undertaking slum-clearance operations, and in 1954 Congress made relocation planning part of the Workable Program for urban renewal, established the Below Market Interest Rate (BMIR) program to increase the supply of low-rent housing for displaced families, and yoked new public housing construction to the size of the relocation task. In Philadelphia's East Poplar area, the RA's Relocation Bureau circulated a mimeographed letter to the owners and occupants of all housing condemned for renewal purposes, advising them that the authority now owned their structure and promising "to assist the family in locating a decent, safe and sanitary dwelling generally as close as possible to your employment as your present dwelling."[15] Yet none of these precautions effectively addressed the housing needs of the thousands of black families trapped in the path of urban renewal. One year after the passage of the Workable Program provisions, critics assailed the renewal program as blatant, unabashed "Negro removal." Dislocating blacks, stated one report, only moves the ghetto elsewhere.[16]

Notwithstanding the creation of a Relocation Office, under the housing coordinator's jurisdiction, during the heyday of urban renewal in the 1950s and 1960s, housing and redevelopment authorities in Philadelphia and other cities bungled the relocation job. Calling it a "startling revelation," Rafsky disclosed in 1956 that 55 percent of the displaced families who moved into "unsatisfactory dwellings in our past experience with relocation were . . . non-white. . . . Housing for minority groups is extremely difficult to find in Philadelphia and even more so in the surrounding area." Conditions worsened by 1960. A study printed that year reported that out of one group of 7,000 families relocated between 1955 and 1960, 80 percent of whom were black, only 1 out of 10 families found satisfactory dwellings. In New York, officials disclosed that 40 percent of the families displaced by urban renewal between 1954 and 1963 moved into another slum area.[17]

Constrained by low incomes and a racially discriminatory housing market, displaced black families searched for housing either on the expanding fringes (the so-called transitional areas vacated by fleeing whites) or in the decaying heart of the black ghetto. Therefore, contrary to its stated objective, urban renewal frequently fostered greater ghettoization and neighborhood disintegration. Several factors explained the pernicious effect of renewal on the black community. A 1955 statement by the Fellowship Commission's Committee for Democracy in Housing condemned the "wall of social prejudice" that prevented blacks from taking part in the postwar migration to suburbia. Black home seekers with incomes under $4,000 faced a dearth of standard housing at affordable rent anywhere in the city. Moreover, little housing existed for single persons, large families, or households headed by senior citizens.[18]

In addition, HHFA researchers discovered that 26 percent of displaced black families in Detroit, Kansas City, Philadelphia, Cincinnati, Cleveland, Baltimore, and Birmingham moved without assistance and presumably relocated into substandard housing. Although between 60 percent and 90 percent of families displaced by urban renewal were "apparently" eligible for public housing, eligibility requirements and tenant-selection criteria barred single persons, as well as very large and very-low-income families, from public housing. Federal studies showed that fewer than 25 percent of families displaced by redevelopment activities were rehoused in government housing projects. For example, while 888 of the 1,480 families that came to the attention of the Philadelphia Relocation Bureau in 1955 "appeared eligible" for public housing, the Housing Authority rejected 638 of the applicants because they were single persons or "unrelated individuals."[19]

Many observers blamed the private sector for obstructing the relocation process. In the 10 key cities scrutinized for a 1955 federal relocation survey, black, low-income families lacked full access to the existing rental housing market and rarely acquired entry to the new private housing within their reach. Landlords rebuffed not only large families but families with histories of irregular rent payments, female-headed families, and families with histories of criminality. Although the survey found that black displacees exhibited a stronger preference for homeownership than white, home purchasers constituted only 9.2 percent among blacks rehoused, compared to 17 percent among white families. The Philadelphia Fellowship Commission (FC) reported blacks as "virtually confined to used housing in certain limited areas of the city." Furthermore, almost all the new housing underwritten by FHA and Veterans Administration mortgages served the white, not the black, housing market.[20]

Federal programs to help displaced families to purchase housing, such as the Voluntary Home Mortgage Credit Program (VHMCP), worked poorly in Philadelphia and other cities. First, like the FHA, all VHMCPs operated through the city's private banks, which, according to the Urban League, had long discriminated against black home seekers. Mortgage lenders not only often forced blacks to make higher down payments but also demanded shorter terms and higher interest rates, which produced higher monthly payments. Consequently, black home seekers with the effrontery to inquire about the VHMCP among local lending institutions approached timorously. Few came at all. During its first year of operation in Philadelphia, VHMCP received just 17 applications and made but 3 loans. Significantly, Rafsky's contact with mortgage lenders and homebuilders disclosed not even an inclination to try low-rent housing construction. Throughout the Philadelphia metropolitan area between 1946 and 1956, amid one of the greatest homebuilding booms in urban American history, fewer than 1 percent of the houses constructed served the already narrowly circumscribed and strained black housing market.[21]

Clearly, poor blacks displaced by urban renewal, as well as more affluent blacks hoping to follow the white exodus to the greener pastures outside the central city, discovered mean fare. For black homeseekers, the question "Where to live?" was answered as much by the whims of the city's real estate and homebuilding establishment as it was by the employment and income constraints of the black household. In 1968 the federal Kerner Commission investigating urban riots bared the awful fact that Philadelphia's Richardson Dilworth had forecast a full decade earlier: A white suburban noose surrounded the black city, suffocating black aspirations for better jobs, education, and housing and strangling any effort to create an integrated urban society. A brief look at the quantity and location of the housing constructed for blacks in the Philadelphia metropolitan area illuminates the seriousness of the problem.[22]

During the suburban housing boom years, 1946–1955, homebuilders in Philadelphia's suburbs (including Camden, Gloucester, and Burlington counties in New Jersey and Bucks, Montgomery, Chester, and Delaware counties in Pennsylvania) made available to blacks a mere 919 units of new housing. Moreover, the location of this black suburban housing belied any dreamlike quality. The bulk of the units of "suburban" housing rose either in satellite cities such as Norristown,

Chester, or Bristol, Pennsylvania, or in Camden County, New Jersey. In addition, suburban housing for blacks fit an urban mold, being largely attached, multifamily, or row housing. For example, the 207-unit Lincoln Park in Delaware County, the 84-unit Flower Manor in Chester, Pennsylvania, the 80-unit Woodbury Park in New Jersey, and the 209-unit Bloomsdale Gardens in Bristol, Pennsylvania, all featured apartment building or row housing design. It is noteworthy, too, that builders constructed almost all this black suburban housing for sale; less than 17 percent served the rental market. As for detached housing—the popular clapboard or red brick colonial adorned with a picket fence—only Morris Milgrim's interracial community of Concord Park in Trevose, Bucks County, and two other developments, in Hammond Heights and Woodbury, New Jersey, offered blacks the ambience of the American Dream.[23]

In providing new housing for blacks, intracity builders performed little better than their suburban brothers. Of the approximately 150,000 units of private housing built in Philadelphia between 1946 and 1955, 1,022, or less than 1 percent, expanded the black housing market. Furthermore, only 28 houses (all but 2 built in Germantown) were detached dwellings. The majority of black housing developments, such as Flamingo Gardens and Girard Court in North Philadelphia and Carver Gardens in West Philadelphia, were apartment residences. City builders constructed the few houses for purchase by blacks in the Germantown and Mount Airy sections, although the sizable Larchwood Gardens, as well as the Eastwick mixed-rent-and-purchase developments, offered housing for blacks near the airport on the marshlands of Southwest Philadelphia.[24]

Whether in city or suburb, the largest proportion of new private housing built for blacks fell short of the contemporary American norms for good housing. Only the housing built in Germantown and Mount Airy, and in Woodbury, New Jersey, met the American postwar standards for housing type, housing space, and neighborhood quality. More often, as with East Poplar's philanthropically inspired Friends Self-Help Cooperative, the housing, in the words of an HHFA market study, nestled in the "heart of the worst slum district." "Once the address [of the cooperative] was announced," explained the HHFA staff researcher, it was "a struggle to persuade potential cooperators to come near the project." Housing experts also scorned Eastwick's inferior location. While "the actual site was not unattractive," the HHFA observed, the interracial development was criticized for its "generally poor reputation—swampy and near a junkyard."[25]

Studies indicated that black families desired neither the romantic white suburb nor such central-city locations as Girard Court, Yorktown, or Flamingo Gardens. The findings of a 1956 environmental survey showed that most black families preferred such neighborhoods as West Philadelphia, Germantown, Mount Airy, and West Oak Lane. One reason was that few blacks chose to risk "pioneering" in suburbia—away from friends, churches, lodges, and familiar stores and job opportunities. Then, too, not many blacks could afford the new suburban housing, not even the rental and purchase housing built especially for black occupancy. Between 1946 and 1959, suburban and city builders priced new, detached, single-family housing for blacks in the $11,500–$12,500 range. In those same years, attached or row housing built for blacks sold for between $9,000 and $10,000. A six-room, detached, single-family house for blacks in Germantown, for example, sold for $13,000 in 1955; row houses there were priced in the $9,100–$12,000 range. Morris Milgrim sold his six-room Concord Park dream homes in Trevose, Pennsylvania, for $12,000 ("no down payment," 30-year mortgage, $75 a month) in 1955.[26]

Typically, blacks achieved homeownership in the city, not the suburbs. Between 1940 and 1950, black homeownership in Philadelphia increased 340 percent. Almost 30,000 blacks owned houses in the "Negro sections" of West Philadelphia, Germantown, Overbrook, and North Philadelphia in 1950. By 1956, the number of owner-occupied black dwellings had risen to 55,411, or 43.8 percent of the total of 126,373 black-occupied dwellings and an 88 percent increase in black homeownership from 1950. At the same time in 1956, 56 percent of Philadelphia's white housing was owner occupied.[27]

These statistics disguise the full extent of the hardship blacks faced in the housing market. In 1950 only 2 percent of black workers earned over $4,000 a year, an income that barely allowed the purchase of an $8,000–$10,000 home. By 1960, 12 percent of Philadelphia blacks earned over $4,000; however, when "family incomes" are considered, close to 38 percent of blacks qualified to purchase housing costing around $9,000.[28]

Clearly, the price tag for homeownership excluded most black home seekers in the Philadelphia area. For one example, throughout the 1960s, the managers of all the largely black-occupied central-city housing projects, such as the Richard Allen Homes, kept a list of FHA and VA reprocessed homes that were available for purchase by successful tenants whose "high" incomes made them "ineligible for continued occupancy" in public housing. Like the other Poplar Area residents, these "over-maximum" tenants craved not only homeownership but housing in a safe, crime-free environment with, to quote one tenant, "just as few bars as possible and with schools that are good." A fortunate very few of these public housing graduates moved into the pleasant row housing found in such black "succession" neighborhoods as North Philadelphia's West Oak Lane. Some bought houses in the spanking new Yorktown development, a federally subsidized row house development in the Temple University redevelopment area and literally in the shadow of the Richard Allen Homes. In many cases, the promise of homeownership flowered and soon wilted somewhere amid the medley of deteriorating row housing fronting the bar-ridden, rodent-infested streets of the North Philadelphia ghetto.[29]

Selecting the Sites

Faithful to the Housing Act of 1954, the architects of CURA assigned to public housing the burden of rehousing the typically poor, black victims of the renewal process. And in Philadelphia, as in other cities across America, this wedding of public housing and renewal greatly accelerated the pace of project construction. It also catapulted the issue of site selection into the limelight.

Since the 1930s, site locations for public housing had proven to be one of the most controversial issues facing city housers and planners. Site selection pitted reform-minded social engineers against white homeowners fiercely opposed to sharing their neighborhoods with black tenants. The revival of public housing construction in the wake of the Housing Act of 1949 had plunged Chicago into two years of warfare between the Chicago Housing Authority and city aldermen championing the interests of white working-class homeowners.[30]

Philadelphia's initial "shelter oriented" redevelopment produced public housing site locations generally stamped noncontroversial; after 1954, however, a new philosophy on sites evolved. Under the Housing Act of 1954 Washington allocated to the city 2,500 units of public housing for the years 1955 and 1956. Facing a June 1, 1956, deadline for securing federal approval of project sites and plans, Rafsky and the Housing Authority in 1955 worked frantically to develop site-selection criteria and identify locations for 21 housing projects.

Philadelphia's postwar system of site selection originated in 1950. That year, at the request of the Housing Authority, the PHA and the CCCP pooled their expertise and created the Joint Committee on Site Selection (JCSS). According to the procedure operating between 1950 and 1955, the authority selected the project sites; these sites were next reviewed by the JCSS and then finally approved by the City Planning Commission. The commission submitted the list of acceptable sites to the City Council only if the sites required a change in zoning, the vacating of city streets, or the demolition of such city-owned property as firehouses or police stations. If the sites survived that gauntlet, they were forwarded to the regional U.S. Housing Authority offices in New York for a final critique and then on to Washington, D.C.[31]

The JCSS represented the first and, for the purposes of racial integration policy, most important hurdle in the site-selection process. The size of the committee and the composition of its membership varied from year to year. Ordinarily, the JCSS included 15 persons— architect-planners such as Oscar Stonorov, Ray Lawson, John Grisdale, and Henry S. Churchill and prominent downtown lawyer-businessmen such as John Bodine and William Ludlow. Dorothy Montgomery and Elfriede Hoeber represented the PHA; Robert Mitchell spoke for city planning. Frank O. Walther of Philadelphia's prominent Girard Trust Corn Exchange Bank chaired the body.[32]

Although the JCSS's site policy in 1954 reflected an enduring environmentalist passion for social engineering, it denoted an ostensible disenchantment with the historic neighborhood-unit model of public housing. Housers still believed in the way-station mission of public housing, but JCSS pronouncements indicated that they no longer saw housing projects as central to neighborhood revitalization. Public housing, affirmed the JCSS, should be small and, in contrast to the superblock designs of the 1930s, an integral part of the existing neighborhood, "not an isolated [entity] separated by industry, highways or other barriers." Rather than the sterile, antifamily elevator apartments scorned by critics, the committee urged the building of low-rise housing on less expensive vacant sites on the urban periphery "so that children can play in their own yards, dig in the dirt, and still be directly supervised by a busy mother working in the kitchen."[33]

In the fall of 1954, with the new housing act in place and talk of urban renewal in the air, the JCSS faced a grueling agenda. Redevelopment officials spoke anxiously about the imminent displacement of hundreds of families from the giant North Allen slum-clearance project and the demolition of 1,279 units of World War II "temporary" housing at the Shipyard Homes, Northeast Village, and Pulaski Homes sites. Pressured to have new public housing sites approved before the expiration of the 1955 fiscal year, the JCSS reviewed four sites: Oxford Village II, Hoffman (at present Haddington), Whitehall in Frankford, and Fitzwater, an old slum in the Thirteenth and Fitzwater neighborhood, situated in the heart of "Negro Philadelphia."[34]

Oxford II, Hoffman, and Whitehall were approved easily; but the JCSS balked at Fitzwater and used its dissent to reassert its commitment to small, low-density, "family-oriented," racially integrated housing. At Fitzwater, the Housing Authority proposed to build an 18-story project that flaunted the already high neighborhood-density rate of 386 persons per acre. Most of the committee members, among them the scrappy Elfriede Hoeber, condemned the poor quality of the Fitzwater neighborhood, calling it "so hopelessly degrading that any new housing there, however desirable, appears a most foolish undertaking. No decent family [Hoeber had a poor Negro woman with some children in mind] will want to live there if it can possibly help it."[35]

Committee members G. Holmes Perkins, Montgomery, and Walther pictured the high-rise Fitzwater project as robbing sunlight from the neighborhood's already penumbral landscape. Moreover, high-rise housing, they contended, excited intergroup tensions, especially since elevator architecture made it impossible for mothers to monitor their children's play. Fitzwater, argued the committee, did not offer reasonable project design or complement the city's anticipated comprehensive plan. Rather than merely "pick" locations such as Fitzwater, sites should be chosen that blended public housing into the residential fabric of the neighborhood.

Members of the JCSS, the FC, and others concerned about housing and intergroup relations questioned the prospects of Fitzwater and the other slum sites for accomplishing the Housing Authority's goal of racial integration. The FC's Committee for Democracy in Housing called for an "extensive change in the character of public housing," mainly "smaller developments of a dispersed and non-institutional nature." And in October 1955 the PHA/CCCP Joint Policy Committee proclaimed that public housing sites and developments "should be designed to minimize concentrations of Negroes and to maximize their distribution in good neighborhoods consistent with the . . . objectives of sound planning."[36]

William Rafsky sympathized with the JCSS's position on the Fitzwater site; however, as Philadelphia's redevelopment czar, he considered the dogged opposition to central-city slum sites to be obstructionist. Late in 1954, in a move to usurp the JCSS's power and centralize control of the site-selection process, Rafsky created a body within the mayor's office called the Inter-Agency Committee on Site Selection (ICSS), which included members of the Housing Authority, the City Planning Commission, the Redevelopment Authority (RA), the Commission on Human Relations (CHR), and development coordinator David Wallace. Understandably, Rafsky's committee promulgated site standards that complemented CURA's goal of stabilizing neighborhoods in the "conservable" zones and deconcentrating population from the decaying slum districts. Therefore, the committee

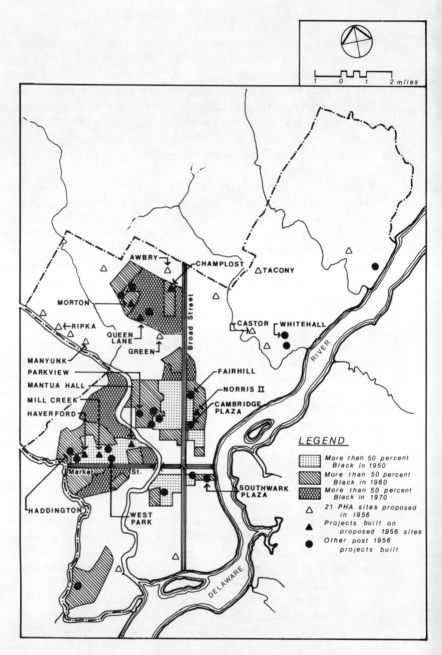

MAP 9: Post-1956 Philadelphia Housing Authority Projects and Racial
Change, 1950–1970

Source: Adkins and Associates, Architects.

preferred public housing locations in the city's white peripheral neighborhoods.

George Schermer, common-sense practitioner of intergroup relations, protested any consideration of public housing sites in already congested all-black areas; but he disputed Rafsky's strategy of deploying public housing as a battering ram against segregation. Reflecting the liberal environmentalist's waning faith in the efficacy of traditional public housing, Schermer advocated a more cautious policy of locating housing projects in "areas where a pattern of racial integration already exists and [which are] sufficiently stable to assure that the introduction of public housing would not result in a rapid transition to all-Negro occupancy.... True integration," urged Schermer, "can only be achieved where color consciousness is obliterated or minimized." He extolled "good livability standards for all" and warned that these standards "should not be compromised because of racial prejudice on the one hand or to promote racial integration on the other."[37]

Few heeded Schermer's admonitions. Rafsky's "Philadelphia's Procedures for Selecting Public Housing Sites," drafted by the Inter-Agency Committee and announced in fall of 1955, embodied fairly well the consensus among housers and planners concerning the role of public housing and racial integration in the urban renewal process. Although housers protested making the sites' contribution to "urban renewal activity the first priority," they applauded the committee's declared goal of "maximiz[ing the] contribution of public housing to low-income families and to the city as a whole." The "Procedures" also favored low-density sites, sites accessible to community facilities, and sites that would enable public housing tenants to become part of the neighborhood.[38] Reservations about urban renewal bias aside, the JCSS concurred wholeheartedly with the "Procedures." On April 4, 1956, the Housing Authority publicly announced its plans to build 2,850 low-rent housing units on 21 "scattered sites" located mainly in the city's white "fringe" neighborhoods—such communities as Olney, West Oak Lane, Manayunk, Roxborough, Rhawnhurst, Fern Rock, and Germantown (see Map 9).

By early 1956, Philadelphia's progrowth coalition had evolved a master plan for renewal that seemingly addressed the twin imperatives of rehousing families displaced by slum clearance and dispersing the black ghetto. Although all the actors in this urban drama agreed that public housing was a crucial part of the plan, the housing no longer wore communitarian colors. Public housing now functioned as a powerful tool for engineering the goal of a better city.

8

From Way Stations to Welfare Centers

Utilizing public housing to achieve urban renewal goals pitted middle-class planners against a white working class that cherished its insularity and feared the power of government to engineer racial change, destroy local property values, and alter an established way of life.[1] Philadelphia's social architects badly miscalculated the intensity of the opposition that would greet the city's housing-site proposals. The debacle that followed erased the last glimmer of missionary zeal from the city's public housing movement. Worn and disillusioned by the experience, planners sought refuge in open housing laws as the antidote to segregation and ghettoization.[2]

Violence in the Neighborhoods

In the spring of 1956 William Rafsky released the names of the 21 sites chosen for new public housing projects. Many of them were located in "conservable" neighborhoods (e.g., Nicetown, Frankford, and Manayunk), but half the sites were in the all-white outlying areas of Olney, Oak Lane, and the Greater Northeast.[3] Rafsky was obviously attempting to accomplish human relations goals as well as renewal goals in his public housing program.

Mayor Dilworth made those goals clear in a May 1956 radio broadcast during which he denounced Philadelphia's "slum situation" 23 times and explained how closely public housing was linked to slum clearance. At the same time, Philadelphia civic organizations, including the PHA, CCCP, Health and Welfare Council, NAACP, and Philadelphia Council of Churches, met at the downtown YMCA to "endorse . . . small, scattered public housing, . . . oppose the use of industrial land, and urge City Council to support these concepts and resist all efforts to ghettoize economically depressed citizens in the least desirable areas."[4]

The impulse toward racial integration and open housing in Philadelphia welled from the offices and boardrooms of established organizations headquartered in the city's downtown, but the forces of particularism, battling to preserve local pride, local values, and local investment, mobilized resistance in the white, working-class neighborhoods. In the postwar era, many of these neighborhoods faced withering assaults from languishing textile and metal manufacturing industries, declining population, inferior services, the steady expansion of the city's black population—and now public housing.

Certain key factors have governed the nature and the intensity of a neighborhood's response to the challenge of public housing and the threatened arrival of black neighbors. First, as Mark Gelfand and Kenneth Jackson have explained, the investment or disinvestment potential of federal policies, particularly HOLC, FHA, VA, and urban renewal, influenced neighborhood real property values. Of greater importance, perhaps, recent research has clearly linked the stability of the neighborhood employment base to the quality and stability of its housing stock. Therefore, residents of such industrially stable neighborhoods as Kensington and Richmond persistently resisted the advance of black home seekers, while their German and Irish cousins in Philadelphia's nineteenth-century "streetcar suburbs" failed to do so. Also, new neighborhoods, such as those in the Northeast, sustained by wartime and postwar industrialism, fought even more strenuously against public housing, perceiving it as the beginning of a black "invasion."[5]

Nationwide, the phenomenal growth of the black city pitted the job opportunities and housing aspirations of blacks against those of the white working class. Where blacks had historically clustered in one large area, or "belt," such as in Chicago, Cleveland, and Detroit, the first black-white confrontations occurred before World War II. In cities with a more dispersed pattern of black settlement, mainly southern cities such as Atlanta, Charleston, and Washington, D.C., and northern cities such as Philadelphia, the confrontations occurred later. In fact, before the war, Philadelphia's black city, like Washington, D.C.'s black alleyworld, remained relatively secret. Only an occasional violent crime or a tenement collapse reminded white Philadelphians of the black presence in their midst.[6]

During World War II, black visibility in Philadelphia increased dramatically. Black transit workers demanded job upgrading, and the housing needs of blacks and whites clashed, if only momentarily, at the Richard Allen Homes. By the early 1950s, racial incidents occurred frequently in the city although Philadelphia escaped any large-scale outbreak of racial violence.[7] Nevertheless, 213 racial incidents during the first six months of 1955 alone reinforced an antiblack climate that cemented the boundaries of the city's North Philadelphia ghetto.

Much of the interracial conflict in the 1950s involved teenagers.

Gangs of young blacks and whites, armed with "zip guns," transformed the frontiers of white and black neighborhoods into war zones where battles raged over the control of precious urban "turf." Elsewhere, blacks charged the police, trolley operators, and the press with discrimination. Newspapers, for example, identified criminals as "Negro" and permitted racial identifiers in employment ads. Not surprisingly, then, any black home seeker who attempted to demolish the barriers separating black and white neighborhoods invited a hostile reception. When in August 1954 a black family bought a rundown storefront residence near Twenty-second Street and Lehigh Avenue, a white crowd "welcomed" them by breaking windows and shouting threats and obscenities.[8]

Antiblack demonstrations in Philadelphia's transitional neighborhoods were neither well organized nor on a grand scale. Yet, while less violent than antiblack demonstrations elsewhere, Philadelphia's numerous incidents of racial conflict warned blacks to beware of trespassing in white neighborhoods. Such neighborhoods as Manayunk, Overbrook, Roxborough, Kensington, Olney, and Frankford, buttressed by the presence of viable industry and good housing stock, staunchly opposed black entry.[9] Some white neighborhoods, especially those in the "New Northeast" section of the city, flourished. The New Northeast became an industrial hub in the 1950s, attracting firms such as Budd, National Biscuit, Crown Cork and Seal, U.S. Rubber, Electric Storage Battery, B. F. Goodrich, and Yale and Towne. At the same time, Rohm and Haas, the Barrett Division of Allied Chemical, Disston Saw, and a host of smaller companies provided steady employment for white homeowners in Kensington and Richmond. Plainly, ample support exists for linking white residential tenaciousness with high rates of homeownership and the presence of a stable neighborhood employment base. Again and again, economically stable white working class neighborhoods fitted the name awarded them by the journalist Peter Binzen, "Whitetown U.S.A."[10]

These white neighborhoods fiercely resisted their selection by Rafsky to be public housing sites. A few experts had anticipated this resistance. George Schermer had warned Mayor Dilworth that once the affected neighborhoods learned of their designation, the outcry would be at best deafening, at worst violent. Schermer favored the passage of state fair-housing laws to achieve residential integration. Once the Housing Authority had determined its course, however, consistent with human relations theory, Schermer implored the agency to flood the white target neighborhoods with educational information about the role and need for integrated public housing.

Shunning Schermer's advice, Allesandroni and the Inter-Agency Committee strategists cloaked the site-selection process in secrecy. Dennis Clark suspected that by waiting until the last moment to spring the news of the 21 sites, Rafsky aimed to mute neighborhood opposition. The tactic failed. At stormy meetings and "information sessions" held at the Housing Authority's Benjamin Franklin Parkway headquarters and in neighborhood schools and recreation centers, furious residents from Olney, Germantown, Manayunk, Roxborough, and other affected sections shouted down authority spokespersons, including Dilworth, who attempted to counter popular arguments that public housing depressed property values and attracted blacks, slum people, criminals, and other "riffraff." At one such gathering, an enraged woman lunged forward and shoved her fist in the mayor's face.[11] At other meetings, representatives of such established local civic organizations as the Greater Olney Community Council, the Rhawnhurst Civic League, and the 21st Ward Council assailed what they described as the arrogance of downtown-based social engineers.

Many neighborhood people regarded the city's public housing plan as a crude, class-based assault on their property and their way of life. From the neighborhood viewpoint, the plan implied nothing less than a bold attempt by slick downtown lawyers and business elites to mold society to suit middle-class requirements without considering the economic and cultural preferences of the people being squeezed into the mold. Philadelphia's Republican controller, Foster A. Dunlap, expressed the neighborhood's grievance beautifully when he blasted the scattered-site proposal as "another case of trying to change people to fit certain theories. Of course, beneath the surface of the plan is the ever-present attempt of the social planners to change our society. The purpose of public housing can best be accomplished when coupled with removal of slums. Open land is not proper for such [housing] projects."[12]

Given the postwar sanctification of domestic values, the anguish of threatened neighborhood homeowners that unfolded in the daily press stirred considerable sympathy citywide. Essentially, the beleaguered neighborhoods appealed to modern America's preference for socially homogeneous communities and the social canon decreeing the sanctity of homeownership and the inviolability of real property. Unlike earlier antiblack protests, these 1956 neighborhood protests neither openly flaunted the race issue nor entertained blatant hate-mongering. Here, the ogre of race lurked just beneath the crescendo of vitriol. Such phrases as "people like us," "undesirables," or the "less ambitious" carried a hardly disguised message.[13]

According to the most frequently heard argument, housing projects despoiled well-maintained, stable neighborhoods. An angry Olney resident launched his diatribe against the Tacony Creek project site by stating that he was "not opposed to blacks." He begged only to raise his two small children in a "decent neighborhood like ours. . . . Most families," he explained, "are young like ourselves, earning $5,000–$6,000 a year. Now the Housing Authority proposes to change the whole character of the neighborhood" by introducing people who are not willing "to make sacrifices like the rest of us."[14] Complained a Germantown site resident, "People have worked all their lives to buy a home and have kept the neighborhood respectable." According to an angry clergyman from the West Philadelphia Greenway site, public housing would "flood the neighborhood with people not used to living in this area . . . creating tension and strcss, and driving down the value of our property, church as well as housing."[15]

Constance Perrin, in her book *Everything in Its Place,* not only described the ideology of American land-use patterns but dissected the norm elevating homeownership over renting. That homeownership norm dominated the 1956 hearings. Time and again, neighborhood spokespersons contrasted the respectability, diligence, and moral superiority of homeowners "like us" with the alleged disreputableness, slothfulness, and property-endangering social traits of tenants living in public housing. "Our neighborhood," proclaimed a member of the Germantown Businessmen's Association, an organization fighting a losing battle against blight and the "invasion" of blacks, "needs wealth creating business and people. . . . Low-cost projects at the rental charged and with the class of tenancy involved . . . [would] not elevate buying power." After hours of haranguing by white doomsday forecasters, John Archer, the black president of the Poplar Area Community Council, remonstrated that "very simply, these people [do not] want their poor relatives living next door!"[16]

Thus it was the low-density, working-class neighborhoods that boasted relatively new housing, high rates of homeownership, and proximity to thriving industries that resisted the intrusion of public housing. The protesters admitted the need for public housing, but not in their white backyards. "Build public housing in the slums where it is needed," exhorted a local clergyman in behalf of 900 Greenway residents who gathered to oppose public housing. In the same vein, Councilman William Hamlin of the 21st Ward, an area already saturated with large housing projects, including the massive Schuylkill Falls, warned Philadelphians living in neighborhoods still untargeted by the Housing Authority to be vigilant, "for the next one might be in your backyard."[17]

A Retreat and Explanations

Philadelphia's site turmoil lacked the political volatility that had surrounded Chicago's public housing furor in 1951–1952 and had produced the nation's most segregative formula for siting public housing. Yet many Philadelphia politicians, among them such stalwart Democrats as William Green and John McDevitt, abandoned Dilworth and his housing brain trust on this politically lethal issue and sought refuge with the forces opposing public housing in the neighborhoods. Anxious to marshal all his available forces, Rafsky enlisted Dennis Clark to soften the opposition of local priests. On another front he dispatched Drayton Bryant to drum up support from "a few pro-public housing realtors." Maury Fagan was drafted to buttonhole "liberal Quaker types," while Schermer canvassed the city's black leadership. But instead of subsiding, public outrage and indignation intensified.[18]

After several City Council members "secretly toured" the 21 public housing sites, the council presented an abbreviated list of sites that included the Northeast Village, Oxford Village, and League Island World War II housing, the Pennsylvania Hospital site in the crowded Forty-fourth and Market area, an industrial tract at Front and Oregon avenues, and the Morton and Germany Hill sites. With the exception of Morton, none of these locations satisfied Dorothy Montgomery. Nor did they complement the long-range objectives of Rafsky's CURA plan.[19]

Philadelphia had negotiated an extension of the federal June 1 deadline. By summer, however, Rafsky, Bacon, and the Inter-Agency Committee were cowed by the intensity of the opposition. Although continuing to view public housing as a vital tool for renewal, Rafsky and the Housing Authority busily scrambled to salvage the city's 2,500 units of public housing and in the process minimized their once paramount concern for low-rent housing sites and design.[20]

In retreat, Rafsky and the Housing Authority first reconsidered the suitability of old, "temporary" wartime project sites, some of which had been rezoned "industrial." It next gave half-serious attention to such isolated and obscure housing sites as the city's prison farm and to Camp Happy, Philadelphia's bucolic retreat for poor children. Finally, in July, it reluctantly approved the Mantua and Oregon Avenue sites, two locations that it had earlier rejected following adverse staff reviews.[21]

Rafsky capitulated bitterly, uttering that "the opposition was so deep-seated in its fundamental attitude that it would take a great deal of doing before we convince the leadership."[22] The development co-

165

ordinator seemingly took the defeat as a personal setback to his efforts to orchestrate a truly comprehensive urban renewal program. But the PHA and the Fellowship Commission (FC) found broader implications in the strident neighborhood resistance to public housing, pronouncing it a defeat for citywide human relations and for racial integration.

Hirsch has argued that rather than ascribe the racial hostility of Chicago's neighborhoods to understandable fears about status, declining property values, or interracial marriage, liberal environmentalists in the Windy City described white neighborhood behavior as "irrational." Similarly, Philadelphia housers and intergroup relations specialists took refuge in psychological interpretations of white racial hostility.[23]

Dissecting the neighborhood reaction to public housing, Dennis Clark uncovered "a certain degree of class prejudice, . . . anti-Negro sentiment which may be the dominant cause of the opposition . . . and ordinary outbursts of neighborhood hysteria based upon misinformation and emotionalism." Housers believed that ignorance underlay the "irrationalism"; accordingly, they blamed the Housing Authority for its failure to educate the public about the wisdom of scattered sites. Montgomery and Fagan, for example, accused the authority and the Inter-Agency Committee of failing to convey to the neighborhoods the message of open "democratic housing." The FC interpreted the controversy as the basic "issue of human beings versus property values," and Elfriede Hoeber of the PHA grieved that the episode only confirmed that the "City Administration is committed to a policy of accepting all public housing sites it can get [and] will [now] rather put housing in poor sites than lose units." The outcome, she lamented, "will result in concentrating rather than dispersing low income and minority families."[24]

Undaunted by the popular outcry against the sites, and Hoeber's pessimism, the PHA, Armstrong Association, Health and Welfare Council, Catholic Interracial Council, and other groups rededicated themselves to the ideal of nonsegregated, humanely situated, low-income housing. The FC in 1956 stressed that "better housing and the sites for them are a community-wide problem and all areas must share in its [sic] solution." Observed the CDH, "Rebuilding old areas at the present densities is merely rebuilding the slum conditions." A telegram to the City Council from eight city agencies hailed public housing as "a basic tool essential to the restoration of good living." Furthermore, stated the telegram, "improperly located public housing is not the answer, but is a denial of the goal of a better city."[25]

The Failure to Integrate

The housing-site debacle sparked a critical reevaluation of Philadelphia's plan to use public housing to engineer racial integration. While in some cases the events of 1956 strengthened the faith of housers and human relations people concerning the need for racial integration, most housers shed their belief in public housing as a means for achieving it. Troubled by the city's difficulties, and aware that 1957 marked the twentieth anniversary of America's public housing "experiment," the PHA and the CCCP remodeled the old JCSS into the Committee on Public Housing Policy, chaired by Jefferson Fordham. In its final report, the so-called Fordham Committee muted its advocacy of interracial housing. Communitywide integration appeared in the report only as an allusion to housing projects conforming socially and architecturally to their neighborhood. Mainly, the committee restated the goal of public housing to provide decent housing for low-income families and underlined public housing's mission to support urban renewal by facilitating slum clearance. Admittedly, the 1956 neighborhood opposition had persuaded Fordham, Walther, and other members of the committee that the imperatives of public relations forbade using public housing to achieve a "balance of income and racial groups" in Philadelphia neighborhoods.[26]

Even as the Fordham Committee intellectually dismantled public housing's role in neighborhood integration, by repudiating the effort artificially to maintain racial balances in public housing, it was extinguishing any fleeting hopes for intraproject integration. Only six years earlier, liberal housers and planners had enthusiastically endorsed the integration policy. Now, in 1957, with 90 percent of the applications for public housing coming from black families, housing and intergroup relations people rejected "steering" as "undemocratic," as violating the spirit of the city's Cooperative Agreement and maintaining white majorities in the Wilson Park, Schuylkill Falls, and Hill Creek projects while denying decent housing to blacks.[27]

In 1955 the PHA and the CHR had launched their assault on the authority's integration program by condemning its discriminatory policy of steering black families into certain projects in order to perpetuate the old "neighborhood formula." As head of the CHR, Schermer ordered an investigation of the Housing Authority's 1952 integration program. To undertake the study, Schermer retained a black sociologist, Robert Johnson, son of the famed black scholar Charles S. Johnson. Johnson submitted a lengthy report based mainly on extensive interviews with Housing Authority personnel. Johnson found

Public Housing and Urban Renewal

TABLE 2: Racial Change in Philadelphia Projects by Percentage Black
Occupancy, 1954 and 1957

Occupancy	1954	1957
Projects over 50% black	88	96
Projects under 50% black	3	6

Sources: Philadelphia Housing Authority, "Facts About Developments of the Philadelphia Housing Authority," January 1977, HADVP; Public Housing Administration Statistical Branch, "Reports on Occupancy," Box 32, Microfilm Reel 39, HUDR.

that, from its first screening of black "pioneer" families for residency in Abbottsford, the authority had engaged in an "invidious process of social segregation" whereby the "best" black families were channeled into such projects as James Weldon Johnson or Schuylkill Falls, while the least desirable or "problem" families gravitated into projects such as the Richard Allen Homes.

The Housing Authority discounted Johnson's findings on methodological grounds. Flaws in his research model aside, Johnson had correctly charged the authority with practicing discrimination to achieve what it considered "a healthy racial balance" in the projects. And, by 1957, the hard evidence portrayed a clear pattern of segregation in Philadelphia's housing projects[28] (see Table 2).

The Fordham Committee and Johnson's reports fueled the disillusionment of Philadelphia housers with social engineering as a solution to the city's mounting problem of racial segregation and ghetto formation. The effusiveness that marked the launching of the Housing Authority's integration program in 1951 had vanished, as had the belief that the Quaker City's history of dedication to human rights predestined interracial harmony. Once, in the early 1950s, the Housing Authority nurtured that interracial vision, and photographs of black and white children eating together and playing together covered the walls of its administration building. By the end of the decade, those pictures had been stored away.[29] After 1958, social reformers seemed less married to "irrationality" as an explanation for racism. In its place Dennis Clark and George Schermer discerned a grievous pattern of human behavior that favored racial segregation in housing. Clark decried segregation as an "invidious force," stalling the progress of urban renewal and threatening the city's business and social life. Almost a full decade before the Kerner Commission envisioned an apartheid urban society in America, Clark invoked the specter of Philadelphia society carved into "vicious islands of mutually suspicious residents: a city sundered into warring 'racial worlds.' "[30]

A look at the outcome of the 1956 public housing integration campaign discloses the consequences of the failure. Between 1956 and 1978, the Philadelphia Housing Authority opened 16 new housing projects. Only 7 of the projects had been among the original 21 sites, and only 2 of the 7, the Germantown and West Oak Lane sites, had attracted significant neighborhood opposition. With the exception of the 189-unit Whitehall project, built on an alternate site in the Frankford section in 1959, the Housing Authority shunned the white strongholds of the Northeast, Roxborough, and Olney, as well as the Italian American bastions of South Philadelphia. Chastened by the intensity of the neighborhood opposition, it also cautiously avoided sites in sections displaying a heavy concentration of homeownership, and in areas where vacant sites appeared suitable for industrial or private residential development.[31]

Throughout the late 1950s and 1960s, the Housing Authority encountered opposition to any form of public housing in white peripheral neighborhoods. Frankford citizens rallied in 1957 to oppose the Adams site, arguing that it would not only crowd the public schools but slow economic growth. In 1969, zoning obstacles dashed the authority's plans to locate a "turnkey project" (privately built housing for transfer to the Housing Authority) on the Woodhaven site. Likewise, when the authority in 1968 resurrected plans to build a 192-unit, low-rent housing project in the 21st Ward, Roxborough neighbors mobilized again, landing 550 telegrams on Secretary of Housing Robert Weaver's desk "opposing [a] Federally Financed Housing Project in the 21st Ward." And, year after year, violent neighborhood opposition blocked the Housing Authority's intention to build a low-income housing project on the South Philadelphia Whitman Park site.[32]

All of the projects planned and built from 1956 to 1967 were sited in ghetto or "transitional" neighborhoods. Even the vigorously contested Whitehall site abutted an old black neighborhood. Champlost Homes, a 102-unit project that featured two- and three-story brick row housing, sat in the path of black Philadelphia's northward advance along a wide corridor stretching from Broad Street to Ridge Avenue, and along Ogontz Avenue to West Oak Lane. Although one of the original 21 sites, Champlost was plainly a black project. Floyd Alston, the ex-manager of the Richard Allen Homes, took the post as chief officer of the Champlost Homes. Blacks regarded Champlost as "highly desirable," and consistent with its location in West Oak Lane, the project attracted the "high type" black families from the inner city.[33]

Blacks similarly made up almost 98 percent of the new tenants who moved into the 19-unit Queen Lane II and the 187-unit Morton housing projects cloistered within Germantown's mushrooming black community. Expediency, more than anything else forced the Housing Authority to spurn the appeals of the PHA and the FC and to keep building public housing on slum-cleared land in and on the flanks of the North and South Philadelphia black ghettos. Between 1956 and 1967, the Housing Authority built Parkview (for the elderly), Reynolds, Norris II, Fairhill, Southwark Plaza, and the gigantic towers of Hawthorne Square, all in South and North Philadelphia. With the exception of Southwark Plaza, which verged on posh Society Hill and had elderly as well as family units, only blacks lived in these projects.[34]

The West Philadelphia ghetto also absorbed its share of public housing. Locked in the heart of the well-established Powelton area, the post-1956 Mantua Hall, Mill Creek II, Haverford, Westpark, and Haddington projects housed an almost exclusively black clientele. In April 1964 a spokesman for the Housing Authority confessed before a meeting of the Council for Equal Housing Opportunity that "it has not been possible to obtain more than a very few white applicants" for the Westpark project. Only six whites lived in Westpark's 381 dwellings.[35]

Black community leaders in the 1960s denounced the Housing Authority's practice of cramming public housing in or near ghetto sites. Enumerating the high-rise scale and ghetto locations of the Reynolds, Westpark, and Hawthorne Square projects, black leaders accused the authority of warehousing as well as ghettoizing the black poor. When in 1968 the authority moved to convert a large private housing development at Tenth and Jefferson streets into public housing, the militant North City Congress protested to Washington, D.C., that it "opposed any additional project type public housing in North Philadelphia." Earlier, Washington had absolved itself of responsibility for site and architectural matters, brushing off complaints as local issues. But faced with increasing objections to federal ghettoization and poor project maintenance, in the late 1960s the federal government moved away from federally built public housing toward the purchase and use of rehabilitated existing housing for low-rent purposes.[36] By then, however, public housing projects had become an integral part of the ghetto housing stock. Data on the changing racial composition of public housing in Philadelphia projects highlight their significance as black shelter (see Table 3). Of the 32 projects studied, 20 of them, comprising 7,259 units, or 71 percent of all Philadelphia public housing, remained virtually segregated throughout the study period.

Despite the integration crusade of the 1950s, the 412-unit Liddonfield Homes and the 340-unit Hill Creek project, both located in the Northeast, continued to be essentially all-white housing in 1968. Of greater interest, perhaps, are the several housing projects that the Housing Authority had once spotlighted for integration: Abbottsford Homes, Passyunk, Bartram Village, Wilson Park, and Schuylkill Falls. Although the three defense housing projects—Abbottsford, Passyunk, and Bartram Village—practically excluded blacks before 1952, and by 1956 the five projects averaged under 9 percent black occupancy, the rate spiraled to almost 50 percent by 1968. Significantly, in that year 442, or 60 percent, of Wilson Park's 746 tenants were black, suggesting that, rather than integration, the changing racial composition of Philadelphia's public housing projects mirrored the greater demand for public housing among blacks in sections such as South Philadelphia and the shifting racial composition of many city neighborhoods.[37]

Shorn of their faith in public housing, and just as dubious about their ability to convert realtors, mortgage bankers, and the white neighborhoods to selfless proponents of racial integration, Schermer, Clark, Fagan, and Montgomery followed the example of the NAACP and took their case for integration to the state legislature and the courts. Proponents of open housing argued that racial segregation in housing existed because white realtors, bankers, and home sellers discriminated against black home seekers. Such state and local ordinances as Philadelphia's Cooperative Agreement had outlawed discrimination in public housing, but by 1959 only six states—Pennsylvania, Washington, Oregon, Massachusetts, New Jersey, and New York—prohibited discrimination in publicly assisted housing. Only New York City forbade discrimination by realtors, builders, and banks in the selling, leasing, or financing of housing.[38]

Despite city and state crusades for open housing, by 1961 the legislative battleground in the war against housing discrimination had become Washington, D.C. John F. Kennedy had campaigned hard among urban black voters in 1960 and had promised to fight for a federal law against housing discrimination. Nationally, the Committee Against Discrimination in Housing (NCADH), a Washington-based group founded in 1950, and in Philadelphia, Walter Wynn of the FC's Council for Equal Housing Opportunity, lobbied to have Kennedy sign an executive order that would, quoting Kennedy, ban discrimination in "all federally aided housing . . . by the stroke of the pen." Wynn's "Fact Sheet" on housing discrimination noted that "discrimi-

TABLE 3: Philadelphia Public Housing Projects, 1938–1974

Project	Units	Year of Occupancy	Percentage Black					
			1952	1956	1960	1964	1966	1968
Hill Creek	258[a]	1938	.7	1.9	1.0	0	1.3	1.5
Johnson Homes	589	1940	98.8	99.0	98.0	100.0	99.8	99.8
Richard Allen	1,324	1942	99.9	100.0	99.8	99.3	99.8	99.6
Tasker	1,077	1941	9.0	23.0	N.A.	38.0	52.0	62.5
Abbottsford	700	1942	.4	9.4	15.5	19.3	40.0	56.0
Bartram	500	1942	.8	9.9	17.0	23.0	34.0	40.0
Oxford	200	1942	0	.7	N.A.	N.A.	1.3	1.5
Passyunk	994	1942	0	4.6	N.A.	18.0	40.0	50.7
Arch	77	1952	51.9	74.0	88.0	98.0	99.0	100.0
Wilson Park	746	1954	—	9.6	12.5	21.0	43.0	60.0
Norris Apartments	326	1954	—	100.0	100.0	97.0	97.0	97.0
Raymond Rosen	1,122	1954	11.0	99.9	100.0	100.0	99.7	100.0
Schuylkill Falls	714	1955	—	11.5	15.4	28.0	56.0	78.0
Liddonfield	412	1955	—	1.9	1.6	1.0	1.0	1.0
Mill Creek	444	1955	—	100.0	100.0	100.0	100.0	100.0
Queen Lane	139	1955	—	92.5	96.4	98.3	97.2	97.2
Spring Garden	203	1955	—	83.3	85.0	97.0	97.0	97.0
Harrison Plaza	300	1956	—	98.6	99.0	97.0	97.0	97.0
Cambridge Plaza	372	1957	—	—	N.A.	N.A.	97.0	95.0
Haddington	150	1959	—	—	N.A.	N.A.	99.0	100.0
Haverford	22	1959	—	—	N.A.	N.A.	99.0	100.0
Whitehall	189	1959	—	—	N.A.	N.A.	20.0	45.0

Development	Units	Year						
Champlost	102	1960	—	—	95.0	96.0	97.2	97.2
Hawthorne Square (Martin Luther King Plaza)	576	1960	—	—	94.7	95.6	97.0	97.0
Mantua Hall	153	1960	—	—	—	N.A.	98.0	98.0
Parkview	22	1961	—	—	—	N.A.	98.4	98.7
Fairhill	298	1962	—	—	—	N.A.	98.0	97.0
Southwark Plaza	886[a]	1963	—	—	—	N.A.	48.5	56.4
Morton	185	1963	—	—	—	—	97.2	97.2
West Park	381	1964	—	—	—	—	98.0	97.4
Paschall	223	1966	—	—	—	—	—	64.6
Norman Blumberg	510	1967	—	—	—	—	—	N.A.
Holmecrest	84[b]	1967	—	—	—	—	—	N.A.
Whitehall II	69[b]	1968	—	—	—	—	—	N.A.
Morton II	65[b]	1969	—	—	—	—	—	N.A.
Liddonfield II	52[b]	1969	—	—	—	—	—	N.A.
Collegeview	54[b]	1969	—	—	—	—	—	N.A.
Emlen Arms	175[b]	1970	—	—	—	—	—	N.A.
Point Breeze Court	72[b]	1971	—	—	—	—	—	N.A.
Plymouth Hall	71[b]	1971	—	—	—	—	—	N.A.
400 North Fiftieth Street	68[b]	1971	—	—	—	—	—	N.A.
Bentley Hall	100[b]	1972	—	—	—	—	—	N.A.
Germantown House	220[b]	1973	—	—	—	—	—	N.A.

Sources: Philadelphia Housing Authority, "Facts About Developments of the Philadelphia Housing Authority," January 1977, HADVP; Public Housing Administration Statistical Branch, "Reports on Occupancy," Box 32, Microfilm Reel 39, HUDR.

[a]Later enlarged to 340 units.
[b]Housing for senior citizens.

nation continued to be the rule in most of the housing built with the assistance of the Federal Government." He pointed out that "80 percent of the federally sponsored public housing is racially segregated and mortgage lending institutions profit from Federal benefits . . . yet deny loans on the basis of race and religion."[39]

On November 10, 1962, Kennedy signed Executive Order 11063, directing all federal departments and agencies to take "necessary and appropriate action to prevent discrimination in housing provided in whole or in part with federal assistance." Furthermore, to help accomplish the goal of open housing, Kennedy established the Commission on Equal Opportunity in Housing, composed of the secretary of the treasury, secretary of defense, attorney general, secretary of agriculture, and secretary of the Housing and Home Finance Administration (HHFA). Whitney Young, the executive director of the Urban League, quickly pointed out to HHFA's secretary, Robert Weaver, that Kennedy's order applied only to new housing and excluded discrimination or segregation resulting from federal action consummated before November 20, 1962. Young and his comrades in arms, Algernon D. Black, chairman of the National Committee Against Discrimination in Housing, James Farmer of the Congress of Racial Equality (CORE), and Roy Wilkins of the NAACP, might have overlooked the law's weakness if the spirit of the executive order had been aggressively promoted. But a year after the law's enactment, Washington had still not created the Commission on Equal Opportunity in Housing, nor had the government disseminated any information to federal agencies concerning the weight of the law.[40]

Throughout the 1960s, the HHFA (which was to become the Department of Housing and Urban Development, or HUD) gathered data on the racial impact of federal programs, on minority occupancy in FHA-guaranteed housing, and on discrimination in public housing and other federally subsidized low-income housing. The reports, letters, and statistical analyses that poured in from throughout the country pictured the implacability of the opposition to integration. The Chicago Housing Authority perpetuated segregation in its housing programs, fully intending, as the Chicago Urban League informed Weaver in 1963, "to erect units for the elderly and fill those units by giving people from the surrounding neighborhoods first preference. If that doesn't perpetuate segregation, I am at a loss to see what will." Meanwhile, in Philadelphia by the end of the decade, black and white housing watchdog agencies voiced similar displeasure at the racially segregative impact of federal housing programs—not the least of the offenders being the Housing Authority itself.[41]

Public Housing Architecture

The architectural consequences of the 1956 debacle proved only slightly less disastrous than the segregative. Despite Montgomery's and Levine's pleas, Rafsky and the Housing Authority substituted expediency for quality. To the credit of the city and the Housing Authority, however, much of their handiwork managed to be fairly well received by critics. On the whole Jeanne Lowe detected in most of Philadelphia's public housing "an unusual sensitivity to the desires and special life style of the poor." As before, the Housing Authority retained prominent architectural firms: Stonorov and Haws, Kahn and Day, Louis McAllister, and David Morgan. Significantly, Lowe's plaudit included the disclaimer that "the quantity scarcely matched the quality." Indeed, despite Rafsky's rummaging for sites in 1956 and 1957, by 1959 the authority had staked out locations for only 14 projects, and 4 sites adjoined existing projects. More disappointing, altogether these 14 projects would provide only 3,441 units of low-income housing.[42]

The architectural critics who gave Philadelphia's projects high marks for design lauded in particular the city's expressed preference for low-rise buildings. Two- and three-story row units constituted a third of the new public housing stock. While the row house addition to Norris, Hill Creek, and Queen Lane lacked distinction, the Morton Homes in Germantown and the Mill Creek addition were noteworthy. At Morton the Housing Authority and its architects—Hatfield, Martin, and White—attempted to make public housing part of neighborhood conservation. Building in a conservation area, the RA used Title I funds to demolish and clear 7.4 acres of the worst housing. For these small parcels, the architects designed clusters of two-story, gable-roofed houses whose red- and white-bricked colonial facades blended nicely with the early-nineteenth-century architectural motif of old Germantown.[43]

The Mill Creek addition also bulwarked RA conservation work in West Philadelphia. Applying International Style design principles, Louis Kahn grouped his two- and three-story red-brick units around small, tenant-maintained garden plots, amid a greenway system of tree-lined pedestrian malls. Miraculously, Kahn successfully shepherded an architectural "frill" through the miserly Public Housing Administration. Washington permitted Kahn to fasten a precast-concrete sunshade above each doorway and window. Take that sunshade away, quipped the architectural critic Phillip Herrera, and instantly the buildings become "typical public housing boxes."[44]

Yet, kudos aside, the Housing Authority situated two-thirds of the city's public housing units in elevator buildings. Although the federal Public Housing Administration opposed slum locations for public housing, the stiffening resistance of white neighborhoods, the stringent government unit-cost formula, and the drying up of Title I slum-clearance funds drove the authority to embrace the tower solution. Blair Lee, the chief executive of the city's largest real estate operation, registered his frustration in a speech before the Philadelphia Real Estate Board during Realtors Week, 1957. Lee's address explained how high land costs compelled the Housing Authority to erect multistory elevator buildings. Somewhat apologetically, Lee remarked that, in the absence of an RA subsidy, the authority could only develop slum sites using high-rise architecture.[45]

Although the authority paraded findings of housing satisfaction among a small group of 65 tenants living in three high-rise projects (Wilson Park, Raymond Rosen, and Schuylkill Falls), few Housing Authority officials, including Executive Director Walter Allesandroni, gladly accepted the elevator policy. In fact, reports of vandalism at Harrison, Norris, and Rosen, plus maintenance problems and hazardous playing conditions at Schuylkill Falls, belied the credibility of the high-rise survey. Therefore it was an anxious executive director who, in November 1958, phoned the PHA seeking allies for his stand against any more high-rise, high-density housing projects. Confided Allesandroni, "Rafsky is under pressure from [City] Council to put some public housing in clearance areas. He's got to put some in slums." But the prospect of a high-rise future for Philadelphia public housing deeply troubled Allesandroni. "Problems in high-rise structures are mounting," he revealed to the PHA. "There is vandalism from outsiders who get into the projects, which have no proper supervision, and nobody is willing to give [the] authority money to do the policing job. Women are raped and their husbands do not testify in court because they fear retribution." Allesandroni related an elevator-door incident at Norris Homes where outsiders, who found the elevator too slow in coming, yanked the door loose and dropped it down the shaft. "Nobody called the police because they felt threatened."[46]

Evidence from policy and housing management records substantiated Allesandroni's concern. As Gwendolyn Wright has observed, however, a tendency arose to blame crime and vandalism on building design rather than internal project conditions. (After 1957, private apartment architecture in Chicago, New York, and other cities often looked just as drab and sterile as public housing.) In the late 1950s, a main problem with high-rise public housing was that it deviated dramatically from the prevailing American norm. While middle-class families, wrote Nathan Glazer, had the economic resources to cope with these normative deficiencies, the structural faults of public housing only aggravated the dilemma of being poor.[47]

Architects and Housing Authority officials by 1960 recognized many of the deficits of public housing living and attempted to ameliorate the problems architecturally; but they usually found their efforts snarled in the thicket of public housing economics and bureaucracy. Southwark Plaza's three 25-story towers rose against the determined opposition of such groups as the PHA and the southern area housing committee of the Philadelphia District Health and Welfare Council (HWC). At its four-block slum site, located in a court- and alley-infested region bordering the city's historic Society Hill, the HWC protested imposing high-density elevator apartments on an already overcrowded district, pleading that row housing would not only ease congestion but would strengthen the Philadelphia "City of Homes" tradition.[48]

Southwark Plaza's opponents lost their battle. Denied Title I assistance, the Housing Authority commissioned the firm of Oscar Stonorov and J. Frank Haws to design an elevator complex that minimized the offensiveness of elevator buildings by balancing the towering edifices with tastefully proportioned low-rise housing. Stonorov felt challenged by limitations of the South Philadelphia slum site and labored to develop a way to insinuate elevator buildings into the already overcrowded environment. "I trust you will understand," wrote Stonorov, "the great pain we are taking in finding new approaches to public housing design, based on the experience of Schuylkill Falls [which Stonorov had designed]. The more I think about the problems of the site and the neighborhood, the more I am still fascinated and wish we could explore all the ranges of possibilities that we have opened up through the [Southwark Plaza] drawings. This one must be good and right all the way through."[49]

Unfortunately, Stonorov, like all public housing architects, was strait-jacketed by cost limitations and the FPHA's edict to avoid "frills." At every turn, Stonorov and Haws encountered the injunction to "use the cheapest materials possible!" Preset concrete slabs replaced wooden floors. Doors disappeared from coat and linen closets [saving $6 a door]. Window openings were narrowed, and it was only after a long struggle that Stonorov won his battle to have elevators stop at each floor rather than at every other floor. As late as 1961, on the grounds of "overdesign," the Housing Authority was bullied by Washington into rejecting the innovative proposal by Ian McHarg, a landscape architect and University of Pennsylvania professor of fine arts, to use earthen mounds to shield the project units from the eyesore of an adjacent commercial laundry.[50]

177

Saving the Central City

To critics such as Montgomery, the Housing Authority's mania for high-rise buildings seemed symptomatic of a malaise afflicting urban renewal in general. In mid-1958, Montgomery impugned the Housing Authority's lack of standards, "making it inevitable," she told G. Holmes Perkins, "that individuals in the community, such as City Council, will propose sites that produce poor public housing, because they don't want to be accused of killing the program." Her depth of concern for the absence of public housing standards matched her deep anxiety about the limited scope and lax pace of urban renewal. Growing day by day more disaffected as a member of the Redevelopment Authority, Montgomery in 1958 waged what she saw as a lonely war against the RA's hodgepodge approach to renewal. In a letter to Wurster, she lamented that "we are getting virtually nowhere [making progress toward the development of the comprehensive plan], because Rafsky . . . [claims] the resources required will not be available in the foreseeable future." Rafsky, she sighed, "makes policy for all the public agencies and the mayor listens to no one else. It really is an extremely frustrating situation. Even Holmes Perkins, now in the Chair of the Planning Commission, is unable to cope with policy formation by the Development Coordinator."[51]

Montgomery's exasperation with the city's renewal program and her discontent at being unable to influence the program's direction peaked in May 1958 when she decided to resign from the RA.[52] She shared the frustration and disillusionment with many of her housing and planning colleagues. Indeed, the outpouring of concern for housing and renewal policy in the late 1950s and early 1960s indicated that housers and planners were engaged in a second, and more introspective, look at housing and urban renewal.

Aware that downtown renewal enjoyed a bedrock of popular support, housers, planners, and progrowth business leaders such as John W. Bodine pondered anxiously the gray and declining conservation areas where, in Rafsky's and Dilworth's estimation, the enormity of the unsolved housing and social problems threatened to undermine the city's goal to be a "blight-free city." Irked by the obstacles to comprehensive renewal, in Philadelphia and elsewhere, in 1960 planner David Wallace derided his fellow renewers as "beggars on horseback." Much like Montgomery and Louis Winnick, Wallace carped that "the mass of people don't know what we're after." Such abstract concepts as "conservation" lacked the tangibility aroused by the Better Philadelphia Exhibit. The broad-gauged renewal implied by conservation, observed Wallace, appealed "to a very small, literate minority of 'professional citizens.'"[53]

Wallace's allusion to "beggars on horseback" struck close to the truth. In the late 1950s the "band of professional citizens"—mainly members of the PHA and the CCCP, groped for a sustainable ideology in an era when ideologies in America were either trampled as subversive or withered amid volumes of data. The frantic explorations of the late 1950s for the "facts and fictions of urban renewal," the "ends and means of urban renewal," or the "elusive goals of urban renewal" hint at the intellectual torment.[54]

Increasingly, planners and other officials saw an invidious relationship between blighted inner cities, white flight, and the prospective bankruptcy of the downtown. Moreover, cities with the greatest slum problems, opined Carter McFarland in 1959, "have the least capacity to deal with [blight]." In fact, as the slums engulfed more of the city and the middle class vanished, fewer tax-ratable properties bore a larger share of the tax burden. Boston in 1959 levied a staggering real estate tax of $101.20 per $1,000 of assessed valuation, which only chased more businesses out of the central city. Not surprisingly, desperate city officials and civic leaders plotted to lure the middle class back to the city. William H. Whyte and Henry S. Churchill, among others, grappled with the "white flight" problem. Whyte, for example, was convinced that, like Rome and Paris, all cities had an eternal appeal to the scholar, the artist, and the young. Accordingly, he deplored the sterile institutional facades of high-rise apartments built for the middle class as well as for the poor. He protested that the city must not only be revitalized; it must be made American—a vital and viable alternative to the apple pie, Chevrolet, picket-fence world of suburbia. In contrast to suburbia, cities, in Whyte's view, offered heterogeneity, a variety of lifestyles, and a housing density and architectural distinctiveness that should be preserved and enhanced through urban renewal.[55]

To the same degree that city officials anguished over the fleeing middle class and planned gleaming skyscrapers and radiant boulevards to lure them back, they expressed a fading concern for the poor, a population that, in Dwight McDonald's words, had become "invisible" in postwar America. Yet, it had been the awareness, if not fear, of the slums that had helped incite the first public housing movement. Notwithstanding the problem of evanescent poverty, evidence accumulated that the "spic and span," "safe and sanitary," way stations of the war years and the early 1950s had become part of the blight. No longer vibrant neighborhoods, public housing projects now seemed an encumbrance or even an embarrassment to the renewal process. Louis Winnick testified that public housing in renewal areas such as East Poplar and Mill Creek actually discouraged investment in middle-income housing.[56] But, ironically, it was Catherine Bauer Wurster who dispelled the last vestige of illusion concerning public housing. In a 1957 article in *Architectural Forum* entitled "The Dreary Deadlock of Public Housing," Wurster contended that public housing officials had reacted to the opposition of NAREB by creating an "overcautious, rigid, uncreative public housing administration"; these officials had architecturally "misapplied" Bauhaus principles to produce institutional fortresses, "islands which turn their backs on the surrounding neighborhoods." She confessed, "Public housing is not the way most American families want to live, it does not reflect our acceptable values as to the way people should live."[57]

Wurster discovered one of the principal weaknesses of public housing in the dichotomy visible in policy between rehousing the poor and housing the middle class. The dichotomy bared itself most conspicuously in the invidious distinction between the homeownership mission of the FHA and the minimal-shelter task assigned the FPHA. This distinction absolved policymakers from any responsibility to consider the total housing project. After Philadelphia's 21-site fiasco, a grieving Dorothy Montgomery conveyed that point in a letter to Wurster. Montgomery wrote that she had "personally come around to the idea that public housing had better stop being a development program [for slum dwellers] and become a housing program instead. . . . It sounds like heresy, but there seems to be many good reasons for a complete review of the program at this time."[58]

In "a spirit of friendly cooperation" with the Housing Authority, Montgomery's review got under way in the fall of 1956 when the PHA and the CCCP together created an Ad Hoc Committee on Public Housing Policy, chaired by Jefferson Fordham. Of all the Fordham Committee recommendations, it was their proposal to have the authority purchase "used" houses in the *C* and *B* renewal areas for service as public housing that hit the mark. While the Housing Authority expressed a few objections to the Fordham report, the authority and Rafsky reacted enthusiastically to the used-house idea. On January 7, 1958, Walter Allesandroni, Blair Lee, Hamilton Vogdes (the authority's director of planning and development), and Jefferson Fordham joined Aaron Levine, Montgomery, and Edmund Bacon in the Washington, D.C., offices of Public Housing Administrator Charles Slusser. While the Philadelphia delegation had planned to discuss a number of Fordham recommendations, Slusser narrowed the discussion to the used-house proposal, which Dilworth had praised as a "flexible approach" to expediting housing for families displaced by renewal.[59]

Grasping at straws, and convinced by the Philadelphians that the used-house idea enjoyed the widespread support of the real estate community, Slusser authorized a 200-unit "pilot" used-house program. The City Council approved the purchase of 200 houses in the Haddington conservation area, a site selected because of the strength of the Haddington Leadership Organization. At the same time the Committee on Public Housing Policy warned that the Housing Authority should not confuse rehabilitation with used-house purchase, but should invest in sound buildings situated in stable zones.[60] Haddington fit the C ("conservable") mold, and although Montgomery described most of the Housing Authority's purchases "as pretty inferior as to lot size, neighborhood condition and interior space," she rejoiced that "at least something is happening to break the log jam on additional units." Having allowed herself a moment of optimism, she quickly lapsed into skepticism. "I sort of begrudge the time we spend [dealing with public housing development policy]," she mused gloomily in a 1958 letter to Wurster, "because the program really is as good as dead." Ironically, between 1959 and 1962 a lawsuit by a Haddington resident, challenging the legality of the Housing Authority's owning and managing properties there, suspended even the popular used-house program.[61]

Contemplating the urban scene, Catherine Bauer Wurster in 1961 somewhat cynically shrugged off the whole renewal effort as "saving the central city." She deplored narrowing the planning vision of the 1920s and 1930s to the singular obsession with the downtown.[62] Others registered similar misgivings. Norton Long worried that renewal had become the "selfish possession of the Downtown"; what had begun as humanitarian slum clearance, rued Charles Abrams, had ended as "a program to rebuild the downtown."[63]

Almost from the dawn of Philadelphia redevelopment, city planners designated the center city as "priority one." As early as 1949, Edmund Bacon had angled for Title I funds to acquire blighted property in the Society Hill neighborhood, an area of two- and three-story eighteenth-century townhouses nestled between Pine and South streets in the shadows of the Delaware River piers. The real impetus for downtown renewal, however, came from the realtor-magnate Albert M. Greenfield, whom Dilworth appointed in 1956 to chair the Philadelphia Planning Commission. Edmund Bacon soon realized that he and Greenfield enjoyed a common interest in downtown renewal.[64] With Rafsky's wholehearted consent, Greenfield helped create the Old Philadelphia Development Corporation (OPDC), a group of prominent civic leaders, business people, and city officials dedicated to preserving the historic area of the central city. The architect Oscar Stonorov and the business leadership of the GPM joined with Greenfield, Bacon, and the OPDC to speed the revival of the central city. Dilworth invited these prominent leaders to City Hall, and with proper fanfare announced the New Philadelphia Movement to "revitalize the Central City, its commercial, financial, industrial, historical and residential sections."[65] By 1960 it was the Center City, University City, and Dock Street projects, not conservation, that stirred the city's imagination.[66]

Meanwhile, public housers and their allies were expressing a growing disillusionment with public housing. Catherine Bauer Wurster, like Dorothy Montgomery and her colleagues at the PHA, no longer harbored the belief that government-built housing would prove the way to rehouse low-income families in healthy, modern communities. Increasingly, the federal bureaucracy and its strict funding formulas seemed to make government an obstacle rather than a partner in the regeneration of the urban scene. More critically, the reformers had lost faith that public housing could aid the cause of racial integration.

Therefore, by 1960 housing activists rejected the strategy of conventional public housing. Although, as the next chapter explains, the rediscovery of the slums and poverty helped usher John F. Kennedy into the presidency, America's rekindled social conscience did not renew the tarnished image of public housing. Instead, under Kennedy, Washington retooled public housing policy and transformed housing projects into welfare centers for the poor.

9

The Vision Eclipsed

If America discovered the big city and urban civilization in the 1920s, then the 1960s witnessed a rediscovery. John F. Kennedy highlighted the city and its problems in his campaign for the presidency, and he used his skills to align urban blacks, ethnic groups, and progrowth disciples behind his New Frontier. But by then, urban renewal had significantly altered the face of the city. Massive slum clearance and city rebuilding had uprooted thousands of families and had exposed festering social chasms and racial cleavages.

In the 1960s the civil rights movement moved from the South into the ghettos of Chicago, Newark, Los Angeles, and Philadelphia. To urban black activists, the source of black America's problems was white racism, and only a revolution in black consciousness and white attitudes about race could solve it.[1] Black activism and the social turmoil of the 1960s directly affected public housing policy. In response to a new social awareness, public housing policymakers recast public housing from way stations into centers for the delivery of social welfare services. Washington's actions made public housing twentieth-century asylums for the poor.

Social Welfare Centers

Although the roots of public housing's transformation from a primarily housing to a social welfare program could be found in the tenant-selection and site-selection policies of the 1930s and in the marriage of public housing and urban renewal in the 1950s, the official rendering of public housing from a housing to a welfare mission occurred in the early 1960s. In addition to the confession of houser disillusionment contained in Catherine Bauer Wurster's "Dreary Deadlock" article, other signs of despair marked the advent of public housing's almshouse era. Most important was the increasingly grim image of the housing project painted by journalists, writers, and scholars.

In a survey of post–World War II society, Harrison Salisbury described the residents of New York City's Fort Green Homes as "deprived of the normal quota of human talent needed for self-organization and self-discipline and self-improvement." Salisbury viewed the Fort Green tenant population as "a living catastrophe . . . [breeding] social ills and requiring endless outside assistance."[2]

While Salisbury was picking through the refuse of the Fort Green Homes, Oscar Lewis, Daniel P. Moynihan, and Nathan Glazer were inventing the "culture of poverty"; not much later, Alvin Schorr discovered the "cycle of poverty." Schorr portrayed the average public housing tenant in 1963 as both poorer and blacker than the typical low-income American. Since 1951, the black population in public housing had increased from 41 percent to 51 percent. Fewer tenants were servicemen, and data indicated that many white families considered public housing to be a last resort. Even more significant, reported Schorr, while the income of public housing tenants had risen 13 percent during the booming economy of the 1950s, American family income nationwide had increased by 44 percent.[3]

Public housing managers in Philadelphia's Richard Allen, Rosen, and Norris projects hardly needed anyone to tell them about the changes in public housing. Reports of broken elevator doors, assaults and rapes, teenage gangs, and the rising incidence of female-headed families regularly crossed the project managers' desks. Convinced that the social and physical deterioration of the project environment reflected the changed social composition of the project population, the Philadelphia Housing Authority in the late 1950s proscribed a whole catalogue of "problem" families, among them "dope peddlers, prostitutes, rapists, thieves, alcoholics, unmarried mothers of two or more children, tuberculars, compulsive gamblers, and families guilty of extremely poor housekeeping." In fact, project managers increasingly singled out the problem family as the root of all evil in public housing. In 1961 the manager of the Rosen project, George Dunn, worried about the large number of public assistance families headed by women. Speaking of one woman at Rosen who wanted to leave the project, Dunn explained, "She is the only one on the floor with a husband. Every day is Sunday in this project."[4]

When John Fitzgerald Kennedy took office in 1961, public housing administrators in Philadelphia were already busy grafting social service onto their historic housing mission. As early as the mid 1950s, in response to what public housing bureaucrats characterized as the "problem family issue," the Philadelphia Housing Association (PHA) and the Citizens' Committee on City Planning (CCCP) had pressed the Housing Authority to station social workers inside the projects. In 1957 the Fordham Committee had importuned the Housing Authority and the Public Housing Administration's commissioner, Charles Slusser, to make social work an integral part of public housing policy. When Slusser turned down the committee's request, the Housing Authority, in close cooperation with the Philadelphia Health and Welfare Council (HWC), inaugurated a Social Service Division (SSD) within the authority. It was a landmark in the history of Philadelphia public housing. The SSD considered public housing tenants to be a "high risk population," tracing their clients' problems, not to a history of poor housing, but to "the stresses that arise from inadequate income," the "lack of prior experience to prepare them for earning a living," and the tenants' "psychologically and socially deprived backgrounds."[5]

During the first year of its operation, the SSD handled 209 cases, almost a fourth of them for "financial" and "housekeeping" problems; at the same time, the SSD established a Big Brother and a housekeeping service program in the projects.[6] Seemingly, the Philadelphia SSD heralded a changing national mood toward poverty. Between 1961 and 1963, under Kennedy, the Federal Public Housing Administration installed social work as a focal concern of national housing policy.

In his bid for the presidency, Kennedy had courted support not only from urban and suburban working-class families but also from city blacks, Hispanics, and progrowth city leaders whose urban renewal plans had been frustrated by tight federal monetary policies. According to John Mollenkopf, under Kennedy and Johnson, Democratic "political entrepreneurs" viewed urban renewal and social programs as a powerful adhesive that would bond a rebuilt New Deal.[7] Kennedy also had campaigned for a vastly expanded urban housing and renewal program that would enlarge the supply of shelter for both low- and moderate-income families. Nevertheless, although the Housing Act of 1961 called for 100,000 new low-income dwellings and enabled cooperatives and limited-dividend housing companies to secure Below Interest Mortgage Rates (BIMRs) for moderate-income housing, by 1963 signs of turbulence in urban America's racial ghettos had surfaced, prompting the National Housing Conference (NHC) to describe the Kennedy record as "not good enough."[8]

In fact, the Kennedy administration dispersed barely $400 million for both housing and urban renewal. Yet the administration toiled unremittingly to mold public housing into an effective instrument for social welfare. To head the HHFA, Kennedy appointed the black economist and authority on housing Robert C. Weaver. To replace Slusser, Kennedy named the executive director of the San Antonio Housing Authority, Marie McGuire, a woman widely respected for pioneering in public housing for the elderly. Both McGuire and her counterpart in the Urban Renewal Administration, William Slayton, oriented the public housing and renewal programs toward "human service" priorities.[9]

McGuire deplored all the negative connotations that adhered to the words "public housing." She repudiated the whole "project" mentality of the federal housing program and strove to transform such existing public housing projects as Philadelphia's Norris, Schuylkill Falls, Rosen, Allen, and Tasker into "bases for the rehabilitation and generation of desires, hopes and energies of people to help themselves."[10] With Weaver and McGuire at the federal helm, the Philadelphia Housing Authority embraced the obligation to service the needs of problem families. A 1963 administrative memo stated that since public housing families "very often bring their behavioral problems with them and cause difficulties for management and other families . . . public housing can provide the necessary physical environment in which efforts at guidance, counseling and education can more readily be made effective." Moreover, McGuire's "people oriented" program demonstrated the way in which housing projects might be transformed into social welfare centers. With federal help, local housing authorities instituted model youth programs, demonstration homemaking programs, and family service centers.[11]

Despite her endeavors to end the "dreary deadlock of public housing," McGuire steadfastly opposed the conventional model of public housing. Where project housing was absolutely necessary, she advocated "vest pocket," architecturally integrated housing designs. The administration retained the architect Albert Mayer to develop guidelines enabling architects to submit creative, noninstitutional designs for public housing. McGuire also urged alternatives to project housing. She vigorously supported experiments with rent supplements, backed used-house programs, and encouraged low-income housing built by the private sector.

Yet, by November 1963, public housing had evolved from a large-scale community-building program aimed at supplying safe and sanitary housing environments to upwardly mobile working-class families into a housing strategy emphasizing the delivery of welfare services to socially and psychologically demoralized tenants.[12]

Two Sides of Urban Renewal

At the same time that policymakers were converting housing projects into centers for the delivery of social services, a rejuvenated urban renewal program flexed its muscle in downtown Philadelphia. Mayor Tate in 1962 appointed Gustav Amsterdam as chairman of the Redevelopment Authority (RA). Emboldened by the city's $120 million share of Kennedy's $2 billion renewal pie, Amsterdam vigorously promoted the RA's favorite projects: Washington Square East (Society Hill), Washington Square West (the Lombard Street area and Jefferson Medical College), and the Temple and University of Pennsylvania developments. These were the projects that inspired Amsterdam to exalt Philadelphia as "a city reborn." A board member of the Old Philadelphia Development Corporation (OPDC), Amsterdam shared that organization's belief that the city's downtown anchored the "heart of a great metropolitan region."

From San Francisco to Philadelphia, urban bulldozers in the early 1960s cleared block after block of aging center-city housing. A portrait of the Society Hill redevelopment area that adorned the cover of the RA's 1962 *Annual Report* showed a rubble-strewn wasteland with outcroppings here and there of preserved buildings.[13] But instead of inspiring exhilaration, redevelopment by 1964 provoked a sense of inexorability; and while the wrecking balls cleared the way for many noteworthy oases of renaissance, among the patches of urban rebuilding were such massive public housing projects as Cambridge Plaza, Norris, and Raymond Rosen, which stood like beleaguered outposts amid the deterioration. Aside from Philadelphia's Penn Center and Society Hill redevelopments, the delightful blending of rehabilitation and rebuilding in East Poplar, and Louis Kahn's artistry at Mill Creek, by 1964 renewal was characterized by rubbish-filled lots and blocks pockmarked with abandoned buildings. Most of North Philadelphia emerged as a wasteland of substandard housing, poor services, poverty, and high crime rates.

Therefore, not everyone gazed approvingly at this display of renewal energy. The massive, government-sponsored destruction of central-city residential property and the glittering office towers and posh apartment complexes that soared out of the rubble sparked criticism from many sides. Martin Anderson, for one, assailed urban renewal programs for using tax money to dislocate poor families while enriching mogul developers. Jane Jacobs decried the government-sponsored destruction of old city neighborhoods whose low-rise architecture and mixed primary uses had been scaled to an intimate and humane urban lifestyle. Herbert Gans, Bernard Frieden, and other urban scholars deplored urban renewal for rending the social fabric of such viable ethnic neighborhoods as Boston's West End and for crassly removing blacks from potentially desirable areas.[14]

But none of these impassioned voices of protest against urban renewal seared the nation's consciousness as much as the rage and fury that in the mid 1960s blazed through the nation's black ghettos.

The Civil Rights Act of 1964 and the other victories of the civil rights movement ignored the pernicious racism stalking the urban ghetto. For urban blacks, the unconquered enemies remained poverty, joblessness, rat bites, lead poisoning, crime, and wretched housing. Whether in Harlem, Washington, D.C., or Watts, the ghetto presented a stultifying, enervating, demoralizing environment.[15] The ghetto rage of the 1960s profoundly affected the history of public housing. And if Philadelphia planners and housing officials had grown complacent and insensitive to the social travail of the ghetto, the violent eruptions of August 1964 awakened their consciousness.

The weeks of July and August 1964 had been extremely hot and steamy for black families living in the aging row houses lining Gratz, Diamond, and Montgomery streets. Not far away, blacks who lived in the Raymond Rosen and the James Weldon Johnson homes endured the same oppressive heat and the same problems. Unemployment exceeded 13 percent for all North Philadelphia blacks in 1964 and approached 21 percent among teenagers and high school dropouts. Joblessness and despair fueled a horrendous cycle of vandalism and violence, prompting the police and the city press to defame the whole region as a "jungle." Thirty-two juvenile gangs rumbled and "bopped" across the intricately defined "turf" lines of North Philadelphia and, all too often, the ugly sound of a pistol shot or zip gun fire reverberated through the sweltering night air.[16]

The 1968 Kerner Commission would report that in Philadelphia, as elsewhere in urban America, blacks regarded the city's white police force with unveiled hatred.[17] On one hot Friday evening in Philadelphia, August 28, 1964, several city police officers vainly attempted to unblock the busy intersection at Twenty-second and Diamond by clearing from it a car occupied by Odessa Bradford and her husband, who were both intoxicated. The police action not only invited a barrage of bricks and stones but also triggered rumors that Mrs. Bradford had been beaten and shot by the police. Despite the pleas of such black leaders as Cecil Moore of the Philadelphia NAACP, the clergyman-activist Leon Sullivan, and comedian Dick Gregory, the ensuing riot lasted three days and engulfed the entire Columbia Avenue area from Broad Street to Twenty-fourth Street. Two people died, 339 were wounded, and the police arrested 308 people.[18]

While the rubble from the riots still strewed Columbia Avenue, anxious representatives of North Philadelphia neighborhood organizations met with other black civic and religious leaders, including the Reverend Joshua Licorish of Zoar Methodist Church, to form the Citizens Emergency Committee (CEC) of North Philadelphia. By August 31, the CEC had drawn up a poverty program to soften the hardships of the community. The CEC ranked the problems, in order of their magnitude, as housing, education, and employment. Their report to Mayor Tate spoke of the "need for immediate as well as long-range community action programs to improve social and economic conditions. The very existence of unemployment, poor housing, and family disorganization," pleaded the CEC, "made possible the opportunity for the easy igniting and rapid spreading of disorder and inciteful conduct such as was exhibited during the crisis of the past few days."[19]

The CEC submitted 10 demands to Tate, including job training for youth, housing-code enforcement, and family counseling. Their demands conspicuously omitted any mention of conventional public housing, but pressed the city to launch an immediate program of housing and/or rehabilitation within the North Philadelphia community. The committee favored the "used-house" program and urged its operation on a citywide basis. And rather than leave the resolution of neighborhood problems to the Housing or Redevelopment Authority, the CEC demanded that "the community organization must play a major role in carrying out either housing conservation or policy making for the poverty program promised by the Mayor's Task Force."[20]

The North Philadelphia riot forced the city to rethink its urban renewal and housing priorities. Despite Kennedy's social agenda for public housing, between 1961 and 1963 it was the enlarged renewal program that had stirred the imaginations of city officials, planners, and policymakers. But by 1964, urban unrest would force a shift in the Redevelopment Authority's posture.

Chaired by Rafsky, and including Bacon and RA director Francis Lammer, Philadelphia's Community Renewal Program (CRP) supervised the production of numerous reports on unemployment, health and welfare, crime, and work opportunities. Renewal program findings underlined the moribund condition of Philadelphia's aging manufacturing economy and the plight of the city's deteriorating slum neighborhoods. CRP data ultimately identified an 11-square-mile area of the city, containing 83,000 families (80 percent of them black), as requiring "reconstruction with substantial demolition." Yet, rather than tie housing decay to the erosion of the city's industrial base, the community renewal data attributed the housing crisis to the disproportionately large share of black, low-income families who were segregated and heavily reliant on health and welfare services. The renewal studies recommended massive and comprehensive antipoverty action for 75 percent of the families living in the city's ghetto areas. Nevertheless, in concert with the 10 North Philadelphia Emergency Committee recommendations, the CRP analysis abjured the public housing solution. Instead, the CRP advocated stronger code enforcement, housing rehabilitation, and the use of FHA financing tools aimed at bringing housing within the reach of low-income families. The CRP studies only lukewarmly endorsed public housing, principally the used-house form. In the main, the CRP analysis prodded the Housing Authority to rely more on social services while ensuring that the neediest families had access to public housing. Not surprisingly, considering the involvement of the PHA and the CCCP in the CRP study, all three organizations took similar positions on city housing issues.[21]

The Great Urban Society

Out of the social ferment of the mid-1960s emerged a new consensus about public housing. Despite the glossy graphics and sentimental verbiage embroidering the Housing and Redevelopment Authority literature, planners and housers scrapped any lingering notions about the regenerative power of public housing. Clearly, urban problems were complex and begged comprehensive solutions. Multiple problems ravaged ghetto neighborhoods, including substandard housing, job discrimination, poor education, crime, and the psychology of poverty.

In view of the persistent shortage of low-income housing, public housing remained stubbornly linked to the solution of the urban crisis. In 1964 housers stressed its welfare role in facilitating housing adjustment for large, elderly, and so-called problem families. Moreover, as one of many agencies dispensing modern social services, public housing operated to restore poor, "disadvantaged" families to "normal" housing. It was for precisely this reason that the CRP studies glorified used housing, housing grants, and FHA rehabilitation and low-rent programs. These housing programs supplied not only more salutary alternatives to the institutionalized housing project but also avoided clustering dependent minorities in the slums. Yet, these programs continued to operate on the assumption that the geographic area for the delivery of meliorative services would be the central city. Under these circumstances, the ghetto became the "model city," a vast staging ground for dispensing social welfare services to the poor.[22]

Mollenkopf has argued that by expanding New Deal and Fair Deal social programs, the Great Society politicians hoped to widen and deepen Democratic party support among blacks, Hispanics, the elderly poor, and the young social activists who now constituted a vocal element in the urban constituency. Although many Democratic city mayors and other officials balked at this political ecumenism, they cooperated as a condition of increased funding for urban renewal.

Socially, the Great Society focused on ghetto poverty. Therefore, Johnson's social architects spotlighted the ghetto as the main stage for the delivery of improved social services. The strategy confirmed public housing's new role as a welfare center. Public housing projects would house preschool programs, job-training centers, welfare offices, health classes, and other public agencies intended to interpose government into the ghetto world and break the cycle of poverty. The Johnson social planners also grappled with dependent relationships. To the dismay of many local housing and redevelopment authorities, the architects of Johnson's Great Society, responding to the hideous evidence of frustration and alienation in the nation's black ghettos, emphasized that neighborhood programs must allow "maximum feasible citizen participation."[23]

Although born and reared in the Texas hill country, Lyndon Johnson imagined the Great Society as an urban society. In 1964 he declared war on urban poverty; later that year, in the wake of the summer ghetto riots, he outlined a massive housing program to address the "problem and future of central cities." One of Johnson's solutions to the problem realized a long-standing dream of city mayors, housers, and planners. After 20 years of debate, Congress in 1965 created the cabinet-rank Department of Housing and Urban Development (HUD). But Johnson's housing legislation went even further. It provided federal funds for urban youth centers and health stations, and for open spaces for parks and playgrounds. In addition, $750 million was allocated for urban renewal, code enforcement, and the building of 240,000 units of new public housing over four years. Finally, an experimental rent-supplement program provided 375,000 units of cooperative, limited-dividend, and nonprofit low-income housing.[24]

Robert C. Weaver, HUD's first secretary, termed the public housing provisions of the new law "flexible"; indeed, of the 60,000 units programmed annually, HUD slated 15,000 to be in "used" and 10,000 to be in "leased" structures. Rent supplements, which the PHA-CCCP Joint Committee had mentioned in their 1965 report, were the most controversial housing innovation in the law. Conceived as a device for "scattering" public housing throughout the urban region, including the suburbs, the act allowed private nonprofit or cooperative housers to build low-income housing with 5.5 percent FHA financing, and to rent the units to elderly, handicapped, or displaced families and to households with incomes below the maximum established for public housing. The new HUD program calculated the economic rent for such housing at 15 percent of a family's income, and ordered rent supplements to cover the difference between a family's ability to pay and the fair-market rent fo HUD-approved shelter.[25]

An AFL spokesman, Boris Shiskin, and Nathaniel Keith, president of the National Housing Conference, conceded the need for rent supplements but begged Washington to program 120,000 units of new public housing annually rather than 60,000. In fact, testifying on the 1965 legislation, National Association of Housing Officials (NAHO) representative Ira Robbins, from the San Francisco Housing Authority, criticized the bill as "marking time rather than scaling the heights of the Great Society." Robbins assailed the rent-supplement provision as an "ill conceived and costly way of housing the poor." But Senator Paul Douglas, a stalwart defender of public housing, shrugged off NAHO's objections. Douglas stated that "dynamism" had long vanished from the housing movement, and he flailed local housing authorities for their abysmal record of housing production. Charging that local public housing authorities had "fallen down on the job and the cities have fallen down on the job," Douglas questioned whether the answer was "merely to say increase the authorizations for public housing. I am for that. But, there must be something more than that done to get housing for the poor. . . . [I]ndeed, the public housing movement, to the degree it is carried out, has become in the North, almost entirely housing for the elderly."[26]

Evidently, neither Douglas, Robbins, Keith, nor Shiskin realized the extent to which cities and their public housing officials had abandoned public housing as a supplier of low-income housing and revamped the program to stress welfare objectives. But Public Housing Administrator Marie McGuire knew it. McGuire, who had been the first to champion public housing as a "welfare center," informed Weaver in September 1965 about public housing's key involvement in the Office of Equal Opportunity's (OEO) War on Poverty program. "Public Housing," she explained, represented a "major community resource" in the War on Poverty. Across the country public housing agencies had provided leadership in designing strategies for community action programs. Many city housing authorities sponsored Neighborhood Youth Corps projects and afforded space for Volunteers in Service to America (VISTA) and Project Head Start. According to McGuire, 97 local housing authorities, including Philadelphia's, employed 2,494 housing project youth in Neighborhood Youth Corps programs, and 524 tenant youth participated in the Job Corps.[27]

To help reconcile the delicate, often volatile concerns of the War on Poverty with the urban housing and renewal mission of HUD, Johnson in October 1965 appointed a Task Force on Urban Problems. Having assembled a distinguished panel, including Philadelphia's development expert William Rafsky, Johnson instructed the commission to attack the problem of urban slums by devising a highly flexible "block grant program to demonstrate how entire urban neighborhoods might be rebuilt socially and physically." The task force's findings became the basis for the Demonstration Cities and Metropolitan Development ("Model Cities") Act, approved by Congress on November 3, 1966. Johnson's Model Cities Act proposed to expand housing, increase jobs, expand urban economies, reduce welfare dependency, and combat disease and crime. Without altering the existing urban renewal appropriation formula, HUD allocated Model Cities grants that equaled 80 percent of the cost of planning model neighborhoods. But, tragically, with the nation slipping deeper into the quagmire of Vietnam, Johnson's agenda of "guns and butter" meant funding Model Cities at only $2.3 billion instead of the $60 billion requested. Yet ultimately 67 cities, among them Philadelphia, participated in the program.[28]

Model Cities attempted to revitalize urban America based on the exhaustive data and recommendations for comprehensiveness contained in local CRP reports. The whole vision encompassed a political as much as a social and economic renaissance. Through Model Cities, Washington hoped to dispatch the "bulldozer syndrome" and encourage local officials to become more responsive to neighborhood concerns and sensitive to the need for community participation. In HUD Administrator Sherry Arnstein's words, Model Cities promised a "massive change in the quality of life and urban neighborhoods." For this to occur, insisted Arnstein, residents would have to play a major part in the planning and administration of the program. Therefore, as a key condition for Model Cities funding, cities not only had to show a financial commitment on the part of the mayor, City Council, and state officials but also had to assure that a mechanism existed for enlisting "maximum feasible citizen participation."[29]

To facilitate this participation, HUD created City Demonstration (Development) Agencies, which functioned to smooth communication between City Hall and the neighborhood. HUD's revolutionary concept of "community participation," however, imagined federal authority wielded on behalf of powerless neighborhoods; it envisioned nothing less than a basic alteration in the configuration of the urban power structure. As Arnstein later confessed, "community participation" failed in Philadelphia, as it did in other cities.

Great Society political entrepreneurs had erected their urban coalition on a crumbling foundation. Political leaders and government agency heads in the 1960s and 1970s confronted a barrage of often conflicting demands for neighborhood participation, black power, ethnic power, social justice, and economic equity. Despite its failure, however, the Model Cities experience in Philadelphia profoundly influenced power relationships, particularly those between tenants, neighborhoods, and the Philadelphia Housing Authority.[30]

For its Model City program, Philadelphia selected the brace of putrefying city neighborhoods north of Vine Street, a region of black poverty and slum housing that had blazed with fury, looting, and gunfire during the 1964 riots. In February 1967, 10 months before HUD announced the city's $278,000 Model Cities planning grant, City Hall formed a partnership with the Area Wide Council (AWC), which included such community groups as the North City Congress (NCC), a group linked closely to another action group, the Philadelphia Council for Community Advancement. A stormy city-AWC relationship ensued, with distrust and bitter invective on both sides. The struggle began immediately, when the Philadelphia Model Cities development coordinator drafted a planning design for neighborhood public housing and slum clearance. Fiercely committed to acquiring independent power, the AWC rejected the coordinator's plan. Amid growing hostility and funding cutbacks in Model Cities, the AWC in March 1969 fashioned its own plan. The AWC blueprint singled out poverty and powerlessness as the root causes of blight and outlined a $250 million Model Cities program, earmarking 50 percent of the federal dollars for economic development, 23 percent for comprehensive education, and 22 percent for physical development—primarily to fund a housing development corporation that would both construct new housing and rehabilitate existing structures. In May 1969 HUD rejected the plan, citing the "heavy involvement of the AWC in the proposed corporations." The AWC forthwith sued to have HUD's decision overturned, but ultimately it lost its case. Without Model Cities funding, the AWC disbanded.[31]

The AWC struggle had further polarized political roles in the turbulent city. Blacks confronted whites; the neighborhoods faced off against City Hall. Community action organizers portrayed City Hall, the Redevelopment Authority, and the Housing Authority as the establishment and themselves as adversaries fighting for neighborhood control.[32] And they portrayed neighborhood groups—public housing tenants, for example—as victims. This polarization of roles compelled the traditional watchdog agency, the PHA, to become an "advocate" for the powerless.

Minority Housing Rights

The impact of all these social changes on public housing appeared in the increasingly acerbic quality of tenant-management relations and in the Philadelphia Housing Authority's difficulty in implementing its celebrated used-house program. In early 1965, Mayor Tate asked Housing Commissioner McGuire to acquire 1,000 to 1,500 houses in the "gray" areas and rehabilitate them for use as public housing. Federal housing people, who toured the city in April, returned to Washington "discouraged, feeling that the effort could not be much of a success in view of the overall condition of the total neighborhood and unrelenting gray areas that remain as the 'environment.'" On every street, the federal inspectors found vacant houses with *For Sale* signs due to code enforcement or abandonment of units. "Evidently," explained one agent, "the owners do not want, or cannot afford, the cost of rehabilitation without getting assurance of rent commensurate with their investment."[33]

A week later, the Public Housing Administration circulated a memorandum among federal agencies entitled "Philadelphia Rehabilitation." The memorandum supported Philadelphia's used-house program and focused on the satisfaction of families living in used housing. It noted especially the "complete integration [of used housing] with the neighborhood and [the] complete removal of any project connotation." Philadelphia has "certainly given the matter a lot of thought and study," concluded George Baily of HUD, "and I am inclined to think that we should take a chance and go along with them."[34]

Weaver enthusiastically supported the "used-house" program, and in June 1967 HUD approved a $70 million contract to enable the Philadelphia Housing Authority to purchase 5,000 rehabilitated, low-rent homes on scattered sites throughout the city. It was the largest single authorization for low-income housing ever made by the federal government. The action by HUD, announced Tate, "removed the last obstacle to putting into effect the city's nationally famed Vacant House Program."[35] Part of the federal government's new Turnkey Program, initiated by the Housing Act of 1965, Philadelphia's used-house operation involved the private rehabilitation of low-rent housing, followed by the Housing Authority's purchase of the repaired unit—in other words, a transfer of the house key from the private developer to the authority. The Philadelphia Plan, as it was also called, represented a joining of HUD and local private capital. "Here is heartening evidence," commented Robert Weaver, "that President Johnson's call to business and labor to take part in solving our urban problems is being put into practice."[36]

Despite Weaver's enthusiasm, Philadelphia's used-house program endured severe buffeting, although it began auspiciously. In 1966, the Housing Authority spotlighted several blocks on Wallace and Mount Vernon streets, in the Fairmount neighborhood, for a 70-unit share of the city's 5,000-unit housing program. Adding further glitter to the project, Smith, Kline and French, a large pharmaceuticals company, pledged to assist a real estate developer in financing the purchase and rehabilitation of the used houses. Indeed, through the SKF Information Center, the firm even helped with relocating the displaced families. Yale Rabin, a young professor of planning at the University of Pennsylvania and a member of the advocacy group Planning for Equal Opportunity, volunteered to work with local organizations as a planner, to draw up house-by-house plans for the used-house site.[37]

But gilt-edged dreams tarnish easily in slum environments. Fairmount contained both a mixed racial and socioeconomic population. Moreover, the Housing Authority's target neighborhood, Mount Vernon east of Fifteenth Street, abutted a renascent area of attractive nineteenth-century Greek Revival and Italianate townhouses that were being rehabilitated by affluent white families. Complicating a situation in which the white gentry confronted nearby poor neighbors, hostile blacks vied with Puerto Rican families for supremacy in the housing being rehabilitated by the Housing Authority. The resultant conflict pitted the white middle-class Fairmount Parents, Business and Neighborhood Association (FPBNA) against the North City Congress (NCC), public housing clients, and the Housing Authority.

The FPBNA feared that the authority's plans to convert several rows of stately "triplexes" (three-story, high-stooped brick houses) into low-income apartments would increase population density and introduce poor, nonwhite renters into a "gentrified" neighborhood of white homeowners.[38] In truth, neither the NCC nor the PHA wanted concentrated triplex apartment housing in Fairmount. They preferred integrated, single-family "used housing," scattered throughout North Philadelphia. Both organizations, however, also distrusted the gentrification agenda of the FPBNA, and side by side with black and Puerto Rican tenants and the Housing Authority, they fought for used housing and to keep Fairmount racially integrated.

The brouhaha over the Fairmount used-house program culminated in a May 25 meeting, called by the PHA, at which the authority defused tensions by agreeing to scatter a limited number of single-family as well as triplex housing units throughout the blocks east and west of Twentieth Street. Moreover, the authority promised to continue its efforts to house families in the Spring Garden area without regard to "social factors." In any case, the Fairmount used-house incident illustrated the volatility of Philadelphia's housing situation in the 1960s.[39]

The Fairmount incident also displayed the PHA's new colors as an outspoken and unequivocal advocate of minority housing rights. Daily immersion in the turbulent urban racial and political milieu of the 1960s had politicized the venerable old housing organization, giving it a far more radical complexion than staid Bernard Newman would ever have imagined. The PHA drifted toward its new advocacy role shortly after health problems forced Dorothy Montgomery to retire in 1965 as managing director and to take a less demanding position as secretary of the association's board of directors. It is surely possible to find symbolic meaning in Montgomery's retirement. While never naive about the racial and economic realities of the housing marketplace, the liberal Montgomery nurtured an idealism about housing and its potential for human betterment that seemed uncomfortably old-fashioned in the abrasive urban climate of the 1960s. The brutality and violence of the ghetto had totally eclipsed the vision of the urban future that Montgomery once had. Tragically, in 1964, Montgomery's friend and ideological companion Catherine Bauer Wurster died while climbing alone in the rugged hills bordering the Pacific shores of California. Eulogized in the *Housing Yearbook* as "the most brilliant light guiding all who seek solutions to American housing, urban renewal, and metropolitan planning," nevertheless, the year she died, the fifty-seven-year-old Wurster had spent most of her time as an academic and like Montgomery had largely abdicated responsibility for the hard decisions of housing and planning to housing authority bureaucrats.

Cushing Dolbeare, Montgomery's assistant, took over as managing director of the PHA. A graduate of Swarthmore College, Dolbeare had spent five years as the associate executive director of the Citizens Planning and Housing Association of Baltimore before joining the PHA staff in 1956. Like her husband, the city planner Louis Dolbeare, Cushing described herself as a "militant liberal."[40] Dolbeare intensified the PHA's activist role without basically altering the organization's structure. A Quaker, Dolbeare owned an especially deep commitment to civil rights. Under Dolbeare's tenure, PHA cooperated with the Urban League to form the Joint Committee on Minority Housing (JCMH) and at the same time escalated its criticism of city housing and renewal policies. In particular, the PHA attacked the Redevelopment Authority's lack of dedication to rehabilitation, especially its massive clearance operations in the Southwest Temple area "which on balance . . . removed more units than have been built."[41] The PHA just as resolutely challenged the RA's penchant for "luxury" projects. In retaliation, the RA declared the PHA "so biased against the RA and its programs that even an attempt [by it] to do an important objective presentation of renewal accomplishments reeks with loaded and biased misstatements."[42]

Charges of unfairness on the part of the PHA evidenced the venerable organization's gradual departure from the progrowth coalition. The bitter site controversy of 1956 had opened the first breach in the city's wall of support for renewal. After 1956, white peripheral neighborhoods no longer shared the downtown's ecstatic vision of a "Better Philadelphia." Similarly, the 1964 riot forced the PHA to reexamine its historically progressive view of housing and renewal. Yet the PHA philosophy remained moderate at least six months after the 1964 riot when Montgomery and her assistant, Dolbeare, asked George Schermer to prepare a "few paragraphs concerning race" for the association's annual policy statement on housing. In his reply, Schermer noted that "it is not enough to improve the racial ghetto to a standard of non-slum, or to declare a policy of free and equal choice of housing. Wholesome, racially inclusive neighborhoods or a process of desegregating the central city ghetto are not likely to develop unless public policy is explicitly committed to those ends and appropriate programs are adopted." Fearful that Schermer's plan for "incentives" and "penalties" to encourage "racial inclusiveness . . . in the planning of all new city and suburban housing" would offend "the very groups that must support the association's other housing initiatives," Dolbeare condensed Schermer's remarks into the form of a brief objective: "We want to end segregation and will deal later with the means of doing so."[43] The PHA's means for ending segregation became apparent in 1965 when the association joined with the Urban League, NAACP, FC, CORE, CHR, and Fair Housing Committee of the Delaware Valley (FHCDV) to "plan and carry out a coordinated attack on racial segregation and discrimination in housing."

The vehicle for waging the assault was the Joint Committee on Minority Housing (JCMH), an organization spawned by the PHA in cooperation with the Urban League. The JCMH, whose letterhead listed everyone in Philadelphia even tangentially concerned with race and low-income housing, fought segregation through a bevy of programs that included community action, education, housing information centers, purchasing power, and law and public policy projects. In the main, however, the JCMH concentrated on the housing plight of the black middle class rather than the black poor.[44]

A few years later, the PHA strengthened its advocacy role when in 1968 it united with the FHCDV to become the Housing Association of the Delaware Valley (HADV). The next year, Dolbeare referred to "housing as a problem, not the problem" and portrayed the PHA as functioning "as an initiator of social change in housing, and as a supporter of needed social change or action in other related areas, such as education, opposition to ABM [antiballistic missile systems] and disproportionate emphasis on military spending, opposition to police repression and the like."[45]

On October 14, 1969, the HADV, braced by Dolbeare and the organization's young, idealistic staff, officially declared its moral opposition to the war in Vietnam and announced that its offices would be closed so that the staff could participate in a nationwide moratorium against the war. In a press release endorsing the moratorium, the HADV president, Bernard Borish, stated that "the U.S. cannot end the exploitation of blacks and poor people or insure real self determination for all communities until we have withdrawn from Vietnam."[46]

The HADV's 1969 agenda called for the enactment of housing allowances, or "income maintenance for low-income households," and pledged the association's resources to eliminating racial discrimination, to "watchdogging" existing programs, to "supporting community self-determination in renewal and Model Cities programs," and to fighting for low-income housing in the Washington Square West renewal area. Dolbeare's cadre of young professionals shared her commitment to an advocacy role for the association. Assistant Director Anne Turner, whose responsibilities included public housing, defined her objective for 1969 as "devising a strategy of action for a citizen housing organization which is truly anti-racist and anti-colonialist." Meanwhile, Sue Carroll, who headed the Housing Authority's Delaware County Training Course, lamented that the HADV did not "have enough of a radical analysis of housing worked out yet to fill out three or four [class] sessions. [Yet,] we've come at least part way in identifying the socialism for the rich/capitalism for the poor syndrome."[47]

The Department of Housing and Urban Development (HUD)

In addition to the HADV, others found public housing an enigma. A HUD analysis of public housing, produced in 1968 by George Schermer, unearthed a number of troubling concerns about the nation's low-income housing program. In *More Than Shelter,* Schermer named poverty as "the root problem" undermining the public housing program. He castigated public housing's management system for discouraging meaningful tenant participation. Nevertheless, like numerous other critics of the federal housing program, Schermer, faced with the severity of the low-income housing crisis, balked at any outright scuttling of the 30-year-old public housing operation. Instead, he strongly urged HUD to involve the tenants themselves in the public housing planning process. Significantly, the HUD Act of 1968, which established a 10-year housing goal of 26 million units of new and rehabilitated housing, also mandated greater tenant involvement in public housing decision making. Moreover, to help reach HUD's ambitious new goal, Congress inaugurated a low-income home-ownership program and funded a new BMIR loan program to enlarge the supply of rent-assisted housing.[48]

Despite the 1968 housing act, the public housing program at the end of the decade remained demoralized and directionless. No less than before, the enduring issue of sites proved a formidable stumbling block. In late 1968, responding to the *Gautreaux* court decision, which had declared Chicago's concentration of high-rise public housing in ghetto areas to be unconstitutional, HUD ordered that for every additional unit of public housing constructed in areas heavily populated by blacks, local housing authorities had to build a similar number of public housing units in neighborhoods outside the ghetto. The HADV welcomed HUD's site directive, although at the same time it reaffirmed its belief that the War on Poverty must precede the battle for housing: "Most people on welfare are poorly housed and . . . most of those in the worst houses are on welfare." Therefore, public housing is no more than "a necessary stopgap."

Understandably, in 1969, as in 1957, the HADV cheered the Philadelphia Housing Authority's announced plan to seed public housing in areas with little or no public housing, including Roxborough, Manayunk, and the Northeast.[49] Yet, no matter how "human scale" the contemplated projects, or how scattered the sites, the Housing Authority's list of project locations disappointed the HADV staff people who scouted them in late 1968. One site, in the Northeast, adjoined the Holmecrest project for the elderly in a Holmesburg slum area; another site, a vacant lot overgrown with weeds and littered with trash, bordered the Chestnut Hill branch of the Reading Railroad; and the Domino Lane site in Manayunk was bathed in the stench and pollution belched forth from a nearby city incinerator. "Are we really going to let them continue to put public housing in the least desirable parts of every community?" asked the HADV's Sue Carroll.[50]

By 1968, blacks constituted 76 percent of the city's housing project population, and housing reformers scorned public housing as a segregated wasteland. Ironically, the HUD actions in the wake of the *Gautreaux* decision intensified the trend toward segregation and therefore reinforced the reformer's disillusionment. HUD removed control over tenant selection from larger cities such as Philadelphia, Chicago, and St. Louis, and devised a new tenant-assignment policy that placed applicants on a citywide waiting list and offered prospective tenants housing in projects with the greatest absolute number of vacancies. Applicants were permitted only three refusals.[51]

Commenting on the new HUD procedures, the HADV's Sue Carroll predicted still greater segregation in public housing. Perhaps, she wrote, whites might be persuaded to move into modernized public housing. (Both the shabby Richard Allen Homes and the aging Tasker project awaited rehabilitation money in 1967.) However, revealing her acute awareness of the dilemma, Carroll noted that "even though the lure of having a shower and an improved unit might attract white families [to such projects as Richard Allen] where previously none dare tread, it is obviously not fair to black families to give whites the better units or to draw them from the waiting list out of turn. Is there any other alternative to writing off the black projects?"[52]

And Philadelphians, especially the housers of 1968 and 1969, seemed increasingly inclined to do precisely that. Occupancy data for 1968 showed that in nineteen of Philadelphia's thirty-two housing projects, black families lived in 95 percent of the units. Blacks comprised over half the population in 83 percent of the city's housing projects.

Racism and Bigotry

Although disillusioned with the segregative results of conventional public housing, and angered at the Housing Authority's attempt to secrete scattered-site housing along unsightly railroad rights-of-way, in the shadow of public incinerators, or in other undesirable corners of the city, in 1969 the HADV once again donned its armor and marched out to save scattered-site public housing from the hostile clutches of the City Council. Determined to sabotage the building of public housing in his district, a Roxborough city councilman had introduced two bills that foreclosed the use of Domino Lane for public housing by rezoning the tract "industrial." The HADV branded the zoning legislation "a blatant attempt to prevent low-income housing from being built outside ghetto areas" and characterized the City Council's action as "racist and bigoted."[53]

If racism and bigotry haunted the chambers of the City Council, they no less intruded into the office suites of the Philadelphia Housing Authority. In a newspaper interview, Frank Steinberg, a home-builder and chairman of the authority, divulged his repugnance to "breaking up the black ghetto by putting public housing units into white areas." Continued Steinberg, "Color likes to live with color. If you can put colored people in the Northwest, colored wouldn't be happy and white people wouldn't be happy. . . . It's only the agitators who want to push them [the blacks] into Roxborough." The incensed HADV petitioned Mayor Tate "to act immediately to remove Frank Steinberg as chairman of the Housing Authority. We believe that now is the time to reconstitute the Authority as a more effective and representative body." Under fire, Steinberg resigned in 1969.[54]

In 1971 Philadelphia elected a mayor dedicated to preserving the racial integrity of white neighborhoods, particularly against threats of public housing. The new mayor was Frank Rizzo, a tough South Philadelphia policeman, who had risen through the ranks to become police chief. Rizzo drew the line against public housing in the Whitman Park area of South Philadelphia, an almost solidly white, working-class neighborhood where 79 percent of the residents were homeowners. The Whitman Park public housing project had been initially proposed in 1956 as Delaware Towers, but the 440-unit high-rise development was defeated then for reasons of size alone. In 1969 the project reappeared on the Housing Authority's drafting boards, this time as Whitman Park. Leaner than in 1956, the new version featured 120 units, and rather than a high-rise design, it offered townhouse dwellings to be erected by a private contractor and "turned over" to the Housing Authority for rental and/or sale to qualified tenants.

Neither the townhouse design nor the incentive of home-ownership persuaded Rizzo. Defying orders from Washington, he blocked all work on the project. In fact, Whitman Park became a symbolic contest pitting black public housing tenants against Rizzo and white Philadelphians resisting government-ordered racial integration. After years of controversy, the black tenants declared victory. In 1976 Judge Raymond Broderick ruled that by failing to build the Whitman Park complex, Philadelphia violated the Fifth, Thirteenth, and Fourteenth amendments to the Constitution, and ordered the project constructed forthwith. Whitman Park Homes opened for occupancy a few years later.[55]

Activism and Advocacy

If local politicians and housing authorities frequently reacted with insensitivity or hostility to the racial implications of public housing, federal officials such as Robert Weaver and Marie McGuire showed a steadfast commitment to public housing's social role. Weaver's 1966 Task Force Report on the Social Concerns of HUD (which the secretary called "the most significant document of all the Task Forces working in 1966") decried the lack of professionalism among public housing managers and bemoaned the absence of "socially oriented staff which can deal effectively with the social-psychological problems of the poor." The 1966 report also deprecated the policy of evicting over-income tenants, which perpetuated ghettos of the poor and discouraged and stymied the creation of social leadership and the development of role models for project families. The task force, chaired by Leonard Duhl of the Harvard Medical School and staffed by, among others, the sociologist Hans Spiegel and Elizabeth Wood, recommended a less rigid model of project management and urged project managers to promote not only homeownership among tenants but also tenant participation and tenant self-reliance, "which must be woven into [public housing's] organizational structure, possibly in the form of an advisory council."[56]

Like community action and neighborhood organization, the appeal for tenant participation and tenant rights became an often heard refrain in the stairwells and courtyards of public housing projects in the late 1960s. And amid the powerlessness and defeatism endemic to project life, telltale signs appeared that, supported by militant organizations, tenant activism was accomplishing change. While hardly democratizing the project environment, successful grass-roots legal actions against the Housing Authority significantly altered the social composition within Philadelphia's housing projects and coerced public housing management into listening to tenant grievances.

Oliva Byrd was one of many unwed mothers who in 1968 sued the Philadelphia Housing Authority for proscribing single, female heads of household under its long-standing policy of excluding "problem" families. A 24-year-old mother of four children, Oliva, who worked from time to time as a waitress and sewing machine operator, lived with her children and welfare-dependent parents in a crowded, substandard center-city apartment. When the Housing Authority rejected her application for housing in the Richard Allen Homes, Oliva appealed to the Community Action Council. In May 1968, on behalf of Oliva and eight other unwed mothers, the state

Supreme Court ruled that the Housing Authority could "not exclude or indifferently treat" any family solely because it included a child born out of wedlock.[57] Furthermore, the court ordered the authority promptly to offer written notice of the reason for refusing any family admission to a project. Although the authority continued to disapprove families engaged in "anti-social, criminal or otherwise undesirable actions," the *Byrd et al.* ruling erected a legal barrier delimiting the authority's power to exercise paternal control over the public housing environment.[58]

If the *Byrd* case hobbled the Housing Authority in its endeavors to enforce moral standards, a second case the same year immobilized the agency. The suit, filed in September 1968 by the Tenant Councils of the Richard Allen and Tasker Homes and resolved in favor of the tenants, took away the project managements' power arbitrarily to make midyear rent adjustments, dictate the use of facilities, and freely hire management staff. For years, the Housing Authority had beseeched Washington to aid them in modernizing the heating and electrical systems of the aging Allen and Tasker projects. At last, in November 1967, HUD announced a nationwide $125 million public housing modernization program to "raise the quality of life of the tenants and enhance their opportunity for economic advancement." But Secretary Weaver attached a proviso to the program: All funded project improvements must be "accompanied by changes in management policies and practices which will feature tenant involvement and programs to improve tenant earnings." Ignoring HUD's injunction, as well as the admonitions of the Richard Allen Homes Tenant Council, in February 1968 Richard Allen management assembled a hand-picked group of tenants and informed them of the modernization program. Rosetta Wylie, an Allen tenant, seized her opportunity. As president of the Allen Tenant Council, and in concert with the Tenant Council of Tasker, Wylie sued the Housing Authority for breach of faith, then promptly telegraphed Weaver requesting him "not to approve [the modernization] funding unless PHA complies with the requirements of HUD." After meeting with Housing Authority representatives in March 1969, Wylie and the chairman of the Tenant Council of Tasker dropped the complaint, but only after extracting from the authority a "Memorandum of Understanding."[59]

The legally binding memorandum set a precedent that altered tenant-management relations in Philadelphia public housing. Among other things, the memorandum forced management to meet monthly with project Tenant Councils; it also compelled project officials to consult with tenants in all hiring decisions and gave tenants first preference in project-related employment. Moreover, management was instructed to provide office space for Tenant Councils, to grant access to a project's community building "on a regular basis," and to supply "24 hour emergency maintenance service."

Of utmost importance to the tenants, the "Memorandum of Understanding" limited the Housing Authority's arbitrary power over rent increases. Not only did the memorandum foreclose management's power to exact mid-year rent adjustments (reflecting, for example, a tenant's raise in pay or the employment of another household member), but tenants were permitted to appeal any increase in rent. In addition, the memorandum prohibited management from arbitrarily evicting tenants for reasons other than the nonpayment of rent, the "serious and intentional" damage to authority property, the serious interference with the rights of other tenants, or "income over the maximum allowable." Finally, the memorandum provided that "any tenant who feels aggrieved by Authority actions in conducting inspections [for housekeeping, etc.], collecting or adjusting rents . . . scheduling evictions or denying transfers, shall be entitled to a hearing."[60]

By mid-1971, an informed, sensitive, and responsive Housing Authority management had increased its social service staff fourfold, gained a "new respect for the self determination of tenants through maximizing the opportunity for locational transfers [to other projects] and increased the income for Continued Occupancy as much as 70 percent for larger families." Nevertheless the litigation that sensitized management to tenant demands for a voice in determining their own housing environment actually compounded the malaise afflicting public housing. Now completely shorn of its way-station function, public housing existed merely as a warehouse for families with the barest means to pay the Housing Authority rents. More often than not, by 1970, those rents were paid from the public assistance provided to poor, black, often female-headed families.[61]

At the same time, the progrowth coalition that had nurtured public housing and urban renewal splintered into warring racial, ethnic, class, and antiwar factions. Political battle lines hardened in a volatile urban environment, forcing such once stalwart progrowth allies as the HADV to carve out an ideological niche farther to the left. Convinced that race, poverty, and public housing formed an invidious nexus, the HADV vigorously opposed the conventional public housing program. "If public housing is provided for low-income families," wrote Ellee Workman of HADV in 1969, "it should be scattered site existing housing which does not earmark families as a public housing family in a community, and which can be purchased by the tenants as their income rises. We should be working to stop public housing," affirmed Workman, "and saying 'projects are bad.' We should not accommodate, but work for change."[62]

Between 1969 and 1971, HADV was transformed from a white middle-class housing organization into a largely black advocacy organization representing grass-roots neighborhood concerns and committed to "institutional change to end racism and exploitation in housing." Evidence of the change appeared in the HADV membership. Old board members, such as Henry Beeritz, resigned, making way for Rose Wylie of the Richard Allen Homes Tenant Council and W. Wilson Goode, a Wharton School graduate and executive director of the Philadelphia Council for Community Advancement. Blacks replaced whites as staff members, and when Cushing Dolbeare resigned in 1971 to head a Washington-based Friends Service project, the HADV board selected as her successor a dynamic black real estate expert once active in the FHCDV, Shirley M. Dennis.[63] Dennis graduated from Temple University and gained housing expertise as a broker for Tucker and Tucker Real Estate. In 1969 she became housing director for the Philadelphia Urban League. After directing the HADV's advocacy housing programs from 1971 to 1979, Dennis left to become executive deputy secretary of the Pennsylvania Department of Community Affairs.[64]

All these changes were still in the wings in November 1970 when the HADV unwrapped a new program, "Toward Ending Racism in Housing." The program focused on institutional change and on exposing "the extent to which housing institutions reflect or intensify racism and exploit the poor." Denouncing the present federal housing program as "inoperable," the HADV expressed horror at the scandalous rate of housing abandonment in the city and pushed for an urban homesteading plan. The association viewed its primary mission, however, as making the city's social institutions (government in particular) more responsive to the shelter needs of neighborhoods. Principally, this involved redistributing social power. According to the HADV, the objective of reform had to be the cultivation of citizen participation—the stimulating of people power. Therefore, in 1969–1970 the Housing Association helped organize Redevelopment Action Groups (RAGs) to prod the Redevelopment Authority to serve residential neighborhoods. The HADV also worked to get more tenant representation and involvement in public housing decision making. In November 1972 the HADV attacked the Housing Authority for refusing to cooperate with the Residents Advisory Board (RAB) and for blatantly ignoring the 1969 "Memorandum of Understanding." Furthermore, it assailed the authority's "indiscriminate labeling of persons as 'desirable' or 'undesirable,' its use of 'undercover agents to spy on tenants,'" and its attempt to evict tenants without due process.[65]

But the Housing Authority's apparent repressive behavior seemed motivated less by any ideological vestiges of the way station than by a desire to preserve a semblance of order, minimize vandalism, and control skyrocketing maintenance costs. Public housing in the mid-1970s represented a gigantic, publicly supported real estate bureaucracy, a human warehousing agency whose clients were either very-low-paid workers or public dependents.

A Failed Policy

Federal housing policy, it has been argued, established the framework for a decentralized program of low-income housing. Most important, federal policy dictated the several themes that informed public housing from 1937 to 1974. Beginning in the 1930s, federal policy heralded public housing as a way station for the upwardly mobile poor; by 1954, public housing had evolved into a tool for accomplishing the progrowth agenda of progressive planners and downtown businessmen; in the 1960s, Washington policymakers described public housing as a center for the delivery of social welfare services; finally, by 1974 public housing bore the stigma of the federal poorhouse.

As surely as public housing mirrored federal policy and the national mood, it reflected even more the housing preferences, redevelopment aspirations, and social prejudices of cities. Two urgent local issues—ghettoization and the redevelopment of the blighted central city—profoundly influenced the direction of public housing policy in Philadelphia.

The Quaker City boasted a long history of vigorous housing reform activity dating from the nineteenth century. But as early as 1934, under the Public Works Administration Housing Division, Philadelphia housing reformers faced the reality that among the city's poorly housed, blacks occupied the worst dwellings. Finding sites for black housing projects confounded city reformers and undermined the communitarian goal of providing good, low-cost housing in low-density communities.

Therefore, postwar urban reformers in Philadelphia mobilized for war on two fronts: against the economic and physical decay of the central city, and against the horror of black ghettoization. Like the hero of Philadelphia's postwar reform, Joseph Clark, city housers and planners regarded the ghetto as the singular obstacle to the goal of urban economic and physical revitalization.

Public housing became an important weapon in the war against the slum and the ghetto. In this crusade, however, reformers forced on it conflicting missions. On the one hand, city reformers, planners, and intergroup relations experts enlisted public housing as an effective means for achieving the goal of a more brotherly Philadelphia. On the other hand, they charged public housing with rehousing poor black families removed from their neighborhoods to make way for the modern office complexes and apartment towers symbolic of the postindustrial city.

An element of tragedy pervades the history of public housing; it began with glowing dreams in the 1920s and ended amid a storm of vilification in the 1970s. Public housing could not, and should not, have been expected to bear the heavy social burden of housing and rehousing the social chaff of urban renewal or the victims of a racially exclusionary housing market. Public housing bore an even greater onus. The government-built and bureaucratically managed complexes contrasted too starkly with American housing norms. That these universally maligned and horribly maintained projects degenerated into warehouses for the urban poor attests to the failure of American housing policy.

How can America decently house low-income families? Housers in Philadelphia in the 1930s so confidently answered that question by pointing to public housing. Tragically, such optimism no longer exists.

Notes,
Bibliographical Note,
Index

Notes

The following abbreviations are used in the Notes to identify sources of materials cited.

AAP	Armstrong Association Papers
CCCP	Citizens' Council on City Planning
CDH	Committee on Democracy in Housing
COEHO	Committee on Equal Housing Opportunity
DHCR	Defense Housing Coordinators Records
FCR	Fellowship Commission Records
FDRL	Franklin Delano Roosevelt Library
FDRP	Franklin Delano Roosevelt Papers
FHCDVP	Fair Housing Committee of Delaware Valley Papers
GPMP	Greater Philadelphia Movement Papers
HADVP	Housing Association of Delaware Valley Papers
HDR	Housing Division Records (Public Works Administration Housing Division)
HUDR	U.S. Department of Housing and Urban Development Records
KP	John B. Kelly Papers
RG, NA	National Archives, Washington, D.C., Record Group
NAACP	National Association for the Advancement of Colored People (Philadelphia Branch) Papers
NECR	U.S. National Emergency Committee Records
OEMR	U.S. Office of Emergency Management Records
PACH	Philadelphia Advisory Committee on Housing
PBRP	Philadelphia Board of Realtors Papers
PHA	Philadelphia Housing Association
PHAR	Philadelphia Housing Authority Records
RAHR	Richard Allen Homes Records
TUA	Temple Urban Archives
ULP	Urban League (Philadelphia Branch) Papers
WCP	Wharton Center Papers
WLRP	William L. Rafsky Papers

Preface

1. William Moore, *The Vertical Ghetto: Every Day Life in an Urban Project* (New York: Random House 1969); Lee Rainwater, *Behind Ghetto Walls: Black Family Life in a Federal Slum* (Chicago: Aldine 1970); and Harrison Salisbury, "The Shook-Up Generation: Problem Youngsters Spring from the Housing Jungle," *New York Times*, March 26, 1958.

Chapter 1. The Roots of Public Housing

1. See Gwendolyn Wright, *Building the Dream: A Social History of Housing in America* (New York: Pantheon, 1981), pp. 193–214; Philadelphia *Inquirer*, June 7, 1925; and Kenneth Jackson, *The Crabgrass Frontier: The Suburbanization of the United States* (New York: Oxford University Press, 1985), pp. 174–177.

2. David P. Thelen, "Social Tensions and the Origins of Progressivism," *Journal of American History* 56, no. 2 (September 1969): 323–341; Roy Lubove, *The Progressives and the Slums: Tenement House Reform in New York City, 1890–1917* (Pittsburgh: University of Pittsburgh Press, 1962), Chapter 1.

3. Lubove, *Progressives and Slums*, pp. 2–6.

4. On efficiency mindedness and progressivism, see Robert Wiebe, *The Search for Order, 1877–1920* (New York: Hill & Wang, 1967); and Robert H. Bremner, *From the Depths: The Discovery of Poverty in the United States* (New York: 1969).

5. Lubove, *Progressives and Slums*, passim.

6. Ibid., pp. 81–115; Anthony Jackson, *A Place Called Home: A History of Low-Cost Housing in Manhattan* (Cambridge, Mass.: M.I.T. Press, 1976), pp. 111–125; and John F. Sutherland, "Housing the Poor in the City of Homes: Philadelphia at the Turn of the Century," in *The Peoples of Philadelphia: A History of Ethnic Groups and Lower-Class Life, 1790–1940*, ed. Allen Davis and Mark Haller (Philadelphia: Temple University Press, 1973), pp. 175–196.

7. Allen F. Davis, *Spearheads for Reform: The Social Settlement Movement, 1890–1914* (New York: Oxford University Press, 1967), pp. 19, 66–70; Jacob Riis, *How the Other Half Lives* (New York, 1890). On Hunter, see Thomas Philpott, *The Slum and the Ghetto: Neighborhood Deterioration and Middle Class Reform, Chicago, 1880–1930* (New York: Oxford University Press, 1978), pp. 29–41. On Veiller, see Lubove, *Progressives and Slums*, pp. 117–184.

8. Gwendolyn Wright discusses the term *houser* as used by Adams and Graham Taylor in her *Moralism and the Modern Home* (Chicago: University of Chicago Press, 1980), pp. 108, 225, 170; see also John F. Bauman, "Disinfecting the Industrial City," The Philadelphia Housing Commission and Scientific Efficiency, 1909–1916," in Michael Ebner and Eugene Tobin, eds., *The Age of Urban Reform: New Perspectives on the Progressive Era* (Port Washington, New York, 1977), pp. 125–128.

9. See Lawrence Veiller, *The National Housing Association: A New Organization to Improve Housing Conditions, Both Urban and Suburban* (New York: National Housing Association, 1910).

10. Davis, *Spearheads for Reform*, pp. 14–17; and Interview, John

Sutherland with Dorothy S. Montgomery, November 3, 1969, TUA. On Cope Prize and workingmen's housing, see Edward D. Boyer to Bernard Newman, June 22, 1913, HADVP; and *Housing Betterment*, May 1916.

11. On the "value of a model block," see Newman to Mrs. Charles H. Frazier, February 29, 1916, Box 1, Folder 148, HADVP.

12. See Howard Gillette, "The Evolution of Neighborhood Planning: From The Progressive Era to the 1949 Housing Act," *Journal of Urban History* 9 (August 1983): 424–425; Roy Lubove, "New Cities for Old: The Urban Reconstruction Program of the 1930s," *Social Studies* 53 (November 1962): 203–206; and Davis, *Spearheads for Reform*, pp. 76–77.

13. See Lewis Mumford, *The Culture of Cities* (New York: Harcourt, Brace & World, 1938), pp. 6–9, 223–295.

14. On Perry's neighborhood unit, see Gillette, "Evolution of Neighborhood Planning," pp. 421–434; Ebenezer Howard, *Garden Cities of Tomorrow* (Cambridge, Mass.: M.I.T. Press, 1965). Also, on Unwin and the translation of Howard's ideas into a town planning movement, see Arthur M. Edwards, *The Design of Suburbia: A Critical Study in Environmental History* (London: Pembridge Press, 1981), pp. 82–96.

15. See John Robert Mullin, "City Planning in Frankfurt, Germany, 1925–1932: A Study in Practical Utopianism," *Journal of Urban History* 4 (November 1977): 3–28; and Lubove, *Progressives and Slums*, pp. 217–256.

16. On housing and World War I, see John F. Sutherland, "World War I Federal Housing in Philadelphia: The Reluctant Departure," paper delivered at Philadelphia Bicentennial Meeting of the American Studies Association, April 1976; and Sadie Tanner Mossell, "The Standard of Living among One Hundred Negro Migrant Families in Philadelphia," *Annals* 97 (November 1921): 174–175.

17. Robert Moore Fisher, *Twenty Years of Public Housing: Economic Aspects of the Federal Program* (Westport, Conn.: 1959), pp. 74–78; Daniel Schaffer, *Garden Cities for America: The Radburn Experience* (Philadelphia: Temple University Press, 1982), pp. 34–35; and Sutherland, "World War I Federal Housing in Philadelphia," pp. 4–7.

18. Sutherland, "World War I Federal Housing in Philadelphia," pp. 10–11; and Jackson, *A Place Called Home*, pp. 158–182.

19. Isadore Lubin to Dorothy Kahn, April 17, 1934, HADVP; Edith Elmer Wood, *Recent Trends in American Housing* (New York: Macmillan, 1931), pp. 72–73; and Sutherland, "World War I Federal Housing in Philadelphia," p. 10.

20. Ibid., pp. 9–11.

21. Fisher, *Twenty Years of Public Housing*, p. 76.

22. On black migration to Philadelphia, see Myra L. Manly, "Where Negroes Live in Philadelphia," *Opportunity: A Journal of Negro Life* 1 (May 20, 1923): 10–15.

23. Armstrong Association, *Report of Negro Population and Industries in Philadelphia*, August 12, 1927, AAP; and Bernard Newman, "Philadelphia's Negro Population," mimeographed, June 10, 1930, HADVP; interview with Shirley Parham, January 17, 1986; Mossell, "Standard of Living," pp. 174–205.

24. Edith E. Wood to Bernard Newman, October 12, 1921, Box 65, Folder 478, HADVP; Wood to Secretary of Commerce Herbert Hoover, n.d., ibid.

25. Newman to Wood, October 17, 1921, ibid.; Newman to Wood, March 10, 1924, ibid.

26. Lubove, *Progressives and Slums*, pp. 217–256. Newman quotes from letter to William Deane Ham, July 16, 1924, Box 32, Folder 112, HADVP; see also Newman to James Ford, executive secretary of Better Homes, Inc., November 8, 1926, Box 31, Folder 46, HADVP.

27. See Newman to John Gries, June 19, 1923, Box 32, Folder 112, HADVP.

28. See James Ford to Newman, September 9, 1927, Box 31, Folder 46, HADVP; and "Campaign for 1923," *New York Times*, April 1, 1923. On the significant role played by women in the Better Homes Campaign, see "Names Suggested for Better Homes Campaign," February 1927, Box 31, Folder 46, HADVP.

29. The secretary of commerce is quoted in *New York Times*, April 1, 1923. On Newman's award of gold medal to best house design, see "Low-Cost Dwellings for Sale in All Parts of City," Box 31, Folder 46, HADVP; see also Better Homes, *Everymans House: A Plan Book of Small Houses*, cited in ibid.

30. On the role of Philadelphia building and loans, see "Low Cost Housing—What the Rest of the Country Can Learn from Philadelphia," *American City*, April 1929, p. 102. On the PHA's Better Housing Building and Loan, see announcement of Better Homes Week, April 25–May 1, 1926, Box 31, Folder 46, HADVP; see also Wood, *Recent Trends*, pp. 44–45, 90.

31. See Newman to Roberta C. Williams, Travelers Aid Society, February 10, 1931, HADVP. On the "education of the builder," see Newman, "What the Rest of the Country Can Learn from Philadelphia." On Whittier Center and housing, see Harry A. Moul, *The Work of the Whittier Center* (Philadelphia: Whittier Center, 1927). On other limited-dividend ventures, see *Five Year Report of the Michigan Boulevard Garden Apartments Building Corporation* (Chicago, 1955), HADVP pamphlets.

32. Lubove, *Community Planning in the 1920s*, pp. 31–48; Schaffer, *Garden Cities for America*, pp. 57–58, 73. Newman was a member of the Regional Planning Federation (RPF) of the Philadelphia Tri-State Region (TSR). See RPF of TSR, *Planned Progress* 2 (March 1929); see also RPF, *Regional Planning: The Region—Past, Present and Future* (Philadelphia: Regional Planning Federation, 1931).

33. Mullin, "City Planning in Frankfurt, Germany," pp. 22; also Eric J. Sandeen, "The International Style Meets the New Deal: Oscar Stonorov and the Mackley Homes Project," paper delivered at the biennial meeting of the American Studies Association, November 6, 1983.

34. On the impact of the Great Depression, see Octavia Hill Association, Minutes, April 16, October 16, and December 17, 1930, Octavia Hill Association Papers, TUA; Jackson, *A Place Called Home*, pp. 180–186; and Editors of Fortune, *Housing America* (New York: Harcourt Brace, 1932), pp. 6–24.

35. See Newman, "What the Rest of the Country Can Learn from Phila-

delphia," pp. 38–41; and Newman to Harold Buttenheim, editor of *American City,* September 19, 1930, Box 32, Folder 60, HADVP.

36. On Buttenheim's crusade to abolish slums, see Harold Buttenheim to Newman, "Revised Draft of Letter to Prospective Members of the American Housing Council," March 21, 1928, Box 32, Folder 60, HADVP; and Buttenheim to Newman, October 4, 1928, ibid.

37. On Housing Conference, see Mel Scott, *American City Planning Since 1890* (Berkeley: University of California Press, 1969), pp. 284–285; and Arthur Evans Wood, "Home and the Housing Expert," *Nation* 133 (December 23, 1931): 693.

38. Wood, *Recent Trends,* p. 190.

39. Chambers, *Seedtime of Reform,* pp. 133–138.

40. On La Follette and the emergence of public works legislation, see Newman to Buttenheim, February 2, 1932, Box 32, Folder 60, HADVP. Newman talked about "Better Homes" on WCAU Radio, circa November 1931, Box 31 Folder 46, HADVP.

Chapter 2. The New Deal Housing Projects

1. On the early depression, see Albert Romasco, *The Poverty of Abundance: Hoover, The Nation, The Depression* (New York: Oxford University Press, 1965), pp. 125–172; also see John F. Bauman, "The City, the Depression and Relief: The Philadelphia Experience, 1929–1941," Ph.D. dissertation, Rutgers University, 1969.

2. On Karl de Schweinitz and the Philadelphia Committee on Unemployment Relief, see Bauman, "City, Depression, and Relief," pp. 134–154.

3. See Arthur M. Schlesinger, Jr., *The Age of Roosevelt: The Coming of the New Deal* (Boston: Houghton Mifflin, 1958), pp. 14–23; also Loula D. Lasker, "The Chance to Rebuild the U.S.A.," *Survey Graphic* 22 (August 1933): 420–421. On FDR and the American Construction Council, see Frank Freidel, *Franklin D. Roosevelt: The Ordeal* (Boston: Little Brown, 1954), pp. 151–158; on the origins of public works legislation, see Nathaniel Keith, *Politics and the Housing Crisis Since 1930* (New York: Universe Books, 1973), p. 22.

4. Eugenie Ladner Birch and Deborah Gardner, "The Seven-Percent Solution: A Review of Philanthropic Housing, 1870–1910," *Journal of Urban History* 7 (August 1981): 403–439.

5. See J. A. McCallum, president of the Philadelphia Housing Association, to Victor Abel, architect of Earlington project, and numerous other correspondence and blueprints relating to the limited-dividend project proposals forwarded to Washington, D.C., all in File H-3000, HDR, RG 196, NA; see also Russell Van Nest Black, regional planner and regional representative of NRA, to Robert Kohn, September 9, 1933, approving "Proposed Low-Cost Housing Project of Hill Creek Homes, Inc.," in File H-3000, HDR, RG 196, NA.

6. On Stonorov, see Eric J. Sandeen, "The International Style Meets the New Deal: Oscar Stonorov and the Mackley Housing Project," paper presented at Biennial Convention of the American Studies Association, November 6,

1983. On Stonorov's social survey, see Mary Susan Cole, "Catherine Bauer and the Public Housing Movement," Ph.D. dissertation, George Washington University, 1975, pp. 215–220, 225–227.

7. On the Carl Mackley Homes, see Juniata Park Housing Corporation, *Carl Mackley Houses, Cayuga Street, Philadelphia, Sponsored by the American Federation of Full-Fashioned Hosiery Workers* (Philadelphia, n.d.), HADV; and PWA Press Release No. 3052, "Carl Mackley Housing," in HDR, RG 196, NA.

8. See "Housing in Philadelphia: Union Sponsored Project Hailed as Model for U.S.," *Christian Science Monitor*, November 2, 1937, p. 7. Note that the project became the center for labor housing agitation; see John Edelman, secretary of the Labor Housing Conference and an officer of the American Federation of Full-Fashioned Hosiery Workers, to Newman, May 17, 1935, HADVP. Catherine Bauer spoke about the Mackley project and its significance in *Modern Housing* (Boston: Houghton Mifflin, 1934).

9. Bauer quote from "Statement on the Housing Situation," August 31, 1934, HADVP; see Bonnie Fox Schwartz, *The Civil Works Administration, 1933– 1934* (Princeton: Princeton University Press, 1984); Charles Ascher, "The Puzzle of Public Housing," *Survey* 70 (August 1934): 242; see also Robert Moore Fisher, *Twenty Years of Public Housing: Economic Aspects of the Federal Program* (Westport, Conn.: Greenwood, 1975), pp. 84–85.

10. "Public Statement on the Abolishment of the Housing Division and the Passage of the National Housing Act," submitted by the Labor Housing Conference, the Housing Study Guild, and the Federation of Architects, Engineers and Chemists, June 25, 1934, HADVP; and National Association of Housing Officials, *Housing Yearbook, 1935* (Chicago: NAHO, 1935), pp. 4–5.

11. On "How to Stall," see Newman to Harold Buttenheim, December 21, 1934, in Box 32, Folder 60, HADVP; and Bernard Newman, "Recommendations on How to Stall on a Federal Housing Program," n.d., circa June 26, 1934, File H-3000.09, HDR, RG 196, NA; Transcript of Conference with Colonel Horatio Hackett, Washington, D.C., June 26, 1934, Series III, Folder 408, HADVP; and Carol Arnovici to Newman, July 7, 1934, ibid.

12. Interview, John Sutherland with Dorothy Montgomery, November 3, 1969, TUA; Mel Scott, *American City Planning Since 1890* (Berkeley: University of California Press, 1969), pp. 324–325. See also Newman's letter to Horatio Hackett, Housing Division, September 25, 1934, requesting that Hackett visit Philadelphia and tour the city with the Unwin party, File H-3000.09, HDR, RG 196, NA.

13. On the Baltimore Housing Conference, see "Summary of Report on the American Housing Program Drafted by European Authorities," October 24, 1934, mimeographed, in Official File, Box 2, FDRL; for quote on "securing adequate housing accommodations," see National Association of Housing Officials, *A Housing Program for the United States* (Chicago, 1934), p. 9, in HADV pamphlets.

14. Interview, John Sutherland with Dorothy S. Montgomery, November 2, 1969, TUA.

15. For quotes, see Harold Ickes to W. Logan MacCoy, May 4, 1934, Central Classified Files, File I-276, Records of the Secretary of the Interior, RG

48, NA; see also A. R. Clas to Executive Director of National Emergency Council, October 14, 1935, Central Housing Committee files, NECR, RG 44, NA.

16. On PACH activities, especially its war on slums, see Philadelphia Advisory Committee on Housing (PACH), Minutes, October 31, 1934, File H-3000.703 HDR, RG 196, NA; on black housing agenda, see Hackett to Newman, March 15, 1935, ibid.

17. On black unemployment, see Joseph H. Willits, "Some Impact of the Depression upon the Negro in Philadelphia," *Opportunity,* July 1933, pp. 200–201.

18. On slum concerns, see Helen Alfred, "The Challenge of the Slums," *Hygeia,* February 1935, pp. 122–127; "Fire Hazards," Philadelphia Housing Association Press Release, September 20, 1923, HADVP; and Newman to John J. Cuerin, July 13, 1934, HADVP.

19. Moore quote in "Statement of J. Hampton Moore," July 4, 1933, found in J. Hampton Moore Collection, in Historical Society of Pennsylvania, Philadelphia; see also Newman to A. R. Clas, July 8, 1935, HADVP.

20. For quote on Chamber of Commerce's cooperation, see Philadelphia Chamber of Commerce, Minutes, April 11, 1935, Minute Books of Philadelphia Chamber found in Historical Society of Pennsylvania, Philadelphia; "Is the Northeast Part of the City?" in *Frankford Dispatch,* February 2, 1934, p. 1; and Jacob Gross, president of South Philadelphia Realty Board, to Ickes, May 9, 1935, in John Ihlder Papers, FDRL.

21. On revival of Democratic party, see Irwin F. Greenberg, "The Philadelphia Democratic Party, 1911–1934," Ph.D. dissertation, Temple University, 1973, pp. 434–533; on Wilson, see Kurt L. K. Rossi, "Philadelphia's Forgotten Mayor: S. Davis Wilson," in *Pennsylvania Dispatch* 51 (April 1984): 154–166; on John B. Kelly and Philadelphia politics, see Scrapbooks of John B. Kelly, in Free Library of Philadelphia, KP. Bernard Newman quoted Ickes on "nonpolitical" nature of public works, in letter to Horatio Hackett, April 1, 1935, File H-3000.73, HDR, RG 196, NA; see also clippings, Philadelphia *Record,* June 23, 1936, Philadelphia *Evening Bulletin,* June 27, 1934, and Philadelphia *Record* August 10, 1934, KP.

22. Philadelphia *Record,* October 20, 1935, KP; for ethnic data, see Philadelphia Housing Association maps showing "Location of Foreign Born Population in Groups of 250 (approx.), 1920, 1930, 1940," n.d., HADVP.

23. On Kelly's pledge to "wipe out all City slums," see Philadelphia *Public Ledger,* August 13, 1935.

24. On Wilson's projects and politics, see *Journal of City Council,* March 8, 1934, and August 26, 1936; and Philadelphia *Inquirer,* October 25, 1935.

25. On black housing, see Works Progress Administration, Philadelphia Property Survey, Philadelphia Surveys, Colored Housing, Bulletins 26 and 27, West and Central Philadelphia Districts A-1 and A-2, April 10, 1936, File H-3000, HDR, RG 196, NA; "Housing Conditions in Philadelphia: Extract from Complaints and Appeals for Help Addressed to the Housing Division," n.d., mimeographed, File H-3000.9, HDR, RG 196, NA.

26. H. Viscount Nelson, Jr., "Race and Race Consciousness of Phila-

delphia Negroes with Special Emphasis on the Years Between 1927 and 1940," Ph.D. dissertation, University of Pennsylvania, 1969, pp. 2–15, 17–18, 95–99, 349–350.

27. On Taylor's Committee on DeSlumming, see Robert Gray Taylor to Newman, February 3, 1934, HADVP; on black middle-class housing, see reports of David Wyatt, secretary of Industrial and Research Department of the Armstrong Association, to Board of Managers of Armstrong Association, December 1934–January 1935, mimeographed, ULP, TUA; see also William N. Blakeney to Newman, October 6, 1933, HADVP.

28. Robert Gray Taylor to Newman, February 3, 1934, HADVP; see also Henry Homer Jefferson to Horatio B. Hackett, May 2, 1935, File H-3000.9, HDR, RG 196, NA.

29. On *Tribune* campaign, see Eustace Gay, managing editor of Philadelphia *Tribune*, to H. A. Gray, PWA Housing Division, December 3, 1936, File H-3000.9, HDR, RG 196, NA; see also Philadelphia *Tribune*, May 28, 1936, December 9, 1937, and July 14, 1938.

30. On blacks and "fashionable" housing such as New York's Dunbar Apartments, see Madge Headley Priest in T. S. Woofter's *Negro Problems in Cities* (New York: Negro Universities Press 1928), pp. 152–170; see also "Transcript of Meeting between Group of WPA Women from 11th and York Streets" (a "committee of twenty-two women mostly negro") and Newman, August 5, 1936, mimeographed, HADVP.

31. See Janice Carp of Neighborhood Center, 422–428 Bainbridge Avenue, to FDR, May 9, 1935, in File H-3000.9 DRF, RG 196, NA. Note W. E. B. Du Bois's views on race relations and segregation in the 1930s in Du Bois, "Postscript," *Crisis*, January 1933, pp. 140–141.

32. See Abbie Johnson, Grand Daughter Ruler, Protective Order of Elks, to Harold Ickes, March 12, 1935, File H-3000.9, HDR, RG 196, NA; Robert Baskerville, Omega Psi Phi, to Ickes, March 23, 1935, ibid.; Arthur DuBois, PWA Housing Division, to Carrie Younker, Philadelphia Federation of Settlements, April 4, 1936, in response to telegrams emanating from March 27, 1936 meeting of 500 tenants, ibid.; and letter of Cornelius Garlick, secretary of Slum Clearance Committee of Philadelphia NAACP, to Horatio Hackett, May 11, 1935, ibid. See also Transcript of conference with Negro groups arranged for by John Edelman, May 21, 1935, mimeographed, HADVP. On housing committee of National Negro Conference, see H. A. Gray to Newman, October 21, 1936, HADVP; for discussion of NNC, see Raymond Wolters, *Negroes in the Great Depression: The Problem of Economic Recovery* (Westport, Conn.: Greenwood Press, 1970), pp. 357–376.

33. See Memorandum, Horatio Hackett to Ickes, April 15, 1935, File I-276, Pa., Records of the Secretary of the Interior, RG 48, NA.

34. Hyman Cunin, assistant architectural engineer, to B. M. Pettit, Initiation Branch, HD, March 23, 1935, File H-3000.703, HDR, RG 196, NA.

35. On Weaver's appointments of R. R. Wright and Crystal Bird Fauset, see Newman to Hackett, May 3, 1935, HADVP; see also Memorandum, A. R. Clas to Ickes, May 23, 1935, recommending Wright "as an outstanding citizen

representing the older Negro interests in Philadelphia," in File I-276, Pa., Records of the Secretary of the Interior, RG 48, NA; see also Philadelphia *Tribune*, August 19, 1937, describing Fauset's political strength as head of the Colored Women's Democratic League.

36. Walter Thomas and Samuel Wetherhill, both of City Planning Commission, to A. R. Clas, May 28, 1935, in File H-3000.2, HDR, RG 196, NA.

37. J. D. Goodman to Newman, October 1, 1935, HADVP.

38. For Newman quotes, see Newman to Meta Herder, St. Paul, Minnesota, June 1, 1935, HADVP; and Newman to Mrs. Allan Reith, Council of Social Agencies, Milwaukee, Wisconsin, January 8, 1934, HADVP.

39. Philadelphia Committee on Public Affairs, "The Public Housing Program in Philadelphia," March 15, 1940, mimeographed, HADVP; see also Newman to Clas, May 31, 1935, File H-3000, HDR, RG 196, NA; and DuBois to Clas, July 25, 1935, File H-3000.2, HDR, RG 196, NA.

40. The *Louisville Lands* case is discussed in Sam Bass Warner, *The Urban Wilderness: A History of the American City* (New York: Harper & Row, 1972), p. 23; and Fisher, *Twenty Years of Public Housing*, pp. 86–89. See also Philadelphia Advisory Committee on Housing, Minutes of Special Meeting, May 9, 1935, HADVP; and Clas to DuBois, March 21, 1936, File H-3001.09, HDR, RG 196, NA.

41. On the record of the Housing Division, see Fisher, *Twenty Years of Public Housing*, pp. 86–87. See also Federal Emergency Administration of Public Works, *The Story of the PWA* (Washington, D.C.: GPO, 1936), HADVP; and Newman to Clas, July 26, 1935, File H-3000.1, HDR, RG 196, NA.

42. Harold Ickes, *The Secret Diary of Harold Ickes* (New York: Simon and Schuster, 1954), I:610.

43. Alfred Fellheimer, "Low-Rent Housing: Planning American Standards for Low-Rent Housing," *American Architect*, February 1935; see also Gwendolyn Wright, *Building the Dream: A Social History of Housing in America* (New York: Pantheon, 1981), pp. 226–227.

44. On Hill Creek Homes, see Memorandum, M. D. Carrel to A. R. Clas, July 16, 1934, File HD-106, HDR, RG 196, NA; and Transcript of meeting of Technical Advisory Committee of PWA, September 11, 1935, HADVP. See also Frank Smith to Newman, October 30, 1937, HADVP; Zane Miller, *Suburb: Neighborhood and Community in Forest Park, Ohio, 1935–1976* (Knoxville: University of Tennessee Press, 1981); Joseph Arnold, *The New Deal in the Suburbs: A History of the Greenbelt Towns Program, 1935–1954* (Columbus: Ohio State University Press, 1971).

45. Arthur DuBois, "A Report to FEA of PWA, Housing Division," n.d., Box 44, Central Housing Committee, NECR, RG 44, NA. See also "Foreward" to Symposium on Legal Foundation of America Housing Program, in *Law and Contemporary Problems* 5 (March 1934): 135–136; and Merlo Pusey, "Our Housing Hodge Podge," *Harper's* 173 (January 1936): 60–61.

46. On efforts to explain housing in terms of slum clearance, see Philadelphia Real Property Inventory, "Release," February 12, 1937, Bulletin 49, "Crime and the Housing Situation," Box 222, File H-3000.3, HDR, RG 196,

NA; and "Housing and Delinquency: Housing in Relationship to Delinquency and Crime," n.d., in Central Classified Files, File I-276, Records of the Secretary of the Interior, RG 48, NA.

Chapter 3. Bauhauses for the Worthy Poor

1. On the tenement collapse of December 1936, see Eugene Pharo, "Philadelphia Named City of Homeless," Washington *Post,* January 10, 1937, p. 7.

2. On public outrage at the tenement collapse, see "Cave-in Toll Mounts as Girl Dies," Philadelphia *Tribune,* December 24, 1936; Philadelphia *Inquirer,* December 31, 1936.

3. On S. Davis Wilson and his crowbar, see "City-Built Homes Planned by Wilson," Philadelphia *Inquirer,* December 31, 1936, p. 1. On the suggestion that the WPA build a barrack for the homeless, see Philadelphia *Record,* December 29, 1936.

4. For Kelly's charge of "skullduggery," see Philadelphia *Inquirer,* December 22, 1936; *Evening Bulletin,* December 22, 1936, and Philadelphia *Inquirer,* December 31, 1936.

5. On the formation of the Tenants' League, see Philadelphia *Tribune,* December 31, 1936; and Philadelphia *Record,* December 29, 1936.

6. On the Tenants' League, see mimeographed flyers, "For Decent Homes at Low Rents!!!" "Stop Unfair Eviction of Mrs. Chandler," and "Defend Your Neighbor," all HADVP. See also Bernard Childs, Executive Secretary of Tenants' League, to Newman, July 9, 1940, HADVP.

7. On the citywide conference, see "Mass Action Sought on Local Housing," Philadelphia *Tribune,* December 9, 1937.

8. On the creation of the Philadelphia Housing Authority, see Newman to H. A. Gray, director of housing, PWA, October 13, 1937, HADVP.

9. Nathaniel Keith, *Politics and the Housing Crisis Since 1930* (New York: Universe Books, 1973), pp. 30–36; on Bauer and the LHC and Bohn, see National Association of Housing Officials, *Summary of Hearings on the Wagner Housing Bill Before the Committee on Education and Labor of the United States Senate, April 20–25, and 29, 1936* (Chicago: NAHO, 1936), p. 43.

10. On the Wagner Act, see Testimony of Helen Alfred, in Senate Committee on Education and Labor, *Hearings on S. 4424: Bill to Provide Federal Assistance to the States and Political Subdivisions for the Elimination of Unsafe and Unsanitary Housing Conditions,* 74th Cong. 2d sess., 1936, pp. 132–133; NAHO, Summary of Hearings, pp. 74–75. On motivation for the Wagner-Steagall Housing Act, see Lawrence M. Friedman, *Government and Slum Housing* (New York: Rand McNally, 1968), pp. 100–103; see also classic account of Wagner Act, Timothy McDonnell, *The Wagner Housing Act* (Chicago: Loyola University Press, 1937).

11. Charles Abrams, *The City Is the Frontier* (New York: Harper & Row, 1965), pp. 21–22.

12. On decentralization implicit in legislation, see John Ihlder to Leon Keyserling, February 27, 1937, Ihlder Papers, FDRL. On the appointment of Philadelphia Housing Authority members, see Philadelphia *Evening Bulletin,*

February 5, 1937; on Barnes's appointment, see Newman to Gray, October 13, 1937, HADVP. Newman saw Barnes as "the only one of the group who, prior to the appointment, showed any interest in housing and his particular interest is in housing for the Negro population," ibid.

13. See Philadelphia Housing Authority, *Minutes*, January–December, 1938, found in Philadelphia Housing Authority Records (PHAR). Hereinafter cited as HA *Minutes*.

14. See Housing Committee of the Committee of Seventy to S. Davis Wilson, n.d., circa 1938, in Series III, Folder 320, HADVP; on other cities, see Keith, *Politics and the Housing Crisis*, p. 152; Devereaux Bowly, *The Poorhouse: Subsidized Housing in Chicago, 1895–1976* (Carbondale: University of Illinois Press, 1978), pp. 27–33; Friedman, *Government and Slum Housing*, pp. 73–146.

15. For Churchill quote, see National Association of Housing Officials, *Practical Standards for Modern Housing: A Report on Physical Standards and Construction Prepared in Collaboration with the American Public Health Association* (Washington, D.C.: NAHO, 1939); see also Mark Gelfand, *A Nation of Cities: The Federal Government and Urban America, 1933–1965* (New York: Oxford University Press, 1975), p. 135.

16. On the positive impact of projects, see Arthur DuBois to A. R. Clas, March 4, 1936, File H-3000, HDR, RG 196, NA; and Civic Club of Philadelphia, Minutes, March 28, 1938, and November 27, 1939, Historical Society of Pennsylvania, Philadelphia.

17. On Old Swedes' site, see "Old Swedes' Site Report," in Central Classified Files, Emergency Housing Corporation Records of the Secretary of the Interior, RG 48, NA; see also Philadelphia Housing Association, maps showing "Location of Foreign Born . . . 1920, 1930, 1940," HADVP; "Outline Map Showing Ratio of Negro Population, 1930," comp. by Research Department of the Armstrong Association and Philadelphia Housing Association, ibid.; U.S. Bureau of the Census, *Fifteenth Census of the United States: 1930*, data taken from "Work Sheets," for Census Tracts 2 A, B, C and 4 A, B, in Free Library of Philadelphia; and "Excerpts from Southwark Public Hearings," April 15, 1940, HADVP.

18. On Tasker site, see Philadelphia Housing Authority, *Building Homes in Philadelphia: Report of the Philadelphia Housing Authority, July 1, 1939–June 30, 1941* (Philadelphia, 1941), pp. 14–16.

19. On Tasker design, see ibid., p. 15; see also Philadelphia Housing Authority, "Project Data," mimeographed, n.d., circa 1963, PHAR.

20. See Robert Weaver, "The Negro and Low-Rent Housing," address delivered at the Eastern Regional Conference of the National Negro Congress, Baltimore, October 7, 1938, TUA; Weaver, "The Negro in a Program of Public Housing," *Opportunity*, July 1938, pp. 198–203; and John Murchison, "The Negro and Low Rent Housing," *Crisis*, July 1935, pp. 199–200.

21. HA *Minutes*, September 27, 1937, December 29, 1937, February 12, 1938, March 11, 1939, and June 12, 1939; see also *Clearing Slums in Philadelphia: First Annual Report of the Philadelphia Housing Authority* (Philadelphia, 1939), HADVP. On James Weldon Johnson, see Philadelphia Housing Authority, *Building Homes in Philadelphia*, pp. 10–13.

22. Newman noted white complaint in a letter to A. R. Clas, May 31, 1935, File H-3000, HDR, RG 196, NA. On Glenwood site, see Philadelphia Committee on Public Affairs, "The Public Housing Program in Philadelphia," March 15, 1940, mimeographed, HADVP.

23. On Richard Allen, see Philadelphia Housing Authority, *Building Homes in Philadelphia*, pp. 17–21; data from U.S. Bureau of the Census, *1940 Census of Population: Selected Population and Housing Characteristics, Philadelphia* (Washington, D.C.: GPO, 1942), p. 63.

24. NAHO, *Practical Standards for Modern Housing*, pp. 7–12, 18.

25. On the expected impact of the "neighborhood unit" design, see Howard Gillette, "The Evolution of Neighborhood Planning: From the Progressive Era to the 1949 Housing Act," *Journal of Urban History* 9 (August 1983): 421–445; Catherine Bauer, *Modern Housing* (Boston: Houghton Mifflin, 1934), pp. 220–221; and Bowly, *The Poorhouse*, p. 84; Interview, John Sutherland with Dorothy S. Montgomery, November 3, 1969, TUA.

26. Wright, *Building the Dream*, p. 230; and Bowly, *The Poorhouse*.

27. See Philadelphia Housing Authority, *Building Homes in Philadelphia*, pp. 10–16; see also Newman, rough draft on "Outstanding Progress in Local Housing," HADVP; U.S. Housing Administration (USHA), *Design of Low-Rent Housing Projects* (Washington, D.C.: GPO, 1939), pp. 30–31; USHA, "Development Cost of a Low-Rent Housing Project," Bulletin No. 4 in Bulletins of Policy and Procedures, HDR; and NAHO, *Report of Committee on Physical Standards and Construction* (Washington, D.C.: GPO, 1939), pp. 5–9. The James Weldon Johnson Homes were considered to be housing for the "finer" poor black families, and it was more than coincidental that the project was named for a "cultured" black literary figure (conversation with Shirley Parham, director of Philadelphia Afro American Museum, May 4, 1984).

28. Bauer, *Modern Housing*, passim.

29. Philadelphia Housing Authority, "Projects Data," n.d., circa 1963, PHAR; on Ihlder, see NAHO, *Practical Standards for Modern Housing*.

30. See draft by Newman, "Outstanding Progress in Local Housing," HADVP; Nathan Straus, "Architects and the U.S.H.A.," USHA Division of Research and Information, Release, n.d. HADVP. See also Newman, "Factors in the Housing Problem," *Annals of the American Academy of Political and Social Science*, March 1937, pp. 2–6.

31. On the sterility and regimentation of housing projects, see USHA, *Design of Low-Rent Housing Projects* (Washington, D.C.: GPO, 1939), pp. 30–31. See also HA *Minutes*, September 6, 1939; Edith Elmer Wood, "One Third of a Nation," *Survey Graphic*, February 1940, pp. 84–89; and Dorothy Canfield, "I Visit a Housing Project," *Survey Graphic*, February 1940, 89–90.

32. USHA, "Initial Steps in Tenant Selection," Bulletin No. 22, in Bulletins on Policy and Procedure, HDR; see also "Suggested Procedures for Initial Tenant Selection on Renting," Bulletin No. 31, ibid.

33. On tenant selection and moral standards, see HA *Minutes*, June 24, 1940, and April 8, 1940; see also John F. Bauman, Edward Muller, and Norman Hummon, "Federal Slum or Waystation? Black Families and Phila-

delphia Public Housing During the 1940s," paper delivered at Ninth Biennial Convention of the American Studies Association, Philadelphia, 1983. Since public housing was restricted to families whose net family income did not exceed five times the rental value of their unit, most clients were respectable, working-class people with incomes under $1,000 a year; ibid.

34. Data from Philadelphia Housing Authority, *Real Property Survey, Philadelphia 1939, General Survey Tables*, vol. 6 (Philadelphia, 1939); see also Dr. Harry Barnes and Charles A. Shorter, Memorandum, "Information re: The Negro Population of Philadelphia and Substandard Housing Conditions," October 25, 1939, ULP.

35. Quote in Wood, "One Third of a Nation," p. 84.

36. See Bernard Childs, *The Amazing Case of Mr. Binns* (Philadelphia: Tenants League of Philadelphia, 1940); Philadelphia Board of Realtors, Minutes, December 18, 1939, June 5, 1940, and November 7, 1940, PBRP, in TUA; Office Secretary of Philadelphia Housing Authority to Newman, September 1, 1928, HADVP.

37. On the death of Wilson and the factions of the Democratic party, see John F. Bauman, "The City, the Depression, and Relief: The Philadelphia Experience, 1929–1941," Ph.D. dissertation, Rutgers University, 1969, pp. 304–313.

38. Philadelphia Housing Authority, *Building Homes in Philadelphia*, p. 28. On the demise of the housing program, see "Statement of Mayor Lamberton to Press," mimeographed, May 13, 1940, HADVP; and Nathan Straus, "Statement before Members of the Philadelphia Housing Authority, 2:30 P.M., Monday," mimeographed, July 1, 1940, HADVP.

39. *Journal of City Council*, June 20, 1940; Philadelphia Housing Authority, "End of the $15,000,000," News Bulletin No. 3, July 12, 1940, HADVP.

40. See Testimony of Carrie Younker, in "Excerpt from Southwark Public Housing [on desirability of a housing project in Southwark area]," April 15, 1940, HADVP.

Chapter 4. Housing America's Homelines

1. See Richard M. Dalfiume, "The Forgotten Years of the Negro Revolution," *Journal of American History* 55 (June 1968): 90–106; and Carl Abbott, "Portland in the Pacific War: Planning from 1940 to 1945," *Urbanism Past and Present* 6 (Winter/Spring 1981): 12–23. See also John Morton Blum, *V Was for Victory: Politics and Culture During World War II* (New York: Harcourt, 1976); and Richard R. Lingemen, *Don't You Know There's a War On?* (New York: Putnam, 1970).

2. Mark I. Gelfand, *A Nation of Cities: The Federal Government and Urban America, 1933–1965* (New York: Oxford University Press, 1975), pp. 125, 136–141; see also Albert Mayer, "Building Our Home-Lines," *Survey Graphic* 29 (February 1940): 55–57; and Loula Lasker, "Homes and Defense," *Survey Graphic* 30 (June 1941): 53–55.

3. "Statement of Mayor Lamberton to Press," mimeographed, May 13, 1940, HADVP; on housing crisis, see Philadelphia Committee on Public Affairs, "The Public Housing Program in Philadelphia," mimeographed, March 15, 1940, HADVP.

4. A. E. Watson, rear admiral, U.S. Navy, Commandant of Philadelphia Navy Yard, to Philadelphia Housing Authority, June 13, 1940, HADVP.

5. Donald Nelson's announcement appeared in the Philadelphia *Record*, September 20, 1940; data extrapolated from itemization of contracts awarded to Philadelphia area manufacturing firms for commodities and plant expansion during October 1940–October 1941; see J. H. Rhoads to E. E. Ashley, October 30, 1941, in Geographic Dockets, Philadelphia, DHCR, RG 207.

6. See A. F. Hinrichs, acting commissioner, Bureau of Labor Statistics, to Edmund Bacon, acting manager of the Philadelphia Housing Association, September 21, 1940, HADVP; Memorandum, Bernice Lapin to E. E. Ashley, April 14, 1942, Box 144, DHCR; U.S. House, Select Committee Investigating National Defense Migration, *Hearings*, 77th Cong. 1st sess., pp. 10,570–10,573.

7. See editorial, "To the Council," in Philadelphia *Record*, September 7, 1940; "Housing Shortage in Key Cities Major Handicap to Defense Plans," Philadelphia *Record*, August 7, 1940; and National Defense Commission, Co-ordinator of Defense Housing, "Locality Information Sheet on Defense Housing Program, Philadelphia," November 28, 1940, Division of Defense Housing Coordinator, Series 23, Office of Emergency Management Records, RG 703.

8. Edmund Bacon to M. D. McClean, general manager, Bendix Aviation Corp., November 21, 1940, HADVP.

9. On wartime housing for blacks, see Philadelphia Housing Association, "Housing for Negroes in Philadelphia," December 29, 1944, HADVP; Loren Green to Richard Ratcliff, September 8, 1943, Box 112, Homes Use Program, DHCR; "WPA Survey Reveals Need for Philadelphia Slum Clearance," Philadelphia *Independent*, June 2, 1940; Pennsylvania State Temporary Commission on the Urban Colored Population, "Report," May 1941, mimeographed, HADVP; and Herbert Garfinkel, *When Negroes March: The March on Washington Movement in the Organization Politics for FEPC* (New York: Free Press, 1969).

10. Philadelphia Housing Authority (aided by the Works Progress Administration), *Real Property Survey, Philadelphia, 1939: General Survey Tables*, vol. 6 (Philadelphia, 1939); and PHA, "Housing for Negroes in Philadelphia," December 29, 1944, HADVP.

11. Program Committee for City-Wide Housing Meeting, "Minutes," November 19, 1940, HADVP; flyer, "Housing and Defense: A City-Wide Meeting, Town Hall," December 10, 1940, in Series III, Folder 183, HADVP.

12. Conference on Planning Problems, Defense, and Urban Rehabilitation, *Proceedings of Conference* (Chicago, 1941), pp. 24–35; Vita of Edmund Bacon, in Philadelphia Housing Association (PHA) office files, Series III, Folder 44, HADVP; and PHA, "Housing Needs in Philadelphia Resulting from the National Defense Program," HADVP.

13. John Palmer Gavit, "Legitimate Military Objective," *Survey Graphic* 29 (January 1940): 122–123; and Mayer, "Building Our Home-lines," p. 56.

14. Edith Elmer Wood, Memorandum on "Federal Administration of Defense and Permanent Housing Activities," mimeographed, n.d. (presumably to FDR), in Samuel I. Rosenman Papers, FDRL.

15. Henry M. Propper, executive vice chairman of the National Committee on the Housing Emergency, Inc., to Coleman Woodbury, assistant administrator of National Housing Administration, June 28, 1944, in Key Official Files, DHCR, RG 207, NA.

16. See Maxey Morrison's series on defense housing in Philadelphia *Evening Public Ledger*, September 24 to September 28, 1940. Note that Philadelphia realtor Arthur Binns called the U.S. Housing Authority a "poison worse than the disease and . . . it will defeat any contribution to the solution of the low-cost housing problem in the present generation." Philadelphia *Record*, February 20, 1940.

17. Morrison, in Philadelphia *Evening Public Ledger*, September 27, 1940.

18. John Green, president of Industrial Union of Marine and Shipbuilding Workers of America, to Franklin D. Roosevelt, July 5, 1940, Official File 63, FDRL; Memorandum from Franklin D. Roosevelt to John Carmody, September 11, 1940, ibid.; Press Release, "Proposed Coordination of Housing Program," August 29, 1940, ibid.

19. Memorandum, Samuel I. Rosenman to Franklin D. Roosevelt, October 15, 1941, in Samuel I. Rosenman Papers, FDRL; Edith Elmer Wood, Memorandum on "Federal Administration of Defense and Permanent Housing Activities," mimeographed, n.d., in Rosenman Papers; Memorandum from H. Smith for FDR, "Program of the United States Housing Authority," October 28, 1941, in Official File 63, FDRL.

20. *Defense Housing Coordination: A Factual Summary of Origin and Operations*, a report forwarded by John H. Fahey, commissioner of Federal Home Loan Bank, November 6, 1941, in Series 21, Administration and Regional Files, DHCR, RG 207, NA.

21. "How Housing Has Been Done," mimeographed, n.d., probably written by Leon Keyserling, in Samuel I. Rosenman Papers, FDRL.

22. PHA, "Too Little and Too Late: War Housing in Philadelphia," March 15, 1942, Box 54, HADVP; PHA, "War Housing in Philadelphia," Confidential Report, n.d., circa July 1942, Box 41, HADVP.

23. Ibid.; "Labor Head Quits," Philadelphia *Record*, April 27, 1941; Philadelphia *Record*, April 26, 1941; Edmund Bacon, Confidential Report, "Defense Housing Activities in Philadelphia, July 19, 1940–June 26, 1942," Box 41, HADVP.

24. Philadelphia *Record*, April 27, 1941.

25. PHA, "Too Little and Too Late."

26. PHA, "War Housing in Philadelphia"; Edmund Bacon, Memorandum, "Defense Problems, Philadelphia Region," October 22, 1941, Box 41, HADVP.

27. PHA, "War Housing in Philadelphia"; "Police to Assist in Housing Survey," Philadelphia *Inquirer*, April 26, 1941.

28. PHA, "War Housing in Philadelphia"; and Report of field trip, Philadelphia, November 24, 1941, Frank A. Vanderlip, Jr., to Ward French, December 9, 1941, in Geographical Dockets, Philadelphia, DHCR.

29. Henry Solotow to J. Bion Philipson, September 17, 1941, Box 42, DHCR, RG 207, NA; and Philadelphia *Inquirer,* August 16, 1941.

30. "4000 U.S. Employees Will Be Shifted from Washington to Philadelphia," Philadelphia *Inquirer,* December 20, 1941; "Federal Workers Swarm into Philadelphia," Philadelphia *Inquirer,* March 23, 1942; "Housing Group Urges 8000 More Family Units," Philadelphia *Record,* February 18, 1942.

31. "Confidential" Press Release, "To the Congress of the United States," from Franklin D. Roosevelt, May 27, 1942, Official File 63, FDRL.

32. See Edmund Bacon, Confidential Memorandum, "Recommendations for War Housing Program," November 16, 1942, Box 41, Folder 185, HADVP; PHA, "War Housing in Philadelphia"; and Henry Propper, "Total War Hits Housing," *Survey Graphic,* August 1942, pp. 341–343.

33. Philadelphia Housing Authority, *Homes for War Workers: Report of the Philadelphia Housing Authority,* July 1942–June 1944 (Philadelphia, 1944).

34. Philadelphia *Evening Bulletin,* June 28, 1941; Philadelphia *Record,* September 6, 1941; and "Mayfair Protests Blacks in Housing," Philadelphia *Record,* June 14, 1942.

35. Confidential Memorandum to Executive Office of the President, Office of Emergency Management, Locality Program Report No. 6, Philadelphia, Pa., February 7, 1942, Box 14, RG 207, NA.

36. "Negroes Plan Suit in Housing Fight," Philadelphia *Inquirer,* September 27, 1942.

37. See Arthur Huff Fauset, "Paying for Defense the Hard Way," Philadelphia *Inquirer,* January 24, 1942; and Charles F. Palmer to Leon Keyserling, February 3, 1942, in Division of Defense Housing Coordination, Series 23, Office of Emergency Management Records, RG 703, NA.

38. Philadelphia *Record,* February 3, 1942, and February 10, 1942; and Philadelphia *Tribune,* March 7, 1942. See also Dalfiume, "Forgotten Years of the Negro Revolution," pp. 90–106.

39. Memorandum, Coleman Woodbury to Samuel I. Rosenman, October 15, 1941, Rosenman Papers, FDRL; see Nathan Straus to Eleanor Roosevelt, October 2, 1941, ibid. See also "Man Who Untangled TVA Is New Housing Czar," Philadelphia *Inquirer,* March 8, 1942; and *New York Times,* February 25, 1942.

40. Mary Simkhovitch, president of the National Public Housing Conference, to Franklin D. Roosevelt, February 25, 1942, Box 142, DHCR, RG 207, NA; and "Housing," *Survey Midmonthly* 77 (March 1942): 80–81.

41. Memorandum, Lawrence A. Appley, executive director, NHA, to Regional Directors, NHA, January 19, 1943, Box 137, DHCR, RG 207, NA; and Memorandum, "Conversion of Existing Buildings for War Housing," from Emmerich to John B. Blandford, n.d., circa January 1943, ibid.

42. "2950 Dwellings to Rise in Philadelphia," Philadelphia *Inquirer,* October 29, 1942; and "Seeks to Broaden Housing Production," Philadelphia *Inquirer,* April 26, 1942.

43. See R. J. Thomas, vice president of the CIO, "War Housing and Production," mimeographed, May 28, 1942, Box 137, DHCR, RG 207, NA.

44. John B. Blandford to William Green, president of the AFL, October 20, 1943, Key Official File, DHCR, RG 207, NA.

45. See Helen Fuller, "From Washington," n.d., unidentified clipping enclosed in letter, Crosby to Emmerich, December 8, 1942, Box 137, DHCR, RG 207, NA; and Bacon, "Recommendations for War Housing Program."

46. Thomas, "War Housing Production."

47. See Albert Mayer, "Why Dreary Housing Projects?" *Survey Graphic* 31 (February 1942): 82; and Philadelphia Housing Authority, *Homes for War Workers.*

48. PHA, "Notes on the War Housing Program," October 20, 1942, Box 41, Folder 185, HADVP; and Philadelphia *Inquirer,* October 29, 1942. See also Federal Public Housing Administration, *Bartram Village: 500 Low-Rent Homes for War Workers under Management of the Philadelphia Housing Authority* (Philadelphia, n.d., circa 1943), HADVP.

49. On Pennypack Woods, see Philadelphia *Record,* May 17, 1942; and Barbara Barnes, "The Defense Worker Is a Family Man," *Evening Bulletin,* February 9, 1942. On project ambience, see "Hill Creek in Bloom: Practical Suggestions for Housing Success," April 1940, mimeographed, Series III, 324, HADVP.

50. On wartime social life in housing projects, see the weekly columns in the Philadelphia *Tribune,* "In and Around the Richard Allen Homes," November 14, 1942, February 12, 1944, PHAR; also see Nellie Reynolds, "Trip Around the James Weldon Johnson Homes," Philadelphia *Tribune,* December 19, 1942; and copies of the Tasker Homes newspaper, *The Speaker,* 1941–1944, PHAR.

51. "Government Houses That City Builders Criticize," *Evening Bulletin,* March 27, 1942; and "Native Son Has Nothing on 'The Neck' Where Shipyard Homes Are Located," *People's Voice,* February 10, 1945.

52. "U.S. Housing Built in Philadelphia Is Half Empty," Philadelphia *Inquirer,* February 21, 1944; and "Negroes Need War Housing but Cannot Obtain It," Pittsburgh *Courier,* March 4, 1944.

53. "Minutes of Housing Committee of Interracial Commission," Box 43, Folder 214, HADVP; "Report of Study Made of Tacony Incidents and Their Causes," ibid.; and Pittsburgh *Courier,* October 16, 1943.

Chapter 5. Race, Redevelopment, and Rehousing

1. John H. Mollenkopf, *The Contested City* (Princeton: Princeton University Press, 1983); Carl Abbott, "Planning for the Homes Front in Seattle and Portland, 1940–1945," in *The Martial Metropolis: U.S. Cities in War and Peace,* ed. Roger W. Lotchin (New York: Praeger, 1984), pp. 163–191.

2. Mollenkopf, *The Contested City.* Among the general explorations of urban renewal are Charles Abrams, *The City Is the Frontier* (New York: Harper and Row, 1965); Martin Anderson, *The Federal Bulldozer* (Cambridge, Mass.: M.I.T. Press, 1964); Jewel Bellush and Maury Hausknecht, eds., *Urban Re-*

newal: People, Politics and Policy (Garden City, N.Y.: Doubleday—Anchor, 1967); James Q. Wilson, ed., *Urban Renewal: The Record and the Controversy* (Cambridge, Mass.: M.I.T. Press, 1966); Jean Lowe, *Cities in a Race with Time: Progress and Poverty in America's Renewing Cities* (New York: Random House, 1967).

3. Arnold Hirsch, *Making the Second Ghetto: Race and Housing in Chicago, 1940–1960* (Cambridge, Mass.: Harvard University Press, 1983); Thomas Lee Philpott, *The Slum and the Ghetto: Neighborhood Deterioration and Middle Class Reform, Chicago, 1880–1930* (New York: Oxford University Press, 1978); Kenneth Jackson, "Race, Ethnicity, and Real Estate Appraisal: The HOLC and the FHA," *Journal of Urban History* 6 (August 1980): 419–453.

4. Lowe, *Cities in a Race with Time*.

5. Ibid. John F. Bauman, "Visions of a Post War City: A Perspective on Urban Planning in Philadelphia and the Nation, 1942–1945," *Urbanism Past and Present* 6 (Winter/Spring 1981): 1–11. On Washington, D.C., see William R. Barnes, "A National Controversy in Miniature: The District of Columbia Struggle over Public Housing and Redevelopment, 1943–1946," *Prologue*, Summer 1977, pp. 91–101.

6. For Ascher quote, see Mark I. Gelfand, *A Nation of Cities: The Federal Government and Urban America, 1933–1965* (New York: Oxford University Press, 1975), p. 125.

7. Bauman, "Visions of a Post-War City"; and Urban Land Institute, *Outline for a Legislative Program to Rebuild Our Cities* (Washington, D.C.: GPO, 1942), pp. 1–7.

8. Charles Ascher, *Better Cities: Building America* (Washington, D.C.: NRPB, 1942). See also Philip J. Funigiello, *The Challenge to Urban Liberalism: Federal–City Relations during World War II* (Knoxville: University of Tennessee Press, 1978), p. 187; Gelfand, *Nation of Cities*, pp. 100, 128–129.

9. See Philip J. Funigiello, "City Planning during World War II: The Experience of the National Resources Planning Board," *Social Science Quarterly* 53 (June 1972): 91–104. On Blandford, see John B. Blandford, "The National Housing Agency: What It Is and What It Can Mean," *Proceedings of the National Association of Housing Officials, 1942* (Washington, D.C.: NAHO, 1942), p. 65; and "Post-War Housing," July 8, 1944, in Key Official File, Commissioner's Meetings, DHCR, RG 207, NA.

10. Bauer discussed her feelings about suburbs in "Cities After the War," in Summary of Proceedings: Annual Luncheon and Conference, PHA, March 25, 1943, HADVP. See also Dorothy Rosenman, *A Million Homes a Year* (New York: Harcourt Brace, 1945); Bauman, "Visions of a Post-War City," p. 3; Catherine Bauer, "Cities in Flux," *American Scholar* 13 (Winter 1943–1944): 70–84; and R. J. Thomas in Foreword to *Memorandum on Post-War Urban Housing* (Detroit: The International Union, United Automobile, Aircraft, Agricultural Implement Workers of America, UAW-CIO, 1944).

11. Kenneth T. Jackson, *Crabgrass Frontier: The Suburbanization of the United States* (New York: Oxford University Press, 1985), pp. 172–218, 231–245.

12. Mollenkopf, *The Contested City*, pp. 20–27; Jackson, "Race, Ethnicity

and Real Estate Appraisal," pp. 231–245; and "Delaware Valley, U.S.A: 1956," a section of the Philadelphia *Inquirer*, September 25, 1956.

13. Hirsch, *Making the Second Ghetto*, pp. 100–104.

14. On pre–World War II ghettoization, see, for example, Kenneth Kusmer, *The Ghetto Takes Shape: Black Cleveland, 1879–1930* (Urbana: University of Illinois Press, 1976); Allan Spear, *Black Chicago: The Making of a Negro Ghetto, 1890–1920* (Chicago: University of Chicago Press, 1967); and Gilbert Osofsky, *Harlem: The Making of a Ghetto* (New York: Harper and Row, 1966). On the growth of the postwar black community, see Karl E. Taeuber and Alma Taeuber, *Negroes in Cities: Residential Segregation and Neighborhood Change* (New York: Atheneum, 1969). An ecological interpretation of the growth of black neighborhoods can be found in Eugene Erickson and William Yancey, "Work and Residence in Industrial Philadelphia," *Journal of Urban History* 5 (February 1979): 147–183.

15. Aspects of black in-migration and the emerging socioeconomic configuration of the post–World War II city have been discussed in several papers. See, for example, H. Viscount Nelson, "The Decline of a Black Community: Philadelphia's Thirtieth Ward, 1940–1960," ms., July 18, 1980; and Leonard Blumberg, "A Study of Negro Migrants into Philadelphia: A Preliminary Report," August 3, 1957, Box 12, Folder 207, ULP.

16. See John F. Bauman, Edward Muller, and Norman Hummon, "Federal Slum or Waystation: Black Families and Philadelphia Public Housing during the 1940s," paper delivered at Ninth Biennial Convention of the American Studies Association, Philadelphia, November 1983; and City of Philadelphia Department of Health, Division of Air Pollution and Environmental Sanitation, "Housing and Neighborhood Evaluation Program," September 10, 1956, Philadelphia City Archives.

17. On black employment, see Philadelphia City Planning Commission, *Socio-Economic Characteristics, 1960–1970, Philadelphia Census Tracts* (Philadelphia, 1970), Philadelphia City Archives; see also U.S. Department of Commerce, Bureau of the Census, *Census of Population, 1940: Selected Population and Housing Characteristics, Philadelphia* (Washington, D.C.: GPO, 1942). The census tracts analyzed were tracts 13, 14, 20, 28, 29, 32, 37, and 47, comprising a sizable portion of the North Philadelphia black community (hereinafter referred to as Census Tract Data); see Census Tract Data, 1950 and 1960.

18. On black income, see Census Tract Data, 1940–1970; see also Commission on Human Relations, "Philadelphia's Non-White Population: 1960, Report No. 3, Socio-Economic Data," Philadelphia City Archives. On the poor quality of black jobs, see Walter Wynn and Charles Shorter to George Schermer, June 21, 1954, Box 12, Folder 206, ULP.

19. On Philadelphia's racial configuration, see Philadelphia Housing Association (PHA), *Some Facts on Philadelphia's Non-White Population and Its Housing: An Analysis of 1950 Census Data Prepared for the Commission on Human Relations* (Philadelphia, 1953), Box 9, Folder 195, NAACPP; see also "Non-White Population and Housing, 1950," PHA *Issues* (November–December 1952), ibid.; and PHA map on "Negro Population, 1910, 1920, 1930, 1940," HADVP.

20. See Morton Grodzins, *The Metropolitan Area as a Racial Problem* (Pittsburgh: University of Pittsburgh Press, 1959); Chester Rapkin and William Grigsby, *The Demand for Housing in Racially Mixed Areas* (Berkeley: University of California Press, 1960), pp. 30–93; and Karl and Alma Taeuber, *Negroes in Cities: Residential Segregation and Neighborhood Change* (Chicago: Aldine, 1965), pp. 40–55.

21. Robert Weaver, *The Negro Ghetto* (New York: Harcourt Brace, 1948), p. 211; for quote, see PHA, "Quality of Housing Occupied by Non-White Families," mimeographed, June 1953, Box 179, Folder 1898, HADVP.

22. "Housing Shortage Here Grows Worse," Philadelphia *Record,* February 3, 1942. Allan Spear discusses earlier black housing problems in *Black Chicago;* and James Borchert explores black housing in the nation's capital in *Alley Life in Washington, D.C.: Family, Community, Religion and Folklife in the City, 1850–1970* (Urbana: University of Illinois, 1980).

23. See PHA, "Quality of Housing Occupied by Non-White Families." See also PHA maps "Average Monthly Rents, 1950"; "Crowding, 1950"; "Dwelling Units Dilapidated or Lacking Private Bath, 1950"; and "Non-White Households, 1950"; all Box 235, Folder 3499, HADVP.

24. On the Temporary Emergency Housing Program, see Wilson Wyatt, "Action on the Housing Front," *Housing* 1, no. 1 (June 1946), pp. 2–3. On Philadelphia's contract for temporary veterans' housing, see Philadelphia Housing Authority, Contract No. 273, signed by Mayor Bernard Samuels, Roland Randall, and John B. Deans, PHAR; also see Philadelphia Housing Authority, "Report for 1950: The Veterans Temporary Housing Program in Philadelphia," n.d., circa December 1951, PHAR.

25. See Philadelphia Housing Authority, "Report for 1950." On promoting homeownership among veterans, see Housing and Home Finance Administration, Press Release, HHFA-2, "Promotion of Home Ownership . . . Is Key to the Government's Program for Disposing of Approximately 160,000 Units of Federally Owned War Housing," n.d., circa September 1947, found with letter, Allesandroni to Charles Lawrence, director of Region II, Public Housing Administration, New York, September 23, 1947, PHAR.

26. G. William Domhoff, *Who Rules America Now: A View for the 80s* (Englewood-Cliffs, N.J.: Prentice-Hall, 1983).

27. On the lineage of American planning, see Mel Scott, *American City Planning Since 1890* (Berkeley: University of California Press, 1969), p. 474; and Donald A. Krueckeberg, "The Culture of Planning," in Krueckeberg, ed., *Introduction to Planning History in the United States* (New Brunswick: Rutgers University Press, 1983), pp. 4–6. On the new role of postwar planners, see Wilson W. Wyatt, "The Effect of the Housing Emergency on Community Development," in *Planning, 1946: Proceedings of the Annual Meeting of the American Society of Planning Officials* (Chicago: ASPO, 1946), pp. 97–110; see also Walter Gropius, "Faith in Planning," in *Planning, 1952* (Chicago: ASPO, 1952), pp. 4–15.

28. On the ascendancy of expertise, see William Graebner, "The Unstable World of Benjamin Spock: Social Engineering in a Democratic Culture, 1917–1950," *Journal of American History* 67 (December 1980): 612–630; and

William H. Whyte, *The Organization Man* (Garden City, N.Y.: Doubleday-Anchor, 1956), pp. 25–35.

29. As one of the most perceptive observers of the nuances of housing and planning, Catherine Bauer was cognizant of the "murky niche" occupied by post–World War II housers. Speaking from what she described as her "soap box" at the 1946 meeting of the American Society of Planning Officials (ASPO), Bauer told the gathering that she "was aware of the martyr complex which is the occupational disease of public housers." See Catherine Bauer, "Is Urban Redevelopment Possible under Existing Legislation?" in *Planning, 1946*, p. 64; see also, Catherine Bauer, "Some Notes on Social Research Regarding Community Planning," mimeographed, February 1949, PHAR. On the views of public health officials regarding housing, see C. E. A. Winslow and F. S. Stuart Chapin, in the American Public Health Association's *Housing for Health* (Lancaster, Pa.: APHA, 1940).

30. Coleman Woodbury and Frederick A. Gutheim, *Rethinking Urban Redevelopment* (Chicago: Public Administration Service, 1949). This was the report of the Chicago conference on "Obstacles to Urban Renewal." In addition to those mentioned in the text, Robert Weaver, Elizabeth Wood, Harold Mayer, Frederick Adams, and Walter Blucher attended the conference.

31. See Bauer's "Some Notes on Social Research," pp. 4, 17, 18, 23–27. See also Louis Wirth, "Housing as a Field of Sociological Research," *American Sociological Review* 12 (April 1947): 137–142; the volume was devoted to the subject of "The American Family and Its Housing."

32. On the planner's definition of the "good city," see Woodbury and Gutheim, *Rethinking Urban Redevelopment*, p. 307. Note that the Philadelphia Housing Authority agreed; see Housing Authority to Mayor Samuels, July 23, 1945, on results of the Bellevue Stratford Meeting, Series III, Folder 324, HADVP.

33. On the issue of population decentralization versus centralization, see William W. Jeanes, "Memorandum on Site Selection," March 1, 1950, Box 84, Folder 365, HADVP. In her 1946 chiding of ASPO for its obliviousness to the importance of housing in urban redevelopment, Bauer stressed that "what we need, first and foremost, is a universally effective housing market, including an expansion of public housing and a whole battery of new instruments to reach the middle group"; see *Planning, 1946*, p. 66. See also "Some Notes on Social Research," pp. 21–22, where Bauer observed that "the whole recent emphasis on social sciences on the significance of the face to face group would seem to belie (or complicate) Isaacs's thesis" concerning the fallacy of the neighborhood unit; and Memorandum from Catherine Bauer to Dorothy Montgomery, April 18, 1949, Box 330, Folder 6427, HADVP.

34. On the Wagner-Ellender-Taft battle, see Lawrence M. Friedman, *Government and Slum Housing* (New York: Rand McNally, 1968), p. 149; Richard O. Davies, *Housing Reform during the Truman Administration* (Columbia, Mo.: University of Missouri Press, 1966), pp. 18, 70; and Nathaniel Keith, *Politics and the Housing Crisis Since 1930* (New York: Universe Books, 1973), pp. 76–85.

35. Friedman, *Government and Slum Housing*, p. 75; and Robert Moore Fisher, *Twenty Years of Public Housing: Economic Aspects of the Federal Program*

(Westport, Conn.: Greenwood, 1959), p. 20. On NPHC's role in battle, see Leonard Freedman, *Public Housing: The Politics of Poverty* (New York: Wadsworth, 1969), p. 76. In 1947 Bauer served as vice-president of the NPHC; R. J. Thomas and Mary Simkhovitch were officers; and Ira Robbins, Robert Taylor, Paul Betters, and Charles Abrams were all directors. See Dorothy Montgomery to Warren J. Vinton, July 5, 1949, Box 278, Folder 4795, HADVP; and Montgomery to Lee Johnson, executive vice-president of NPHC, May 20, 1948, Series III, Folder 254, HADVP.

36. William Slayton, "The Operation and Achievement of the Urban Renewal Program," in Wilson, ed., *Urban Renewal*, pp. 189–231; Davies, *Housing Reform during the Truman Administration*, pp. 11–12, 29; and Keith, *Politics and the Housing Crisis*, p. 91.

37. Abrams, *The City Is the Frontier*, pp. 75–76; and Freedman, *Public Housing*, p. 76.

38. Domhoff, *Who Rules America Now?*

39. Harold Wolman, *Politics of Federal Housing* (New York: Dodd Mead, 1971), p. 37.

40. See Weaver, *Negro Ghetto*, pp. 197–198; Abrams, *Forbidden Neighbors*, pp. 312–315; and Jackson, "Race, Ethnicity, and Real Estate Appraisal," pp. 419–453.

41. On the creation of the Racial Division, see Department of Interior, USHA Ordinance No. 96, April 14, 1938, Historical File, HDR, RG 207, NA.

42. On the Horne demotion, see Philip Klutznik, commissioner of housing, to Frank S. Horne, April 17, 1945, Historical File, Race Relations, HUDR; and Note to Mr. Krooth from John W. Shively, August 9, 1946, Historical File, Race Relations, 1944–1948, HUDR, RG 207, NA.

43. On segregated war housing, see Philadelphia Housing Authority, "Housing for Negroes in Philadelphia," mimeographed press release, December 29, 1944, HADVP; and the Reverend W. L. Johnson, Housing Committee of Philadelphia NAACP, "Housing Committee Report," September 28, 1945, Folder 316, NAACP. On "any project" facing "same racial problem," see Transcript of telephone conversation between W. W. Jeanes of the PHA and Roland Randall, December 16, 1946, Box 54, Folder 325, HADVP. Stuyvesant Town is discussed in Abrams, *Forbidden Neighbors*, p. 250.

44. On *Shelly v. Kraemer*, see Abrams, *Forbidden Neighbors*, p. 297; and George and Eunice Grier, *Equality and Beyond: Housing Segregation and the Goal of the Great Society* (Chicago: Quadrangle, 1966), pp. 51–52.

45. Davies, *Housing during the Truman Administration*, pp. 40–115.

46. On reform and planning, see David Wallace, "Renaissancemanship," *Journal of the American Institute of Planners* 26 (August 1960): 157–176; Edmund Bacon, "How City Planning Came to Philadelphia," n.d., circa 1943, Series III, Folder 60, HADVP; Lowe, *Cities in a Race with Time*, pp. 321–323; and James Reichly, *The Art of Government* (New York: Fund for the Republic, 1959), pp. 107–135.

47. Lowe, *Cities in a Race with Time*, p. 322.

48. On Montgomery appointment, see PHA press release on Dorothy Schoell (Montgomery) appointment, December 29, 1943, HADVP; also see

Interview, John Sutherland with Dorothy Montgomery, November 3, 1969, TUA.

49. On state redevelopment law and creation of city redevelopment authority, see Wallace, "Renaissancemanship," p. 159; National Housing Administration, "Comparative Digest of the Principal Provisions of State Redevelopment Legislation," April 1, 1947, mimeographed, HADVP; and *Martha Belovsky v. Redevelopment Authority of City of Philadelphia*, brief for the Redevelopment Authority, No. 68, by Abraham Freedman, June Term, 1946, PHAR.

50. On early activities of RA, see Redevelopment Authority of City of Philadelphia, *Our City: Today and Tomorrow* (Philadelphia, 1948), HADVP.

51. See Dorothy S. Montgomery to Mrs. William Wurster (Catherine Bauer), October 30, 1947, Box 330, Folder 6427, HADVP.

52. Harvey Molotch, "The City as a Growth Machine: Toward a Political Economy of Place," *American Journal of Sociology* 83 (1982): 309–329; and Mollenkopf, *The Contested City.* On the CCCP, its founding, and its role in Philadelphia's urban renewal, see Citizens' Council on City Planning, "A Chronological History of the CCCP," in CCCP, Box 1, TUA; see also CCCP, *Annual Reports*, 1945–1965, Box 1, TUA.

53. On the Better Philadelphia Exhibit, see Lowe, *Cities in a Race with Time*, pp. 322–323; see also Dorothy Montgomery to Bryn J. Hovde, May 21, 1951, Box 170, Folder 1657, HADVP; Edmund Bacon, "A Case Study in Urban Design," *Journal of the American Institute of Planners* 26 (August 1960); and Henry S. Churchill, "City Redevelopment," *Architectural Forum*, December 1950, p. 72.

54. On the Housing Authority's postwar housing program, see Roland R. Randall, James McDevitt, Raymond Rosen, et al. to Edward Hopkinson, chairman of Planning Commission, July 23, 1945, PHAR; and Statements of Harry Block, President of CIO Council, and Dorothy Schoell (Montgomery), PHAR, at Housing Authority Meeting on Post-War Housing held at the Bellevue Stratford Hotel, May 19, 1945, Series III, Folder 324, HADVP.

55. On the Housing Authority's six-year program, see Housing Authority to Mayor Samuels, July 23, 1945, PHAR; and "Notes on Housing Authority Hearings of Saturday, May 12, 1945 at Bellevue Stratford," mimeographed, Series III, Folder 324, HADVP.

56. See Statement of Joseph S. Clark, Democratic candidate for city controller, "Delay Endangering Philadelphia Housing Program," August 1949, PHAR; Montgomery to Wurster, October 30, 1947, Box 330, Folder 6427, HADVP; and issue of politics raised in HA *Minutes*, September 29, 1948.

57. PHA press release, June 17, 1947, Series III, Folder 325; and Montgomery to Warren J. Vinton, July 5, 1949, Box 278, Folder 4795, HADVP.

58. For assault on Samuels and the Republican machine, see Joseph R. Fink, "Reform in Philadelphia, 1946–1951," Ph.D. dissertation, Rutgers University, 1971; Philadelphia *Record*, October 19, 1943; Lowe, *Cities in a Race with Time*, p. 325; and Richardson Dilworth, Press Release, August 10, 1949, Series III, Folder 566, HADVP.

59. See Greater Philadelphia Movement, *Report of Activities*, 1949–1965,

GPMP, TUA; and Greater Philadelphia Movement, Minutes, September 28, 1949, GPMP, TUA.

60. On the Greater Philadelphia Movement, see Lowe, *Cities in a Race with Time*, pp. 324–325; and Kirk Petshek, *The Challenge of Urban Reform: Policies and Programs in Philadelphia* (Philadelphia: Temple University Press, 1973), pp. 156–157.

61. On scandal and reform, see William W. Jeanes, president of PHA, to Hon. Frederic Garman, president of City Council, April 28, 1949, PHAR; and William Reinhardt to C. Jared Ingersoll of Greater Philadelphia Movement, August 8, 1949, Box 84, Folder 361, HADVP. The whole story was told by Walter Phillips in a WFIL radio speech; see Transcript, "Remove Political Road Blocks and Build Houses," January 26, 1950, Box 84, Folder 357, HADVP.

62. On Kahn quote, see Associated City Planners, "Excerpts from Report on the Triangle Development," March 22, 1948, p. 12, HADVP; also see Churchill, "City Redevelopment," p. 76.

63. On Moses and urban renewal, see Lowe, *Cities in a Race with Time*, pp. 45–98. On Pittsburgh, see Roy Lubove, *Twentieth Century Pittsburgh: Government, Business and Environmental Change* (New York: Wiley, 1969), pp. 106–176; Woodbury and Gutheim, in *Rethinking Urban Redevelopment*, p. 10, stated that "Philadelphia had given more thought to selling urban redevelopment and had more promising experiments under way than any other locality."

64. See Philadelphia City Planning Commission, Division of Land Planning, map "Redevelopment Areas," certified January 9, 1948, and map revised February 1952, Box 234, Folder 3470, HADVP. Walker referred to commission's "housing orientation," in Philadelphia Chapter AIA, *Challenge 1950: Yearbook of Philadelphia Chapter AIA* (Philadelphia, 1950), HADVP.

65. Edmund Bacon, "Personal History," n.d., Series III, Folder 44, HADVP. Lowe called Bacon "shelter oriented"; see *Cities in a Race with Time*, p. 333. Petshek emphasized that "Bacon never modified his personal priority, which was design." He claimed that Bacon was reluctant to see the city's total development; see *Challenge of Urban Reform*, p. 101. See also Wallace, "Renaissancemanship," p. 161. On Bacon file, see "The City: Under the Knife, or All for Their Own Good," *Time*, November 6, 1964, pp. 69–70.

66. In the *Time* article cited in note 65 Bacon was quoted as saying that "Elliel Saarinen was my great master and teacher. He emphasized design as the relationship of form and space; so the real design problem is the city. Saarinen taught us that harmony of form and mass doesn't stop at the property lines but continues." See also Elliel Saarinen, *The City: Its Growth, Its Decay, Its Future* (Cambridge, Mass.: M.I.T. Press, 1943); and Bacon, "A Case Study in Urban Design."

67. Baltimore's Waverly section, referred to in Wallace's "Renaissancemanship," p. 160; "The Philadelphia Cure: A Big Job Is Divided into Small Parts for Easy Handling," *Architectural Forum*, April 1952, pp. 64–79; see also Lowe, *Cities in a Race with Time*, pp. 334–335.

68. On the rehabilitation strategy and "Yardville," see John A. McDermott, "Operation Fix-Up," mimeographed, October 26, 1954, HADVP.

69. Ibid.; see also Jack Diegel, "Report on Philadelphia Conservation Activities," September 12, 1951, HADVP pamphlet; and Redevelopment Authority of Philadelphia, *Operation Fix-Up: A Program to Help Improve Your Neighborhood* (Philadelphia, 1949), HADVP pamphlet.

70. On East Poplar, see Wallace, "Renaissancemanship," p. 162; ACTION Research Memorandum, "Case Study: Quaker 'Self Help' Rehabilitation Program in Philadelphia," n.d., circa 1956, HADVP pamphlet; and "Blighted Area of Philadelphia Is Being Transformed," Philadelphia *Dispatch*, November 8, 1953.

71. On Bosworth, see ACTION Research Memorandum, "Case Study"; see also Kevy Kaiserman, chairman of Redevelopment Authority, to Dorothy Montgomery, April 3, 1951, Box 249, Folder 3985, HADVP. Bosworth asked for buffer in letter to Allesandroni, November 17, 1953, PHAR.

72. See Jane Jacobs, *The Death and Life of Great American Cities* (New York: Vintage, 1961), pp. 112–221; Herbert J. Gans, *The Urban Villagers: Group and Class in the Life of Italian-Americans* (New York: Free Press, 1962), pp. 3–41; ACTION Research Memorandum, "Case Study."

73. Citizens' Council on City Planning, *Planning Progress in Philadelphia, The Annual Report of the Citizens' Council on City Planning, 1948–1949*, Box 1, CCCP.

74. On architectural firms for first projects, see listing of all firms holding public housing contracts in Philadelphia AIA, *Challenge 1950*. Lowatt's appointment announced in HA *Minutes*, August 29, 1949. See also "Statement of Architectural Fees Approved by the Public Housing Administration for Low-Rise Projects," mimeographed, n.d., circa 1949, Box 278, Folder 4795, HADVP.

75. Philadelphia Housing Authority, "Project Data," August 1964, PHAR; see also *Project Analysis: Spring Garden: PA-2-20* (December 1954), PHAR; a similar *Project Analysis* was compiled and published for each of the first 10 projects.

76. On Wilson Park, see Philadelphia Housing Authority, *Plan for Wilson Park: A Low-Rent Housing Development of 742 Homes* (Philadelphia, 1952), pp. 3–13, HADVP; on the first Wilson Park tenants, see Philadelphia *Evening Bulletin*, July 20, 1954; also Philadelphia Housing Authority, *Wilson Park: A Proposed New Site for Federally-Aided Low-Rent Public Housing*, n.d., HADVP pamphlet.

77. On Schuylkill Falls, see Germantown *Courier*, April 1, 1954; *Suburban Press*, September 9, 1954, and September 30, 1954.

78. On the Rosen project, see "Housing Project Dream Home to Family of Five," Germantown *Courier*, January 8, 1955; Lloyd King, "Rosen Project Results in Good Planning and Extensive Work," Philadelphia *Tribune*, August 9, 1955; Lloyd King, "Rosen Home Family Finds Happiness in New Apartment," Philadelphia *Tribune*, August 12, 1955.

79. Interview with David Wisdom at his office in Germantown, May 1, 1984. Wisdom was a young architect under both Oscar Stonorov and Louis I. Kahn. Kahn graduated from the University of Pennsylvania in 1924; on his ideas see "Toward a Plan for Midtown Philadelphia," *Perspecta: The Yale Archi-*

tectural Journal 2 (1953): 10–23; Mill Creek discussed in "The Philadelphia Cure," *Architectural Forum,* April 1952, pp. 64–79.

80. Southwest Temple discussed at some length in RA of Philadelphia, *A New Philadelphia Rises: 1958 Annual Report* (Philadelphia, 1959), and in RA of Philadelphia, *The Skyline Changes: 1959 Annual Report* (Philadelphia, 1960), both TUA.

81. On Norris, see "First Slum Clearance," Philadelphia *Daily News,* August 8, 1951; also Philadelphia Housing Authority, *Project Analysis: Norris* (October 1954), PHAR; on Harrison project see interoffice memorandum, Lancelot Sims to Hamilton Vogdes, February 20, 1953, submitting report on Harrison meeting with Redevelopment Authority to discuss land cost and density, PHAR.

82. See Clarence Shenton, "Richard Allen Homes Inspection Reveals No Sign that This Project is Becoming a Slum," *Evening Bulletin,* July 27, 1949.

83. On "normalcy," see David Walker's comment in "Report of Proceedings: The Philadelphia Housing Authority Public Hearings on Proposed Sites Held at Board of Education Building," mimeographed, October 4, 1950, PHAR; also, see transcript of Public Hearings on Redevelopment Proposal, East Poplar Redevelopment Area, Project "A," November 12, 1952, PHAR; and memo, Drayton Bryant to members of Subcommittee on Tenant Selection and Occupancy, January 9, 1952, Box 230, Folder 3341, HADVP.

84. Also on "normal" communities, see PHA, *Plan for Wilson Park* and "Housing Project Dream Home to Family of Five," Germantown *Courier.*

85. On a normative aspect of public housing, see Devereaux Bowly, *The Poorhouse: Subsidized Housing in Chicago, 1895–1976* (Carbondale: University of Illinois Press, 1975); Freedman, *Public Housing: The Politics of Poverty;* Hirsch, *Making the Second Ghetto,* passim; and especially Earl W. Morris and Mary Winter, *Housing, Family and Society* (New York: John Wiley, 1978), pp. 328–329.

86. On compromising with quality, see Wisdom Interview; and Memorandum, Lancelot Sims to Hamilton Vogdes, July 6, 1951, PHAR; also John Kervick, director of New York Field Office of Public Housing Administration, to Philadelphia Housing Authority, August 1, 1952, PHAR.

87. On splashboards, see Bid Documents: Review Reports, Project PA-2-20, Technical Comments, February 1953, PHAR; on landscaping for Spring Garden, see Draft of Lawns and Planting Specifications: Review Report, Project PA-2-20, Technical Comments, February 2, 1955, PHAR; also H. Allen Lincoln to Hamilton Vogdes, February 2, 1953, on landscaping specification for East Poplar, PHAR.

Chapter 6. The "Sunlit Years"

1. On urban progressivism see Robert Wiebe, *The Search for Order, 1870–1920* (New York: Hill and Wang, 1967), pp. 111–196; Samuel P. Hays, "The Politics of Reform in Municipal Government in the Progressive Era," in Samuel P. Hays, *American Political History as Social Analysis: Essays by Samuel P. Hays* (Knoxville: University of Tennessee Press, 1980), pp. 205–232. On Phila-

delphia's "sunlit hour," see James Reichley, *The Art of Government* (New York: Fund for the Republic, 1959); see also Kirk Petshek, *The Challenge of Urban Reform: Policies and Programs in Philadelphia* (Philadelphia: Temple University Press, 1973), p. 286; and Dennis Clark, "The Urban Ordeal: Reform and Policy in Philadelphia, 1947–1967," Integrative Paper Series, no. 1, n.d., TUA.

2. On integration movement, see Dennis Clark, "Public Housing Integration: One of Those Liberal Causes," ms., n.d., copy provided by Dennis Clark.

3. On the city charter, see Philadelphia Housing Association and City Charter Commission, "Housing and the City Charter: Recommendations of the Philadelphia Housing Association and the City Charter Commission," mimeographed, April 1950, HADVP; David Wallace, "Renaissancemanship," *Journal of the American Institute of Planners* 26, no. 3 (August 1960): 159; and Jeanne Lowe, *Cities in a Race with Time: Progress and Poverty in America's Renewing Cities* (New York: Random House, 1967), pp. 326–330.

4. Petshek, *Challenge of Urban Reform*, pp. 50–53, 286.

5. Interview with George Schermer, Washington, D.C., February 17, 1983; Petshek, *Challenge of Urban Reform*, pp. 286–294; and Reichley, *Art of Government*, pp. 19–22.

6. Dorothy S. Montgomery to Bryn J. Hovde, November 14, 1951, Box 170, Folder 1657, HADVP; and Hovde to Montgomery, November 18, 1951, ibid.

7. On Joseph Sill Clark, see Reichley, *Art of Government*, pp. 107–115; Petshek, *Challenge of Urban Reform*, p. 286; Lowe, *Cities in a Race with Time*, p. 330; see also Steve Neal, "Joseph Clark: Our Last Angry Man," *Today Magazine*, Philadelphia *Inquirer*, August 3, 1975. For Clark's social philosophy, see his "The Future of Urban Shelter," speech given at meeting of Metropolitan Housing and Planning Council, Chicago, May 6, 1955, Box 9, Folder 196, NAACP.

8. On Philadelphia as a city whose goal remained the private quest for wealth, see Sam Bass Warner, *The Private City: Philadelphia in Three Periods of Its Growth* (Philadelphia: University of Pennsylvania Press, 1968).

9. On U.S. Conference of Mayors, see Mark I. Gelfand, *A Nation of Cities: The Federal Government and Urban America, 1933–1965* (New York: Oxford University Press, 1975), pp. 186–189; see also Clark, "Urban Ordeal."

10. Nathaniel S. Keith, *Politics and the Housing Crisis Since 1930* (New York: Universe Books, 1973); and Clark, "Future of Urban Shelter."

11. On "best men," see Martin Schiesl, *The Politics of Efficiency: Municipal Administration and Reform in America, 1880–1920* (Berkeley: University of California Press, 1977), pp. 133–171. On Rafsky appointment, see Petshek, *Challenge of Urban Reform*, p. 56; Wallace, "Renaissancemanship," p. 161; and Walter Allesandroni to Dorothy Montgomery, April 8, 1952, Box 232, Folder 3408, HADVP.

12. See Lowe, *Cities in a Race with Time*, pp. 331–332.

13. On Philadelphia's Cooperative Agreement, see Statement by Sidney Schulman, counsel of Committee on Democracy in Housing, Philadelphia, n.d., circa 1950, made at City Council *Hearings*, Box 84, Folder 359, HADVP;

and Dorothy S. Montgomery to Philadelphia Housing Authority, May 20, 1950, ibid.

14. See Montgomery to Mayor Bernard Samuels, May 5, 1950, HADVP.

15. "Cooperative Agreement of June 1950, Between the Philadelphia Housing Authority, the City, and the School District of Philadelphia," mimeographed, n.d., Box 229, Folder 3315, HADVP.

16. Arnold R. Hirsch, *Making the Second Ghetto: Race and Housing in Chicago, 1940–1960* (Cambridge, Mass.: Harvard University Press, 1983), pp. 154–170.

17. See Clark, "Future of Urban Shelter." See also Joseph Clark's observations about people and events in his daily journal, February 20, 1952, and July 21, 1954, William L. Rafsky Papers; note in particular Clark's comment on August 11, 1953, that he "lunched with Rafsky and George Schermer. We reviewed the over-all housing problem of the community, which gives me serious concern [for] the impact of them on the race relations problem."

18. On Schermer's appointment, see Edward Turner, president of Detroit Branch, NAACP, to John W. Flammer, acting secretary of the Philadelphia NAACP, December 30, 1952, Box 4, Folder 98, NAACPP; and Clark to Charles Shorter, NAACP, January 29, 1954, Box 3, Folder 86, NAACP.

19. On activities of the committee, see Subcommittee on Housing of Interracial Committee, Minutes, January 20, 1944, Box 72, Folder 103, HADVP.

20. The Fellowship Commission (FC) Records at TUA disclose very little about the beginnings of the organization. Moreover, the records are currently unprocessed. See Philadelphia Fellowship Commission, Minutes of Council, November 26, 1949, FCR; and Fellowship Commission, Standing Council, "List of Officers," n.d., circa 1950, FCR.

21. On Quaker interracial activities, see William M. Dwyer, "Experiment in Housing," reprint from *Commonweal*, n.d. (1960), Box 10, Folder 199, NAACP.

22. See Charles Abrams, "The Housing Problem and the Negro," *Daedalus* 95 (Winter 1966): 72–73; Memorandum from Joseph Ray, Race Relations Service, to Albert Cole, August 13, 1954, "Racial Policy to Govern Administration of HHFA Program," Committee Files, Minority Housing Conference, December 9–10, 1954, HUDR, RG 207, NA.

23. Cole quoted in Joseph Ray, "Findings and Recommendation [of] Conference of Race Relations Officers, Public Housing Administration, Washington, D.C.," May 3–7, 1954, Race Relations Program File, HUDR. See also Memorandum, Joseph Ray to Albert Cole, August 13, 1954, HUDR, RG 207, NA; and Al Thompson, "Procedures and Techniques Employed by Racial Relations Officials in Analyzing a Community to Determine Effective Demand Among Minority Groups," September 14–18, 1953, Program Files, Race Relations, HUDR, RG 207, NA.

24. See Memorandum, Joseph Ray to Albert Cole, August 13, 1954, HUDR, RG 207, NA.

25. See Alene D. Simkins, "What Intergroup Professionals Ought to

Know about Integration in Public Housing," paper presented at meeting of National Association of Intergroup Relations Officials, November 12, 1952, Program Files, Race Relations, HUDR, RG 207, NA.

26. See George B. Nesbitt, special assistant to director (Race Relations), to Howard Wharton, supervisor of Area I, August 19, 1954, Program Files, Race Relations, HUDR, RG 207, NA.

27. For a discussion of Whyte, Janowitz, and the concept of community in postwar America, see Zane Miller, *Suburb: Neighborhood and Community in Forest Park, Ohio, 1935–1976* (Knoxville: University of Tennessee Press, 1981), pp. 29–31; see also Howard Gillette, "The Evolution of Neighborhood Planning from the Progressive Era to the 1949 Housing Act," *Journal of Urban History* 9 (August 1983): 421–445; David Reisman, *The Lonely Crowd: A Study of the Changing American Character* (New Haven, Conn.: Yale University Press, 1950), pp. 36–82, 188–224; and William H. Whyte, *The Organization Man* (Garden City, N.Y.: Simon and Schuster, 1956), pp. 69–154.

28. Gillette, "Evolution of Neighborhood Planning," p. 101. On 1951 meeting, see Frederick Gutheim, *Housing as Environment: A Report on the Research Conference "The Role of Social Research on Housing Design" Sponsored by the Committee on Housing Research, Social Science Research Council* (New York: Columbia Institute for Land Use, 1953), pp. 2, 9, 22.

29. See John Dean, "The Myth of Housing Reform," in *Urban Housing*, ed. William L. C. Wheaton et al. (New York: Free Press, 1966), pp. 255–258.

30. For Bauer quote, see "The Increasing Social Responsibility of the City Planner," *Proceedings of the American Institute of Planners Conference* (1950), HADVP. Catherine Bauer expressed her belief in research in a letter to Montgomery, n.d., Box 330, Folder 6428, HADVP; Mel Scott described Wurster as an "actionist" in *American City Planning Since 1890* (Berkeley: University of California Press, 1969), pp. 475–477.

31. For data, see Philadelphia Housing Association (PHA), *Relocation in Philadelphia* (Philadelphia: PHA, 1958), p. 57; the PHA analyzed families dislocated from the North Allen, Norris, and Harrison sites, all in the Southwest Temple Area; if single and nonrelated persons had been included, there would have been 1,556 cases. See also Redevelopment Authority of Philadelphia, "Notice of Public Hearing" on East Poplar land acquisition and clearance, July 15, 1952, PHAR; see also mimeographed information and maps on "East Poplar Development: 203 Low-Rent Homes," PHAR.

32. On the opening of the Rehousing Bureau in 1950, see Memorandum to Subcommittee on Tenant Selection, from George J. Dunn, director of Management, Philadelphia Housing Authority, on "Relocation in East Poplar," November 19, 1952, Box 230, Folder 3349, HADVP; and PHA, *"Mill Creek Relocation: A Report on the Relocation Operation for the Mill Creek Low-Rent Housing Development,"* 1933, HADVP pamphlets. On "dark and dingy" tenements, see report by Chester Hayes, director of Relocation of Redevelopment Authority, "East Poplar, Project A, Unit Number 7," June 27, 1951, Box 249, Folder 987, HADVP.

33. On Resolution 3630, see Memo from Walter Allesandroni to Super-

visors and Managers, PHA, May 28, 1952, "Revised Occupancy Policy of the Philadelphia Housing Authority," Box 232, Folder 3412, HADVP. For a general discussion of Philadelphia's integration efforts, see Clark, "Public Housing Integration." For the PHA view, see Elfriede Hoeber, "Human Relations Aspects in Housing," March 13, 1952, Box 235, Folder 3491, HADVP; see also Philadelphia Housing Authority, *Summary of the Integrated Occupancy Program*, March 6, 1953, HADVP pamphlets.

34. See "Outline Calendar of the Integration Program," mimeographed, n.d., Box 180, Folder 1931, HADVP; and Clark, "Public Housing Desegregation."

35. On Wilson Park, see Anna McGarry's "Report of Investigation of Wilson Park Opposition in South Philadelphia," n.d., Box 235, Folder 3495, HADVP; William Gray, "City Housing Backed by Fellowship Groups," *Daily News*, February 25, 1952; "Council Kills Biased Housing," Pittsburgh *Courier*, March 8, 1952; and P. Blair Lee to Joseph Clark, February 19, 1952, Box 232, Folder 3405, HADVP.

36. "Facts about Integration Policy of the Philadelphia Housing Authority," May 26, 1952, PHAR; and William Gray, "Housing Rule Hailed as 'Brotherly Living,'" *Daily News*, June 5, 1952.

37. Clark, "Public Housing Desegregation"; see also Philadelphia Housing Authority, *Summary of the Integrated Occupancy Program*.

38. On Abbottsford, see Anna McGarry, "Report of the Abbottsford Homes Community Council Held Thursday, October 2, 1952," Box 235, Folder 3493, HADVP; see also, Joseph Clark's journal, August 13, 1952, WLRP.

39. See Elizabeth Fetter to Joseph Clark, August 29, 1952, Box 235, Folder 3492, HADVP.

40. On criticism concerning the slow progress of Housing Authority integration program, see Philadelphia Fellowship Commission, Committee on Democracy in Housing (CDH), Minutes, March 15, 1955, Box 271, Folder 4620, HADVP; at that meeting, Drayton Bryant explained for the authority that "two-thirds of the families placed in 1954 were Negroes and 80 percent of all of the present applicants for public housing are Negroes. One of the basic questions which must be faced in this whole picture is, should we attempt to maintain some degree of integration over a long period of time rather than let the matter take its course. *The latter may mean that all public housing will be completely Negro in a very few years* [author's italics]. . . . The Authority in its whole integration program has attempted to work on the basis of the spirit of the [Cooperative] agreement rather than on the letter as it was written." Statistical data from Public Housing Administration Statistical Branch, *Reports on Occupancy*, Box 32, Microfilm Reel 39, PA-1-1 to PA-5-2, HUDR, RG 207, NA.

41. On the high-rise decision, see Montgomery to Mrs. William Wurster, July 15, 1951, Montgomery to Wurster, June 12, 1951; and Montgomery to Wurster, June 22 1952; all in Box 330, Folder 6428, HADVP.

42. On AIA meeting, see Montgomery to Wurster, November 1, 1951, Box 330, Folder 6429, HADVP. On standards, see John Taylor Egan to

Montgomery, March 13, 1951, Box 278, Folder 479, HADVP; and draft of letter "not sent," Montgomery to Egan, May 1951, ibid.

43. The Philadelphia Housing Authority in 1951 sincerely studied the social ramifications of public housing architecture, and members made trips to Chicago and New York City, among other places. See Philadelphia Housing Authority, Minutes, August 13, 1951; and Interview with Drayton Bryant, April 16, 1972, Philadelphia, Pa. On Wallace Study, see Anthony F. C. Wallace, "The Houser and the Social Scientist," May 7, 1953, paper presented at Philadelphia Housing Association meeting, Box 144, Folder 1144; and Wallace, "Material for Philadelphia Housing Association," November 12, 1952, Box 144, Folder 1142, HADVP.

44. Anthony F. C. Wallace, *Housing and Social Structure: A Preliminary Survey with Particular Reference to Multi-Storey Public Housing Projects* (Philadelphia: Redevelopment Authority of Philadelphia, 1952).

45. On Wurster's fear concerning Wallace's study, see Wurster to Anthony F. C. Wallace, December 16, 1951, Box 330, Folder 6429, HADVP; and Wurster to Montgomery, December 17, 1951, ibid.

46. Wallace, *Housing and Social Structure*.

47. Ibid., p. 91. Lee Rainwater made similar observations about the social environment of public housing projects in "Fear and the House-as-Haven in the Lower Class," *Journal of the American Institute of Planners* 32 (1966): 23–31.

48. Wallace, *Housing and Social Structure*, pp. 6–59. Wallace clarified his aim and control variables in "Wallace Material," Box 144, Folder 1142, HADVP.

49. See Catherine Bauer Wurster, "Clients for Housing: The Low-Income Tenant, Does He Want Supertenements?" *Progressive Architecture*, May 1952.

50. Ibid; for problems of supertenements, see discussion of Fort Green Houses in Harrison Salisbury's "Shook-Up Generation: Problem Youngsters Spring from the Housing Jungle," *New York Times*, March 26, 1958.

51. On "problem" family issue, see "Special Report to the Advisory Committee of the Philadelphia Housing Authority on the Relocation of 342 Families from the Site of the East Poplar Project," October 8, 1952, Box 230, Folder 3355, HADVP.

52. Carol Stack, *All Our Kin: Strategies for Survival in a Black Community* (New York: Harper and Row, 1974); and Joyce Ladner, *Tomorrow's Tomorrow* (Garden City, N.Y.: Doubleday, 1971).

53. On defining "problem" families as opposed to "stable" families, see Subcommittee on Tenant Selection and Occupancy, Minutes, November 19, 1952, Box 230, Folder 3349, HADVP; see also "Special Report to the Advisory Committee of the Philadelphia Housing Authority on Relocation of 342 Families."

54. Subcommittee on Tenant Selection and Occupancy, Minutes, November 19, 1952, Box 230, Folder 3349, HADVP; and Subcommittee on Tenant Selection and Occupancy, Minutes, May 25, 1953, Box 82, Folder 106, HADVP.

55. On the "changed type of applicant," see Memorandum, Drayton Bryant to Walter Allesandroni, June 3, 1953, Box 230, Folder 3353, HADVP.

56. See Wurster, "Clients for Housing"; see also Wurster to Wallace, December 16, 1951, Box 330, Folder 6429, HADVP.

57. See Martin Meyerson and Edward C. Banfield, *Politics, Planning and the Public Interest* (Glencoe, Ill.: Free Press, 1955); and testimony of James W. Follin, director of Slum Clearance, Redevelopment Division, HHFA, *Hearings on Housing Act of 1954 Before the Committee on Banking and Currency*, U.S. Sen., 83rd Cong., 2d sess., March 10, 1954, pp. 91–93.

58. On Philadelphia's enthusiasm for urban redevelopment in the early 1950s, see Philadelphia *Evening Bulletin*, November 12, 1952. On waning esteem for public housing, see Catherine Bauer, "The Dreary Deadlock of Public Housing," *Architectural Forum* 106 (May 1957): 140–142, 219, 221; Keith, *Politics and the Housing Crisis;* Leonard Freedman, *Public Housing: The Politics of Poverty* (New York: Holt, Rinehart and Winston, 1969), p. 103; and Gelfand, *A Nation of Cities*, p. 205.

59. See Richard O. Davies, *Housing Reform during the Truman Administration* (Columbia, Mo.: University of Missouri, 1966), pp. 122–127; and Robert Moore Fisher, *Twenty Years of Public Housing: Economic Aspects of the Federal Program* (Westport, Conn.: Greenwood, 1959), p. 21.

60. See Davies, *Housing Reform during the Truman Administration*, pp. 131–136; Keith, *Politics and the Housing Crisis*, pp. 105–107; and "Congress' Housing Cuts Doom Projects Here," Philadelphia *Inquirer*, July 27, 1951.

61. Copies of the Gwinn Amendment form containing a list of all organizations deemed subversive by the attorney general ("Attorney General's List") were filed in all tenant record folders, RAHR, PHAR.

62. On "red-baiting" and public housing, see Freedman, *Public Housing*, p. 66. On the Marter case, see Henry J. Cadling, chairman of American Friends Service Committee, to P. Blair Lee, July 3, 1952, Box 232, Folder 3415, HADVP. On Bryant, see Memorandum, Drayton Bryant to members of the Philadelphia Housing Authority concerning "*Daily News* Article of June 23rd," June 25, 1952, Box 232, Folder 3414, HADVP.

63. See Bennett Berger, *Working Class Suburb* (Berkeley: University of California Press, 1960); and Herbert Gans, *The Levittowners: Ways of Life and Politics in a New Suburban Community* (New York: Pantheon, 1967). On Eisenhower cuts, see Keith, *Politics and the Housing Crisis*, pp. 110–113; see also "Keep the Housing Program," Philadelphia *Inquirer*, May 8, 1953.

64. On Eisenhower's "dynamic conservatism," see Gelfand, *A Nation of Cities*, pp. 167–170.

65. On Colean and urban redevelopment, see Scott, *American City Planning*, pp. 498–499; and Gelfand, *A Nation of Cities*, p. 172.

66. On Philadelphia precedents for Colean's approach, see Memorandum, Montgomery to Board of Directors of Philadelphia Housing Association, May 8, 1953, submitting draft report of "The Housing Code and City Housing Policy," mimeographed, n.d., HADVP.

67. For Clarence Mitchell quote, see Confidential Memorandum, Frank S. Horne to Albert M. Cole, November 19, 1953, concerning "Proposals for

the Presidents Advisory Commission on Housing," Program Files, Race Relations, HUDR. Walter White and Clarence Mitchell, in a Memorandum to Albert Cole, "Memorandum on the Promotion of Housing Segregation by Federal Agencies," May 6, 1953, complained that in all federally aided projects segregation or discrimination "is left almost entirely to the discretion of the private developer, lender or the local public agency."

68. See Frank Horne, *Analysis of the Report of the President's Advisory Commission on Housing Policies and Programs*, January 6, 1954, Program Files, Race Relations, HUDR, RG 207, NA.

69. On the creation of the URA and the Workable Program, see Ashley A. Foard and Hilbert Fefferman, "Federal Urban Renewal Legislation," in *Urban Renewal: The Record and the Controversy,* ed. James Q. Wilson (Cambridge, Mass.: M.I.T. Press, 1966), pp. 71–125; Scott, *American City Planning,* pp. 500–501, 520; and Wolman, *Politics of Federal Housing,* p. 38.

70. On Housing Act of 1954, see Foard and Fefferman, "Federal Urban Renewal Legislation," pp. 96–97; and Freedman, *Public Housing,* pp. 82–84.

71. On Philadelphia's reaction to the Housing Act of 1954, see "Philadelphia Public Housing Program Seen Headed for Quick Death," in Philadelphia *Daily News,* October 14, 1954; Philadelphia *Tribune,* July 17, 1954; and Philadelphia *Inquirer,* July 30, 1954.

72. On Clark's new appointments to Redevelopment Authority's Development Committee, see Petshek, *Challenge of Urban Reform,* p. 138; and Scott, *American City Planning,* p. 522.

73. See Martin Meyerson, "Memorandum on Policy and Programs for Housing to Development Committee of Redevelopment Authority," May 28, 1955, Box 321, Folder 6161, HADVP.

74. On citizen participation and PHA role, see PHA, *Citizen's Guide to Housing and Urban Renewal* (Philadelphia: PHA 1960), p. 21; and Montgomery and Aaron Levine to Allesandroni, March 28, 1955, submitting "A Recommendation for Policy on Site Selection for Public Housing," February 24, 1955, PHAR. For a good general discussion of the subject, see Hans B. C. Spiegel, "Citizen Participation in Federal Programs: A Review," *Journal of Voluntary Action Research,* Monograph No. 1 (1971): 4–31.

75. See draft of "A Statement on Housing and Urban Renewal Policy for Philadelphia," August 5, 1955, Box 321, Folder 6163, HADVP; and William L. C. Wheaton et al., "A Statement on Housing and Urban Renewal Policy for Philadelphia," mimeographed, October 1955, Box 168, Folder 1617, HADVP.

76. See Montgomery to G. Holmes Perkins, August 15, 1955, Box 321, Folder 6164, HADVP; see Montgomery to Dilworth, January 8, 1957; Montgomery to Dilworth, March 21, 1956; and Dilworth to Montgomery, January 17, 1957; all in Box 117, Folder 567, HADVP.

Chapter 7. Public Housing and Roundhouse Renewal

1. See David A. Wallace, "Renaissancemanship," *Journal of the American Institute of Planners* 26 (August 1960): 161.

2. Arnold R. Hirsch, *Making the Second Ghetto: Race and Housing in Chicago, 1940–1960* (Cambridge, Mass.: Harvard University Press, 1983), pp. 162–180.

3. On Rafsky's elevation to development coordinator, see Kirk Petshek, *The Challenge of Urban Reform: Policies and Programs in Philadelphia* (Philadelphia: Temple University Press, 1973), p. 97.

4. See map, "Renewal Areas," Redevelopment Authority of City of Philadelphia, April 1957, HADVP; and Redevelopment Authority of City of Philadelphia, "Summary of Urban Renewal Policy and Programs," mimeographed, n.d., circa February 1956, Box 249, Folder 3988, HADVP.

5. See Dorothy S. Montgomery to G. Holmes Perkins, January 11, 1956, Box 221, Folder 3046, HADVP; on Rafsky's priorities, see Office of Development Coordinator, *A New Approach to Urban Renewal for Philadelphia*, December 1956, HADVP pamphlets.

6. Dennis Clark used the expression "roundhouse renewal" in a letter to William Rafsky, December 16, 1955, Box 272, Folder 4624, HADVP. See also Interview with Dennis Clark, April 22, 1983; Interview with George Schermer, Washington, D.C., February 18, 1983; and Wallace, "Renaissancemanship," p. 161.

7. Mel Scott, *American City Planning Since 1890* (Berkeley: University of California Press, 1969), p. 532; and Philadelphia Housing Association (PHA), *Citizen's Guide to Housing and Urban Renewal* (Philadelphia: PHA, 1960), p. 10.

8. On the leadership program, see PHA, *Citizen's Guide*, p. 11; see also Office of Development Coordinator and Housing and Home Finance Agency, *Partnership for Renewal: A Working Program, A Summary of the Accomplishments of Philadelphia's Experiment in Improving Housing and Neighborhood Conditions through City–Citizen Cooperation* (Philadelphia: City of Philadelphia, 1960), pp. 17–19. William F. Rafsky, "Summary of Activities," June 18, 1956, Box 1, WLRP, TUA, is a detailed daily log of meetings and activities with reflective annotations. Both Clark and Dilworth urged all their department heads to keep such logs.

9. See Wallace, "Renaissancemanship," p. 161.

10. Hirsch, *Making the Second Ghetto*, pp. 100–134. On Bacon-Wallace strategy, see Rafsky, "Summary," April 19, 1956, June 18, 1956, and February 28, 1956.

11. See Henry Beeritz to Montgomery, October 10, 1956, Box 117, Folder 567, HADVP; and Rafsky, "Summary," August 24, 1956, and September 20, 1956.

12. On conservation areas, see Petshek, *Challenge of Urban Reform*, p. 142; OCD/HHFA, *Partnership for Renewal*, p. 77; and PHA, *Citizen's Guide*, p. 11.

13. See Chester Hayes, Redevelopment Authority, and David Antebi, Philadelphia Housing Association, "Management Memo on Redevelopment Authority Relocation," November 14, 1955, Box 245, Folder 3588, HADVP; see also Charles Abrams, *The City Is the Frontier*, (New York: Harper and Row, 1965), pp. 133–134; and William Alonzo, "Critics, Planners and Urban Renewal," in James Q. Wilson, ed., *Urban Renewal: The Record and the Controversy* (Cambridge, Mass.: M.I.T. Press, 1966), p. 447.

14. Memorandum, George B. Nesbitt, assistant to commissioner (Race Relations), to J. W. Follin, urban renewal commissioner, July 25, 1956, "Review of Relocation of Families, Through September 1955," Program Files, Race Relations, HUDR, RG 207, NA.

15. On relocation problem, see PHA, *Relocation in Philadelphia* (November 1958), HADVP pamphlets; see also Redevelopment Authority of Philadelphia, Francis J. Lammer, executive director, "To the Present Owner, Tenant, or Occupant of the Above Premises," March 21, 1955, PHAR.

16. See PHA, "Facts on Philadelphia's Negro Population and Its Housing," October 1953, HADVP; and Statement of the Reverend William E. Fantroy, chairman of Housing and Urban Renewal Committee of Minister's Alliance, Washington, D.C., Before Subcommittee No. 1 of House Committee on the District of Columbia, *Hearings of H. R. 6312, Amendment to the Redevelopment Act of 1954*, Subject Correspondence Files, Robert Weaver, 1961–1968, Folder: Program for Community Improvement, HUDR, RG 207, NA. Also see Committee on Equal Housing Opportunity (COEHO) of Philadelphia Fellowship Commission, Minutes, November 28, 1961, where under "Report on the Development of Southwest Temple Area," Richard Watson reported "much concern over the lack of integration in this [Southwest Temple Redevelopment] area; the opinion was that people were being moved from one miserable ghetto to a much nicer ghetto, but that the ghetto itself was not changing," Box 179, Folder 1893, HADVP.

17. See Testimony of William L. Rafsky, Housing Coordinator, before Subcommittee on Housing, House of Representatives Committee on Banking and Currency, October 1, 1955, Folder 184, ULP; see also "Supplement to Housing Services Department Memo," February 1, 1960, Box 16, ULP; and Report to Urban Renewal Administration, n.d., circa 1963, Box 749, Program Files, Race Relations, HUDR, RG 207, NA. An indication of the enormity of the living conditions endured by Philadelphia's low-income blacks can be found in letters to the Philadelphia Housing Authority requesting public housing. One letter, from a desperate woman, pleaded that she had "lived at her Jefferson Street address for five years. . . . We have 2 rooms, a bedroom and a kitchen. We do not have any sink or running water. We use water from the bathroom which is not sanitary. We have five in our bedroom, one a baby. My husband only works now. He did not go to school, but that is completed," RAHR file, RAH 3560, PHAR.

18. Committee for Democracy in Housing (CDH), Fellowship Commission (FC), "Statement for House Investigation Sub Committee of the House Committee on Banking and Currency Sitting in Philadelphia, October 11–13, 1955," Folder 84, ULP.

19. On relocation studies, see PHA, *Relocation in Philadelphia;* see also Memo, Nesbitt to Follin, July 25, 1956, Program Files, Race Relations, HADR, RG 207, NA.

20. CDH, "Statement for House Investigation"; and Lewis J. Carter, "Urban Renewal and Non-White Families in Philadelphia: A Statement of Facts and Opinions Presented to National Urban League Urban Renewal Institute, April 19–20, 1956," Folder 183, ULP.

21. Rafsky Testimony, Subcommittee on Housing; Lewis Carter, "Statement of the Armstrong Association before the Sub Committee on Housing of the Banking and Currency Committee, October 14, 1955," Folder 183, ULP; and "Supplement to Housing Services Department Memo," February 1, 1960, Box 16, Folder 195, ULP.

22. National Advisory Commission on Civil Disorders, *The Kerner Report* (New York: Bantam Books, 1968), pp. 406–407.

23. See PHA, "New Housing Available to Negroes: A Report on the Dwelling Units Available to Negro Occupancy, 1946–1953," September 3, 1953, Box 11, Folder 175, ULP; see also PHA, "New Housing Available to Negro Occupancy, July 1953–June 1955," April 1956, ibid.; and John F. Kain and John M. Quigley, *Housing Markets and Racial Discrimination* (New York: Columbia University Press, 1975).

24. Ibid.; see also PHA, "Philadelphia New Construction by Wards, 1946–1948," Box 85, Folder 384, HADVP; and PHA, "New Private Housing Available to Negroes, Philadelphia Metropolitan Area, 1946–1953," ibid.

25. For a critique of the Friends coop, see Frank S. Kristoff, FHA, "An Analysis of the 1954–1955 Housing Demand of the Philadelphia, Pa. Housing Market Area," April 1, 1954, Box 6, Market Analysis Reports, 1948–1957, HUDR, RG 207, NA.

26. Interview with George Schermer, Washington, D.C., February 17, 1983. PHA, "New Private Housing Available to Negroes." Note that in COEHO, Minutes, November 28, 1961, Richard Watson reported that the housing developer Mr. Denny "complained that he cannot sell within the un-demolished area from 12th Street to Broad Street immediately adjacent to his own project [Yorktown], because people did not wish to be neighbors to a slum. . . . [Moreover] he is building middle class housing, and families with middle incomes want to live in the suburbs." See Box 179, Folder 1893 HADVP.

27. PHA, "New Private Housing Available to Negroes"; and PHA, "New Housing Available to Negroes: A Report on the Dwelling Units Available to Negro Occupancy, July 1953–June 1955," Box 11, Folder 175, ULP.

28. CHR, "Philadelphia's Non-White Population: 1960"; and PHA, "Some Facts on the Philadelphia Negro Population," n.d., circa 1960, Box 12, Folder 206, ULP.

29. Federal Housing Administration, Philadelphia, "FHA Acquired Properties Available for Sale or Rent," August 1, 1968, PHAR; and letter from anonymous tenant to the Philadelphia Housing Authority, May 23, 1966, RAHR, RAH 4181, PHAR. See also Alton Berry, manager of the Richard Allen Homes, to anonymous tenant, September 12, 1963: "We have at management office a list of 61 reprocessed homes." Ibid.

30. Hirsch, *Making the Second Ghetto*, pp. 171–211; and Lawrence M. Friedman, *Government and Slum Housing* (New York: Rand McNally, 1968).

31. See "A Site Selection Policy for Public Housing," Philadelphia Housing Association *Issues*, January–March 1952, p. 5. See also Frank O. Walther, chairman of Joint Committee on Site Selection, to Professor Ian McHarg, School of

Fine Arts, University of Pennsylvania, November 2, 1954, asking McHarg to become a member; Box 234, Folder 3457, HADVP.

32. ˙On composition of JCSS, see several typed lists of "Members of Joint Committee on Site Selection," October 4, 1954, and January 19, 1955, Box 234, Folder 3460, HADVP.

33. See "A Site Selection Policy for Public Housing"; and Henry S. Churchill, Jefferson Fordham, Martin Meyerson, William L. C. Wheaton, Dorothy S. Montgomery, et al., "A Statement on Housing and Urban Renewal Policy for Philadelphia," October 1955, Box 168, Folder 1617, HADVP.

34. Frank O. Walther to P. Blair Lee, November 12, 1954, Box 234, Folder 3457, HADVP; Philadelphia Housing Authority, Site "Data Sheets," on Fitzwater Site No. 134, Whitehall Site No. 292, Oxford II Site No. 351, all dated November 1, 1954; ibid.

35. On the Fitzwater controversy, see William Rafsky to Walther, December 3, 1954, where Rafsky agreed with Walther that "the density is much too high. I have urged both the planning commission and the Housing Authority to do everything possible to reduce it. . . . The problem is, as you know, that the Housing Authority must meet the cost limitations imposed on it by the Public Housing Administration regulations. Some time has been spent in examining the possibility of using other open sites, but the time it would take to get these ready and obtain approval all the way from the neighborhood up through the City Council would have meant not being able to meet the deadline of the 1955 fiscal year." Box 234, Folder 3458, HADVP. See also Elfriede Hoeber to Dean G. Holmes Perkins, December 24, 1954; ibid.

36. Memorandum, William Gray, CDH, to P. Blair Lee, April 1, 1955, PHAR; and G. Holmes Perkins, president of PHA, to William Rafsky, March 14, 1955, Box 234, Folder 3461, HADVP. Later, Rafsky reported that he was in agreement with all the points made by Perkins. "We are now reviewing the whole procedure [for site selection] in an attempt to relate planning, human relations, and family and social problems to site selection." See Rafsky to Perkins, March 24, 1954, Box 234, Folder 3462, HADVP.

37. See Commission on Human Relations (probably authored by George Schermer), "Human Relations Factors in the Selection of Sites for Public Housing," July 20, 1955, Box 235, Folder 3510, HADVP; note also Montgomery's jottings on the margin of her agenda at a meeting of the RA, September 29, 1955, to discuss Schermer's "Human Relations Factors" report: "If [public] housing were available in all part of city," she wrote, "if none were excluded— if there were a comprehensive plan and program to achieve it?"

38. See "Philadelphia's Procedures for Selecting Public Housing Sites," January 10, 1956, Box 284, Folder 4977, HADVP; and "Public Housing Dilemma: What Next for City," Philadelphia *Sunday Bulletin*, April 28, 1956.

Chapter 8. From Way Stations to Welfare Centers

1. Kirk Petshek, *The Challenge of Urban Reform: Policies and Programs in Philadelphia* (Philadelphia: Temple University Press, 1973), p. 139.

2. Arnold R. Hirsch, *Making the Second Ghetto: Race and Housing in Chicago, 1940–1960* (Cambridge, Mass.: Harvard University Press, 1983).

3. On publishing sites, see Walter Allesandroni to Edmund Bacon, April 2, 1956, PHAR, stating that "we are submitting to you at this time for approval by the Philadelphia City Planning Commission a list of 21 sites. . . . These sites will make possible the construction of the 2,500 homes." See also Philadelphia *Evening Bulletin,* June 4, 1956.

4. "Radio Report to People by Richardson Dilworth, Recorded 5/1/56," Box 117, Folder 567, HADVP; "Civic Groups Urge City to OK 21 Housing Sites," Philadelphia *Daily News,* May 15, 1956; and "Mayor Presents Data on Projects," Philadelphia *Evening Bulletin,* May 26, 1956.

5. Mark I. Gelfand, *A Nation of Cities: The Federal Government and Urban America, 1933–1965* (New York: Oxford University Press, 1975), pp. 216–222; and Kenneth Jackson, "Race, Ethnicity, and Real Estate Appraisal: The HOLC and the FHA," *Journal of Urban History* 6 (August 1980): 446–447.

6. Kenneth L. Kusmer, *A Ghetto Takes Shape: Black Cleveland, 1870–1930* (Urbana: University of Illinois Press, 1976); Peter O. Muller, Kenneth C. Meyer, and Roman Cybriwsky, *Philadelphia: A Study of Conflicts and Social Cleavages* (Cambridge, Mass.: M.I.T. Press, 1976); and Thomas L. Van Valley, Wade Clark Roof, and Jerome E. Wilcox, "Trends in Residential Segregation, 1960–1970," *American Journal of Sociology* 82 (January 1971): 826–843.

7. See Allen Winkler, "The Philadelphia Transit Strike of 1944," *Journal of American History* 57 (June 1972): 73–89; and Vincent P. Franklin, "The Philadelphia Race Riot of 1918," *Pennsylvania Magazine of History and Biography* 99 (June 1975): 336–350.

8. See George Schermer, "Semi-Annual Analysis of Tension Reports, First Half of 1955, Compared with Last Half of 1954," October 5, 1955, Box 4, Folder 95, NAACP. On the nature of tensions, see, for example, NAACP to George Schermer, April 28, 1955, Box 4, Folder 97, NAACP; see also Memorandum, Charles Shorter to Maurice Fagan of the Fellowship Commission, March 20, 1956, on "Cases Handled by NAACP [of alleged police mistreatment]," Box 1, Folder 105, NAACP; "Survey of Racial, Religious and National Designations in the Philadelphia *Evening Bulletin,* Monday June 4–June 10, 1951," Box 1, Folder 316, NAACP; and Commission on Human Relations (CHR), "Summary of Neighborhood Tensions or Threatened Tensions around Housing Situations," October 13, 1943, Box 54, Committee on Community Tensions, FCR.

9. Hirsch, *Making the Second Ghetto,* pp. 40–99; on Overbrook Improvement Association, see Memo, Clarence Pickett to Committee on Community Tensions, "West Philadelphia," n.d., circa 1957, Box 4, Folder 97, NAACP.

10. See Eugene P. Ericksen and William L. Yancey, "Work and Residence in Industrial Philadelphia," *Journal of Urban History* 5 (February 1969): 147–183; see also Philadelphia *Inquirer,* Section on *Delaware Valley U.S.A. 1956,* September 25, 1956, and *Delaware Valley U.S.A.,* October 4, 1960.

11. Ericksen and Yancey, "Work and Residence in Industrial Philadelphia," pp. 147–183; "Opponents of Castor Site Meet Public Housing Com-

mission," Frankford *News Gleaner*, May 16, 1956; Germantown *Courier*, February 9, 1956, and February 16, 1956; and Philadelphia *Evening Bulletin*, April 20, 1956.

12. "One Thousand Protest Plan in Logan," Philadelphia *Evening Bulletin*, April 4, 1956; "Eight Hundred Add to Housing Site Protest," *Daily News*, April 11, 1956; CDH Minutes, April 17, 1956, Box 272, Folder 4624, HADVP; and Hirsch, *Making the Second Ghetto*, pp. 193–211. For Dunlap quote, see "Resident's Petition Demands Housing Project Be Dropped," Mayfair *Times*, May 3, 1956.

13. Philadelphia *Evening Bulletin*, April 14, 1956; Philadelphia *Daily News*, April 11, 1956; and *Suburban Press*, May 24, 1956.

14. Morely Cassidy, a vehement opponent of public housing, wrote this account in "Why Housing Is Fought," Philadelphia *Evening Bulletin*, April 24, 1956.

15. On Germantown protest, see "No Unanimity on Public Housing Plans for City," Philadelphia *Evening Bulletin*, April 22, 1956; and "Many Protest at Hearings on New Housing Site," Philadelphia *Evening Bulletin*, June 4, 1956. The protest continued into 1957, and at the November 1957 elections an unofficial referendum was held on public housing; the result was 658 against and 8 for. See also David Luithein, president of the United Northeast Civic Association, to State Representative Harry R. Comer, May 27, 1957, PHAR.

16. Constance Perrin, *Everything in Its Place: Social Order and Land Use in America* (Princeton: Princeton University Press, 1979); for quote by Germantown businessmen on class of tenants in public housing, see "Notes on the Citizens' Meeting on Public Housing," November 20, 1956, Box 278, Folder 4813, HADVP.

17. On Hamlin, see Germantown *Courier*, February 9, 1956; and Philadelphia *Evening Bulletin*, April 12, 1956.

18. The site controversy of 1956 unfolds in Rafsky, "Summary." See, in particular, April 4, 13, and 25, 1956, where Rafsky solicited aid from Bryant, Dennis Clark, and Schermer; see also entries for April 6, 1956, and July 26, 1956. See also "Mann Asserts Public Housing Looks Like Slave Labor Camp," in Philadelphia *Inquirer*, May 16, 1956; and "Many Protest at Hearings on New Housing Sites."

19. On this "secret tour," see *Suburban Press*, June 17, 1956; Montgomery's views are noted in Rafsky, "Summary," April 20, 1956.

20. On "holding off public housing," see Rafsky, "Summary," October 25, 1956. Rafsky argued "that we would not want to lose any sites, but would accept alternative public housing sites if Council insisted" (ibid., April 20, 1956). See also ibid., October 25, 1956, and June 28, 1956.

21. On Camp Happy and other alternative sites, see ibid., April 19, 1956, June 3, 1956, and June 19, 1956.

22. Ibid., May 7, 1956.

23. Hirsch, *Making the Second Ghetto*, pp. 207–208.

24. Interview with George Schermer, February 15, 1983; Maurice Fagan

to Charles Slusser, commissioner of Public Housing Administration, July 24, 1956, Box 272, Folder 4625, HADVP; "Statement on Public Housing," April 1956, Box 272, Folder 4623, HADVP; and Elfriede Hoeber, "Review of Public Housing Policies," June 25, 1956, mimeographed, Box 282, Folder 4921, HADVP. For Clark quote, see CDH Minutes, May 15, 1956, Box 272, Folder 4624, HADVP.

25. "Low-Cost Housing Basic in Restoration of Good Living," Philadelphia *Tribune*, May 28, 1956. See also CDH Minutes, April 17, 1956, Box 272, Folder 4624, HADVP.

26. On Fordham Committee report, see Committee on Public Housing Policy, Jefferson Fordham, Chairman, Minutes, December 12, 1956, Box 282, Folder 4934, HADVP; and Jefferson Fordham et al., "Basic Policies for Public Housing of Low-Income Families in Philadelphia: A Report on Public Housing Policy," mimeographed, November 1957, Box 282, Folder 4905, HADVP.

27. Note that the Fordham Committee found that "the well-meaning efforts at artificially controlling the proportion of racial groups in individual projects are unsupportable. Government may not make selection of tenants dependent in any degree upon their race, religion, or national origin, even though professedly for their good. . . . The Commission believes that there is no discrimination and no segregation in a moral and legal sense where the free and bona fide working of reasonably necessary regulations incidentally result in the admission of different percentages of white and non-white applicants than would otherwise occur." Fordham et al., "Basic Policies."

28. See Robert L. Johnson, "Review of Integration Program of Philadelphia Housing Authority," mimeographed, 1957, Box 235, Folder 3516, HADVP. See "Comments by the Staff of the Philadelphia Housing Authority on Dr. Johnson's study," n.d., in Box 235, Folder 3516, HADVP; also Montgomery "Memorandum on Public Housing Policy," July 26, 1957, Box 282, Folder 4905, HADVP; and Commission on Human Relations, "Findings of the Commission and Policy Statement Relative to Non-Discrimination and Racial Integration on the Operation of the Philadelphia Housing Authority," October 31, 1957, in Box 235, Folder 3517, HADVP; whether or not the questions surrounding Johnson's study were responsible, shortly after submitting his report Robert Johnson took his own life.

29. Clark, "Public Housing Desegregation"; see also the collection of photographs found in the public relations files of the Housing Authority, PHAR.

30. Dennis Clark, "Racial Change in Philadelphia," mimeographed, 1958, Box 235, Folder 3519, HADVP.

31. Maps showing the location of Philadelphia Housing Authority projects and other descriptive information concerning Housing Authority developments can be found in Philadelphia Housing Authority, "A City-Wide Program of Low-Cost Homes," June 1959, PHAR; and Philadelphia Housing Authority, "Developments of the Philadelphia Housing Authority," June 1, 1961, ibid.

32. See Philadelphia Housing Authority, "Report of Proceedings: Public Hearing for Adams Terrace and Champlost Site," April 25, 1957, PHAR; and

Drayton Bryant to Dorothy S. Montgomery, February 7, 1958, Box 330, Folder 3327, HADVP.

33. See "Thirty-Five Year Old Floyd W. Alston to Manage West Oak Lane Project," Germantown *Courier,* December 24, 1960. Note that Richard Allen tenants seeking transfers called Champlost "highly desirable"; Richard Allen Homes Project Records, File RAHR 4283, PHAR.

34. Public Housing Administration Statistical Branch, *Reports on Occupancy,* Box 32, Microfilm Reel 39, PA-1-1, Pittsburgh, Pa. 5-2, McKeesport, HUDR, RG 207, NA; see also maps of Philadelphia Housing Authority projects cited in note 31; and data on "Percent of Public Housing Units Occupied by Non-Whites in Philadelphia, December 1953–January 1956," n.d., mimeographed, Box 180, Folder 1931, HADVP.

35. On Westpark, see COEHO, Minutes, April 21, 1964, Organization Research File, Folder 65, ULP.

36. On NCC, see Telegram, Alvin C. Echols, executive director of NCC, to Robert C. Weaver, Box 344, Subject Correspondence Files, Weaver, 1961–1968, HUDR, RG 207, NA. On HUD, see Elder Gunther, deputy assistant secretary of HUD, to Mr. Walter Worthington, Hill District Council, Pittsburgh, circa March 1968, ibid.

37. PHA Statistical Branch, *"Reports on Occupancy."*

38. See Commission on Race and Housing, *Where Shall We Live: Report of the Commission on Race and Housing* (Berkeley: University of California Press, 1958), pp. 44–45. See also Commission on Human Relations, "Practical Framework for a Program for the Housing Industry," May 10, 1956, Box 235, Folder 3513, HADVP; Committee on Equal Housing Opportunity (COEHO), of the Fellowship Commission, "Equal Housing Opportunity: Real Estate Dilemma," mimeographed, n.d. (1959–1960), Box 178, Folder 1869, HADVP; and "Existing Fair Housing Legislation in Other States and Cities," May 26, 1958, Box 272, Folder 4631, HADVP.

39. "Action by !!! A Stroke of the Pen is Needed Now!!!" COEHO, *Action Letter* 1, October 19, 1961, Box 179, Folder 1893, HADVP.

40. See Arthur M. Schlesinger, *A Thousand Days: John F. Kennedy in the White House* (Boston: Houghton Mifflin, 1965), pp. 928–931. Executive Order 11063 and its impact is discussed in Robert Weaver of the President's Commission on Equal Housing Opportunity to Whitney Young, May 6, 1963, Subject Files, Intergroup Relations, HUDR; and Algernon D. Black, James Farmer, Roy Wilkins, and Whitney Young, "Statement Regarding Implementation of the Executive Order Barring Discrimination in Federally-Aided Housing," n.d., circa May 1963, Subject Files, Intergroup Relations, HUDR, RG 207, NA.

41. See, for example, Robert C. Weaver, "Report on Effects of Executive Order on Equal Opportunity in Housing for Period January 3–June 14, 1963," Subject Files, Intergroup Relations, HUDR, RG 207, NA; Memorandum, Howard Wharton to Robert Weaver, April 23, 1964, concerning "Status of Complaints," ibid.; and Sherwood Ross, public relations director, Chicago Urban League, to Weaver, March 15, 1963, ibid.

42. On site quality, see Jeanne Lowe, *Cities in a Race with Time: Progress and*

Poverty in America's Renewing Cities (New York: Random House, 1967), p. 358; Petshek *Challenge of Urban Reform,* p. 157; William H. Whyte, "Are Cities Un-American?" *Fortune,* September 1957; and "Twenty-One Projects Now Planned Include No High-Rises," *Evening Bulletin,* April 29, 1956.

43. See Whyte, "Are Cities Un-American?" On Morton, see Phillip Herrera, "Philadelphia: How Far Can Renewal Go?" *Architectural Forum,* September 1964); and Philadelphia Housing Authority, *Biennial Report, 1963–1964* (Philadelphia, 1964), pp. 18–19.

44. Herrera, "Philadelphia: How Far Can Renewal Go?"

45. See P. Blair Lee, "Philadelphia's Housing Program: Its Opportunities and Problems; Its Contribution to the City's Renewal," remarks to the Philadelphia Real Estate Board, April 4, 1957, Box 230, Folder 3223, HADVP.

46. On the high-rise survey, see "Operation Contact: 65 Families Living in 11 Elevator Buildings Are Visited by Staff of the Philadelphia Housing Authority," mimeographed, June 1955, Box 229, Folder 3305, HADVP; see also "Notes on Telephone Conversation with Mr. Allesandroni," November 19, 1958, Box 279, Folder 4824, HADVP.

47. Gwendolyn Wright, *Building the Dream: A Social History of Housing in America* (New York: Pantheon, 1981), pp. 237–239; and Whyte, "Are Cities Un-American?" On evidence of vandalism, see Memorandum, Gennie B. Groskin, supervisor of resident aides, Philadelphia Housing Authority, to George Dunn, Division of Housing Management, March 1, 1957, PHAR. Groskin commented on the low standards under which families were living in public housing. She noted the destruction of property, "throwing fire extinguishers out the windows," and "tampering with fire alarms and fire hoses."

48. On Southwark Plaza, see Marie E. Pierro, chairman of housing committee of Southern Area Philadelphia District Health and Welfare Council, to P. Blair Lee, October 10, 1957, Box 278, Folder 4818, HADVP.

49. In 1959 Stonorov headed the firm of Oscar Stonorov, Architect, J. Frank Haws, Architect, and Louis Gust Vastardis, Town Planner. Stonorov discussed his plans for Southwark Plaza in a letter to Hamilton Vogdes, n.d., found in sheaf of official correspondence on Southwark Plaza, PA-2-53, PHAR. See also Interview with David Wisdom, Architect, May 1, 1984; Wisdom described Stonorov as "breezy and bluff," and recalled the architect regularly bringing eggs from his Phoenixville farm to his Philadelphia office.

50. See "Development Plan for Southwark Plaza," typed, n.d.; Frank Haws to Hamilton Vogdes, May 4, 1959; and Haws to Vogdes, April 11, 1960; all in Southwark Plaza file, PHAR. On landscaping Southwark Plaza, see Ian L. McHarg to Thomas McCoy, executive director of the Philadelphia Housing Authority, June 21, 1963; and Vogdes to Stonorov and Haws, February 11, 1963; both in ibid.

51. On Montgomery's criticism of public housing standards and city redevelopment policy, see Montgomery to G. Holmes Perkins, August 15, 1958, Box 221, Folder 3046, HADVP; evidence of her frustration also surfaced in a letter to Wurster, April 3, 1958, Box 330, Folder 6431, HADVP. On high-rise projects, see James A. Sutton of Joint Committee on Public Housing Development Policy to P. Blair Lee, May 18, 1949, Box 279, Folder 4831, HADVP.

52. On the reorganization of the Redevelopment Authority and Montgomery's decision to resign, see Montgomery to Dilworth, May 21, 1958, Box 117, Folder 568, HADVP.

53. David A. Wallace, "Beggars on Horseback," in *Ends and Means of Urban Renewal: Papers from the Philadelphia Housing Association's Fiftieth Anniversary Forum* (Philadelphia: Philadelphia Housing Association, 1961), p. 55. John W. Bodine, a long-time member of the CCCP and president of Penjerdel, a Philadelphia-based regional planning group, expressed his reservations about the goals of renewal in an address before the 1963 meeting of ASPO. Bodine talked about the "Indispensable One Hundredth of One Per Cent," the Montgomerys, Bacons, Clarks, Dilworths, CCCPs, and Housing Associations, whose pro-growth intensity was responsible for Penn Center and Old Philadelphia triumphs of the city's renewal program. But when "we turn to what the future holds, we must recognize the emergence of several disquieting circumstances. . . . The political climate is changing. The architects of municipal reform are off the scene. . . . As in many other communities, more and more questions are arising about the adequacy of mere physical renewal. Do the many families dislocated by renewal merely represent a shifting about in the hard core of our underprivileged? Is the environment of the typical housing project really conducive to less delinquency and better family living? Are the spectacular downtown improvements for the benefit of only a few of our more well-to-do citizens? Are our existing social agencies, including our school system, really equipped to deal with the increasing proportion of our city population that seems destined for joblessness and dependency?" See *Planning, 1963* (Chicago: American Planning Association, 1963), p. 202.

54. See William G. Grigsby, "Housing and Slum Clearance: Elusive Goals," *Annals of the American Academy of Political and Social Science* 352 (March 1964): 110.

55. George Schermer noted the link between white exodus and blight in an interview with me on February 17, 1983. See also Abrams, *City Is the Frontier,* pp. 24–29. On planners' perception of the invidious relationship between white flight, blight, and the downtown, see Carter McFarland, "Urban Renewal," in *Urban Housing,* ed. William L. C. Wheaton et al. (New York: Free Press, 1966), p. 430; Howard W. Hallam, "Citizens and Professionals Reconsider the Neighborhoods," *Journal of the American Institute of Planners* 25 (August 1959); Henry S. Churchill, "Neighborhood Esthetics," in Philadelphia Housing Association, *Forum on Neighborhoods Today and Tomorrow,* No. 4 (May 1958); and Whyte, "Are Cities Un-American?"

56. On diminishing interest in the poor, see Leonard Freedman, *Public Housing: The Politics of Poverty* (New York: Wadsworth, 1969), pp. 95–97, 105; see also Louis Winnick, "Facts and Fictions in Urban Renewal," in *Ends and Means of Urban Renewal,* pp. 23–25; Jewel Bellush and Murray Hausknecht, "Public Housing: The Context of Failure," in *Urban Renewal: People, Politics and Planning,* ed. Bellush and Hausknecht (New York: Doubleday—Anchor, 1967), p. 451.

57. Catherine Bauer Wurster, "The Dreary Deadlock of Public Housing," *Architectural Forum* 106 (May 1957): 141, 112; see also Freedman, *Public Hous-*

ing pp. 90–91, 116–117, 181–185; and James Q. Wilson, "Citizen Participation in Urban Renewal," in James Q. Wilson, ed., *Urban Renewal: The Record and the Controversy* (Cambridge, Mass.: M.I.T. Press, 1968), pp. 408–409.

58. Wurster, "Dreary Deadlock," p. 221. Grigsby agreed; see "Housing and Slum Clearance," p. 107; and Montgomery to Wurster, June 3, 1956, Box 330, Folder 6431, HADVP.

59. See Memorandum, C. Carter McFarland to Walker Mason, deputy administrator of HHFA, on meeting with Philadelphia Housing Authority, January 15, 1958, Chief Administrator's Files, Albert Coles, 1953–1958, HUDR; see also "Minutes of Special Meeting to Discuss Conference with Charles Slusser," January 7, 1958, Box 281, Folder 4877, HADVP; Howard Hallam to Files, on Meeting with Slusser, January 15, 1958, Box 278, Folder 4818, HADVP; and Montgomery to Wurster, April 7, 1958, Box 330, Folder 6431, HADVP.

60. See "Report to Citizens' Council on City Planning and Philadelphia Housing Association from Committee on Public Housing Development Policy on Recommendations Concerning Used-House Program," March 5, 1959, Box 279, Folder 4827, HADVP; and "Housing Board to Purchase 25 Private Houses," *Evening Bulletin,* March 6, 1958.

61. See Montgomery to Wurster, April 3, 1958, Box 330, Folder 6431, HADVP.

62. Wurster spoke about "saving the central cities" in a talk at American Institute of Planners Convention, Detroit, November 27, 1961 (see "Urban and Regional Structure: The Belated Challenge and the Changing Role of the Physical Planner," Box 330, Folder 6431, HADVP). In the talk Wurster said the postwar "boom in babies and incomes descended on us willy-nilly, and the housing shortage brought another rash of hasty *ad hoc* measures. We were equally unprepared to cope with the flood of automobiles, and the social and geographic mobility which poured middle-class tract-houses all over the hinterland, and Negroes into the cities with new hopes and demands. It was a moment to guide growth and change toward a rational pattern of development and a sensible structure of cities. But we missed our big chance."

63. See Norton Long, "Local Government and Renewal Policies," in Wilson, ed., *Urban Renewal,* pp. 426–427; and Abrams, *The City Is the Frontier,* p. 166.

64. On central-city priority, see Rafsky, "Summary," January 25, 1956, February 3, 1956, February 13, 1956, and April 5, 1956. Note that Greenfield was a director of the Yellow Cab Company, on the Board of the Philadelphia Transportation Company, and active in the Urban Land Institute and the Greater Philadelphia Movement. He generously backed Dilworth's mayoralty bid. See also Philadelphia *Evening Bulletin,* January 17, 1956; and Conrad Weiler, *Philadelphia: Neighborhood, Authority and the Urban Crisis* (New York: Praeger, 1974), p. 108.

65. On the OPDC, see Lowe, *Cities in a Race with Time,* pp. 344–347; and Rafsky, "Summary," January 11, 1956, February 23, 1956, and September 11, 1956. On the New Philadelphia Movement, see Dilworth to Montgomery, June 8, 1956, Box 117, Folder 567, HADVP.

66. See Rafsky, "Summary," April 28, 1957. On center-city projects, see Lowe, *Cities in a Race with Time*, pp. 379–385.

Chapter 9. The Vision Eclipsed

1. On the 1960s and the rise of black power, see Allen J. Matusow, *The Unravelling of America: A History of Liberalism in the 1960s* (New York: Harper and Row, 1984); and Milton Viorst, *Fire in the Streets: America in the 1960s* (New York: Simon and Schuster, 1979).

2. Harrison Salisbury, "The Shook-Up Generation: Problem Youngsters Spring from the Housing Jungle," *New York Times*, March 26, 1958.

3. On public housing and the "cycle of poverty," see Oscar Lewis, *La Vida: A Puerto Rican Family in the Culture of Poverty* (New York: Random House, 1966); Leonard Freedman, *Public Housing: The Politics of Poverty* (New York: Wadsworth, 1969), pp. 109–111; and Alvin Schorr, "Slums and Social Security," in *Urban Renewal: People, Politics and Controversy*, ed. Jewel Bellush and Maury Hausknecht (Cambridge, Mass.: M.I.T. Press, 1967), pp. 415–419.

4. On "problem" families, see Memorandum from George Dunn, May 29, 1957, Box 285, Folder 5006, HADVP; for the "Every day is Sunday" quote, see Memorandum for the Files, Subject: "Interview with George Dunn," October 29, 1961, Box 281, Folder 4890, HADVP.

5. On the SSD, see Osborne McClain, "A Beginning Social Service Program in Public Housing: A Six Month Statement of the Social Service Division," n.d., Box 233, Folder 3430, HADVP; and Harriet Bury, Health and Welfare Council, "Social Service in Public Housing," draft, mimeographed, n.d., circa 1961, Box 285, Folder 5829, HADVP. McGuire also expanded public housing's mission to include the elderly. See "Single Persons Over 65 to Get Public Housing," *Evening Bulletin*, December 16, 1958; also Memo 188, George Dunn to all managers, June 27, 1958, where Dunn said that the "number of tenants over 65 is increasing and this is because we have encouraged it to do so," PHAR.

6. On the 209 cases, see Osborne McClain, "One Year of Service in 1966: A Report from the Social Service Division, Philadelphia Housing Authority," mimeographed, January 18, 1962, Box 233, Folder 3434, HADVP.

7. John H. Mollenkopf, *The Contested City* (Princeton: Princeton University Press, 1983), pp. 81–96.

8. On the NHC complaint, see Nathaniel Keith, *Politics and the Housing Crisis Since 1930* (New York: Universe Books, 1973), pp. 142–147; and William L. Slayton, "The Operation and Achievements of the Urban Renewal Program," in *Urban Renewal: The Record and the Controversy*, ed. James Q. Wilson (Cambridge, Mass.: M.I.T. Press, 1968), p. 194.

9. Regarding Slusser and McGuire, see "Legislative History of Public Housing Traced through 25 Years," *Journal of Housing* 8 (1962): 442–445. Herbert Gans espied the change in planning in "City Planning in America: A Sociological Analysis," in Gans, *People and Plans: Essays on Urban Problems and Solutions* (New York: Basic Books, 1968), pp. 66–71. See also Lawrence Daverr, acting commissioner, Public Housing Administration, to Norman Ma-

son, March 14, 1960, Subject Correspondence Files, Mason, 1960, HUDR, RG 207, NA. Also, a new approach to housing low-income families was urged in a Policy Memo from Mason, "Some Recent Management Achievements and Some Major Problems," n.d., circa January 1, 1960, ibid.

10. See HHFA Department Study Draft, "A Demonstration Program to Deal with Human Problems Related to Urban Renewal and Housing Program," n.d., circa 1963, Box 114, Correspondence Files, Weaver, HUDR, RG 207, NA.

11. On "people oriented" programs, see Robert Weaver to Marie McGuire, October 23, 1963, Box 116, Subject Correspondence Files, Weaver, 1961–1968, HUDR, RG 207, NA; and Memorandum, Assistant Commissioner of Public Housing Administration (Slayton), to Administrator HHFA, October 21, 1963, ibid. See also William Slayton to Ralph Thacker, director of Neighborhood Organizations, August 5, 1963, Box 116, Subject Correspondence Files, Weaver, 1963, HUDR, RG 207, NA.

12. See Albert Mayer to Robert Weaver, June 17, 1963, Policy Memos, Subject Correspondence Files, Weaver, 1961–1968, HUDR, RG 207, NA; see also Confidential Memo, "Legislative Proposals for 1964," Marie McGuire to Robert Weaver, April 12, 1963, Box 116, Subject Correspondence Files, Weaver, 1963, HUDR, RG 207, NA.

13. See Maurice White, "Redevelopment Authority: Housing Concerns Did Not Go Unnoticed in 1960s Movement," part 8 of a series on Redevelopment in Philadelphia, Philadelphia *Tribune*, November 3, 1978, p. 8. See also *Old Philadelphia Development Corporation to Build Center City Anew* (Philadelphia, 1966), HADVP pamphlets; *15th Annual Report of the Redevelopment Authority of City of Philadelphia* (Philadelphia, 1961), HADVP pamphlets; and *1961 Annual Report of the Redevelopment Authority of the City of Philadelphia* (Philadelphia, 1962), HADVP pamphlets.

14. See Martin Anderson, *The Federal Bulldozer* (Cambridge, Mass.: M.I.T. Press, 1964); Jane Jacobs, *Death and Life of Great American Cities* (New York: Vintage, 1961); Herbert Gans, *The Urban Villagers: Group and Class in the Life of Italian Americans* (New York: Free Press, 1962); and Marc Fried, "Grieving for a Lost Home: Psychological Costs of Relocation," in *The Urban Condition*, ed. Leonard Duhl (New York: Basic Books, 1963).

15. See Kenneth Clark, *Dark Ghetto* (New York: Harper and Row, 1965); Elliot Liebow, *Talley's Corner: A Study of Negro Streetcorner Men* (Boston: Little Brown, 1967); and William K. Tabb, *The Political Economy of the Black Ghetto* (New York: Norton, 1970).

16. A good description of the North Philadelphia riot site can be found in Lenore Berson, *Case Study of a Riot: The Philadelphia Story* (New York: Institute of Human Relations Press, 1961), pp. 25–35. The riot area is also discussed in Peter O. Muller, Kenneth C. Meyer, and Roman Cybriwsky, *Philadelphia: A Study of Conflicts and Social Cleavages* (Cambridge, Mass.: M.I.T. Press, 1976).

17. *Report of the National Advisory Commission on Civil Disorders* (New York: Bantam, 1968), pp. 251–259.

18. Berson, *Case Study of a Riot*, pp. 1–25.

19. See Citizens Emergency Committee of North Philadelphia, Minutes, August 29, 1964, Box 37, Folder 38, WCP; note that among the organizations participating in the meeting were the Congress of Racial Equality (CORE), the NAACP (represented by Delores Tucker), the North City Congress (represented by Wilson Long), and representatives of several black churches.

20. Memorandum, Citizens Emergency Committee of North Philadelphia to the Honorable James H. J. Tate, mayor of Philadelphia, August 31, 1964, Box 37, Folder 38, WCP.

21. Government Consulting Service, Fels Institute (University of Pennsylvania), *Community Renewal Program of Philadelphia*, draft, June 15, 1966, HADV pamphlets; and Community Renewal Program Committee, *A Preliminary Report on Findings and Proposals for Review and Discussion*, October 1964, HADV pamphlets.

22. See Memorandum, Members of Subcommittee on Existing Housing of Housing Policy Committee to Board of Directors, PHA, October 1964, Box 166, Folder 1596, HADVP.

23. Mollenkopf, *The Contested City*; also Keith, *Politics and the Housing Crisis*. Keith agrees that by 1964 urban renewal had clearly supplanted low-income housing as the target of conservative critics, a turn of events, argues Keith, that reflected the small amount of public housing built (p. 155). See also Bernard Frieden and Marshall Kaplan, *The Politics of Neglect: Urban Aid from Model Cities to Revenue Sharing* (Cambridge, Mass.: M.I.T. Press, 1977).

24. See Robert Caro, *The Years of Lyndon Johnson: The Path to Power* (New York: Random House, 1981); Keith, *Politics and the Housing Crisis*, p. 160; and Mel Scott, *American City Planning Since 1890* (Berkeley: University of California Press, 1969), pp. 610–615.

25. See "1965: Housing Comes of Age," in *Housing Yearbook*, 1965, pp. 109–111. On rent supplements, see Leonard Freedman, *Public Housing: The Politics of Poverty* (New York: Wadsworth, 1969), p. 130; and Harold Wolman, *Politics of Federal Housing* (New York: Dodd Mead, 1971), pp. 44–46.

26. See Testimony of Boris Shiskin, Nathaniel Keith, Robert Weaver, and Ira Robbins before Senate Subcommittee of the Committee on Banking and Currency, *Hearings on S. 1354: Housing Legislation of 1965*, 89th Cong. 1st sess., pp. 74, 267–268, 431; and Keith, *Politics and the Housing Crisis*, p. 184.

27. For views of the War on Poverty, see Francis Fox Piven and Richard A. Cloward, *Regulating the Poor: The Functions of Public Welfare* (New York: Vintage, 1972); and Daniel P. Moynihan, *Maximum Feasible Misunderstanding* (New York: Free Press, 1969). On the key involvement of public housing in the War on Poverty, see Memorandum, Marie C. McGuire to Robert Weaver, September 14, 1965, "Public Housing's Involvement as a Major Community Resource in OEO Program," Box 168, Subject Correspondence Files, Weaver, HUDR, RG 207, NA.

28. See Frieden and Kaplan, *Politics of Neglect*, pp. 36–59; Wolman, *Politics of Federal Housing*, p. 43; and Scott, *American City Planning*, pp. 622–667.

29. Arnstein quoted in Frieden and Kaplan, *Politics of Neglect*, p. 77. For Philadelphia's experience with Model Cities, see "Maximum Feasible Manip-

ulation: As Told to Sherry Arnstein," in *Perspectives on the American Community*, 2d ed., ed. Roland Warren (New York: Rand McNally, 1973), pp. 409–419.

30. Frieden and Kaplan, *Politics of Neglect*, pp. 69–74.

31. On the failure of AWC, see "Poverty War Bogs Down Here: Lack of Leadership Cited," Philadelphia *Inquirer*, March 21, 1965; see also "Maximum Feasible Manipulation," pp. 409–427; Philadelphia Crisis Committee, "Chronological Fact Sheet on Model Cities Controversy—Issue: Meaningful Citizen Participation," September 22, 1969, FCR; Memorandum, Cushing N. Dolbeare, Housing Association of Delaware Valley, to Executive Committee, Philadelphia Fellowship Commission, September 22, 1969, "Model Cities Suit," FCR.

32. Stokely Carmichael and Charles V. Hamilton, *Black Power: The Politics of Liberation in America* (New York: Random House, 1967); Charles Sacrey, *The Political Economy of Urban Poverty* (New York: Norton, 1973); and Piven and Cloward, *Regulating the Poor*.

33. See Memorandum, Marie McGuire, commissioner of public housing, to Robert Weaver, April 12, 1965, Box 168, Subject Correspondence Files, Weaver, 1965, HUDR.

34. Memorandum, "To Whom it May Concern: Re: Philadelphia Rehabilitation," April 19, 1965, Box 168, Subject Correspondence Files, Weaver, 1965, HUDR, RG 207, NA.

35. See Office of the Mayor (Tate), News Release, June 21, 1967, where Tate announced Robert C. Weaver's approval of the $70,000,000 used-house contract, Box 230, Folder 3329, HADVP.

36. The "turnkey" provision of the 1965 Housing Act allowed local housing authorities to purchase units that could be separated from the rest of a project, making way for Philadelphia's used-house program. See Henry J. Aaron, *Shelter and Subsidies: Who Benefits from Federal Housing Policies* (Washington, D.C.: Brookings Institution, 1972), p. 119.

37. On the Spring Garden program and Yale Rabin, see the "confidential" daily log of Anne M. Turner (Staff person, HADV), July 1, 1966, Box 285, Folder 5010, HADVP; and Memorandum, Emily Achtenberg to Public Housing Committee of HADV, May 18, 1967, "Issues in the Spring Garden Area," ibid.

38. On the FPBNA versus the NCC, see ibid. See also "Statement of Policy for the Fairmount P.B.N. Association, 2223 Fairmont Avenue, Philadelphia, Pa., April 1967," ibid.

39. See daily log of Anne M. Turner, May 10, 1967; and Memorandum from Emily Actenberg, May 18, 1967; both in Box 285, Folder 5010, HADVP.

40. See Obituary, "Catherine Bauer Wurster, The First Lady of Housing, 1907–1964," in *Housing Yearbook* (1965), 47. On Cushing Dolbeare, see letter of congratulations from Francis J. Lammer, executive director of Redevelopment Authority, to Cushing Dolbeare, June 4, 1965, Box 250, Folder 4001, HADVP; and biographical sketch of Dolbeare in Memorandum for Bette Marsh, United Fund, "Further Material on Cushing Dolbeare," n.d., Box 1, Special Collection, HADVP. Note that Cushing Dolbeare's husband was the

Harvard-educated regional planner Louis Dolbeare, a member of the ACLU, Americans for Democratic Action, and West Mount Airy Neighbors.

41. On the formation of JCMH, see Memorandum, Andrew Freedman, director of Urban League, and Cushing Dolbeare, to Joint Committee on Minority Housing, October 14, 1969, HADVP; on tensions between HADV and RA, see daily log of Cushing Dolbeare, November 1, 1965, Box 250, Folder 4004, HADVP.

42. Daily log of Cushing Dolbeare, November 1, 1965, Box 250, Folder 4004, HADVP.

43. George Schermer, reply to Cushing Dolbeare's request for "a few paragraphs on race," n.d., 1966, HADVP.

44. On the creation of the JCMH, see Eleanor Workman, administrative assistant, to Phyllis Smollensky, March 8, 1968, Box 150, Folder 1934, HADVP; and Memorandum from Workman, "Future Structure of JCMH," March 28, 1968, ibid.

45. See Cushing Dolbeare, preliminary draft, "Housing Associaton Program, 1969–1970," September 1969, Box 21, Housing 1968–1974, FCR.

46. HADV on Vietnam, see "Agenda," Executive Committee of HADV, October 9, 1969, Box 1, Special Collection, HADVP; and "Cushing Dolbeare Announced Opposition to War in Vietnam," HADV News Release, October 14, 1969.

47. "Turner Draft [of goals for 1970]," August 28, 1969, Box 21, Housing, 1968–1969, FCR; F. C. Carroll to Dolbeare and Staff, August 28, 1969, ibid.

48. See George Schermer Associates, *More Than Shelter: Social Need in Low and Moderate-Income Housing* (Washington, D.C.: GPO, 1968), pp. 39, 64; Aaron, *Shelter and Subsidies*, p. 120; Devereaux Bowley, *The Poorhouse: Subsidized Housing in Chicago, 1895–1976* (Carbondale: University of Illinois Press, 1978), p. 189.

49. See Bowley, *The Poorhouse*, p. 190. On housing and poverty, see HADV, "Statement on Public Housing Sites Presented to the Philadelphia Housing Authority," December 1968, Box 284, Folder 4994, HADVP. Ellee Workman of the HADV stated the housing organization's revised viewpoint quite bluntly: "We must take the kind of action which shows a commitment to what we say. If we are against projects and for more aggressive use of other programs [i.e., housing grants] we should be working to stop projects . . . , but we have them so let's make them a better place—or make their site selection criteria a little better" (Workman's daily log, February 12, 1969, ibid).

50. See Sue Carroll's daily log, December 9, 1968, December 10, 1968, and December 17, 1968; and Susan Beetle's daily log, December 12, 1968; both Box 284, Folder 4994, HADVP.

51. See Lee Rainwater, *Behind Ghetto Walls: Black Families in a Federal Slum* (Chicago: Aldine, 1970); and Bowley, *The Poorhouse*, pp. 189–194.

52. See Memorandum, Susan Carroll to Public Housing Subcommittee on Tenant Assignment, September 4, 1968, "Tenant Assignment in Public Housing," Box 285, Folder 5016, HADVP.

53. Data from Public Housing Administration, Statistical Branch, *Reports on Occupancy*, Box 32, Microfilm Reel 39, HUDR, RG 207, NA. See Edward Sims, "Statement before City Council, re: Bills 835 and 845," February 26, 1969; and HADVP; also Charles Campbell, "Statement before City Council, re: Bills 835 and 845," February 6, 1969; both Box 284, Folder 4994, HADVP.

54. Eugene Mayer, "Philadelphia Housing Authority Opposes Forced Mixed Housing," *Sunday Bulletin*, March 16, 1969; Peter Binzen, "HUD Disavows Steinberg Idea for Housing," Philadelphia *Evening Bulletin*, March 18, 1969; and Michael Strong, acting president of HADV, to Mayor Tate, March 21, 1969, Box 284, 4994, HADVP.

55. On Whitman Park and Mayor Frank Rizzo, see Joseph Daughen and Peter Binzen, *The Cop Who Would Be King* (Boston: Little Brown, 1977); Staff of Philadelphia City Planning Commission, "Whitman Public Housing Background Paper," December 21, 1976, mimeographed, HADVP; and Urban Coalition Task Force, *Facts You Should Know about the Whitman Park Court Case* (December 1976), HADVP pamphlets.

56. See Thomas Morehouse, Abner Silverman, Hans Spiegel, George Williams, and Elizabeth Wood, "The Social Concerns of HUD: Report of Work Group on Social Concerns [to Weaver]," August 23, 1966, Box 305, Subject Correspondence File, Weaver, HUDR, RG 207, NA; see also Memorandum, Ashly Foard to Weaver, February 10, 1967, ibid., recommending against sending report on social concerns to Congress, since it "could be used to attack and discredit the Department." The paper, said Foard, "suffers from the jargon of the sociologist and statements that are inaccurate such as public housing was initially designed to serve the *lowest* income group."

57. The Philadelphia Housing Authority, "Policy on Tenant Admissions and Continued Occupancy," July 1, 1964, had specifically barred unmarried mothers of two or more children evidencing "an irresponsible and continuous pattern of illegitimacy," Box 277, Folder 4783, HADVP. See Affidavit of Oliva Byrd, filed in U.S. District Court, Philadelphia, against the Philadelphia Housing Authority, circa April 1968, and record of settlement, May 20, 1968, Box 285, Folder 5002, HADVP. See also "Revised Philadelphia Housing Authority Policy on Tenant Admission and Continued Occupancy," May 15, 1968, which excluded the above proscription of unwed mothers, Box 277, Folder 4793, HADVP. The new policy also provided for a review committee hearing on all cases of rejection.

58. Affidavit of Oliva Byrd and record of settlement.

59. On the tenants' challenge to modernization procedures, see telegram, Richard Allen Tenant Council, Rosetta Wylie, president, to Robert Weaver, September 23, 1968, objecting to modernization program "unless PHA complies with the requirements of HUD Low Rent Management policies that tenants participate in management." Box 344, Secretaries Correspondence Files, Weaver, HUDR, RG 207, NA. See also "Complaint before the Secretary, Department of Housing and Urban Development, Richard Allen Tenant Council and Tenant's Improvement Council of Tasker Homes versus Philadelphia Housing Authority," circa September 1968, PHAR.

60. "Memorandum of Understanding between Tenant Improvement Council of Tasker Homes, the Richard Allen Tenant Council, and Philadelphia Housing Authority," March 1969, PHAR.

61. See "Programs, Policies and Procedures," *Open Circuit*, a mimeographed newsletter published by the PHA and circulated among management, July 1971, PHAR. Aaron points out in *Shelter and Subsidies*, p. 114, that "the numbers of black families eligible for public housing so visibly exceeded the number of units available for occupancy that [despite laws] Local Housing Authorities had broad discretion in screening applicants."

62. See Workman daily log, February 12, 1969.

63. On Dolbeare's resignation, see Cushing Dolbeare to M. C. Strong, June 17, 1971, Box 51, Special Collection, HADVP. The transformation of the HADV into an advocacy organization was visible from the changing composition of the organization's board of directors and staff; see 1968–1969 Directories of Board and Staff listed in HADV, *Issues*, no. 1 (December 1969), and HADV, *Annual Report* (1971–1972), Box 1, File 12, RG 29, Annual Reports, Newsletters, HADVP. In 1974, in response to Richard Nixon's "abandonment of low-income housing program," Cushing Dolbeare founded and headed the Ad Hoc Low-Income Housing Coalition, in Washington, D.C., a public-interest group concerned primarily with the housing needs of low-income, inner-city families.

64. Official biography and vita of Shirley Dennis given to me by the Pennsylvania Department of Community Affairs, June 25, 1984.

65. On HADV's new mission, see "Toward Ending Racism in Housing: New Program Directions," *Issues*, no. 2 (November 1970); and Memorandum, Shirley Dennis to Members of HADV Executive Committee, November 8, 1972, Box 1, Special Collection, HADVP. After 1974, under Shirley Dennis, the HADV increasingly advocated the urban homesteading program and became a strong voice warning of the danger of housing abandonment in the city.

Bibliographical Note

Philadelphia has been an important stage for housing activities since the 1890s. During the period covered in this book, 1920–1974, many of the most prominent public housers, architects, and city planners were active in Philadelphia and kept extensive records of their involvement in the city's housing and urban renewal programs. Considerable information also exists about Philadelphia's black community and the saga of race relations in the twentieth-century city.

Much of the record of housing, race, and renewal in twentieth-century Philadelphia is conveniently located in one place, the Urban Archives at Temple University. The richest collection stored there may be the Housing Association of Delaware Valley (HADV) papers. The entire history of public housing and renewal is documented in the papers of the Philadelphia Housing Association (PHA). And several other collections, among them the papers of the Citizens' Council on City Planning (CCCP) and the Greater Philadelphia Movement (GPM) proved extremely useful. The Urban Archives also contain collections critical for understanding the black community's involvement in housing and renewal. Most valuable of these are the papers of the Philadelphia NAACP, the Urban League, and the Wharton Center. For the 1950s, the records of the Philadelphia Fellowship Commission (FC) and the Philadelphia Board of Realtors proved indispensable.

The Philadelphia City Archives, located in the City Hall Annex, contain records of local public agencies, including the Redevelopment Authority, the Planning Commission, and the Housing Authority. Planning commission materials include a number of important studies of housing conditions based on census data as well as other planning studies relevant for a better understanding of neighborhood decline. Another segment of the historical record of the Housing Authority has resided for years in the basements of housing projects—including valuable correspondence concerning project design, construction data, and project maintenance information. The important minute books of the Housing Authority are shelved in the agency's downtown offices and are particularly useful for understanding the evolution of public housing policy.

Much of the story of urban housing, race, and renewal is lodged in Washington, D.C., in the National Archives. The records of the Housing and Home Finance Administration (HHFA) proved especially useful. The records of the Department of Housing and Urban Development harbor a wealth of urban history and document the odyssey of federal housing and renewal policymaking from the creation of the National Housing Agency through the termination of conventional public housing.

The Samuel I. Rosenman and John Ihlder papers, both located at the Franklin Delano Roosevelt Library, Hyde Park, New York, proved most useful for documenting the gestation of public housing and for illuminating the struggle to preserve public housing.

In researching this book I also consulted numerous journals and periodicals. Among the most important were the *Proceedings of the National Conference on City Planning, Journal of the American Institute of Planning, Housing Yearbook, Planning, Journal of Housing, Survey,* and *Survey Midmonthly.*

Index

Index

Dolbeare, Louis, 258–259
Domhoff, William: on postwar urban crisis, 192; on Wagner-Ellender-Taft Act, 44
Domino Lane site, and segregated public housing, 200–201
Douglas, Paul, on public housing, 192
Downtown renewal: as "priority one," 181; promoted by Gustav Amsterdam, 187
DuBois, Arthur, on Housing Division architecture, 39
Duhl, Leonard, 203
Dunbar Apartments, 34
Dunlap, Foster A., opposes twenty-one sites, 163
Dunn, George, 117
Durkheim, Emil, 8

Earle, George, 31; and origins of Philadelphia Housing Authority, 43–44
East Poplar redevelopment area: Bacon's design of, 110; criticism of, 110; and Francis Bosworth, 108; map of, 109; and Mayor's Committee on Neighborhood Improvement, 107
Edelman, John: and Carl Mackley Homes, 24–25; helps form Labor Housing Conference (LHC), 25
Eisenhower, Dwight David, and political opposition to public housing, 137–138
Emergency Fleet Corporation, and World War I housing, 11
Executive Order 8802, and expansion of black work force during World War II, 58
Executive Order 11063, and open housing, 171, 174

Fagan, Maurice, 123, 129; and campaign for twenty-one sites, 165
Fair Housing Committee of Delaware Valley (FHCDV), merges with Philadelphia Housing Association (PHA), 198
Fairmount Parents, Business, and Neighborhood Association (FPBNA), and used-house program, 196
Farmer, James, 174
Fauset, Arthur Huff, 36, 68
Fauset, Crystal Bird, 219; selected to membership on Philadelphia Advisory Committee on Housing (PACH), 36
Federal Housing Administration (FHA): discussed by Kenneth Jackson, 95; and racial policies, 95; and wartime urban planning, 81
Federal Public Housing Authority, 177
Federal Works Agency, and Lanham Act, 62
Fellowship Commission of Philadelphia (FC): and failure of relocation effort, 151; and Joseph S. Clark, 119; opposition of, to slum sites for public housing, 166; origins of, 122
Finnegan, James, aids Joseph S. Clark politically, 119
Fitzwater Site: discussed, 157; Rafsky on, 247
Flamingo Gardens, as private black housing, 153–154
Ford, James, and Better Homes Movement, 15
Fordham, Jefferson, 141–142
Fordham Committee: created in 1957, 167; and Philadelphia disillusionment with public housing, 167–168; and racial quotas in public housing, 250; and social work in public housing, 184–185; and used-house program, 180
Fox, Hannah, 5
Frankford, and neighborhood opposition to public housing, 162
Frankford Arsenal, 57
Freedman, Abraham, 97–98
Frieden, Bernard, 187
Friends Neighborhood Guild, 108, 123
Fuller, Helen, criticizes National Housing Agency (NHA) on war housing record, 71

Gans, Herbert, as critic of urban renewal, 187
Garden cities, and Ebenezer Howard, 9
Gautreaux decision, and housing segregation, 200
Gavit, John, 60
Geddes, Patrick: influences communitarian housers, 8, 9; and Saarinen's theory of organic decentralization, 105
Gelfand, Mark, 161
Ghettoization, 245
Girard Court, and private black housing, 153
Glazer, Nathan, 176; on culture of poverty, 184
Glenwood Cemetery site, 47
Gloria Dei (Old Swedes') Church site: 28, 46; as Italian neighborhood, 46
Goode, Wilson, on board of Housing

Index

Index